OXFORD MODERN LANGUAGES
AND LITERATURE MONOGRAPHS

Editorial Committee

FLOWER POETICS IN NINETEENTH-CENTURY FRANCE

PHILIP KNIGHT

CLARENDON PRESS · OXFORD

1986

Oxford University Press, Walton Street, Oxford OX2 6DP
Oxford New York Toronto
Delhi Bombay Calcutta Madras Karachi
Kuala Lumpur Singapore Hong Kong Tokyo
Nairobi Dar es Salaam Cape Town
Melbourne Auckland
and associated companies in
Beirut Berlin Ibadan Nicosia

Oxford is a trade mark of Oxford University Press

Published in the United States
by Oxford University Press, New York

British Library Cataloguing in Publication Data
Knight, Philip
Flower poetics in nineteenth-century France. —
(Oxford modern languages and literature monographs)
1. French poetry — 19th century — History and
criticism. 2. Flowers in literature
I. Title
841'.8 PQ433
ISBN 0–19–815833–5

Library of Congress Cataloging in Publication Data
Knight, Philip
Flower poetics in nineteenth-century France.
(Oxford modern languages and literature monographs)
Bibliography: p.
Includes index.
1. French poetry — 19th century — History and
criticism. 2. Flowers in literature. 3. Symbolism
in literature. 4. Baudelaire, Charles, 1821–1867.
Fleurs du mal. 5. Nerval, Gerard de, 1808–1855 —
Criticism and interpretation. 6. Romanticism — France.
I. Title. II. Series.
PQ433.K55 1986 841'.009'36 85–21731
ISBN 0–19–815833–5

Set by Dobbie Typesetting Service, Plymouth
Printed in Great Britain
at the University Printing House, Oxford
by David Stanford
Printer to the University

PREFACE

The poetry of Baudelaire has a unique significance for the nineteenth century and beyond, and it appeared under a title (*Les Fleurs du Mal*) which uses a flower figure to refer to poetry. This fact alone suggests that the flower image had considerable importance for Baudelaire, and that it might have had some importance for his Symbolist successors and even conceivably for his Romantic predecessors. But there exists no survey of the importance of flower figures for the poetry and poetics of this period. There are works studying related fields like mystical thought and 'le sentiment de la nature',[1] and there are excellent studies on Baudelaire's relations with mysticism and with nature.[2] But neither in these works nor elsewhere can one find an overall view of the flower rhetoric of this most floral of poets. Nor has the popular flower literature which grew up during the Romantic period received adequate attention. And scholars have never taken proper notice of the frequent use and striking elaboration of flower imagery (often specifically related to poetics) in the work of poets writing at the mid-century or later — Nerval, the Parnassians, and the Symbolists.

This book therefore aims to show what role the flower figure played in French poetry and poetics during the nineteenth century. It indicates general trends in the use of poetic flower imagery, and notes the influence of popular flower publications on serious writing. But it gives most attention to the ways in which flower rhetoric contributed to poetic theory and practice. It opens with an introductory chapter surveying the flower tropology of earlier periods, both to indicate the sources of much nineteenth-century imagery and to provide a context for studying its unprecedented

---

1. B. Juden, *Traditions orphiques et tendances mystiques dans le romantisme français (1800–55)* (Klincksieck, 1971), G. Charlier, *Le Sentiment de la nature chez les romantiques français, 1760–1830* (Fontemoing, 1912), and E. Guitton, *Jacques Delille et le poème de la nature de 1750 à 1820* (Klincksieck, 1974).
2. J. Pommier, *La Mystique de Baudelaire* (Les Belles Lettres, 1932), and F. Leakey, *Baudelaire and Nature* (Manchester UP, 1969).

elaboration in this period. Subsequent chapters follow chronological order where possible. Chapter 2 outlines the Romantic development of idealizing flower languages in poetry, and Chapter 3 studies Baudelaire's use of these languages and his ironic revisions of them. Chapter 4 notes how other writers of Baudelaire's time (Nerval and the Hellenists) made their own adaptations of Romantic flower rhetoric, while Chapter 5 shows how radically this was transformed by the Symbolists, following Baudelairian and Hellenist precedent.

During this period flower figures served the poets in many ways, and even came to provide the one indispensable emblem of continuity and change in poetry. Indeed by the mid-1880s it was clear that the rhetoric of flowers had influenced the transformation of poetic language itself. This study therefore ends at that time, since henceforth poets were dependent on this Symbolist achievement.

From the beginnings of Romanticism to the flowering of Symbolism, flower rhetoric made a highly significant (and unjustly neglected) contribution to poetic theory and practice. The history of nineteenth-century French poetry is also the history of its flower poetics.

ACKNOWLEDGEMENTS

I am much indebted to Dr A. W. Raitt of Magdalen College, Oxford, for his constant encouragement of this study, which is an abridged version of a thesis supervised by him. His great knowledge and kindness have been invaluable to me.

I am also grateful to the University of Alberta (Edmonton, Canada), and to colleagues in its Department of Romance Languages.

ACKNOWLEDGEMENTS

CONTENTS

CONVENTIONS ADOPTED

Titles of poems. This is a study of the poetry of a tradition dominated by short poems, many of which were first published independently. It is therefore convenient to treat each one as a separate work, and in this book each title is in italic whatever its first mode of publication.

Place of Publication. In footnotes and bibliography mention of place of publication is here omitted for all books in English published in London, and all books in French published in Paris. Most university presses are noted in abbreviated form throughout.

Abbreviations for periodicals. In footnotes and bibliography the following abbreviations are used:

Revue des deux mondes	*RDM*
Revue d'histoire littéraire de la France	*RHLF*
Revue des sciences humaines	*RSH*

Abbreviations for volumes of poetry. These are given in a footnote immediately before first use, and only used in a single chapter or section.

Je cueille modestement des fleurs en attendant qu'il me vienne de l'esprit.

(A. de Musset, *Fantasio.*)

Flores vero persecutus est nemo quod equidem inveniam, nec nos nunc scilicet coronas nectemus — id enim frivolum est — sed de floribus quae videbuntur digna memorabimus.

(Pliny the Elder, *Naturalis historia.*)

1

FLOWER FIGURES
BEFORE 1820

I. Introduction: 'le culte des fleurs'

> I bring thee the flower which was in the beginning, the glorious
> lily of the great water.
>
> > (Inscription from the Egyptian temple of Denderah.)

> > The eye reads omens as it goes,
> > And speaks all languages the rose.
>
> > (R. W. Emerson, *Nature*, 1836.)

In 1896 Gabriel Viaud made this claim: 'En aucun temps le culte
des fleurs n'a été plus vif que de nos jours.'[1]. He was pointing to
a striking cultural phenomenon in nineteenth-century France which
had its literary counterpart. This study will describe the extensive
use of flower figures in French poetry and poetics in that period,
but it cannot ignore Viaud's assumption that there has always been
a 'culte des fleurs'. By the end of the nineteenth century, indeed,
many had commented on the nearly universal significance of the
flower in primitive and ancient culture.[2] Thus A. de Gubernatis
asserted in 1878: 'l'homme, à l'état de nature, a toujours retrouvé
une analogie si intime entre . . . la vie des plantes et celle des hommes,
qu'il a toujours supposé une correspondance fatale entre les uns et
les autres'.[3] More recent scholars might revise this phrasing, but
would not deny that plant life had a grandly inevitable status in
primitive symbolism.

From the first, no doubt, man has perceived 'how intimately his
own life is bound up with that of nature'.[4] Finding analogies
between human life and that of plants, primitive man understands
them in a wider context. According to Eliade, here correcting earlier
scholars such as Frazer, vegetation is never worshipped for itself but
rather because it 'embodies the sacred' and is 'the manifestation
of the life that renews itself periodically'.[5] Lévi-Strauss insists,

however, that primitive consciousness is not 'dominée par l'affectivité et noyée dans la confusion et la participation', but rather 'une pensée rompue à tous les exercices de la spéculation'.[6] Faced with nature's phenomena, primitive man interprets them in a language already capable of classification, combination, and contrast, and his plant symbolism will be complex in its rhetoric.

Eliade (like Frazer before him) pays much attention to the widespread occurrence of plant symbolism in cyclical fertility rites. When these entail (or imply) a ritual form of sacrifice it is common for the floral symbolism to combine the two thematic extremes of the cycle of death-and-renewal. According to the two myths preserved in ancient literary culture, violets grew from the blood of Attis, red roses and anemones from that of Adonis. By their blood-like colours these flowers stand metaphorically for human death and suffering; but they function, too, as metonymies for all vegetation with its powers of renewal. Here then are floral myth-symbols which express several immense binary themes (man/nature, death/life, change/continuity) while reconciling their contradictions. Separated from the sacrality of the primitive context, these flowers seem to prefigure later Western ones by their rhetorical complexity, and their meanings could even seem to imply a universal flower symbolism based on the intrinsic 'natural' appropriateness of (particular) flowers for particular rhetorical uses.

Some commentators do indeed envisage a cross-cultural flower symbolism more or less constant in meaning, semiologists and psychologists among them.[7] Thus Jungian psychology, assuming that the 'basic forms of the archetype are common to all nations and times', considers the flower directly related to the *mandala* which is the pre-eminent archetype figuring necessary processes of psychic death and rebirth.[8] Freud, too, sees no radical discontinuity between mythical and subsequent symbolic language, since he derives his interpretation of dream symbols from 'myths . . . from folklore . . . and from poetic and colloquial uses of language'; his declaration that 'blossoms and flowers represent the female sexual organs' is perhaps the *ne plus ultra* of the universalist interpretation of flower symbols.[9] Such confidence about a flower rhetoric semantically stable over time and across cultures makes large assumptions about human perceptions, mind, and language.[10]

For the present purpose it is not necessary to decide whether the significance of Attis' violets seems decipherable because they have 'universal' meaning or because they belong to Western tradition. This chapter will, however, attempt a survey of the literary uses of the flower figure in early Western tradition and in pre-nineteenth-century France. For without some awareness of this continuous intertextual 'culte des fleurs', it will not be possible to see its elaboration in the French nineteenth century for what it is: a new flower rhetoric for a new poetics.

II The Flower in Literary Tradition

> Voici des millions d'années que nous servons de texte de comparaison aux mortels.
>
> (*Les Fleurs animées*, 1846.)

i. Antiquity

In Hellenic culture, the early flower figures still recall their cultic origins. The Homeric *Hymn to Demeter*, among the earliest Attic poetry, includes a 'flower catalogue' in its opening account of the Rape of Persephone.[11] These flowers evoke both the beauty and the vulnerability of Demeter's daughter, and the miraculous many-blossomed narcissus is termed both 'beautiful plaything' and 'fatal snare' (it leads to the girl's abduction). Since the narcissus was associated with the underworld and with Demeter herself, the flower becomes an emblem of the myth as a whole, in a context at once literary and theophanic.

Although cults and myths celebrating a fertility goddess (Demeter, Gê, or Cybele) survived into the Classical period and beyond, Aristotelian method produced, in the works of Theophrastus, investigations of the plant world unconcerned with religious symbolism. These count, indeed, as the major works of botanical science in antiquity, since Pliny's later encyclopaedic *Naturalis historia* is a compendium of previous writers on the subject.[12] Yet within the culture which could demythologize flora so rigorously, literary tradition preserved and adapted the earlier connotations of this same flora.

The flower references in Homer already exemplify this. Narcissi and hyacinths bloom to celebrate the marital reconciliation of Zeus and Hera, veiled in a cloud of gold on Ida (*Iliad*, xiv. 346–51). The epithet for dawn, 'rosy-fingered' (*Odyssey*, xvii. 1), relates the colour and brilliance of the rose to the renewal of daylight. The violet is found in the *locus amoenus* around Calypso's cave (v. 72), a flowery pastoral landscape apparently withdrawn from the sufferings of life. Moreover, the episode of the lotus-eaters (ix. 80–103) speaks of a 'flowery food' which brings forgetfulness. These episodes, later to become common topoi, yield a connotation of the flower often found in Classical Antiquity: pleasure plucked from the vicissitudes of life. Indeed floral garlands very early stood for celebration: pleasure-giving flowers are associated with athletic or poetic success (Pindar) and with the pleasures of beauty, love, and conviviality (Sappho). All these connotations of the figure are also found in Latin literature.

Yet in Classical literature this same figure also evokes the ephemeral nature not only of pleasure but of life itself: the natural world provides the transition. 'Fair the spring violet but soon it fades', says Theocritus,[13] and Florus tells the whole life-story of the rose in five lines, each one a day in its life. For Mimnermus the very pattern of life is that of a flower: 'Youth's fair flower hath no tomorrow' (GT 191). Horace, in the same tradition, juxtaposes transient flower and short-lived man, and adds a practical conclusion concerning pleasure:

> huc vina et unguenta et nimium brevis
> flores amoenae ferre iube rosae,
> dum res et aetas et sororum
> fila trium patiuntur atra.
>
> (*Odes*, II. iii.)

This thematic dichotomy (pleasure/transience) is assumed too in Horace's witty use of the verb *carpere*, usually denoting the picking of flowers, in his advice to Leuconoe, 'carpe diem' (*Odes*, I. xi. 8). Ausonius' description of the rose's life-cycle in *De rosis nascentibus* leads to advice like Horace's: 'Collige, virgo, rosas dum flos novus'. A poem of Catullus's, cynical footnote to this tradition, points out that the *flos* of virginity fades when picked, 'carptus defloruit' (*Carmina*, lxii. 43).

The Classical flower figure bears, then, no simple theme. Moreover the Homeric examples themselves contain ambiguities: Calypso's garden is beautiful, but it is 'also a garden of lust, death, prey',[14] while the pleasure given by the lotus results in an almost suicidal escapism. Greek tragic realism joins here with the sombre view of plant life elsewhere reflected in the ontological myths of such flowers as the rose, the anemone, the narcissus, the hyacinth. In the pastoral genre, however, ancient literature sets up 'a false relation with nature',[15] in which flowers represent an ideal beyond suffering. A whole tradition of Theocritan idyllic landscape lies behind a description like this of Virgil's: 'hic ver purpureum, varios hic flumina circum / fundit humus flores' (*Eclogues*, ix. 40–1). Even this landscape can become expressive of emotional unease, as in Theocritus' lines:

> Now let the briar and the thistle flower
> With violets; and the fair narcissus bloom
> On junipers: let all things go awry,
> And pines grow pears, since Daphnis is for death.
>
> (*Idylls*, i. 131–4, GT 543.)

But the flowers here represent a stylized disordering of the pastoral setting, which remains ideal. This tradition more typically assumes the undimmed perfection of flowers, a brilliance which links them with the unchanging stars: Columella calls them 'terrestria sidera' in his *De re rustica*.

Outside the pastoral genre, other versions of the idealized spring landscape enlist plant imagery, among them Virgil's Elysium (*Aeneid*, vi. 638 ff.) and Ovid's golden age of *ver aeternum* (*Metamorphoses*, i. 1 ff.). But un-ideal nature, the world of 'lust, death, prey', counters this ideal everywhere in the literature of antiquity. Significantly, the common personification of spring (Chloris/Flora) is herself a victim of rape, and Ovid associates her with the violent origins of at least one flower: 'feci de sanguine florem' (*Fasti*, v. 201–23). Claudian's version of the Persephone story, *De raptu Proserpinae* (AD 395?), is an entire discourse built on a similar paradox. The idealized setting for the abduction (Sicilian Henna) is radiant with spring flowers (ii. 88–100), yet after the rape the land of death far outshines it in beauty: 'perpetui flores, quos nec tua protulit Henna' (ii. 289). This is a complex inversion of pastoral, an almost mystical treatment of nature and death, made possible by the literary tradition and its cultic origins.

But before the end of the Classical period, the flower also provided metaphors for aspects of literature itself. One such figure was the floral garland: beautiful materials carefully selected and woven together with artistry. Thus 'Simonides called Hesiod a gardener, Homer a maker of garlands. Hesiod created stories . . . Homer wove them into garlands'.[16] Pindar calls an ode in praise of an athletic victor a 'gleaming crown', and composition 'weaving an intricate hymn'. In a similar way, writers who gather materials to dispose them with care in an intricate pattern are sometimes compared with bees making honey culled from flowers. When writers on rhetoric characterize one of the three styles of oratory as 'flowery' (in Cicero *floridum* or *florens*, in Quintilian *antheron*), they emphasize its pleasing intricacy.[17] Dionysius applies this epithet to Hesiod, Sappho, and Anacreon, while Quintilian praises a whole passage as a 'flower' (*anthos*) apparently because it is brilliant, highly wrought, and pleasant.

It was early accepted that poems were themselves 'flowers of the muses': Plutarch quotes the term in a fragment of Sappho. But no single work in antiquity did more to establish this conceit than Meleager's 'garland' (*Stephanos*) of poems, a selection compiled in about 90 BC from six centuries of Greek poetry and forty-six authors. Many of the poems in the collection are indeed highly floral in reference. But Meleager's own poetry is especially notable for its floral epithets, not merely comparing girls with flowers ('lovely rose of Peitho', 'freshest flower of flowers') but using the garland conceit with great subtlety ('Is the rose Dionysios' garland, or he himself the garland's rose?')[18] Moreover, his introductory poem (GT 625) insists on the full meaning of the title metaphor by characterizing many of the poets as particular flowers. Thus not only gods and girls, but poems and poets are flowers, and the garland is an 'anthology'—a 'selection of (the best) flowers'. Other poetic anthologies followed Meleager's (although Diogenianus (*c.* AD 150) was the first to use the term as title), for the analogy between poetry and flowers was now definitively established. The very concept of anthology henceforth contains the metaphor: the finest writing is flower-like.

ii. *The Middle Ages*

As Western Christians explored their inheritance, they were to discover flowers in their Judaeo-Christian as well as their classical sources. From Genesis onwards, flowers represent abundance and fulfilment in the Old Testament no less than in Classical Antiquity. But in the Hebrew Scriptures, pleasurable fullness typically depends on the Lord of Israel: when he wills it, 'laetabitur deserta . . . et florebit quasi lilium'.[19] In only one book, the *Canticum canticorum*, is there floral imagery celebrating spring, beauty, and erotic love, apparently without reference to ethical monotheism.[20] Even the ubiquitous metaphor for mortality becomes a call to faith: 'omnis caro faenum et omnis gloria eius quasi flos agri . . . exsiccatum est faenum et cecidit flos; verbum autem Domini manet in aeternum.'[21] And when a New Testament text gives this passage an eschatological sense (since Christians are 'renati non ex semine corruptibili sed incorruptibili', Pet. 1: 23–5) it only underlines man's dependence on the eternal God. The Jesus of the Gospels tells his disciples to imitate the divinely-sustained lily: the message here is no less theocentric.[22]

Following its Scriptures, the Christian West was to see flowers, along with all natural things, as signs of God's overarching plan in creation, as 'res et signa'.[23] This is a tradition neatly exemplified in lines by Alan of Lille (d. 1203):

> Omnis mundi creatura
> quasi liber et pictura
> nobis est in speculum.
> Nostri status pingit rosa
> nostri status decens glosa
> nostrae vitae lectio.[24]

From the decline of the Classical world until the high Middle Ages, Christian culture avoided celebrating the mere pleasurable beauty of flowers and saw them as signs to be interpreted, lessons in the 'book of nature'. For St Bernard, even the stoniest (less flowery) parts of nature can yield the 'honey' of a Christian interpretation.[25] Yet the emblematic meanings attributed to flowers were derived from disparate sources (colour symbolism and Classical plant-lore among them) and thus never seem to have formed one accepted system of interpretation.[26]

But another floral tropology, more directly related to Christian concerns, was eventually developed from Scripture itself. A prophecy in Isaiah could suggest that Christ was the 'flos Dei' (c.890) and the incarnation a double flowering: 'Aureo flore . . . florens rosa / processit'.[27] The many allegorizing interpretations of the *Canticum*, from Origen to St Bernard, provided further floral epithets for Christ and Mary. By the twelfth century floral references to Christ (including 'flos florum') were commonplace, while Marian devotion had developed such imagery even more enthusiastically: Mary is 'flos de spina, spina carens, / flos spineti floria . . . flos campi, convallium / singulare lilium' (ML 229). The lily was a favourite emblem of Mary's purity, but she could also be described as a rose and, by cumulative hyperbole, as 'flos florum'. The figure of the *hortus conclusus* was applied to Christ, Mary, the Church, and the heavenly paradise. Widespread mystical elaborations of the flower figure like these are without parallel in Classical culture.

Imagery derived from biblical sources is found, too, in secular contexts. So the twelfth-century *Carmen de rosa* can use liturgical and Marian language creatively in a poem of secular love: the poet calls the girl 'virgo gloriosa', 'mundi rosa', and 'florem floridum'.[28] Provençal troubadour poetry too, secular though it is, often echoes religious language, as in these lines of Bernart de Ventadorn, recalling the spouse of the *Canticum*: 'joi de la flor, / e joi de me e de midons major'.[29] At the same time, Classical sources could be made to bear religious meanings. Christian typology had long seen Classical idealized landscapes as 'types' of its own *loci amoeni* and the flowers of pastoral could thus represent a Christian idea of perfection. Radbert's *Egloga duarum sanctimonialum* assumes a Theocritan heaven of 'flores et lilia' in which Christians can already participate,[30] and Bernard of Cluny reminds Christians in his *De contemptu mundi* to look forward to a 'patria splendida terraque florida, libera spina', eternal 'pascua vivida' (ML 223–6). Thus much literary floral imagery was Christian in some sense, either by derivation from biblical sources, or by typological use of Classical sources.

But by a singular development of the twelfth century (whether literary or more broadly cultural), the flower came once more to bear connotations forgotten since Classical times and only equivocally related to doctrinal Christianity: sensuous beauty, elegance, *amour-passion*.[31] In the secular Latin lyric, spring love is a common topos, as in the poem which begins 'Aprilis tempore . . . / pratum roseis armatur floribus / iuventus tenera fervet amoribus' (ML 316). The French idyllic romance *Floire et Blancheflor* is an elegant display of many kinds of flower figure (including 'pasque florie'), exceptional only in its extended use of such imagery.[32]. While numerous works of the twelfth and thirteenth centuries bear similar titles, others contain elegant comparisons between 'puceles' and flowers, particularly roses. Again, poems based on the 'debate of love' (like *Florence et Blanchefleur* or the *Dieu d'Amors*) give rich descriptions of eternal spring in the 'champ fleuri' where love dwells: a bower which is at the same time a profane *hortus conclusus* and a version of pastoral.[33]

The first part of the *Roman de la Rose* may be seen as a *summum* of such secular flower imagery.[34] The poem opens in flowery spring, 'Ou temps amorous plain de joie' (l. 48), with 'flors indes et perses' (l. 63). In the garden of Deduit, moreover, there are 'flors de diverses colors' (l. 1402), and the poet himself calls love's garden a 'paradis terrestre' (l. 636) and a 'leu plesant et delitable' (l. 1412). The poem's whole allegorical structure depends, indeed, on the lover's susceptibility to the overwhelming charm of the garden, and of the rose he especially desires: 'ce bouton que plus me plesoit / Que nus des autres ne fesoit' (ll. 1687–88). Yet the poem is by no means a straightforward celebration of this (secular) pursuit, for the conventional garden and flower imagery (Christian by derivation or typology) suggests an ironical perspective on it. Oiseuse and Deduit, for example, when they welcome the lover to the enclosed garden each wear a pagan 'chapel de roses' (cf. Sap. 2: 8). This is very much an earthly paradise, like Eden a garden in which a sin is committed. As Raison remarks of love, 'Ce est enfers li doucereus, / C'est paradis li dolereus' (ll. 4327–8). Adam picks an apple, the lover a rose: for all its beauty, this 'bouton' is (doctrinally) a flower of evil. The poem is both sensuous and ironic in its development of secular and Christian flower imagery.

So, too, Dante's *Divina commedia* achieves a union of the secular and mystical connotations of the rose in its triumphant final vision (*Paradiso*, xxx–xxxi). Since it is Beatrice who conducts Dante to his vision of the 'candida rosa', the flower represents in one sense the higher meaning of courtly love. But it is also a polysemic mystical symbol: it is Mary, Christ, the Church triumphant, the heavenly paradise, and a comprehensive symbol of the creator's love.[35] Connotations of the flower from literary and devotional traditions are brought together here in a single multifoliate rose.

Dante's immense symbolic flower-structure is of course without precedent as a literary form. Yet even its formal aspects owe something to earlier linguistic and cultural tradition. The flower was associated with perfection in forms like the elative *flos* (as in *flos aetatis*), the metaphorical *rosa mundi*, and the intensive form *flos florum*. So too the concept of anthology was invested with Christian meaning in the Latin monastic *florilegia*, selections of specially edifying texts and aids to salvation (flowers).[36] All these usages suggest that the flower could be an appropriate 'abstract' symbol for perfection, quite apart from its possible thematic connotations.

Dante's creative use of both abstract and connotative flower symbolism is the medieval high point of both traditions.

iii. France from the Renaissance to pre-Romanticism

Within French literary culture, the use of flower figures to indicate perfection became firmly established in the sixteenth century, and earlier superlative uses no doubt had some part in this. The Latin elative passed into the vernacular in such forms as 'la fleur de la Grèce' (Du Bellay), or 'La Fleur et antiquité des Gaules' (a book title of 1532). The concept of the medieval *florilegium* could give rise to titles like that of an early printed book: 'Les Fleurs . . . des faits merveilleux de Dieu' (1483). The singular form even became interchangeable with the plural (no doubt because of their equally superlative associations), so that an Italian title 'Fiori di virtu' (1475) could come into French as 'Fleur [sic] de vertu' (1530). Thus literary anthologies could bear titles which used these forms indiscriminately: 'Les Fleurs de Poésie Francoyse' (1534), 'La Fleur de Poésie Francoyse' (1543). The title given to a collection of Marguerite de Navarre's poems wittily combines the two kinds of superlative flower (and superlative pearl): 'Les Marguerites de la Marguerite des Princesses' (1547).

Certainly the superlative associations of the flower are exuberantly expressed and developed in Renaissance poetry. It everywhere celebrates, for example, the brilliant diversity of flowers. A *Blason du jardin* by G. Corrozet is a simple case: 'Jardin plaisant, doux, delectable . . . Jardin semé de toutes fleurs / Painctes de diverses couleurs'.[37] Ronsard praises floral diversity in various rhetorical contexts, sometimes in terms which suggest parallels in *émail* or *peinture:*

> Puis de livre ennuyé, je regardois les fleurs,
> Fueilles, tiges, rameaux, especes et couleurs,
> Et l'entrecoupement de leurs formes diverses,
> Peintes de cent facons, jaunes, rouges et perses,
> Ne me pouvant saouler, ainsi qu'en un tableau
> D'admirer la Nature, et ce qu'elle a de beau.[38]

Indeed for him flowers are typical figures of nature itself, which because it is 'variable en ses perfections' provides a model for 'copieuse diversité' in art.[39]

The beautiful brilliance of flowers is always assumed in the genres derived from Classical pastoral, and is often associated with immaculate female beauty. In Baïf's, Ronsard's, or Belleau's imitations of Theocritus or Ovid, the shepherdess's beauty emulates that of flowery nature:

> Plus esclattant luit ta beauté fleurie
> Qu'au beau Printemps la diverse prairie.[40]

Ronsard bases many figures on emulative comparisons between woman and flowers, presenting a naiad 'Qui comme fleur marchoit dessus les fleurs' (C i 27), or envisaging the rape of Cassandre as she gathers flowers, 'fleur, mille fleurs ravissant'. Such metaphors were so frequent during this period that the *flos florum* conceit naturally suggested itself. Marot uses this as a simple epithet for a woman ('Gris, Tanné, Noir, porte la fleur des fleurs'), but Ronsard's development of it is more subtle than Meleager's, more extended than a Marian hymn:

> En vain pour vous ce bouquet je compose,
> En vain pour vous, ma Deesse, il est fait,
> Vostre beauté est bouquet du bouquet,
> La fleur des fleurs, la rose de la rose.

> (C i 174.)

Such beauty is perfection indeed, since the flower imagery already stands for the perfection of perfection.

Renaissance poets also developed another topos from Classical and Christian tradition: the flower of transience. A poem of Jean Lemaire de Belges opens with the *flos foeni* (Isa. 40: 6–8), 'Nostre age est bref ainsi comme des fleurs', but continues more Hellenistically:

> Force se perd, toute beauté finit
> Et se ternit ainsi comme la rose.[41]

This poem concludes didactically with 'trois pensées', but as familiarity with ancient culture grew during the sixteenth century, the Horatian or Ausonian *carpe* replaced more pious advice. Thus there were imitations of Ausonius' *De rosis* by Des Periers, Du Bellay, Baïf, and Pontus de Tyard, besides Ronsard's definitive version in the ode beginning 'Mignonne, allons voir . . .':

> O vrayment marastre Nature,
> Puis qu'une telle fleur ne dure
> Que du matin jusques au soir! . . .
> Cueillez, cueillez vostre jeunesse:
> Comme à ceste fleur la vieillesse
> Fera ternir vostre beauté.[42]

Here is a delicate balance between charm and tragic poignancy, making the floral analogy more than the pretext for a *pensée* (pious, tragic, or opportunistic). Ronsard develops the same figure in his poem on the death of Marie ('Comme on voit sur la branche . . . ') where the final tribute suggests the poetic 'survival' of flower and woman after death, as the poet offers 'ce panier plein de fleurs, / Afin que vif et mort ton corps ne soit que roses' (C i 184). This is a flower figure expressing the poet's power to challenge mortality, in a complex rhetoric elaborated from the traditional association between beauty and flowers.[43]

It is not surprising to find that literary commentary, reflecting poetic practice, also makes considerable use of floral tropes. Ronsard can allude at the same time to anthology and to the Classical conceit of the bee-like poet: 'je choisiray les belles fleurs des Muses / Afin d'en esmailler un livre en vostre nom'.[44] He describes the aesthetic value of 'copieuse diversité' in a similar figure:

> De cette fleur que voici,
> Et de celle, et celle aussi,
> La mouche son miel facconne
> Diversement . . .

(C i 362-3.)

Ronsard could appeal, too, to Classical rhetorical theory, where ornate diversity had also been considered 'flowery'. Recalling Quintilian, he claims in comments on the *Franciade* that the epic poet must enrich his diction 'de comparaisons bien adaptées de descriptions florides, . . . de fleurs poëtiques' (C ii 1019). And if both poetic method and epic style can be characterized in floral imagery, so too can the distinction between two kinds of poetry.

> Poëme et Poësie ont grande différence.
> Poësie est un pré de diverse apparence
> Orgueilleux de ses biens et riche de ses fleurs,

Diapré, peinturé de cent mille couleurs,
Qui fournist de bouquets les amantes pucelles,
Et de vivres les camps des abeilles nouvelles.
Poëme est une fleur . . . [45]

This passage brings together several aspects of Renaissance flower poetics: diversity, rich ornateness, brilliance, perfection, and *copia*/anthology. The image of the flower garland bears all these meanings while suggesting as well the intricate organization proper to poetry. Fittingly, the opening lines of Ronsard's *Ode à Michel de l'Hospital* (C vi 386) summarize the poetic act in this metaphor and Belleau uses it in *Au Sieur Salomon*:

Ainsi tu vas triant au jardin des neuf soeurs
D'industrieuse main les mieux fleurantes fleurs
Pour te ceindre le front d'une couronne torte.[46]

Using diversely floral materials, the poet achieves a single highly-wrought garland—an appropriate superlative figure for a poetry giving diverse significance to the flower trope in practice and theory. Not until the nineteenth century was the flower again to play such a role in French poetry and poetics.

In the century following the death of Ronsard, many floral conceits passed from earlier sources into baroque and *précieux* poetry. The poems of the *Guirlande de Julie* (1634) made decorative use of old-fashioned floral emblematics (modest violet, pure or royal lily, etc.) and of the conventional tribute to beauty, in the service of fashionable *galanterie* and *esprit*.[47] So too devotional flower imagery, anthology titles, and the topos of the transient rose were all adapted to the new sensibility, and the brilliance of flowers was exuberantly celebrated.[48] But seventeenth-century writers sometimes raised new questions about how art is related to the beauty of flowers. Malherbe begins a poem saluting beauty in woman and nature with an aesthetic paradox:

Sus, debout, la merveille des belles!
Allons voir sur les herbes nouvelles
Luire un émail dont la vive peinture
Défend à l'art d'imiter la nature.[49]

Here floral brilliance is in competition with art, and is said to be triumphant. For other poets the aesthetic challenge of nature's 'peinture' is most acutely evident in the newly imported tulip. Saint-Amant calls this flower 'bizarre et merveilleuse', and Bussière exclaims:

> Mais ô ciel quel est ce prodige! . . .
>
> De quelle Circé voy-je icy
> Les merveilles sur cette tige! . . .
>
> Glorieuse, elle se joue
> Des traicts les plus subtils de l'Art.[50]

Nature reveals, in the tulip, almost magical aesthetic powers: disquietingly, it imitates art.

In the wider context of society, too, new approaches blurred the distinction between art and floral nature. Flowers ('new' or domestic) were collected and observed as botanical specimens or collectors' items; they were painted in new ways (in non-emblematic still life), and used as the basis for decorative patterns and vignettes. In the radical cultural realignment of the mid-seventeenth century, besides, flowers were excluded from Le Nôtre's highly stylized gardens, while *orangerie* flowers, flower painting, and floral decoration thrived.[51]

At the same period, literary taste began to allow much less importance to flower imagery. In poetry it survived listlessly in the decorative genres derived from pastoral, as an elegant motif furnished by tradition, while allusions to the ancient flowers of the muses became slight figures for the rococo delights of poetry. Boileau, it is true, makes this trope into a trenchant comparison between poet and gardener, as he archly imagines their situations reversed:

> [Si . . .] Tout à coup devenu poète et bel esprit,
> Tu t'allais engager à polir un écrit
> Qui dît, sans s'avilir, les plus petites choses,
> Fît des plus secs chardons des oeillets et des roses,
> Et sût même au discours de la rusticité
> Donner de l'élégance et de la dignité.[52]

These lines recall Ronsard only to differ from him on the dignity of 'la rusticité': they are a Classical *art poétique* in themselves. Reference to poetic flowers was usually a less pointed commonplace, as in Saint-Aulaire's *Élégie* of 1710, where the muse is surrounded by 'mille fleurs sur le Parnasse écloses', and offers 'couronnes de roses' to poets.

When writers 'discovered' nature in the mid-eighteenth century, the flowers they found there were scarcely the 'fleurs des Muses' of rococo taste. For the flowers of nature had an important place in the two new versions of pastoral informed by the new 'sentiment de la nature': Descriptive poetry and Sentimental prose writing.[53] The most important influence on Descriptive poetry was Thompson's *Seasons* (available in the Bontems translation from 1759), an influence attacked by Bernard in 1760:

> Aussi voit-on dans nos champs littéraires
> Changer l'émail de nos vives couleurs
> Et par l'effet des teintes étrangères
> Dénaturer nos primitives fleurs.[54]

The metaphor in this defence of Boileau hints that flowers are not irrelevant to the new controversy: Thompson does, indeed, provide enthusiastic descriptions of 'unnumbered flowers' in his 'Spring'. In French Thompsonian *Saisons* (like Bernis's of 1763 or Saint-Lambert's of 1769) floral description is less important than rhetorical forms like 'Flore nous appelle' and 'Naissez, brillantes fleurs'. Later imitators of Thompson's panoramic description like Delille (*Les Jardins*, 1782) paid more attention to nature's 'piquante irrégularité' when speaking of flowers, and even their frequent use of apostrophe ('Fleurs charmantes! par vous la nature est plus belle') was intended to emphasize the importance of 'sensations' and 'sentiments' as 'la source des plaisirs que nous causent les scènes champêtres'.[55] This genre therefore revealed, and helped effect, a major shift in taste: the flowers of nature's 'rusticité' were now associated with personal perception and emotion.

The literary treatment of floral nature was transformed in a similar (but much more radical) way by writers not constrained by the conventions of poetry. In *Julie ou la Nouvelle Héloïse* (1760), Rousseau not only praises rustic life, but provides in Julie's 'Élysée' a notable pre-Romantic 'agréable asile'. This is a garden which seems to Saint-Preux 'le lieu le plus sauvage, le plus solitaire de la nature' (even 'une île déserte') and which, with its wild and domestic flowers growing 'éparses de tous côtés', appeals to his 'imagination du moins autant qu'à [ses] sens'.[56] Yet Rousseau's distinctive approach to floral nature is most clearly shown in his 'ferveur' for botany after

1763–4. When he speaks of 'herborisation' in *Les Confessions* (XII) and *Les Rêveries du promeneur solitaire* (VII), his use of poetic vocabulary ('prairie émaillée', 'brillantes fleurs') points to the imaginative significance of his interest in botany. Although claiming this is an 'étude oiseuse' with no utilitarian purpose, he presents it as a retreat from society into rustic nature, a way to 'purifier [son] imagination' through contact with the innocence of plants. Besides, this activity produces the *herbier*, an anthology not only of plants but of remembered (recreatable) feelings, each dried flower a nostalgic emblem of happiness in a rustic setting: 'je n'ai qu'à ouvrir mon herbier, et bientôt il m'y transporte'.[57]

With this sentimental botany Rousseau opened up a new range of emotive possibilities for the literary flower: an emblematics of pathos, dependent on memory and personal sensibility, and typically related to the wilder parts of nature. This was a botanical sentimentality which (after 1790) Senancour was to exploit with introspective subtlety over forty years of writing, and of which Ballanche provides the characteristic outline in a work of the seventeen-nineties: 'Le jeune homme, dont toutes les fibres sont en harmonie avec la nature, essaie ses premières jouissances à la campagne: c'est là que, ne cueillant qu'avec choix les fleurs des plaisirs les plus purs, il se prépare un riche herbier de souvenirs.'[58] But two other pre-Romantic writers carried the new 'botany' into prose fiction. Bernardin de Saint-Pierre first presented *Paul et Virginie* as part of his *Études de la Nature*, almost as a work of botanical description intended to 'peindre un sol et des végétaux différents de ceux de l'Europe'.[59] His *île déserte* is, however, a pastoral idealization: the two children grow like 'deux bourgeons' (p. 88), flowers of 'beauté morale' (p. cxlv) amidst tropical rusticity, and an idealizing flower imagery is found at every level of the narrative. The flower message in Virginie's letter from Europe appeals in more ways than one to the sensibility of pathos: the emblematic *violette* (humility) and *scabieuse* (mourning) not only evoke past love and present separation, but anticipate the sentimental end as well. These are the 'signes mémoratifs' of a primary code of the feelings, but they are also complex figures conferring form on the narrative.

Chateaubriand's use of flowers in *Atala* is not dissimilar, for here a luxuriant landscape again furnishes an all-pervasive flower imagery used to give literary form to the central pathos of the narrative.[60]

The floral imagery related to virginity is especially notable. It begins as metaphorical substructure linked with landscape: 'les vierges [sont] des fleurs mystérieuses qu'on trouve dans les lieux solitaires' (p. 23). But a particular flower, the 'rose de magnolia', is associated emblematically with the virginal Atala: in death she is symbolized by a 'fleur de magnolia fanée' (p. 62) and even becomes a 'rose mystique' (p. 58), alive in heaven and in Chactas's memory. For good measure there is a reference to the biblical *flos foeni* ('J'ai passé comme la fleur', p. 62), yet the flower imagery in this work is an original synthesis: Christian flowers become indistinguishable from those of Florida, or from the sentimental flowers of innocence, memory, and loss.[61]

While prose fiction, by assimilating the sentimental *herbier*, found new literary uses for flower imagery, pre-Romantic poetry was more hesitant since it was still constrained by conventional diction. Léonard, in lines on his return to France, hints at the poetic possibilities of the new sensibility:

> Les voilà ses jonquilles d'or,
> Ses violettes parfumées!
> Jacinthes que j'ai tant aimées,
> Enfin, je vous respire encore.[62]

Other poets fittingly revived the conventional flowers of transience and loss, André Chénier among them:

> Je meurs. Avant le soir j'ai fini ma journée.
> A peine ouverte au jour, ma rose s'est fanée.[63]

Millevoye provides a neo-classical rationale for such figures:

> Les dieux aiment les fleurs qui parent la victime;
> Couronne-toi de fleurs une dernière fois,
> Lyre! . . . [64]

Indeed such neo-classicism dominated the poetry of the first two decades of the Romantic century, along with the still influential Descriptive tradition. The latter is exemplified in Chênedollé's roll-call of the 'riantes tribus du royaume de Flore':

> Le crocus au front d'or, l'hépatique empourprée . . .

> Et l'aimable pervenche aux pétales d'azur
> Et l'humble violette à l'haleine embaumée.[65]

Although this poem ends with the flowers' destruction as pathetic victims of frost, the diction here recalls Delille, and the list of flowers (one attribute for each) suggests a botany undisturbed by sentimentality. Poetic flower imagery was to be successfully integrated with the new sensibility only when poetry had learned with the prose writers to give free expression to the feelings. For it was to the tradition of Rousseau that the young Romantics turned as they rejected Delille (Lamartine planned in 1816 to 'mettre Atala en vers') not least because Rousseau, Bernardin de Saint-Pierre, and Chateaubriand had revealed in nature a new suggestiveness.

And sentimental flower imagery could serve as a reminder that the floral tropology of earlier periods had been capable of a wide range of emotional expression. Chateaubriand's debt to Christian imagery was clear, as was Bernardin de Saint-Pierre's reliance on earlier pastoral and emblematics. At the same time as they assimilated the pre-Romantic feeling for nature and its flowers, the young Romantics were directed towards neglected aspects of the Western *culte des fleurs*. Indeed many forgotten aspects of literary flower tradition were to become available after 1820. While Classical literature was already familiar, knowledge of medieval literature was to grow rapidly, along with interest in Ronsard and his period.[66] The flower imagery of the literary past was to prove indispensable in the elaboration of a specifically Romantic flower poetics.

III. Flowers in Esoteric Tradition and German Romanticism

i. Esoteric tradition

The Romantics inherited a literary tradition in which flowers could stand for human feelings (love, pathos, the sense of transience), for various kinds of perfection (human, Christian, literary), and for poetry itself. But they were aware that other more esoteric traditions had also made use of flower imagery. Of these, only the tradition associated with Orpheus had any intrinsic link with literature, for from the outset this figure appears not only as priest-interpreter of nature but also as musician-poet.[67] By Renaissance times, Orpheus is for Ficino the model for an artist enabled by inspiration (*furor poeticus*) to capture natural and cosmic harmonies, and Ronsard can present a poet with similar powers:

Il cognoist la nature et les secrets des Cieux,
Et d'un esprit bouillant s'eleve entre les Dieux.
Il cognoist la vertu des herbes et des pierres,
Il enferme les vents, il charme les tonnerres.[68]

The poet's privileged knowledge of plant-life helps confirm his status
as mystical seer-poet or *vates*. This concept has its counterparts in
the nineteenth century.

But other traditions of esoteric thought helped to establish plant-
life (especially flowers) as a phenomenon of occult significance either
spiritual or analogical. Thus Hermes Trismegistus, in one of the
central texts of the *corpus Hermeticum*, inspires his disciple to say:
'Now that I see in mind, I perceive myself to be the All. I am in
heaven and earth . . . I am in beasts and plants.'[69] Elsewhere this
tradition assumed the esoteric unity of the cosmos by crediting
flowers with occult astrological powers. Flower symbolism is found,
moreover, in the alchemical tradition: *le grand œuvre* (or the higher
mysticism associated with it) could be characterized by the alchemist
Nicholas Flamel as 'une belle Fleur en la sommité d'une montagne
très haute . . . un beau rosier fleury au milieu d'un grand jardin'.[70]
Cabbalistic tradition provided further imagery: the flower-shaped
sepiroth (symbolizing the ten 'manifestations' of spiritual reality)
of the 'tree of life'.[71] All these traditions—hermetic, alchemical,
and cabbalistic—flourished during the sixteenth and early seven-
teenth centuries, and all provided precedents for the esoteric flower
emblem of the Rosicrucian manifestos of 1614–16[72]. For the late
eighteenth century the *rose croix* was still a recognized occult
emblem.[73] But new forms of theosophical mysticism were to
prepare the way for further mutations of mystical flower symbolism.

The two eighteenth-century theosophers most influential on later
writers were Swedenborg (1688–1772) and Saint-Martin (1743–1803),
and both found some place for flowers and plants in the systems
they developed to counteract contemporary materialist tendencies.
For Swedenborg the spiritual world, more real than the material,
is united with it by *correspondentia*, 'collectively . . . [and] in every
part of it'. Thus 'a garden in general corresponds to heaven as to
intelligence and wisdom, and heaven is called in the Word the garden
of God and paradise'.[74] Furthermore, 'everything in the vegetable
kingdom has a certain relation to something in man' and this is no
mere emblematic relation but one validated by visionary experience:

'when I have been in gardens and have noticed the trees, fruits, flowers and herbs, I have seen their correspondences in heaven, and conversed with those in whom they were.' Thus garden-analogy becomes flower-vision and flower-speech, as the initiate greets the spiritual in the natural world. Saint-Martin's description of the cosmos is apparently more sceptical:

Les merveilles du Seigneur semblent jetées sans ordre et sans dessein dans le champ de l'immensité. Elles brillent éparses comme les fleurs innombrables dont le printemps émaille ses prairies. Ne cherchons pas un plan plus régulier pour les décrire. Principe des êtres, tous tiennent à toi.[75]

Yet behind the flower-like wonders of nature Saint-Martin perceives another kind of reality, 'comme une fleur est la réunion visible de toutes les propriétés qui existent invisiblement, depuis sa racine jusqu'à elle'. Naturalists describe only the visual aspects of things, whereas the theosopher seeks 'ce que nous n'y voyons pas'.[76] The natural flower, typifying all natural phenomena, is an 'emblème' pointing to spiritual reality, for 'le but du mystère de la nature est de nous élever . . . jusqu'à des régions vraiment analogues avec nous'.[77] Not surprisingly, Saint-Martin draws imagery for man's spiritual condition from plant-life: his soul is a 'plante fertile' and 'les hommes . . . qui meurent sont des plants en pépinière que l'on transplante'.[78]

Imagery of this latter kind was taken over by theosophical followers of Saint-Martin: in Fabre d'Olivet's neo-masonic rite a red *immortelle* is the 'emblème' of the initiate's soul, 'object d'une céleste culture', while for Ballanche the spiritual part of man is 'une fleur intellectuelle croissant sur une tige terrestre, une fleur immortelle'.[79] Such metaphors are related to the traditional typology of paradise, and Swedenborg was not alone in providing a theosophical variant of this typology. For Magneval the spiritual world open to the initiate is like a 'vaste champ où règne une verdure continuelle . . . que dominent les sept montagnes de roses'.[80] Nodier parodies such supernatural imagery, no doubt, when he makes the 'créature aérienne' of *Trilby* (1819) say: 'J'habiterais, si je l'avais voulu, de riantes demeures, sur des lits de mousse . . . ou dans le calice embaumé d'une rose qui ne se flétrit que pour faire place à des roses plus belles.'[81] More seriously, Ballanche's visionary Orpheus describes the final *palingénésie* of heaven-on-earth as a flowery synaesthesia: 'Lyre, beauté, grace, amour, souffle de la vie, âme, éclat et baume des fleurs, mélodies de l'air, ombrage sacré des bois, verdure calme des prairies . . . Nous tresserons des guirlandes de fleurs, de fleurs immortelles.'[82] These flowers are figures of realized eschatology (Christian and theosophical in origin), but also elements in an Orphic vision related to earlier anti-materialist views of universal harmony.[83]

Indeed the concept of a harmony by which the various parts of nature are connected with one another was found in many forms during the pre-Romantic period. Charles Bonnet held that in nature 'Tout est systématique . . . tout y est combinaison, rapport, liaison, enchaînement'.[84] Bernardin de Saint-Pierre celebrated the *Harmonies de la Nature*: 'Soyez mes astres, filles du ciel et de la terre, divines Harmonies. C'est vous qui assemblez et divisez les éléments, et qui organisez tous les êtres qui végètent ou qui respirent . . . Avec les feux de l'amour vous touchez la matière.'[85] Auguste Gleizes's account of the perceived unity of nature is even closer to Orphic, hermetic, and theosophical thought: 'Un amour universel unissait tous les êtres, il était dans l'air, dans l'eau, dans les plantes; il pénétrait tous les corps, on le respirait dans toute la nature.'[86] While Delisle de Sales claimed Pythagorean authority for his views on the 'âme universelle', Fabre d'Olivet translated the *Carmen aurea* and concluded in his commentary that 'l'Analogie est la grande loi des êtres'.[87] Whatever the differences between such systems, plant-life is seen in all of them as part of a large cosmic system, and everywhere significant relationships are found between plants, other parts of nature, and human feeling.

Plant-life is evoked, too, among the 'merveilles de la nature' which point to the transcendental. Thus Chateaubriand sees the complex 'amours des plantes', and Bernardin his 'harmonies végétales', as pointers to the deity, while for the theosophical Eckhartshausen the smell of flowers is enough: 'Je respire l'ambroisie des fleurs, je me délecte aux doux parfums de la rose . . . Quel est l'être à qui je suis redevable de tout cela?'[88] In an early fragment Ballanche provides a more pessimistic note, addressing spring: 'Tu m'apportes bien les douces émanations des fleurs, mais tu as oublié les riantes illusions de l'avenir. J'ai reconnu que le bonheur était une plante étrangère, qui croît dans les champs du ciel, et qui ne peut s'acclimater sur la terre.'[89] But Senancour finds a new sceptical use for this topos in a celebrated passage of *Oberman*:

Une jonquille était fleurie. C'est la plus forte expression du désir: c'était le premier parfum de l'année. Je sentis tout le bonheur destiné à l'homme. Cette indicible harmonie des êtres, le fantôme du monde idéal fut tout entier dans moi: jamais je n'éprouverai quelque chose de plus grand, et si instantané.[90]

Balancing his terms, Senancour confers momentary objectivity on the spiritual world perceived, while noting that this perception is a 'fantôme'. And the non-mystical insight which follows, a simple analogy between flower and woman, is presented as a mysterious paradox:

Je ne saurais trouver quelle forme, quelle analogie, quel rapport secret a pu me faire voir dans cette fleur une beauté illimitée, l'expression, l'élégance, l'attitude d'une femme heureuse dans toute la grâce et la splendeur de la saison d'aimer.

Thereafter these two perceptions become a single image of desired happiness and beauty, yet the 'image élyséenne' so formed is an image of the unattainable, an 'ombre indiscernable, errante, égarée dans le ténébreux abîme'.[91]

Thus Senancour makes use of pre-Romantic theosophical and anti-materialist terms in a context agnostic about mysticism. The *jonquille* becomes a figure for the power of the imagination, the emblem of a subjective ideal: 'Si [cette lumière] nous égare, elle nous éclaire et nous embrase.' And if Senancour's conceptual structure here anticipates that of much nineteenth-century poetry, so too does his metaphorical procedure. For he shows how 'analogie' and 'rapport secret', starting with flower-sensations of two kinds (smell and sight) can form a complex figure for the imaginative ideal, a flower 'puissante de tout le prestige de l'inconnu'.

ii. German Romanticism

Certain German writers, investigating the affinities between mystical and imaginative ideals with even more persistence than Senancour, gave floral tropology an importance it did not have for their French literary contemporaries (1790–1820). Goethe, for example, could treat flowers on several levels: in description throughout his literary work, in the alchemical 'Fair Lily-Maiden' or his *Märchen* (1795), and in his botanical study, with its prototypical 'symbolische Pflanze' (later 'Urpflanze').[92] With Jean-Paul Richter, however, the mystical orientation of Romanticism is clearly established. He seeks to perceive the 'flowery universe' not just as an artist (like Goethe) but as a visionary, and discerns the spiritual everywhere in nature, even in a single flower. In *Siebenkäs* he describes the 'second universe' of the spirit as a flower-bearing paradise, and throughout his work uses the dream-like commerce of flowers with stars (or sky) as a figure for the visionary imagination.[93] Thus in *Die unsichtbare Loge* (1792) the flower which effects the hero's initiation into the higher spiritual world is blue like the sky: 'Il avait la sensation de se fondre en une rosée, que venait aspirer le calice d'une *fleur bleue*; puis la fleur, en se balancant, l'éleva dans les airs et l'emporta vers une chambre haute.'[94] This is a mystical symbol even more striking than the giant dream-flowers elsewhere in the same work.

Novalis' symbolic blue flower grows out of the same mystical culture as Jean Paul's. From the first lines of *Heinrich von Ofterdingen* the flower arouses mystical longing in the hero: 'die blaue Blume sehn' ich mich zu erblicken . . . es ist, als hätt' ich vorhin geträumt, oder ich wäre in eine andere Welt hinübergeschlummert.'[95] The décor of the subsequent dream sequence (blue grotto, miraculous light, blue sky) implies that the flower ('eine hohe lichtblaue Blume') has supernatural attributes. Yet it is also associated with human love: the miraculous flower is also a woman's face. The flower imagery of Klingsor's tale suggests, besides, that love and the miraculous are indeed defining attributes of the main symbol, for here both Eros and Fabel are associated with a floral manifestation of harmony (p. 310). Flowers participate, too, in the final sequence of marriage and reconciliation, as the plants regain souls and voices lost since the *Urzeit* of primeval harmony: 'Alles sprach und sang' (p. 340). It would seem, indeed, that the flower stands in this work for a nature transfigured by wonder-working imagination and by love.

The *Blumensehnsucht* of Novalis was no isolated phenomenon, for mystical and oneiric flowers were common topoi in the work of his German contemporaries and followers.[96] Only E. T. A. Hoffmann, however, gave flowers of this kind a dominant place as images of the poetic imagination. Thus in *Der goldene Topf* (1814) the alchemical *Feuerlilie* represents the glamorous world of the imagination into which Anselm desires to be initiated: it gives 'die Erkenntnis des heiligen Einklangs aller Wesen'. Only by rejecting philistinism and everyday life does Anselm become worthy to receive the flower as dowry, and live with Serpentina 'in Poetry'.[97] By contrast, the complex aesthetic argument and form of *Prinzessin Brambilla* (1820) are centred on the concept of irony, the reflecting mirror of the *Urdarquelle*. Yet the birth of Princess Mystilis in the *Lotosblume* anticipates symbolically the final triumph of the ironic imagination. Besides, plant-imagery dominates *Meister Floh* (1822): it ends with a double marriage (the thistle Geherit and the tulip Gamaheh, King Sekakis and the Flower Queen) which is also a *Blumentod* giving everlasting harmony and repose from conflict. Hoffmann's flowers (like Novalis' blue flower) are figures which, while owing something to mystical and occult tradition, point to the power of the imagination and beyond that to a high view of Romantic Art itself.

Flowers, as figures for a harmonious other world, were also associated by some German Romantics with music: both music and flowers, after all, traditionally appear in paradise typology.[98] While Novalis introduces music and flowers together at moments of transcendent dreamlike harmony, Tieck describes the experience of music in terms of a flowery dream-paradise. In a similar way, the trancelike synaesthesia described in the well-known passage of Hoffmann's *Kreisleriana* also results characteristically from the experience of music. It is an 'Übereinkunft der Farben, Töne und Düfte. Es kommt mir vor, als wenn all auf die gleiche geheimnisvolle Weise durch den Lichstrahl erzeugt würden und dann sich zu einem wundervollen Konzerte vereinigen müssten.'[99] The sensation Kreisler goes on to describe is quite unlike this concert of the senses, for here it is smell and colour which produce dream and music: it is set off by a personal 'emblematic' association, with the smell of particular flowers ('der dunkelroten Nelken') evoking a particular musical timbre.

Possibly because the French Romantics were themselves attracted both by the concept of synaesthesia and by flower emblematics, this flower-piece was to gain more notice than either Novalis' or Hoffmann's own more ambitious flower figures. Indeed French writers of the nineteenth century were not to develop flower imagery rivalling theirs until the second half of the century, and then largely from indigenous sources. Yet Jean Paul and Hoffmann were widely read in France after 1830, and could at least provide precedents for the imaginative use of the flower figure; even Novalis may have exerted a 'secret' influence of the same kind.[100] Certainly German Romanticism, like the French pre-Romantic 'mystical' tradition, helped to make floral tropology part of the new sensibility. Madame de Staël might be characterizing either tradition when she praises the German writers for their 'sentiment de l'infini' and describes the poet's task in mystical terms: 'errer par la rêverie dans les régions éthérées, oublier le bruit de la terre en écoutant l'harmonie céleste, et considérer l'univers entier comme un symbole des émotions de l'âme'.[101] She also reminds her readers of C. H. von Schubert's dictum; 'les fleurs se tournent vers la lumière, afin de l'accueillir'.[102]

2

FLOWER LANGUAGES
IN
FRENCH ROMANTICISM

I. Nature's Flowers and Poetic Freedom

> Nymphe tendre et vermeille, ô jeune Poésie,
> Quel bois est aujourd'hui ta retraite choisie?
> Quelles fleurs, près d'une onde où s'égarent tes pas,
> Se courbent mollement sous tes pieds délicats?
> Où te faut-il chercher? Vois la saison nouvelle . . .
>
> Et Jupiter se plaît à contempler sa fille,
> Cette terre où partout, sous tes doigts gracieux,
> S'empressent de germer des vers mélodieux . . .
>
> Des vers, s'ouvrant en foule aux regards du soleil,
> Sont ce peuple de fleurs au calice vermeil.
>
> (André Chénier, 'Fragments de *Bucoliques*'.)[1]

When Delille pronounced in 1808 that in the plant realm 'tout est désenchanté', he no doubt held the new systematic botany more responsible than his own poetic tradition.[2] Rousseau, however, had insisted on the suggestiveness of flowers even while recognizing the claims of the new science, and noted in his botanical dictionary (under 'Fleur'): 'Si je livrais mon imagination aux douces sensations que ce mot semble appeler, je pourrais faire un article fort agréable aux bergers, mais fort mauvais pour les botanistes.'[3] The young Romantics were to associate the flowers of nature with 'douces sensations' in many ways, and they were to find more than one *langage des fleurs* expressive of the feelings. Even the traditional figure for poetry was early adapted for this purpose. Hugo, dedicating his first large-scale work (a Classical tragedy) in 1817, writes:

> Ce ne sont pas de ces fleurs immortelles
> Dont Racine se pare au céleste banquet;

Ce sont des fleurs simples et naturelles
Comme mon cœur; Maman, je t'en offre le bouquet.[4]

Marceline Desbordes-Valmore, in some lines of 1818, also invokes a poetry of the heart:

Ô douce Poésie!
Couvre de quelques fleurs
La triste fantaisie
Qui fait couler mes pleurs.[5]

These two sentimental uses of the traditional figure may be contrasted with Chénier's delicate neo-classical elaboration of it, but taken together these three examples suggest the importance of the flower figure even at the opening of the first Romantic decade.

Flower language was implicated from the first in the reaction against Classical diction and Descriptive poetry, since flowers had been an inescapable subject in the latter. As early as 1804 Senancour had accused the 'genre pastoral, le genre descriptif' of overworking terms like 'l'émail des prés' and so trivializing 'l'objet qu'[ils] prétendaient agrandir'.[6] In 1809, Viollet-le-duc had reproached the genre itself for its banality:

Décrivez, décrivez, peignez, peignez sans cesse,
Qu'à la fin d'une image, une image se presse.
Un insecte, une fleur, un caillou, chaque objet
Peut d'un poème entier devenir le sujet.[7]

By the mid-twenties, many shared these negative views. Nodier picks out scholastic flower-imagery for special condemnation, in lines celebrating the 'triomphe du romantique':

C'en était fait de Rome antique
Et du Parnasse de Chompré.
Adieu le bagage de Flore
Et le vermillon suranné
Dont ses fleurs ont illuminé
Les vieux doigts de la vieille Aurore.[8]

Forced to admit the aridity of the old modes, H. de Latouche finds a metaphor which links a ubiquitous Descriptive subject with the traditional figure for poetry:

> Ils sont beaux les vallons de l'antique Ausonie!
> Mais peut-être ce sol éclatant de couleurs,
> Longtemps sollicité s'est épuisé de fleurs.[9]

Hugo criticizes the deadening effects of scholasticism on poetry in the image of a petrified flower: the 'forme primitive' of the flower remains, but its 'parfum' is lost (A i 282–3).

But such writers could deprecate petrified flowers, or those of *Parnasse* and *Ausonie*, without disqualifying the flower as a metaphor for art. Latouche suggests a tolerant enlargement of the old image to allow for the new growths: 'Toute idée est féconde et la ronce a du miel'. Hugo, in the preface to his 1826 *Odes et Ballades*, is more radical:

La pensée est une terre vierge et féconde dont les productions veulent croître librement, et, pour ainsi dire, au hasard, sans se classer, sans s'aligner en plates-bandes comme les bouquets dans un jardin classique de Le Nôtre, ou comme les fleurs du langage dans un traité de rhétorique. (A i 280–1.)

Using a contrast familiar in Descriptive poetry itself (Kent versus Le Nôtre), Hugo is here denying that diction should be controlled by genre-related conventions. Yet his imagery implies a more total liberation for poetry. These 'productions' which resist arrangement in flower-beds are the organic growths of creativity in its natural fertile state. The central passage in the preface goes on, besides, to develop these metaphors, as the new freedom is pictured as 'une forêt primitive du Nouveau Monde': the symmetry, topiary, and 'bouquets' of Versailles are to be replaced by the 'sauvages harmonies', 'végétation profonde', and floating 'îles de fleurs' of the forest of *Atala*.

Hugo's choice of metaphor raises a question about the subject matter of the new poetry: were the floral parks and 'prés' of the school of Delille to give way to tropical exoticism? Little in Hugo's 1826 volume suggests this. Nor does contemporary Romantic poetry admit it as a real option: four lines in Vigny's *Eloa* (1822) reveal its limitations (with their 'jasmin des Florides' and 'non-pareille'), despite the hope voiced by F. Denis and Sainte-Beuve in 1824 that such 'images étrangères' might provide a new source of inspiration for poetry.[10] Only E. Souvestre, writing in 1830, anticipates the later uses of such imagery in the poetry of escape:

Ô terre des Incas! dans tes grandes savanes
J'irais chercher un nid au milieu des lianes,
Et dans l'ombre et les fleurs, là, comme enseveli,
Rêver et m'endormir au chant du bengali.[11]

Exoticism in Chateaubriand's manner was perhaps a less fertile source of inspiration, in the 1820s, than orientalism. Hugo himself, in *La Fée et la Péri* in the 1826 volume, presents the Orient in terms which might justify it as poetic material:

Mais Dieu qui pour l'Asie a des yeux moins austères,
   Y donne plus de fleurs aux terres . . . ! . . .
L'Orient fut jadis le paradis du monde.
Un printemps éternel de ses roses l'inonde,
Et ce vaste hémisphère est un riant jardin.

(A i 548–9)

This is the Orient which, as the inspiration of *Les Orientales* (1829), is compared to a 'mosquée . . . épanouie au soleil comme une large fleur pleine de parfums' (A i 579). And when Hugo characterizes the Orient as especially flowery, as Edenic spring, or as sleepily fragrant, he is emphasizing its attractions as a new terrain for escapist pastoral. The poems of the 1829 collection are undeniably escapist, and this volume proclaims its forgetfulness of the present 'préoccupations graves du public'. Much of the incidental orientalism of early Romanticism, indeed, makes use of the flowers of an exotic pastoral landscape to achieve a distancing timelessness:

Aux bords du Bendemir est un berceau de roses
Que jusqu'au dernier jour on me verra chérir.
Le chant du rossignol dans ses fleurs demi-closes
   Charme les flots du Bendemir.[12]

Amable Tastu's flowers here, like those of Souvestre, anticipate the flowers of a later poetry of free imaginative evocation. Whether as elements in a charmed landscape, or as a metaphor for poetic escapism, the flowers of exotic pastoral suggest new possibilities for poetry: Hugo's use of flower terms in the rhetoric of poetic freedom is by no means arbitrary.

A few months before Hugo's 1826 preface, Sainte-Beuve had made his own abjuration of Descriptive method ('copie fidèle et monotone de la nature inanimée') and proposed a new function for natural settings in poetry. French poets should, like the English *lakistes*, learn to 'associer à ces peintures les impressions qu'elles faisaient naître, et de les vivifier par un reflet des sentiments humains'; unlike prose-writers (Rousseau, Bernardin, Chateaubriand) they had too long ignored 'une source nouvelle d'émotions et d'images'.[13] As Sainte-Beuve knew, a few of Lamartine's earliest *Méditations* had drawn (ambiguous) attention to this procedure:

> Je promène au hasard mes regards sur la plaine,
> Dont le tableau changeant se déroule à mes pieds. . . .
> Mais à ces doux tableaux mon âme indifférente
> N'éprouve devant eux ni charme ni transports.[14]

In these lines, Lamartine speaks of Descriptive method only to reject it. Typically, neither Lamartine nor Hugo dwell on 'doux tableaux' of this kind, since any such description might be too reminiscent of Delille: the natural scenes in their early poetry are as large and undetailed as the emotions they reflect. Indeed, 'peintures' of landscapes including flowers are rare in the Romantic poetry of the first period, and the few examples of such floral 'tableaux' are carefully legitimized by an emotive context. Madame Tastu's nostalgic *Scènes du passé* include

> Verts gazons où fleurit la blanche marguerite,
> Ombrage qu'au printemps la violette habite.[15]

Jules Lefèvre attempts an unhappy alliance of flowers and elegiac feeling:

> L'aubépine est en deuil, et les faibles pervenches
> De leurs boutons fleuris s'échappent sans couleurs.[16]

But the emotion-filled flower imagery which elsewhere pervades Romantic poetry is not based on any association of 'sentiments' with 'peintures' of the kind proposed by Sainte-Beuve in 1825.

Yet the Descriptive model, in diction and method, could still exert some attraction even at the end of the twenties. Sainte-Beuve himself, as Joseph Delorme, borrows from a 'bagage de Flore' which belongs as much to Delille as to the Pléiade or to Chénier:[17]

> Printemps, que me veux-tu? pourquoi ce doux sourire,
> Ces fleurs dans tes cheveux et ces boutons naissants?

> (p. 27.)

> Fleurs, ne vous pressez pas d'éclore.
>
> (p. 128.)

Yet Sainte-Beuve, no doubt aware of the problems posed by such flower diction, displays an ambiguous attitude to the countryside which is the subject of Descriptive poetry. In a poem like *Le Bonheur champêtre*, it becomes an idyllic illusion contrasted with urban reality ('J'ai regagné la ville . . . / Adieu l'illusion!') and the contrast itself is summarized in a flower metaphor:

> la fleur, où d'abord l'œil se pose
> Pâlit sous le regard et n'est plus une rose;
> Le calice a jauni.
>
> (p. 58.)

In his own review of the second edition of the work, besides, he characterizes Delorme as an urban poet: 'il vivait dans un faubourg, ne connaissait d'arbres que ceux de son boulevard, de fleurs que celles qui poussaient dans les fentes des pavés de sa cour.'[18] But Sainte-Beuve is here perhaps less concerned to refuse the Descriptive model than to disclaim the 'douleurs philosophiques et aristocratiques' of a Lamartine or a Hugo: in *Le Cénacle*, after all, he had called himself an 'humble fleur pâlissante, / Le bluet du sillon' (p. 65).

Gautier sets similar limits to the poetic space of his own first poems. He too is 'urban' ('il n'a vu du monde que ce que l'on en voit par la fenêtre'), and he too prefers a small-scale rusticism to the Romantic grandiose:

de petits paysages à la manière des Flamands, d'une touche tranquille, d'une couleur un peu étouffée, ni grandes montagnes, ni perspectives à perte de vue, ni torrents, ni cataractes. Des plaines unies . . . d'humbles coteaux rayés où serpente un chemin . . . un ruisseau qui gazouille sous les nénuphars . . . une marguerite qui tremble sous la rosée . . . Voilà tout.[19]

This claim is borne out by the reduced *paysage* of a poem like *Le Sentier*:

> C'est plaisir de le voir en mai, lorsque les fleurs
> Étalent à l'envi sur ses bords leurs couleurs,
> Rouges coquelicots et marguerites blanches,
> Asphodèles, bleuets, chrysanthèmes, pervenches
> Sous la goutte de pluie inclinant leur azur;

> Violettes, trésor de parfums: un jour pur
> En fait éclore assez pour combler des corbeilles.[20]

Apart from its inventive versification, this passage is recognizably Descriptive in character: it relies on the pleasures of seeing and describing, avoids strong emotion, and ignores society. Indeed, when Gautier defends such poetry against the new requirements of 'l'art social', his metaphorical language contains an appeal to the self-sufficient beauty of flowers: 'L'art, c'est la liberté, le luxe, l'efflorescence, c'est l'épanouissement de l'âme dans l'oisiveté'.[21] His poetry is to be free (like Hugo's in *Les Orientales*) to ignore the concerns of *cité* and *ville*, finding precedent in the idleness associated with pastoral and Descriptive tradition.

The more sophisticated Gautier of the influential *Mademoiselle de Maupin* (1835–6) could still recognize the attraction of the old rustic modes:

N'as-tu jamais remarqué comme l'ombre des bois . . . les riantes perspectives, l'odeur du feuillage et des fleurs, tout ce bagage de l'églogue et de la description, dont nous sommes convenus de nous moquer, n'en conserve pas moins sur nous . . . une puissance occulte à laquelle il est impossible de résister?[22]

And he could present the escapist aspects of poetry in similar terms:

— Mais, hélas! le monde de l'âme n'a pas d'Ardennes verdoyantes, et ce n'est que dans le parterre de poésie que s'épanouissent ces petites fleurs capricieuses et sauvages dont le parfum fait tout oublier.[23]

The flowers of rustic escapism here serve as an appropriate analogy for an art forgetful of social concerns, and in a poem of 1838 Gautier makes them central to his polemic against Hauréau's views on social utility:

> Il est dans la nature, il est de belles choses,
> Des rossignols oisifs, de paresseuses roses,
> Des poètes rêveurs . . .
>
> Ils resteront des mois assis devant des fleurs,
> Tâchant de s'imprégner de leurs vives couleurs; . . .
>
> Vos discours sont très-beaux, mais j'aime mieux des roses.[24]

Flowers are invoked too in the preface to *Mademoiselle de Maupin*, specifically as an analogy for art. Like art, they are 'useless' but indispensable because of their beauty: 'il n'y a qu'un utilitaire au

monde capable d'arracher une plate-bande de tulipes pour y planter des choux'.[25] Attacking a variety of utilitarian views, Gautier can make the flowers of 'l'églogue' and 'la description' into new 'fleurs des Muses', in the service of aesthetic autonomy.[26] For him, as for Hugo, a renewed flower rhetoric has helped define a radical artistic freedom.

II. Emblems and Metaphors

In their reaction against Classical diction, the Romantic poets soon learned to adapt another aspect of flower rhetoric to their own sensibility, and to make use of flowers as emblems (or metaphors) for meanings and feelings. They were to develop the concept of the *langage des fleurs* with particular assiduity. This term designated, at first, a Turkish custom reported by Lady Mary Wortley Montagu: the use of a secret flower code for love messages in the harem.[27] Bernardin de Saint-Pierre spoke of similar oriental flower codes,[28] and M. Hammer provided in 1809 a glossary for 'ce langage mystérieux d'amour et de galanterie'.[29] It was this concept of a flower code able to express a range of feelings[30] which provided the model for the popular flower emblematics of the nineteenth century. In 1810–11 three pioneering works of flower lore provided glossaries of flower-meanings (derived from mythology, folklore, and literature) without paying marked attention to 'galanterie'.[31] Subsequent flower dictionaries, while often based on one or more of these works, adapted their 'meanings' for sentimental salon use: they invoke the Turkish *selam* (as the flower language was called after a note in Byron), no less than Western emblematic tradition.[32]

But the *selam* was itself a subject of literary interest. For the Hugo of 1820 these 'doux messages / Où l'amour parle avec des fleurs!' (Ai 293) typify the escapist charms of the Orient. Musset addresses a flower which has been sent to him as a 'mystérieuse messagère':

> As-tu pour moi quelque message?
> Tu peux parler, je suis discret.
> Ta verdure est-elle un secret?
> Ton parfum est-il un langage?[33]

Indeed as a wordless language which is both *doux* and mysterious, the *selam* could hardly escape the attention of writers. Sainte-Beuve

in 1824 quotes approvingly Fernand Denis's comment on it: 'Messager plus discret que notre écriture, maintenant si connue, son parfum est déjà un langage, ses couleurs sont une idée.'[34] Balzac, who presents the *selam* in great detail in *Le Lys dans la vallée* (1837), calls it 'une science perdue en Europe où les fleurs de l'écritoire remplacent les pages écrites en Orient avec des couleurs embaumées'.[35] Both Balzac and Gautier, besides, draw attention to the 'allegorical' aspects of such flowers and Gautier points out that in the *selam* 'Chaque fleur est une phrase'.[36] Senancour makes explicit the implied comparison between this flower-language and literary forms: 'les orientaux, s'attachant à interpréter les nombreuses différences qu'on remarque dans les parfums ou dans les nuances des fleurs, en forment une suite d'emblèmes et une espèce de langue poétique ou romanesque.'[37] The flower code could provide a model (if one were needed) for the semantic use of flowers in poetry.

Nor was the emblematic ascription of meanings to particular flowers uncommon in early Romantic writing. The procedure could be followed straightforwardly ('C'est l'amandier qui porte l'espérance / . . . Le lilas blanc recèle la constance')[38] or with botanical and psychological precision, as by Nodier addressing the *anémone des bois*: 'Ta tige courbée sur elle-même est l'emblème de la mélancolie.'[39] Desbordes-Valmore structures whole poems around it, as in *L'Églantine* ('Églantine! humble fleur, comme moi solitaire'), or gives narrative significance to emblematic procedure: 'Et j'ai vu tout un sort dans ce rapide emblème'.[40] The flower sonnets in Balzac's *Illusions perdues* depend, too, on the emblematic principle:

> Chaque fleur dit un mot du livre de nature:
> La rose est à l'amour et fête la beauté,
> La violette exhale une âme aimante et pure,
> Et le lis resplendit de sa simplicité.[41]

It is perhaps less the 'livre de nature' which speaks here (and in the preceding examples) than the popular flower dictionary: the 'meanings' of such single flowers are not inconsiderable, but the procedure itself limits their emotional effects. Not surprisingly, later writers were to find the concept of the *langage des fleurs* more useful than emblematic practice.

Yet in relation to flowers considered generically (*les fleurs, la fleur, une fleur*) the Romantics made use of a wide range of emotive connotations, adapting older figures to convey the sensibility of pathos or mysticism in a new 'emblematics' of meanings and feelings. Since (for example) the pathos of mortality underlies much Romantic sensibility, the ancient topos of transience is widely used. Hugo juxtaposes it with *selam* sentimentality in *Regret* (1821):

> Tu mets tous tes amours, vierge, dans une fleur.
> Mais à quoi bon? La fleur passe comme la vie.
>
> (A i 451.)

Lamartine sets out the biblical simile in *La Poésie sacrée*:

> L'homme vit un jour sur la terre
> Entre la mort et la douleur; . . .
>
> Il tombe enfin comme la fleur.
> (G 78.)

Even in its simplest form, the figure remains current well into the second decade of Romantic poetry. Hugo uses it in his *Soirée en mer* of 1836:

> Sur votre plus belle rose,
> Sur votre lys le plus beau,
> Savez-vous ce qui se pose?
> C'est l'oubli pour toute chose,
> Pour tout homme le tombeau!
> (A i 974.)

Gautier's *Comédie de la Mort* (1838), for all its varied flowers of death, does not neglect the basic figure:

> Ne laissez pas mourir, vous qui donnez la vie,
> La pauvre fleur qui penche et qui n'a d'autre envie
> Que de fleurir un peu.[42]

Desbordes-Valmore had early developed from it a whole graveyard genre ('C'est ici le mélange / Des roses et des pleurs') often made more poignant by personal reference:

> Toujours je pleure au nom de mon enfant;
> Je le revois dans la fleur éphémère.[43]

Indeed for Romantic poets the flower is an almost inescapable image for the death of vulnerable beings like women and children. Thus Musset uses the figure in the simple apostrophe form ('Tu t'es

évanouie! ô toi, fleur solitaire')[44] as does Hugo, referring in
Fantômes (*Les Orientales*) to the death of young women: 'Toutes
fragiles fleurs, sitôt mortes que nées!' (A i 667). But in this latter
case Hugo heightens the pathos by contrasting the flowers of
mortality with the 'roses de la vie, / Beauté, plaisir, jeunesse, amour!'
(A i 671).

Indeed the ancient figure coupling these 'roses de la vie' with the
concept of ephemerality was revived in a number of Romantic forms.
Lamartine employs the full Horatian *carpe diem* in his *Élégie*—

> Cueillons, cueillons la rose au matin de la vie;
> Des rapides printemps respire au moins les fleurs.

> (G 143.)

—and it was also taken up by Hugo, Vigny, and Sainte-Beuve. But
the new sensibility was not well served by this 'formule brutale et
impérieuse'[45]—Desbordes-Valmore, like Amable Tastu, follows
Thomas Moore in replacing Horatian pleasures by Romantic
'dreams':

> Hâtons-nous de cueillir et les fleurs et les songes,
> Les songes et les fleurs ne seront plus demain.[46]

Often the elegiac component here (the *fleur fanée*) is used by itself
to convey a disillusion for which there is no remedy:

> Le charme des fleurs que je cueille
> Sous mes doigts se fane et s'effeuille:
> Non, je ne veux plus espérer![47]

Tastu's world-weariness is echoed by many poets including Hugo
('Toutes fleurs pour moi sont fanées'), Lamartine ('ce désert de la
vie / Où toujours sous mes pas chaque fleur s'est flétrie'), and
Desbordes-Valmore ('Plus d'espoir . . . plus de fleurs').[48] Hugo uses
a heightened form of the image in 1839, contrasting present
disillusion with past hopes:

> Fleur lumineuse à l'ombre épanouie.
> Cette vision
> S'est évanouie!

> (A i 1110.)

Such ephemeral flowers make a considerable contribution to the
imagery of Romantic melancholy.

The flowers of memory find fewer poetic uses. Some of Desbordes-Valmore's flower images, it is true, express simple nostalgia for *le sol natal* (Ô mon pays . . . une fleur me parlerait de toi') or for youth:

> Qui n'a cru respirer, dans la fleur renaissante,
> Les parfums regrettés de ses premiers printemps?[49]

As feeling-filled emblems of past experience, such figures recall Rousseau's or Senancour's mnemonic emblematics. But if similar emblems were commonly put to sentimental uses (as in the 'fleur bleue d'Allemagne' of Hugo's *Ruy Blas*), they did not become a major topos of Romantic poetry. Although there is a 'fleur séchée dans un album' in a Lamartine poem of 1827 ('Et je trouve, en tournant la page, / La trace d'un beau jour'), it evokes the past without emotion (G 1198). Yet there are other flower figures representing a means of survival for experiences from the past, a denial of the passage of time. Lamartine, adapting Ausonius and Ronsard, tells the *bien-aimée* of *Chant d'amour* that although her beauty will fade 'comme une fleur passée', it will be preserved in the *album* of the poet's heart:

> Là, ta beauté fleurit pour des siècles sans nombre;
> Là ton doux souvenir veille à jamais . . . [50]

Love inspires Hugo, too, to deny the passage of time:

> Je puis maintenant dire aux rapides années:
> — Passez! passez toujours! je n'ai plus à vieillir!
> Allez-vous-en avec vos fleurs toutes fanées;
> J'ai dans l'âme une fleur que nul ne peut cueillir!
> (A i 878.)

These are flowers preserved from withering by almost mystical powers of feeling, eternally alive in the poet's soul.

More common, no doubt, were the flower figures which draw directly on mystical tradition (Christian or theosophical) to deny mortality. Sainte-Beuve (imitating Wordsworth) promises Laure survival after death:

> Tu fleuriras, ange toi-même,
> Fleuron du sacré diadème.[51]

Lamartine's Jocelyn anticipates heaven in similar terms, praying to be carried off to a land 'Où de nectar les fleurs sont toujours pleines':

> Car l'âme aussi veut le ciel pour éclore
> Et la prière est le parfum des cœurs.

(G 641.)

The most powerful statement of such imagery is found in a prose work, Balzac's *Séraphîta* (1835), in which the mystical androgyne is assumed as a 'fleur du ciel', a 'fleur des Mondes', into the spiritual realm.[52]

When characterizing the innocence and purity of women and children, moreover, Romantic poets use a related type of flower imagery, derived in part from the Christian connotations of virginity but owing something to their sentimental developments in pre-Romantic works like *Paul et Virginie* or *Atala*. Hugo, in one of his first successful poems, *Les Vierges de Verdun*, celebrates the innocent vulnerability of his heroines by invoking the flowers of the victim, and tells the *vierges* that the same flowers ('ces symboles touchants') will become their martyrs' crowns (A i 301). More commonly, a celestial innocence is presented as the normal attribute of admirable young women. Gautier describes the girl in *La Jeune fille* as 'un souvenir des cieux, / Une fleur au désert'[53] and Sainte-Beuve can write:

> Aimer, c'est croire en toi, c'est prier avec larmes
> Pour l'angélique fleur éclose en notre nuit.[54]

Such imagery, linking mystical and sentimental traditions, does not lack erotic overtones. Gautier's *Magdalena* is a 'pâle fleur d'amour éclose au paradis', Vigny's Eloa is 'comme un beau lys' but susceptible to seduction, and even Séraphîta is an object of sentimental love.[55] Balzac draws out many of the implications of this imagery by contrasting the carnal and 'celestial' views of womanhood in *Le Lys dans la vallée*,[56] and Hugo sums up these ambiguities in *Date lilia* (1834):

> Elle! tout dans un mot! c'est dans ma froide brume
> Une fleur de beauté que la bonté parfume!
> D'une double nature hymen mystérieux!
> La fleur est de la terre et le parfum des cieux!

(A i 913.)

The unequivocal innocence of childhood is celebrated by several Romantic poets. Hugo's *La Prière pour tous* provides a heightened form of this type of sentimental piety, in which children become 'flowers' with a sentimental or expiatory function:

> Pour ceux que les vices consument,
> Les enfants veillent au saint lieu;
> Ce sont des fleurs qui le parfument,
> Ce sont des encensoirs qui fument,
> Ce sont des voix qui vont à Dieu!
>
> (A i 797.)

And in part VII the poem takes on an ecstatic intensity:

> Jasmin! Asphodèle!
> Encensoirs flottants! . . .
>
> Fleurs dont la chapelle
> Se fait un trésor! . . .
>
> Fêtes réjouies
> D'encens et de bruits!
> Senteurs inouïes!
> Fleurs épanouies
> Au souffle des nuits! . . .
>
> De la terre entière,
> Des champs de lumière
> Parfums les plus doux!
>
> (A i 798–9.)

Lines like these display the new evocative power of this type of imagery.

Indeed, Hugo might almost be illustrating here the poetic method recommended by Pierre Leroux in an article of 1829: 'cette manière qui consiste à ne développer jamais l'idée morale, mais à lui substituer un emblème ou un symbole'.[57] This is a 'style symbolique' which presents 'l'abstrait sous des formes matérielles, souvent ravissantes' using beautiful natural objects as expressive emblems for idealized feeling and meaning. Here is a poetics well exemplified by the connotative flower imagery developed in the first two Romantic decades.

The flower imagery of pathos and sentimental mysticism could also prompt new ways of speaking of poetry itself. Thus Lamartine makes the transient flower into an ambitious synaesthetic figure for poetry.

> La fleur tombe en livrant ses parfums au zéphire;
> A la vie, au soleil, ce sont là ses adieux;
> Moi, je meurs; et mon âme, au moment qu'elle expire,
> S'exhale comme un son triste et mélodieux.
>
> (G 76.)

Or he can transform the Horatian formula to suggest that ephemeral experience can only be made to survive in the *album* of poetry:

> Vous tomberez ainsi, courtes fleurs de la vie!
> Jeunesse, amour, plaisir, fugitive beauté!
> Ainsi vous tomberez, si la main du génie
> Ne vous rend l'immortalité!
>
> (G 13.)

Hugo presents *Les Feuilles d'automne*, moreover, as an elegiac poetry concerned with ephemerality ('les mille objets de la création qui souffrent ou qui languissent autour de nous, une fleur qui s'en va . . . ') and the poems themselves are released to the world as 'des feuilles flétries, / . . . toutes défleuries' (A i 715, 806). The flowers of pathos can furnish new variants on the flower figure for poetry.

On the other hand it is the flowers of sentimental mysticism which provide the model for an image in Vigny's preface to *Chatterton* (1834), where the mere *homme de lettres* is presented as ignorant of the distant mysteries of poetry: 'il les respire de loin comme de vagues odeurs de fleurs inconnues'.[58] For Hugo, again, the sentimental devotion to a pure woman gives rise to an image for the poet's mysterious task:

> Oh! vous faites rêver le poète, le soir! . . .
> Car l'âme du poète, âme d'ombre et d'amour,
> Est une fleur des nuits qui s'ouvre après le jour
> Et s'épanouit aux étoiles!
>
> (A i 778.)

The language Gautier adopts in *Mademoiselle de Maupin* to praise virginal purity ('une chaste fleur . . . un beau lis') is similar to that he uses for beauty itself: 'Fleur éphémère et fragile qui croit sans être semée, pur don du ciel! . . . tu es admirable et précieuse comme

. . . le parfum du lis séraphique'.[59] Hugo employs flower imagery when attributing his best inspiration to children:

> l'enfance aux riantes couleurs
> Donne la poésie à nos vers, comme aux fleurs
> L'aurore donne la rosée.
>
> (A i 750.)

Elsewhere, emphasizing the mystery of the 'enfances sublimes' of musicians or poets, he characterizes the child's creative gift as a flower: 'Qui fait naître la fleur au penchant des abîmes . . . ?' (A i 1101). Musset combines the theme of ephemerality and the child-like poet in a single flower image, in some lines to Sainte-Beuve:

> Ami, tu l'as bien dit: en nous, tant que nous sommes,
> Il existe souvent une certaine fleur
> Qui s'en va dans la vie et s'effeuille du cœur.
> 'Il existe, en un mot, chez les trois quarts des hommes,
> Un poète mort jeune à qui l'homme survit.'[60]

For all these writers the Romantic flower imagery of pathos and sentimental mysticism has prompted a new kind of commentary on poetry, beauty, and creativity. It has suggested ways of adapting the traditional metaphor for poetry to the idealizing sensibility of Romanticism.

III. 'Le langage des fleurs': Nature, Mysticism, and Poetry

Il faut, pour connaître la nature, devenir un avec elle. Une vie poétique et recueillie, une âme sainte et religieuse, toute la force et toute la fleur de l'existence humaine, sont nécessaires pour la comprendre, et le véritable observateur est celui qui sait découvrir l'analogie de cette nature avec l'homme, et celle de l'homme avec le ciel.

(Madame de Staël, *De l'Allemagne*.)[61]

During the Romantic period flowers became essential to another type of discourse, derived from mystical currents in earlier French and German thought: the flowers of nature became typical signs and expressions of the mystery of nature and man's (the poet's) relationship with it.

The pantheism popular in the early Romantic period provided one congenial context for the development of this 'symbolic' use of

flowers, since it could see the whole of creation as a sign with hidden meaning, as a writer in *Le Globe* reported in 1825:

Un symbole est un signe, mais un signe qui non seulement rappelle, indique une pensée, c'est encore un signe qui l'exprime et la *contient* . . . Or c'est précisément le grand dogme de l'école actuelle, que la nature est le reflet, ou, pour mieux dire, la forme vivante de la pensée de son auteur. Toute la nature est donc le symbole du Dieu qui vit en elle, ce n'est plus un vain théâtre pour les yeux, c'est un sanctuaire tout rempli de l'être invisible, où retentit sans cesse l'hymne religieux.[62]

So Lamartine, for one, assumes the symbolic character of nature when affirming the presence of God in it:

> Pour qui ne l'y voit pas tout est nuit et mystères, . . .
> Mais cette langue, en vain par les temps égarée,
>   Se lit hier comme aujourd'hui;
> Car elle n'a qu'un nom sous sa lettre sacrée,
>   Lui seul! lui partout! toujours lui![63]

A stanza from Hugo's *Pan* emphasizes that not only the whole creation but particular parts of it are symbolic expressions of God:

> C'est Dieu qui remplit tout. Le monde, c'est son temple.
> Œuvre vivante, où tout l'écoute et le contemple!
> Tout lui parle et le chante. Il est seul, il est un.
> Dans sa création tout est joie et sourire;
> L'étoile qui regarde et la fleur qui respire.
>   Tout est flamme et parfum!
>
> (A i 804.)

Here the flower is itself an 'œuvre vivante': by breathing out its fragrance it participates in the life of God-filled nature and expresses its meaning. Such pantheism has general theoretical implications for nature poetry, as both Lamartine and Hugo realized.[64] Hugo attempts, indeed, to draw practical conclusions from these in some lines probably written soon after 1830:

> Le poëte dit: La poésie, c'est
> Le poëme de Dieu traduit en langue humaine.
> Je tire du lac bleu, des cieux, des arbres verts,
> La vie intérieure et j'en remplis mes vers;
> La chose dans le mot revit, plus belle encore.
> L'étoile se fait verbe et la fleur métaphore.
>
> (A i 1529.)

If the poet is to transpose the language of God's poem, he must be able to discern the 'vie intérieure' hidden in each part of nature.

Others during this period celebrated the same poetic faculty without recourse to pantheistic beliefs. Victor Cousin had done so in his lectures of 1818, declaring that since 'la forme' of each thing in nature is 'la manifestation de l'interne' and 'l'intérieur seul est beau', the artist's task is to express the inner beauty of a nature in which 'tout est symbolique'.[65] Jouffroy, too, considers that everything in nature is 'symbolique' and that 'Tout parle, tout vit dans la nature . . . et nous parle un langage mystérieux'.[66] This interests 'les artistes, les poètes' more than others since they 'connaissent et entendent infiniment mieux le langage des symboles que le reste des hommes'.[67] Sainte-Beuve attributes similar ideas to his Joseph Delorme:

Le sentiment de l'art implique un sentiment vif et intime des choses. L'artiste, comme s'il était doué d'un sens à part, s'occupe paisiblement à sentir, sous ce monde apparent, l'autre monde tout intérieur . . . il a reçu en naissant la clef des symboles et l'intelligence des figures.[68]

Expressing the same concept in poetic terms in 1830, he writes of poets:

> Ils comprennent les flots, entendent les étoiles,
> Savent les noms des fleurs, et pour eux l'univers
> N'est qu'une seule idée en symboles divers.[69]

By naming flowers as 'symboles' capable of yielding their hidden meaning to poets, Sainte-Beuve is rewriting Ronsard's Orphic statement of poetic inspiration in Romantic terms. Like Hugo (but without the latter's religious vocabulary), he is attempting to define a new poetic approach to the mystery of nature.

All such discourse about nature differs from that of Descriptive poetry by its dependence on idealist systems of various kinds (theism, *illuminisme*, Platonism, Orphism). Indeed literary thought after 1830 turned with interest to the theosophical ideas of an earlier generation.[70] Thus Sainte-Beuve himself was moved to include in *Volupté* (1834) an account of the thought of Saint-Martin. The hero Amaury, rejecting Lamarckian materialism, comes in a visionary moment to see that 'toutes les choses visibles du monde et de la nature' are signs to be interpreted, and finds himself able to

dégager quelques syllabes de cette grande parole qui, fixée ici, errante là, frémissait partout dans la nature . . . La Création . . . se rouvrait à l'homme, ornée de vases sonores, de tiges inclinées, pleine de voix amies, d'insinuations en général bonnes, et probablement peuplée en réalité d'innombrables Esprits vigilants. Au-dessous des animaux et des fleurs, les pierres elles-mêmes. . . les pierres des rues et des murs n'étaient pas dénuées de toute participation à la parole universelle.[71]

As one of the three realms, the plant world ('tiges inclinées', 'fleurs') has its part in the revelation of the inner life of nature. Balzac does not fail to include flowers, either, in his summary of Swedenborg's doctrines in *Séraphîta*. He presents visionaries as 'Esprits angéliques' for whom

tout ici-bas porte sa signifiance. La moindre fleur est une pensée, une vie qui correspond à quelques linéaments du Grand-Tout . . . Enfin tout parle aux Esprits. Les Esprits sont dans le secret de l'harmonie de créations entre elles; ils s'entendent avec l'esprit des sons, avec l'esprit des couleurs, avec l'esprit des végétaux.[72]

In this Swedenborgian view of nature, as in Sainte-Beuve's *martiniste* one, to attribute meaning to flowers is to endow them with life and 'voices'. It is, at the same time, to see flowers as participating with the rest of nature in the 'parole universelle' or in the 'harmonie de créations entre elles'. When the initiated understand the meaning of nature, they participate not only in the communicative life of each part, but in the unity of the whole.

As writers assimilated these views in the eighteen-thirties, the theme of participation in nature's life became more widespread.[73] Amongst those who speak of plant-life in this context is Lamartine:

> Car dans l'isolement mon âme qui déborde
> Au monde végétal s'unit par sentiment.
> Et si Dieu réduisait les plantes en poussière,
> J'embrasserais le sol et j'aimerais la pierre.[74]

For Maurice de Guérin the 'floraison' of spring is 'l'expression de l'amour, c'est l'amour lui-même qui célèbre ses doux mystères dans le sein de chaque fleur'. Accordingly, he dreams of participation in it: 's'identifier au printemps, forcer cette pensée au point de croire aspirer en soi toute la vie, tout l'amour qui fermentent dans la nature, se sentir à la fois fleur, verdure, oiseau, chant . . . volupté, sérénité'.[75] And if Guérin speaks of approaching love through nature, George Sand evokes in *Lélia* (1833) the opposite process, as

Sténio approaches nature through love: 'grâce à l'amour, il couronnait les plus belles scènes de la nature avec une grande pensée . . . celle de Lélia . . . Alors, Lélia était partout, dans l'air, dans le ciel, dans les eaux, dans les fleurs, dans le sein de Dieu.'[76] Gautier, however, in two important passages in *Maupin*, links participatory feeling of this kind with the motif of initiation into nature's meaning. In the first, his hero d'Albert is alone in a moonlit garden, although sensing the presence of 'une population de fantômes inconnus et adorés':

— Je ne pensais pas, je ne rêvais pas, j'étais confondu avec la nature qui m'environnait, je me sentais frissonner avec le feuillage, miroiter avec l'eau, reluire avec le rayon, m'épanouir avec la fleur.

D'Albert understands the nightingale's song ('comme si j'eusse eu le secret du langage des oiseaux') as it tells of his future bien-aimée:

Il donnait une voix à ma rêverie . . . Elle s'élevait lentement avec le parfum du cœur d'une large rose à cent feuilles . . . Jamais je n'ai eu tant d'amour dans le cœur; j'aurais pressé la nature contre mon sein.[77]

The second passage celebrates the realization of this dream of love in nature imagery recalling the earlier scene:

Ah! je vis maintenant . . . Mille voix mystérieuses me chuchotent à l'oreille . . . les marguerites me rient doucement, et les clochettes murmurent mon nom avec leur petite langue tortillée: je comprends une multitude de choses que je ne comprenais pas, je découvre des affinités et des sympathies merveilleuses, j'entends la langue des roses et des rossignols, et je lis couramment le livre que je ne pouvais même pas épeler . . . c'est l'amour, c'est l'amour qui m'a . . . donné le mot de l'énigme.[78]

This passage is a synthesis of several strands of French and German nature mysticism. Besides recalling Swedenborg, Saint-Martin, Senancour, Hugo, and Lamartine, it suggests the Hoffmann of whom Sainte-Beuve wrote in 1830 (addressing poets as 'mystiques sans foi'): 'comme il aurait voulu vous retremper au sein d'une nature active, aimante et pleine de voix et de parfums'.[79] And for a poet/lover like d'Albert, no less than for other Romantic *illuminés*, to participate in nature's mysteries is to gain understanding of the secret language of nature and of flowers.

Despite its apparent significance for the renewal of the poetic treatment of nature, mystical thought of this kind was not early or easily assimilated into poetic use. Once more Hugo led the way, however, providing in *Les Chants du Crépuscule* (1835) two important accounts of the relationship between poetry and the mysteries of nature, and associating flowers with both terms. In 'L'Aurore s'allume' he presents the poet's approach to nature as an initiation into its meaning. Like Pythagoras and Moses, the poet must seek the truth ('Vérité . . . / Tige où tout fleurit') to be found in nature, the meanings of the 'parole obscure' spoken by each of its parts and written in the 'livre salutaire' of the whole. The ultimately pantheistic sense of this language is not in doubt ('Création pure! / Etre universel!') and flowers are invoked to express it: 'Fleurs où Dieu peut-être / Cueille quelque miel!' (A i 869–73). By contrast the other poem, *A Mademoiselle J.*, dwells on the spontaneous loving communion with nature once experienced by the young poet and now wistfully remembered:

> Alors, du fond de vingt calices,
> Rosée, amour, parfums, délices,
> Se répandaient sur mon sommeil;
> J'avais des fleurs plein mes corbeilles; . . .
>
> Tandis que tout me disait: J'aime!
> Écoutant tout hors moi-même,
> Ivre d'harmonie et d'encens,
> J'entendais, ravissant murmure,
> Le chant de toute la nature
> Dans le tumulte de mes sens!

Yet Hugo here, like Gautier's d'Albert, associates flowers not merely with participation in nature's life but also with mysterious meaning, since 'roses par avril fardées' are amongst the phenomena which

> Me parlaient cette langue austère,
> Langue de l'ombre et du mystère,
> Qui demande à tous: Que sait-on?
> (A i 879–80.)

As a discourse in the form of a question, this 'langue' remains obscure, although it none the less provides 'notes' and 'mots' for the Hugolian philosopher-poet (here invoked as Orpheus/Plato). In his Orphic role, the poet understands the enigmatic language of nature and of flowers, and includes in his own poetry some sense of its mystery.

In these poems the flower is seen as one phenomenon (privileged no doubt) amongst others in nature. Elsewhere, though, Hugo uses flower figures almost as shorthand symbols for the mysterious link between nature and the poet. Even as a child the poet can hear 'le bégaiement confus des sphères et des fleurs'.[80] Later he is one of those who have 'dans le cœur cette fleur large et pure, / L'amour mystérieux de l'antique nature'.[81] The poet may even be characterized as himself a flower:

> Va t'épanouir, fleur sacrée,
> Sous les larges cieux du désert![82]

For although the poet's duty to society may call him back from his desire to blossom amidst the things of nature, his 'meilleure pensée' comes from 'ce que murmure leur voix'. While Hugo can see all his literary productions together as 'des fleurs de toute espèce', the flower figure has for him a special affinity with the mystical poetics of nature: 'Poème. Végétation où Pan respire'.[83]

Similar views of poetry (if not always accompanied by flower imagery) were not uncommon by 1840.[84] Alphonse Esquiros called on poets to immerse themselves in the natural universe ('harmonieux et sympathique') and find the meaning behind the 'voiles du symbole' so that (for example) 'l'arbre parle à l'âme du poète'.[85] Victor de Laprade, even more singlemindedly, could affirm the necessity for his poetry 'de sympathie pour la nature, de douce volupté à se pénétrer de ses harmonies, d'intelligence de ses rapports secrets avec le monde invisible'.[86] Thus in the longest piece in his *Odes et poëmes* (1843) the poet learns (from the nature spirit Hermia) how to read 'le symbole' and 'les divins caractères' of nature, how to discover the 'rapports secrets' by which 'Chaque degré de l'être aux autres correspond'. Because of her love for the poet, Hermia also teaches him her special knowledge of the secret life of flowers, with their 'rêves', 'plaisirs', 'amours', and 'langue habile aux tendres mélodies'.[87] This knowledge is presented, in fact, as the particular local instance confirming the ability to understand nature as a whole. Accordingly, a reviewer of this volume could characterize it in these words: 'Tout vit, tout parle, tout a une existence particulière. Les arbres des forêts et les fleurs des jardins conversent entre eux et avec le poëte.'[88] Indeed by this date a reference to the poet's participation in the language of flowers might have been sufficient to indicate both Laprade's view of nature and his idea of nature poetry.

Metaphysical views of nature similar to Laprade's were widely
entertained at this time.[89] Many poets were content, indeed, to treat
them as the subject matter of didactic verse without reference to the
nature poetics of a Hugo, an Esquiros, or a Laprade. Some lines
of Ferdinand de Gramont show the persistence of the type of flower
reference associated with pre-Romantic views of natural harmony:

> Dans l'œuvre universel il n'est rien d'isolé:
> Le métal en cristaux végète et s'organise;
> La fleur a ses amours, et le ver qu'on méprise,
> Transformé lentement, au ciel s'est envolé . . .
>
> Tout s'enchaîne, se suit, se déduit, s'harmonise.[90]

Nerval's view of nature in *Pensée antique* (1845) is based on a more
mystical aspect of such thought:

> Respecte dans la bête un esprit agissant:
> Chaque plante est une âme à la nature éclose;
> Un mystère d'amour dans le métal repose;
> 'Tout est sensible!' . . . [91]

In Lamartine's *Les Esprits des fleurs* (1847) flowers themselves are
represented as the type of all sentient matter:

> Non: chaque atome de matière
> Par un esprit est habité;
> Tout sent, et la nature entière
> N'est que douleur et volupté!
>
> (G 1216.)

Alphonse Constant takes up once more the theosophical and literary
theme of a universe 'formé de visibles paroles', declaring that

> Rien n'est muet dans la nature:
> Les Astres ont une écriture,
> Les fleurs des champs ont une voix.[92]

Hugo himself provides a summary of these themes in *Ce que dit la
bouche d'ombre* (1855):

> tout a conscience dans la création;
> Tout parle: l'air qui passe et l'alcyon qui vague,
> Le brin d'herbe, la fleur, le germe, l'élément.
>
> (A ii 801.)

All such accounts of nature, whether they speak of its harmony and sentience or of its 'language', were derived from a body of thought in which such concepts had long been considered interrelated. These poetic expositions are noted here because they provide further variants on the concept of the *langage des fleurs*. But like all expressions of these ideas they also contribute, by their insistence on the interaction between all natural phenomena (reflected in the recurring stylistic pattern 'Tout sent', 'Rien n'est muet', etc.), to a climate of thought hospitable to the concept of synaesthesia.[93]

Writers as dissimilar as Voltaire and Madame de Staël had earlier proposed that the perception of analogies between sense experience of various kinds might be one manifestation of the unity of nature.[94] Madame de Staël was no doubt aware of the theories of Castel:

Les analogies des divers éléments de la nature physique entre eux servent à constater la suprême loi de la création, la variété dans l'unité, et l'unité dans la variété. Qu'y a-t-il de plus étonnant, par exemple, que le rapport des sons et des formes, des sons et des couleurs?[95]

In a similar way Senancour, who discusses in *Oberman* the parallels (and differences) between hearing, sight, and sound,[96], allows elsewhere in the same work that a 'suite de couleurs' or a 'suite d'odeurs' are as liable as 'la mélodie des sons' to produce at particular moments a 'sentiment de l'infini' in man: 'il lui arrive qu'une perception subite lui montre les contrastes et l'équilibre, le lien, l'organisation de l'univers'.[97] It will be recalled that Senancour's reflections on the *jonquille* follow a not dissimilar pattern: the smell of the flower produces a perception of the 'harmonie des êtres', while its appearance suggests a related image of human love. Senancour thus not only notes that experience in different senses may provoke an awareness of general unity, but also advances a model for this process: a flower which evokes the harmonies of nature and love by appealing to both smell and sight.

The concept of the *langage des fleurs* as *selam*, itself a harmonious link between nature and love, had always had some dependence on the appeal of flowers to these two senses. The emblematic meanings attributed to them by the earliest flower dictionaries were based (when they were not derived from folklore, literature, or etymology) on either colour or 'parfum'. Thus for Madame Maugirard in 1810 the *tubéreuse* is 'le symbole de la volupté' because 'son parfum est enivrant', while the *scabieuse* represents 'le mystère' because of its 'teintes sombres'.[98] Senancour himself, in a curious work of 1823 reflecting knowledge of such manuals, claims to bear in mind when setting up his own flower glossary 'non seulement l'odeur, mais aussi la forme, la couleur même et le port des végétaux'.[99] By 1833 at least ten such dictionaries had been published and all of them presented the *selam* as a synaesthetic code to some degree. Indeed commentators during this period could point to either smell or sight as the sense field appropriate to the *langage des fleurs*. Thus T. Thoré could claim in 1836 (perhaps with the *selam* in mind) that 'avec les parfums on peut exprimer toute la création aussi bien qu'avec les lignes et la couleur'.[100] By contrast, F. Portal could note in 1837 that 'le selam des Arabes paraît avoir emprunté ses emblèmes à la langue des couleurs'.[101] The flower language not only constitutes an emblematic code but contains as well two distinct languages, each one (as Thoré puts it) 'un aspect des harmonies de la nature'.

By the mid-thirties, however, writers could relate the *langage des fleurs* to a third aspect of such harmonies—music itself.[102] Balzac provides some etiological commentary on this application of the principle of *harmonie* in his celebration of the *selam* in *Le Lys dans la vallée*.[103] He invokes the theory of analogy between music and colours ('J'inventai donc la théorie du père Castel au profit de l'amour') after explaining that the colours of the bouquet 'avaient une harmonie, une poésie . . . comme les phrases musicales'. He is thus insisting on the aesthetic character of the *selam*, and can speak in turn of 'cette œuvre poétique' and 'ces symphonies de fleurs', recalling contemporary theories of the *synthèse des arts*.[104] At the same time he associates this synaesthetic hymn of love with spirituality, in a comparison reminiscent of Ballanche or of his own *Séraphîta*:

Que donne-t-on à Dieu? des parfums, de la lumière et des chants, les expressions les plus épurées de notre nature. Eh! bien, tout ce qu'on offre à Dieu n'était-il pas offert à l'amour dans ce poème de fleurs lumineuses qui bourdonnait incessamment ses mélodies au cœur . . . ?[105]

Castel's theories, the *synthèse des arts*, and the associations of spiritual typology also contribute to Félicien Mallefille's synaesthetic celebration in *Le Concert des fleurs*, written a year before Balzac's novel.[106] In this *conte*, however, the *langage des fleurs* has little in common with the *selam*: the hero is an old Breton peasant who in a lifetime's devotion to flowers has 'appris leur langage'. The narrator discovers him finally in a Paris street giving 'des concerts de fleurs' by means of a 'boîte de verre' so manipulated that the compartments (containing flowers) are opened in sequence, 'avec une sorte d'harmonie dans leur jeu':

D'abord je ne compris rien, ne vis rien, n'entendis rien . . . Mais peu à peu le parfum des fleurs enfermées dans la boîte se répandit dans l'air . . . et commença à m'enivrer . . . J'entendis une musique céleste, je vis des jardins pleins de verdure et de fraîcheur . . . mon oreille s'ouvrit à des paroles d'amour, ma bouche frissonna sous des baisers.[107]

This curious fiction combines *le merveilleux* with irony (since this 'poète inconnu' is finally incarcerated as a madman) and certainly owes something to Hoffmann. And its floral concert enlarges Senancour's project for a 'clavecin des odeurs' to include four (perhaps five) senses in this mystical barrel-organ of synaesthetic art. The association between the synaesthetic and the expressive faculties of flowers could scarcely be more explicit, and once more both are made to serve the concepts of harmony and love.

George Sand's interest in theories of analogy is firmly announced as early as 1834: 'Tout est harmonie, le son et la couleur; sept tons et sept couleurs s'enlacent et s'émeuvent dans un éternel hyménée.'[108] Equally evident by this date is her interest in the harmonies of nature.[109] At the end of the decade, moreover, she relates these ideas to the *langage des fleurs* in a garden passage in *Consuelo*, musing on 'le rapport de la musique et des fleurs':

Il y avait longtemps que l'harmonie des sons lui avait semblé répondre d'une certaine manière à l'harmonie des couleurs; mais l'harmonie de ces harmonies, il lui sembla que c'était le parfum. En cet instant, plongée dans une vague et douce rêverie, elle s'imaginait entendre une voix sortir de chacune de ces corolles charmantes, et lui raconter les mystères de la poésie dans une langue jusqu'alors inconnue pour elle.[110]

The subsequent glossary of the flowers' 'voix' follows emblematic convention ('la rose lui disait ses ardentes amours, le lis sa chasteté céleste', etc.), yet these must be seen in relation to the theoretical structure of the passage. The flowers' 'parfums' become (emblem-atical) 'voix', and both together become music, the flowers 'unissant leur voix dans un choeur aérien' of 'harmonies idéales'. Moreover, these smells and voices are not only musical but poetic, speaking in a new way about the 'mystères de la poésie'. Sand finds in the *langage des fleurs* a complex statement about the harmonies of the senses, the arts, nature, and poetry.

Such imaginative elaborations of the concept of the flower language reveal serious literary and theoretical concerns, and suggest why it was capable of attracting literary attention during so much of the nineteenth century. In the forties and fifties, indeed, the concept is found together with these literary associations even in contexts marginal to serious writing. Thus a passage from the journalistic *belles-lettres* of Alphonse Karr evokes an ordinary garden transformed by adolescent love into 'un autre pays, une ravissante contrée', in these words:

les fleurs n'exhalent pas seulement de suaves parfums, mais d'enivrantes pensées d'amour. Chaque arbre, chaque plante y conte, dans un langage plus noble que la poésie et plus doux que la musique, des choses dont aucune langue humaine ne saurait même donner une idée . . . l'air est rempli de chants.[111]

And Karr acknowledges the literary associations of such discourse, for his lengthy description concludes: 'Allez donc chercher ces poétiques contrées'. The chapter on 'La Musique des fleurs' contributed by Méry to Grandville's keepsake album *Les Fleurs animées* is equally dependent on literary tradition:

Qui de nous, dans le recueillement d'une belle nuit, au milieu des bruits étouffés, des murmures mystérieux des eaux, de la terre et des bois, n'a pas demêlé distinctement le chant varié des Fleurs? . . . Le son est invisible, insaisissable comme le parfum. Le parfum flotte, pénètre, s'échappe comme le son: l'un est la musique de l'homme, l'autre est la musique de la nature et la voix des fleurs. La musique ordinaire ne sert plus qu'à faire souhaiter plus ardemment les beautés idéales et mystérieuses de la musique des fleurs.[112]

Unlike some of his predecessors, Méry neither heightens nor explains the mystery by reference to love, and he presents it (appropriately for a keepsake readership) as accessible to all. Yet for him too, these sounds are 'idéales et mystérieuses': as in all such synaesthetic pieces, the language and music of flowers are figures for mysterious powers of expression and perception.

All these accounts provide, in fact, a similar model for the literary imagination. They propose that nature, and man's relation to it, are characterized by 'des harmonies jusqu'alors inconnues', and offer extraordinary beauties to those who can understand them. They suggest that the mysterious voices of nature—from the emblematics of the flower dictionary to the higher synaesthetic mysteries of the *langage des fleurs*— may serve as patterns for literary language to emulate. Indeed, they challenge poets to find a language which can embody—or rival—that of nature.

IV. 'Fleurs du bien' and 'fleurs du mal'

At the mid-century the language of flowers was established, in the several versions associated with nature mysticism, as a suggestive concept rather inviting enthusiastic speculation than indicating any particular stylistic procedure. Yet most commentators agreed not only on the general benevolence of nature's message but on its beneficent connections with literature. George Sand was so optimistic on these points that she could suggest an awareness of nature's harmonies gained through botanical studies was a necessary qualification for poets:

Le poète et l'artiste ne peuvent que gagner dans les études naturelles, et les lois de la vie sont tellement harmonieuses dans leur enchaînement, que pour bien comprendre l'énigme de la vie humaine, il faut comprendre celle du moindre atome admis au privilège de la vie.[113]

This is an extreme form, no doubt, of the general Romantic idealization of the relationship between the poet and the harmonies of nature.

Another conception of the way nature's harmonies might be relevant to poetic procedure had been put forward by Lamartine in 1835:

Il y a des harmonies entre tous les éléments, comme il y en a une générale entre la nature matérielle et la nature intellectuelle. Chaque pensée a son reflet dans un objet visible qui la répète comme un écho, la réfléchit comme un miroir, et la rend perceptible de deux manières: aux sens par l'image, à la pensée par la pensée, c'est la poésie de la double création! Les hommes appellent cela comparaison: la comparaison, c'est le génie . . . Comparer c'est l'art ou l'instinct de découvrir des mots de plus dans cette langue divine des analogies universelles.[114]

Starting from the familiar doctrines of nature mysticism, Lamartine here elaborates a theory of poetic comparison reminiscent not only of Leroux's appeal in 1829 for a 'style symbolique' but of Fourier's theories. The type of comparison proposed by Lamartine is well exemplified (in a minor but universally known form) by flower-dictionary emblematics, and Fourier himself was well aware that his system of 'analogie universelle' followed the same principles as the 'fariboles analogiques intitulées le *langage des fleurs*'. Attacking their authors as 'sophistes' for restricting analogy to flowers alone, he insists that the procedure is of universal validity:

L'analogie est complète dans les différents règnes; ils sont, dans tous leurs détails, autant de miroirs de quelque effet de nos passions; ils forment un immense musée de tableaux allégoriques où se peignent les crimes et les vertus de l'humanité.[115]

Fourier's universal glossary of emblematic meanings differs from flower dictionaries not only in scale but in emphasis, since the latter had always stressed positive virtues and feelings along with the more attractive flowers. Fourier's project, however, is to find analogies for all human attributes ('les crimes et les vertus') including negative ones. In the realm of plant analogies he is free to range descriptively, with none of the limitations of the glossary genre. Thus while *jonquille* becomes in his system the 'hiéroglyphe' of maternal love, the *hortensia* is read as 'la coquette prodigue' and the *balsamine* as 'le portrait de l'égoïste industrieux'.[116] In the same way A. Toussenel, in a *fouriériste* article of 1846, sees the rose (traditionally enough) as 'la jeune fille', but cacti and 'les plantes vénéneuses' as 'les sociétés limbiques'.[117] In such ways, Fourier's principles of *analogie* could serve as a reminder that flower analogies need not be restricted to idealized images of virtue, happiness, love, or charming *peines d'amour*.[118]

The attribution of negative meanings to flowers was indeed sanctioned by literary tradition (the flowers of transience) and by early Romanticism (the flowers of pathos). These conventional figures are still found in the poetry of the twenty years after 1830: they play a considerable role, notably, in the extended *carpe diem* of Gautier's *Comédie de la Mort* (1839). Yet during this period there are occasional indications of new developments in prose flower imagery which suggest the literary possibilities of a more sophisticated floral tropology using negative connotations.

Given the inescapable conventions associating flowers with beauty and positive connotations, these new figures all include some element of paradox. Indeed each one appears to be an *ad hoc* formulation, an individual achievement of irony. Thus Musset, in a passage attacking heartless urban pragmatism, speaks of 'les froides substances de ce nénufar monstrueux que la Raison plante au cœur de nos villes' in terms ironically recalling pastoral and oriental associations.[119] Gautier provides an important series of similar figures in *Mademoiselle de Maupin*. One inspiration for them is d'Albert's 'dépravation horrible',[120] a corruption of the pastoral innocence of youth:

Printemps au-dehors ... neige de fleurs à tous les buissons, blanches illusions épanouies dans nos âmes, pudique rougeur sur nos joues et sur l'églantine ... Hélas! — cela a peu duré ... Le germe de corruption qui était en moi s'est développé bien vite.

(p. 188.)

Thus he can describe his character as monstrous and paradoxical, in a set piece of tropical anti-pastoral:

C'est un étrange pays que mon âme, un pays florissant et splendide en apparence, mais plus saturé de miasmes putrides et délétères que le pays de Batavia ... — les larges tulipes jaunes, les nagassaris et les fleurs d'angsoka y voilent pompeusement d'immondes charognes. La rose amoureuse ouvre ses lèvres écarlates ... mais il y a cent à parier contre un que, dans l'herbe, au bas du buisson, un crapaud hydropique rampe sur des pattes boiteuses.

(pp. 249–50.)

These attractive flowers conceal horrors, so that behind their apparent meaning is a repulsive truth. In the passage in which Théodore/Maupin describes the sufferings caused by *l'idéal*, Gautier follows a similar procedure. There is first a pastoral evocation— 'Idéal, fleur bleue au cœur d'or, qui t'épanouis tout emperlée de rosée sous le ciel du printemps, au souffle parfumé de molles rêveries'[121]— then an ironic reversal: 'fleur si douce et si amère, on ne te peut arracher sans faire saigner le cœur à tous ses recoins . . . Ah! fleur maudite, comme tu avais poussé dans mon âme!' Finally, the full presentation of a 'negative' flower image: 'Plante de l'idéal, plus venimeuse que le mancenillier ou l'arbre upas, qu'il m'en coûte, malgré les fleurs trompeuses et le poison que l'on respire avec ton parfum, pour te déraciner de mon âme!' (p. 234). All these flowers are idealizing emblems paradoxically made to speak of corruption, monstrosity, suffering, or poison.

Elsewhere in *Maupin* Gautier creates an even more ambitious figure, based on the emblematic meaning of the 'fleurs de la passion'

(p. 201) and the Christian typology of the 'rose mystique' (p. 203). Drawing a contrast between the joyous materialism of paganism and the melancholic asceticism and 'rêvasserie' of Christian culture, he exclaims:

Virginité, plante amère, née sur un sol trempé de sang, et dont la fleur étiolée et maladive s'ouvre péniblement à l'ombre humide des cloîtres . . . rose sans parfum et toute hérissée d'épines, tu as remplacé pour nous les belles et joyeuses roses baignées de nard et de falerne des danseuses de Sybaris!
Le monde antique ne te connaissait pas, fleur inféconde . . .

(p. 205.)

While Gautier can use a 'negative' flower figure to comment on the Christian origins of one aspect of Romantic modernity, Musset employs similar figures in *Lorenzaccio* to speak of art itself. After defining the artist's task ('Réaliser des rêves, voilà la vie du peintre'), the painter Tébaldeo continues: 'Hélas! les rêves des artistes médiocres sont des plantes difficiles à nourrir, et qu'on arrose de larmes bien amères pour les faire bien peu prospérer!' At the same time he suggests that the present corruption and sufferings of Florence ('ma mère') may nourish the work of its artists: 'Mais des gouttes de sang de ma mère sort une plante odorante qui guérit tous les maux. L'art, cette fleur divine, a quelquefois besoin du fumier pour engraisser le sol et le féconder.'[122] With these precedents, it is not surprising to find writers by the end of the thirties occasionally using strong negative flower imagery to present an alternative to the pervasive sentimental idealization of Romanticism. A character in Borel's *Madame Putiphar* (1839) argues for pleasures other than those of sentimental virtue, and alludes at the same time to flowers:

Croyez-moi, soyez sage; descendons ensemble dans l'abyme du mal, et descendons-y en habit de fête; descendons-y joyeux. On dit que tout au fond il est jonché de fleurs où s'enivrent des plus rares plaisirs, des plaisirs proscrits, ceux qui ont osé . . . descendre ses ravins affreux. Ne faisons pas fi du crime: . . . il a des beautés secrètes.[123]

And Balzac can contrast the pastoral flowers of virtue with the 'fleurs vénéneuses' of modern immorality, in Sabine's remark in *Béatrix* (1839): 'Car il y a des fleurs du diable et des fleurs de Dieu'.[124] These figures all present, in fact, ironic views of the idealizing sensibility of Romanticism and of its hero/artist.

They remain, however, isolated cases, and there are few significant parallels in the poetry of the period. Writers could not easily assimilate, no doubt, a type of flower symbolism so different in tone from the idealizing flower language of *selam*, nature mysticism, and synaesthetic theory: hardly anyone was subversive enough to question the contemporary consensus on the high value and beauty of flowers. A thinker as serious as Jouffroy could provide a 'philosophical' justification for this affirmative view, even while questioning the main premiss of the *langage des fleurs*:

Voyez cette rose, humide de rosée, se balancer sur sa tige — symbole de la grâce et de la volupté, elle nous séduit et nous attire — le besoin de l'union se déclare; nous la cueillons; mais en vain la mettons-nous en contact avec tous ceux de nos sens qui peuvent la percevoir; elle demeure froide et insensible; elle ne répond pas.[125]

In another passage he 'proves' that human response to the beauty of flowers is not merely conventional but a matter of instinctive *sympathie*:

Prenons, Messieurs, deux plantes; prenons d'une part cette plante élégante et riche en couleur, d'une odeur suave, qu'on appelle la rose, et à côté de cette rose mettons une autre plante, l'*aconit* . . . plante de couleur terne, plante sombre, plante qui cache sa fleur; placez une créature humaine en présence de ces deux plantes, et demandez-lui de rendre compte de ses impressions. Cette créature humaine vous répondra que l'une des plantes lui plaît, et que l'autre lui inspire une sorte de répugnance.[126]

For this thinker the beauty of flowers raises questions about their expressiveness, but he does not fail to insist on the mysterious relationship linking them with positive human feelings.

Poets and prose writers were, of course, investigating the same questions and celebrating these mysteries in their own fashion, both in their flower emblematics of meaning and feeling and in their commitment to the flower languages of nature. But the enthusiasm of intellectuals and men of letters was equalled in intensity by the *culte des fleurs* in bourgeois popular culture, which although less arcane shared many of the same assumptions. From the second decade of the century the popular flower dictionary had insisted on the beauty of flowers while presenting them as a symbolic language of innocent love. With early authors like Madame de Genlis, praise of flowers is already indispensable to the genre: flowers are 'ce que la Nature a de plus gracieux', 'ces êtres presqu'animés, sur la surface de la terre qu'elles embellissent', or simply 'Fleurs aimables!'[127]

A manual of 1821 further idealizes flowers by relating them to the innocent paradise where primitive people first chose flowers as a language because their

aspect doux et riant pouvait le mieux exprimer les sentimens heureux qui les animaient: ainsi naquit le langage des plantes, des fleurs et des couleurs . . . un langage qui rappelle cet âge d'or tant vanté des poètes, ces jours fortunés où régnaient l'innocence et la justice.[128]

By 1840 a number of such works were in circulation and the style and concerns of the genre well established. In that year Hostein, in his *Flore des dames ou Nouveau Langage des fleurs*, speaks of the 'culte qu'on . . . voue' to flowers, notes their 'ingénieuses propriétés de langage' and repeatedly praises love and the 'dames' of the title: 'Ainsi les femmes aimeront toujours les fleurs'. These elements are found together in the rather unaccomplished octosyllabics with which he introduces the 'Emblèmes des fleurs':

> Livre charmant de la nature,
> Que j'aime ta simplicité!
> Ta science n'est point obscure,
> Tu nous plais par la vérité,
> Nous retiens par la volupté,
> Et nous charmes par ta parure.
> Mais des plus tendres sentiments
> Les fleurs nous fournissent l'image.[129]

These verses capture the typical stylistic notes of these works: an innocent sentimentality and enthusiasm which brings together flowers, femininity, love, and innocence in a suggestive unity of idealization.

But Hostein's volume contains not only a flower glossary but 'des poésies nouvelles de nos célébrités contemporaines' — a not uncommon feature of these manuals, which sometimes become almost mini-anthologies. Authors of these works had always had a tendency to quote at least brief poetic extracts to lend authority to their emblematic attributions and create the appropriate sentimental atmosphere. Appealing to the same market (largely bourgeois and feminine), publishers of a similar genre had also been using literary extracts to enhance its tone: this was the keepsake, an album of engravings (usually English) accompanied by a collection of poems, *nouvelles*, literary *précis*, or anecdotes. Significantly, many of these works bore titles which have a clear relation to the floral sentimentality of emblematic manuals. Between 1836 and 1840 alone seven keepsakes were published under flower titles: *La Perceneige* (1836), *Ne m'oubliez pas* (1837), *Le Dahlia, heures de loisir* (1837), *L'Anémone* (1838), *Les Bleuets* (1839), *Les Violettes* (1840), and *Fleurs de littérature contemporaine* (1840).[130] The keepsake resembled the flower manual in its pervasive tone of sentimental but virtuous femininity and its allusive treatment of literature. But it also often appealed to flower sentimentality in content as well as title: Marceline Desbordes-Valmore's flower poems were especially popular and her *Myosotis* is quoted in several such works. The relationship between the two genres is made explicit in Alhoy and Rostaing's *Les Fleurs historiques* (1852), a collection of stories based on associations between emblematic flower meanings and historical anecdotes. The preface assumes readers familiar with the style of the flower dictionary, as it presents a male character gently parodying the tone of flower idealization: 'Fleurs, fleurs! admirables productions de la nature, vous vous disputez l'amour des cieux et de la terre, vous seules avez le don d'embellir l'amour même; vous êtes l'emblème ou plutôt l'idéal de la beauté et de la candeur!'[131] By the close ('ce n'est pas plus difficile que cela, ma chère Hélène') this passage has confirmed that at mid-century the idealizing association of flowers with love, beauty, and innocence was a commonplace.

No doubt the most successful of such volumes was a work of 1846-7 in which the flower sentimentality of the manuals is totally integrated in the keepsake form: *Les Fleurs animées*. Karr's introduction emphasizes love of the flowers of nature ('on aime les fleurs mais seulement pour elles-mêmes'), but Grandville's illustrations depict particular flowers as women of variously picturesque appearance and dress, in a clever variant of emblematic procedure. Méry's sentimental texts are anecdotes about flowers become women, and his introduction explains the transformation in terms of emblematics and poetry: 'Voici des millions d'années que nous servons de texte de comparaison aux mortels; nous défrayons à nous seules toutes les métaphores: sans nous la poésie n'existerait pas . . . La vie des fleurs nous ennuie.'[132] Women and flowers are idealized together throughout, so that even 'les beautés idéales et mystérieuses de la musique des fleurs' can be seen as characteristic of both. The popular appeal of this general concept was so great that two vaudeville plays bearing the same title were produced in

1846.[133] The work's popularity is confirmed by its publishing record (three reprints between 1847 and 1857) and by other flattering imitations, like the keepsake called *Fleurs et jeunes filles ou les fleurs animées* (1854). With the Grandville work (which Méry praised under his own name four years later as 'cette œuvre empreinte d'une poésie si douce, si gracieuse et si élevée'),[134] the idealization of women and flowers in the context of popular culture was complete.

The relationship between publications of this type and serious writing cannot be easily defined, but evidently involved reciprocal influence. In any case flower ideology was clearly an important factor in mid-century culture, widely diffused in both literary and paraliterary forms, and limited to no single social or political milieu.[135] Thus after 1840 it even extends to popular devotional writing: the anonymous author of *Les Fleurs* (a pious volume of 1854) praises virtues as flowers and flowers as virtue, even claiming that 'celui qui s'adonne à la culture des fleurs semble devenir meilleur'.[136] So too the *fouriériste* Toussenel participates in the ideology of flower manual and keepsake when he states that 'la fleur, poésie de la végétation et miroir des passions humaines, chante de sa voix parfumée l'*Hosanna in excelsis* à l'amour'. And he inevitably dedicates his work to a woman, praising Madame Henriette L—— as the 'bienfaitrice' of the 'frais paradis' of her garden, where her presence is 'le secret de l'éclat et du parfum de [ses] fleurs'.[137] Poetry, women, flowers, and perfection are the constant elements of this pervasive ideology.

During the Romantic period the flower had come to have unprecedented importance both for serious writers and for wider culture. In the literary world floral tropology had been elaborated to express various aspects of the new sensibility. The flowers of pastoral and Description had been transformed to define a new sense of artistic freedom. The traditional flower metaphors of transience, love, and spirituality had been assimilated to a floral tropology of pathos and sentimental idealization, and the ancient figure of the flowers of the muses adapted accordingly. At the same time, writers had developed from anti-materialist views of nature a new literary ideology of the *langage des fleurs*, proposing a privileged participation in nature's meanings and synaesthetic mysteries. Serious writers usually understood flower rhetoric in terms of the idealization of human sentiment or nature's mysteries, and only occasional prose-writers gave ironic negative connotations to flower imagery. But popular flower literature insisted even more single-mindedly on the idealization of innocence, love, and nature. For Romantic culture as a whole the flower had become an indispensable emblem of the new sensibility.[138]

3

BAUDELAIRE'S FLOWER POETICS

Germinations, éclosions, floraisons,
éruptions successives, simultanées,
lentes ou soudaines, progressives
ou complètes . . .

(P ii 138.)

Dans l'ordre poétique et artistique,
tout révélateur a rarement un précurseur.
Toute floraison est spontanée
individuelle.

(P ii 581.)

Le temps des Byron venait.

Car Byron était *préparé*, comme Michel-Ange.

Le grand homme n'est jamais aérolithe.

(P ii 68–9.)

I. Baudelaire's Flower Imagery before 1855

i. Childhood and youth

Tel petit chagrin, telle petite jouissance de l'enfant, démesuré-
ment grossis par une exquise sensibilité, deviennent plus tard
dans l'homme adulte, même à son insu, le principe d'une œuvre
d'art.[1]

Baudelaire's use of flower metaphors in and for poetry is
unprecedented not so much in its extent and variety as in the ways
it corresponds to a particular cast of mind. This latter may already
be discerned in what we know of the poet's childhood, for example
in his claim that 'tout enfant, j'ai senti dans mon cœur deux
sentiments contradictoires, l'horreur de la vie et l'extase de la vie'
(P i 703). Such attitudes have their iconographical counterparts in
two contrasting pictures familiar to Baudelaire in childhood:

Charles les avait suspendus lui-même dans sa chambre; celui à l'huile, vieux tableau, est un Saint-Antoine dans sa solitude, où il se croyait obsédé par le démon ou un mauvais ange; il a près de lui une croix.

M. Baudelaire s'était amusé à faire pendant à ce tableau, un tableau profane. A la place du saint il a mis une bacchante qui tient une thyrse au lieu de la croix de Saint-Antoine; elle est entourée d'amours au lieu d'anges.[2]

Madame Aupick's apparently naïve description registers a series of bi-polarities, opposing sacred to profane, Christian to classical, self-denial to self-indulgence, and even vice to virtue. And the contrast between cross and thyrsus, between the Christian emblem of sacrificial death and a Hellenic fertility emblem (in form, a stick entwined with flowers) produces a further series: death/life, sacrifice/fertility, self denial/creativity. Looking at these pictures the young Charles was no doubt aware (however intuitively) of some of these thematic paradoxes, in which the flowers of the thyrsus have a significant place.

Baudelaire himself, writing about De Quincey near the end of his life, insisted that childhood environment has a determining influence on adult creativity:

Chagrin d'enfant, principe d'œuvre d'art. Le logis de l'enfant, un arbre, des fleurs, une chambre sombre. L'enfant de génie né dans un tel logis ne ressemblera pas à l'homme de génie né dans un milieu différent.

(P i 520.)

In stating that a childhood awareness of flowers counts among the determinants of an artist's cast of mind, Baudelaire would seem to have consulted his own experience as well as De Quincey's. But whereas the child De Quincey had been 'enfermé dans un beau et silencieux jardin', it is hard to point to any equivalent paradise in Baudelaire's case. Publicly at least, he remembers only

> Notre blanche maison, petite mais tranquille;
> Sa Pomone de plâtre et sa vieille Vénus
> Dans un bosquet chétif cachant leurs membres nus.

(P i 99.)

The tone here veers from nostalgia to disdain, suggesting that the only flowers in this Neuilly 'garden' were Pomona's plaster bouquet. The other poem about 'notre ancienne vie' evokes a more disturbing memory:

> La servante au grand cœur dont vous étiez jalouse,
> Et qui dort son sommeil sous une humble pelouse,
> Nous devrions pourtant lui porter quelques fleurs.[3]

These lines suggest unease about the servant and the poet's mother, and equivocations about the 'duty' of bringing flowers as tributes to the dead.[4] The flowers in these evocations of childhood hint at memories of uneasiness or even perhaps *chagrin d'enfant*.

Several general references to the state of childhood in Baudelaire's writings, however, associate it rather with 'l'extase de la vie'. It is characterized as 'le beau temps . . . où nos yeux clairs riaient à toute la nature' (P i 560), or as a 'paradis parfumé / . . . Où dans la volupté pure le cœur se noie', 'le vert paradis des amours enfantines' (P i 63–4). And children are like flowers in this paradise of ecstasy:

Le rire des enfants est comme un épanouissement de fleur. C'est la joie de recevoir, la joie de respirer, la joie de s'ouvrir, la joie de contempler, de vivre, de grandir. C'est une joie de plante.

(P ii 534.)

Moreover the child is like the artist in his joyful receptivity of new beauty:

L'enfant voit tout en *nouveauté*; il est toujours *ivre*. Rien ne ressemble plus à ce qu'on appelle l'inspiration, que la joie avec laquelle l'enfant absorbe la forme et la couleur . . . C'est à cette curiosité profonde et joyeuse qu'il faut attribuer l'œil fixe et animalement extatique des enfants devant le *nouveau*, quel qu'il soit, visage ou paysage, lumière, dorure, couleurs.

(P ii 690.)

These references, consistent in orientation over a period of twenty years of writing, represent a view of childhood dependent on Romantic literary sources but no doubt also on personal memory. The child-poet of *Bénédiction* is also reminiscent of mystical and literary tradition:

> Pourtant, sous la tutelle invisible d'un Ange,
> L'Enfant déshérité s'enivre de soleil,
> Et dans tout ce qu'il voit et dans tout ce qu'il mange
> Retrouve l'ambroisie et le nectar vermeil.
>
> Il joue avec le vent, cause avec le nuage
> Et s'enivre en chantant du chemin de la croix.

(P i 7–8.)

Yet despite the literary framework, these lines seem to tremble on the edge of psychological self-revelation. And significantly, the flowery 'ambroisie' and 'nectar vermeil' which help attest the child's powers of communion with nature are associated with two kinds of inebriation, as the child 's'enivre de soleil' and 's'enivre en chantant du chemin de la croix'. Although the mature Baudelaire is here presenting the archetypal Romantic poet (both mystical and suffering), he is perhaps also confessing that the child-poet aware of 'soleil' and 'croix' (*l'extase* and *l'horreur*) is his own youthful self.

All that is known of the poet's adolescent schooldays suggests that the youth's personality was indeed torn between some such 'sentiments contradictoires' as he claimed to have known since childhood. Schoolmasters, classfellows, and his own correspondence testify to an alternation between piety or hard work on the one hand and apathy, rebelliousness, or sensual fantasy on the other.[5] The latter are emphasized in his own account of this period, in the lines written to Sainte-Beuve five or six years later. He recalls the oppressively sensual atmosphere of *ennui* in which he read *Volupté*, and then describes the work in terms which evoke the same atmosphere:

> Et puis venaient les soirs malsains, les nuits fiévreuses . . .
>
> Les soirs italiens, de molle insouciance . . .
>
> —Quand la sombre Vénus, du haut des balcons noirs,,
> Verse des flots de musc de ses frais encensoirs . . .
>
> J'en ai tout absorbé, les miasmes, les parfums,
> Les doux chuchotements des souvenirs défunts,
>
> —Chapelets murmurants de madrigaux mystiques;
> —Libre voluptueux, si jamais il en fut.

> (P i 207.)

It is almost as if 'les miasmes, les parfums' emanate from the flowers (the 'frais encensoirs') of 'la sombre Vénus', as if it is impossible not to be overpowered by a force of sensuality controlling past and present.

Such 'molle insouciance' seems to have alternated with periods when Baudelaire could appear 'sérieux, studieux et religieux'.[6] His success in Latin verse composition in the last three years at school, for example, is evidence of considerable commitment to study. Even in this austere discipline the schoolboy was capable of bold stylistic initiatives. Thus in the composition for the *Concours général* for 1837 he elaborates on the proposed subject by describing the re-growth of flowers after a volcanic eruption ('culmina floribus ornant') and contrasts the abyss which swallowed up the inhabitants with the roses now growing on the site:

> Atque immanis ubi populos absorpsit hiatus
> Gemmavere rosae, velantque vireta ruinas.
>
> (P i 233–5.)

Another composition written at Louis-le-Grand in the same year ends on a similar note of Romantic pathos, with its description of French exiles consoled by the fragrance of breezes 'Quae forsan patriis flores libavit in hortis'. By introducing these Romantic figures into 'le classique carcan', the schoolboy shows he is not merely 'triomphant et mutin',[7] but already aware of the ironic possibilities of the flowers of pathos.

The mature poet was to be concerned both with exile and the flowers of the homeland, the abyss and the roses growing over it, and his creative power was to derive in large part from the dialectic between horror and consolation. He was to realize very early that only by a rebellious process of self-exile and an unprecedented exploration of the abyss could he develop a poetic vision larger than the pieties of family, school, and society.

ii. *Flowers of irony*

> Une fleur qui ressemble à mon rouge idéal.
>
> (P i 22.)

The young Baudelaire was never to reassume the appearance of piety observed at school, and the poems written after he began living (from the end of 1839) in Bohemian and literary Paris are soon boldly marked by self-discovery and self-assertion. A poem he copied into Félicité Baudelaire's album ('Vous avez, chère sœur dont le cœur est poète' (P i 202)) praises her 'âme mondaine' and expresses nostalgia for simple piety ('cette dévotion des champs'). Some lines addressed to his half-brother treat the distinction between sacred and profane even more boldly while discussing the expression 'mon ange' from the viewpoint of a pedantic libertine ('Il est de chastes mots que nous profanons tous', P i 202).

The poem which most clearly shows the young man's new independence was probably written soon afterwards: 'Je n'ai pas pour maîtresse une lionne illustre'.[8] The poem is clearly intended to shock, most obviously by its celebration of a prostitute as 'maîtresse':

> Pour avoir des souliers elle a vendu son âme;
> Mais le bon Dieu rirait si près de cette infâme
> Je tranchais du Tartufe, et singeais la hauteur,
> Moi qui vends ma pensée, et qui veux être auteur.

(P i 203–4.)

The similarity between self-prostituting writer and woman makes it impossible for him to judge her according to the criteria of society. By choosing to be a writer, the poet has made himself free to construct an independent value-system in which appreciation of the woman's value is proudly solipsistic:

> Invisible aux regards de l'univers moqueur
> Sa beauté ne fleurit que dans mon triste cœur.

These lines define (and are inseparable from) the structural opposition on which the poem is built: beauty flowering subjectively for the poet where objectively there are no qualities to be admired at all. The degradation of this 'pauvre créature' is gloatingly presented in a list of extreme personal and social defects. For only by seeming to claim that the woman has no objectively admirable qualities can the poet make clear his own power to change degradation into beauty, transforming a 'pauvre créature' into a 'reine'.[9] This is the beauty of a flower rooted in personal and social *mal* but blossoming through the poet's consciousness into his verse: a fully grown *fleur du mal* in a poem written before he was 21 years old. Very possibly, then, this poem was one of the 'fleurs . . . singulières' mentioned with apparent casualness in a letter promising to send some verses to his mother (CP i 88).

Odd as it may seem that the mature Baudelaire's most typical use of poetic flower imagery should be so clearly implied at this early point, it is by no means out of character. The poem about Sara, with its insistent paradox, is an appropriate test piece for a young poet used to entertaining 'sentiments contradictoires'. Moreover, the inversion of accepted pieties follows naturally from his desire to assert liberation from his family and their social values. Their shocked reaction to 'un ordre d'idées dérangées par une surabondance de mauvais principes' was predictable in its turn, as was the initiative of the sea voyage intended to 'donner un autre cours à ses idées'.[10] But if Charles left France 'sans témoigner de répugnance', he returned with all his 'mauvais principes' intact, and asserted his independence once and for all: 'Je me suis sauvé, et j'ai été dès lors tout à fait abandonné' (CP ii 153). However his circumstances were to change in the next few years (the Hôtel Pimodan, the *conseil judiciaire*, the attempted suicide, the début as journalist-critic), the young Baudelaire never denied his decision to be a poet or repented his 'mauvais principes'.

For from the first he seems to have understood that for him the poetic enterprise must in some way involve the rejection of accepted values. The poem about the prostitute Sara is no doubt his first serious attempt at this, and here he relies to some extent on existing tradition. Other writers of the period had shown some interest in the idea that unexpected beauties might be found in *le laid*.[11] Others too had made use of the contrast between virtue and vice suggested by the theme of the paradoxically virtuous prostitute.[12] Indeed, flower metaphors had sometimes been used in this context. For from its association with virtue in devotional and sentimental tradition, the flower was an appropriate figure to make explicit, by oxymoron, the suggestive contrasts inherent in this theme. Gautier had recently retouched an ancient version of it in his Magdalena (that 'pâle fleur d'amour éclose au paradis') and Eugène Sue gave it the modern urban form of a prostitute nicknamed 'Fleur de Marie' in his *Mystères de Paris* of 1842. These women are seen as beautiful innocent flowers in spite of their (past or present) lack of virtue, and Gautier's Magdalena could be recognized in Sue's praise of his prostitute's argot nickname: 'Ne dirait-on pas un beau lis élevant la neige odorante de son calice immaculé au milieu d'un champ de carnage? Bizarre contraste, étrange hasard!'[13] Here it is an irony of situation which produces the moral and aesthetic oxymoron. Baudelaire's more complex rhetoric reveals his originality. By insisting on the woman's objective unattractiveness (ironizing the conventional idealization of women) and the poet's equal degradation, it emphasizes the remarkable transforming powers of a poet who can find beauty where no traditional or Romantic poet would look for it. The beauty which 'ne fleurit que dans mon triste cœur' is not merely achieved in spite of degradation, but created by means of a rhetoric of degradation and anti-idealization.

This is a rhetoric already capable of a variety of poetic strategies in the early work, where the theme of prostitution often provides its form. In *Les Deux Bonnes Sœurs*, for example, he presents the 'poète sinistre' as an unrepentant enemy of socially idealized values ('ennemi des familles, / Favori de l'enfer, courtisan mal renté') to such a degree that (like the hero of *Don Juan aux enfers*) he can welcome not merely debauchery but death itself. His riposte to Le Vavasseur's idealizing sonnet (itself an attack on Baudelaire's poem) suggests that the prostitute's justification for rejecting accepted pieties is not unlike the poet's:

> Elle croit, elle sait, cette vierge inféconde
> Et pourtant nécessaire à la marche du monde,
> Que la beauté du corps est un sublime don
> Qui de toute infamie arrache le pardon.
>
> (*Allégorie*, P i 116.)

In *La Muse vénale* the poet can insist again on his social marginality and on his own powers of ironic transformation:

> Sentant ta bourse à sec autant que ton palais,
> Récolteras-tu l'or des voûtes azurées?
>
> (P i 15.)

Or he can suggest that all poetic idealization must be read ironically since the poet (like the prostitute) is forced to 'Chanter des *Te Deum* auxquels tu ne crois guère', or (like the *saltimbanque*) to disguise suffering by laughter. Only a discourse ironically aware of the limits of idealization, it is implied, can be true to experience. Indirectly, Baudelaire provides justification here for the formulation of experience as oxymoron ('De terribles plaisirs et d'affreuses douceurs', P i 115) towards which an anti-idealizing rhetoric seems to be leading him in several early poems. The poem 'Tu mettrais l'univers entier dans ta ruelle' ends triumphantly with two extreme figures of this kind ('O fangeuse grandeur! sublime ignominie!', P i 28) after emphasizing that the 'Femme impure' is helping to create the poet by means of the degradation she imposes on him. The poet's insistence on his own degradation plays a similar role in relation to the theme of lesbianism, since Baudelaire can see the lesbian as 'Prêtresse de débauche et ma sœur du plaisir', sister like other 'femmes damnées' to the poet who is 'favori de l'enfer'.[14] Here too the rejection of accepted morality leads to a complexity of experience appropriately formulated in contrastive figures:

> Ô vierges, ô démons, ô monstres, ô martyres,
> De la réalité grands esprits contempteurs,
> Chercheuses d'infini, dévotes et martyres,
> Tantôt pleines de cris, tantôt pleines de pleurs.
>
> (P i 114.)

Even before planning the collection to be called *Les Lesbiennes* (advertised from 1845 to 1847), the young poet had learnt that contrastive formulations were poetic figures well adapted to his rhetoric of anti-idealization.

During this period, Baudelaire was clearly aware of the prestige of the Romantic *culte des fleurs*, or at least of some of its manifestations. The parody of Arsène Houssaye's *Sapho*, in which he collaborated in 1845, suggests, indeed, that he and his literary friends considered the more obvious forms of flower symbolism fatuously conventional. The parody associates a flaccid subject and verse-form with an over-pointed use of flower manual codes:

> Si bien que vous trouvant, quand vous venez le soir,
> La cause de ma joie et de mon désespoir,
> Mon âme les compense, et sous les lauriers roses
> Étouffe l'ellébore et les soucis moroses.[15]

It relies too on the code meaning of the *tubéreuse* ('la volupté'):

> Comme de ses chansons chaudement amoureuses
> Émane un fort parfum de riches tubéreuses, . . .
>
> Je baisse pavillon, — pauvre âme adolescente
> Au feu de cette amour terrible et menaçante.
>
> (P ii 4.)

The parody, written at a time when Baudelaire's *Les Lesbiennes* had been announced,[16] perhaps refers knowingly to his own interest in 'la perfide atmosphère / De tes tristes cités, corruptrice Lesbos' (P ii 5). But whatever their intention, the parodists' playful treatment of flower symbolism shows their awareness of a literary culture in which flower symbolism could provide contrastive tropes or even a metaphor for Sappho's 'amour terrible et menaçante'.

Indeed, the Baudelaire who during this period could adopt the *persona* of Sappho ('Car Lesbos entre tous m'a choisi sur la terre / Pour chanter le secret de ses vierges en fleur', P i 151) was himself experimenting more seriously with subversive flower symbolism. *La Fanfarlo* provides a model for this subversiveness when it juxtaposes Madame de Cosmelly's innocence and her sentimental love of flowers with Samuel Cramer's aggressive negativism:

C'est la haine de tous et de nous-mêmes qui nous a conduits vers ces mensonges . . . Nous nous sommes tellement appliqués à sophistiquer notre cœur . . . qu'il est impossible que nous parlions le langage des autres hommes. . . . nous avons altéré l'accent de la nature, nous avons extirpé une à une les pudeurs virginales.

(P i 559–60.)

Recognizing here the anti-idealization of Cramer's poems *Les Orfraies* (as we detect that of Baudelaire's *Lesbiennes*), Madame de Cosmelly replies:

'Encore des Orfraies! . . . voyons, donnez-moi votre bras et admirons ces pauvres fleurs que le printemps rend si heureuses!'
    Au lieu d'admirer les fleurs, Samuel Cramer . . . commença à mettre en prose et à déclamer quelques mauvaises stances composées dans sa première manière.

Baudelaire and Cramer are clearly aware that idealizing flower sentimentality is the ideological opposite of their own experience, theories, and writing.
    It is possibly to Baudelaire's own 'première manière' that the poem *Une martyre* should be attributed.[17] Its subject certainly suits that of *Les Lesbiennes*, with its background in 'un amour ténébreux, / Une coupable joie et des fêtes étranges / Pleines de baisers infernaux' (P i 112). Here again is the contrast between Romantic idealized values ('amour', 'joie', 'fêtes', 'baisers') and subversive moral negativity ('ténébreux', 'coupable', 'étrange', 'infernaux'). The poem presents a woman's corpse in a flowery secret boudoir (reminiscent of Paquita's love bower in Balzac's *La Fille aux yeux d'or*), after the fatal enactment of 'des désirs errants et perdus'. The atmosphere is charged with a deadly and wayward eroticism:

        Dans une chambre tiède où, comme en une serre,
            L'air est dangereux et fatal,

Où des bouquets mourants dans leurs cercueils de verre
Exhalent leur soupir final.

(P i 112.)

In a situation which would seem to exclude any moral or aesthetic idealization of this perverse 'martyre', Baudelaire introduces conventional sentimentality only to qualify it: the 'bouquets' are enclosed 'comme en une serre' and 'dans leurs cercueils de verre', and all the adjectives are negative ('tiède', 'dangereux', 'fatal', 'mourant', 'final'). But his description of the severed head is a bold experiment in poetic style. First the head is presented as a ghostly horror ('Semblable aux visions pâles qu'enfante l'ombre'), then realistically as the head of a voluptuous woman ('avec l'amas de sa crinière sombre / Et de ses bijoux précieux'), then 'comme une renoncule'. This flower simile only heightens the effect of paradox, not just 'visually' (through the discrepancy in size between head and flower), but semantically too. There is an ironic boldness in the introduction of floral beauty into this setting, and the irony is confirmed by the *renoncule*'s ambiguous flower-code meaning — 'perfidie', 'ingratitude', 'remords', or 'la toilette'.[18] And the antithetical rhetoric of this simile is that of the whole poem, contrasting floral sentimentality with the subversive beauty of a transient flower.

By locating visual and poetic beauty in degradation and death, Baudelaire transforms the 'cadavre impur' into a 'forme immortelle'. The poem *Une Charogne* works in a similar way.[19] Once more a conventional idealization ('mon âme', 'un beau matin d'été si doux') is quickly subverted, here by an 'objet' apparently fit only to evoke disgust: 'une charogne infâme'. The first two stanzas move through different types of anti-idealization: from animal's carcass to 'femme lubrique' ('les jambes en l'air') to rotting meat 'cooked' and decomposed by the sun's rays. Then (after a transitional 'Et') the text produces its boldest antithetical image, yoking perfection and degradation in an oxymoron, and then in a flower figure:

Et le ciel regardait la carcasse superbe
Comme une fleur s'épanouir.

(P i 31.)

This image is a striking inversion of the ancient *flos foeni*, for here it is not the beautiful ephemeral flower which suggests death and decomposition but the reverse. It is no mere decorative surprise, however, for the carcass/flower, superlative both in terms of idealization ('superbe', 'fleur') and of degradation ('la puanteur était si forte') becomes an absolute symbol of the creative and destructive powers of 'la grande Nature'. Later references to grass, insects, water, wind, and the human world ('un vanneur', 'l'artiste') suggest the same vast natural context of decomposition and transformation. The poet goes on to insist in the envoi that the idealized beloved herself '(Étoile de mes yeux, soleil de ma nature') is part of 'la grande Nature' and thus subject to the same processes:

> Quand vous irez, sous l'herbe et les floraisons grasses,
> Moisir parmi les ossements.

(P i 32.)

Already implicitly flower-like through the poet's idealization, she too will fade and decompose after death, but just as the carcass can 'comme une fleur s'épanouir' so her own decomposition can take on 'la forme et l'essence divine' of poetry.[20] The flower images in this poem mediate between nature (decomposition and transformation) and poetry (anti-idealization and idealization) to develop a new rhetoric out of the flower of transience.

The flower imagery of both these poems derives its almost numinous intensity from being placed against a background of negative facts and values in contrast with which the flowers' traditional idealizing qualities only show more brightly. Well before 1846, Baudelaire had learnt how to 'tirer parti de la laideur elle-même' but in that year he proposed a theory of anti-idealization in the semi-serious context of the *Choix de maximes consolantes sur l'amour*:

Pour certains esprits plus curieux et plus blasés, la jouissance de la laideur provient d'un sentiment encore plus mystérieux, qui est la soif de l'inconnu, et le goût de l'horrible. C'est ce sentiment, dont chacun porte en soi le germe plus ou moins développé, qui précipite certains poètes dans les amphithéâtres et les cliniques, et les femmes aux exécutions publiques. Je plaindrais vivement qui ne comprendrait pas; — une harpe à qui manquerait une corde grave.

(P i 548-9.)

But he is aware too that the 'goût de l'horrible' is only the ground base in a more complete harmony. Advising the reader on how to react when 'l'héroïne de votre cœur, ayant abusé du *fas* et du *nefas*, est arrivée aux limites de la perdition', he proposes a more inclusive definition of 'l'idéal' than the conventional Romantic one:

Dites hardiment, et avec la candeur de vrai philosophe: 'Moins scélérat, mon idéal n'eût pas été complet. Je le contemple, et me soumets: d'une si puissante coquine la grande Nature seule sait ce qu'elle veut faire. Bonheur et raison suprêmes! Absolu! *résultante* des contraires! Ormuz et Arimane, vous êtes le même!

(P i 550.)

This more complete 'idéal', resulting like oxymoron from contrary qualities, reflects 'la grande Nature' itself, with its creative and destructive aspects — *Ormuz* and *Arimane*. After the assertive negativism of his early period, Baudelaire seems indeed, at certain times in the mid-forties, to be seeking a positive counterpart to 'le goût de l'horrible'. His use of contrastive formulations (including flower imagery) could only provide the required dualism at the rhetorical level. At certain times after 1842, however, Baudelaire seems to have thought some positive value might be found in aspects of the *rêve hellénique* cultivated by some of his contemporaries.[21]

    The cult of aesthetic formalism and the *impassible*, already coming to be associated with Hellenism in this decade, seems not to have seriously tempted Baudelaire. The poet of *Une charogne* and *Une martyre* could have little use for the Hellenist idealization of the Venus de Milo, hailed as a 'grand poème de marbre' by Banville or as the symbol of the 'impassible' by Leconte de Lisle.[22] The sonnet *La Beauté* (if it dates from this period) may be read as a critique of such attitudes, since Beauty is represented as a woman whose coldness promises danger for the poet rather than inspiration.[23] Baudelaire's interest in antiquity was directed rather to an area he could reproach the Hellenist Louis Ménard with neglecting: 'le côté panthéistique et naturaliste de la question'.[24] Attracted by the idea of a primitive humanity in communion with nature and its deities, Baudelaire sought in it an ideal of innocence, health, and abundance:

> Alors, l'homme et la femme en leur agilité
> Jouissaient sans mensonge et sans anxiété . . .
>
> Cybèle alors, fertile en produits généreux, . . .
>
> Abreuvait l'univers à ses tétines brunes.

(P i 11–12.)

It is in fact the very possibility of unironic poetic idealization that is celebrated in this image of a youthful humanity

> qui va répandant sur tout, insouciante
> Comme l'azur du ciel, les oiseaux et les fleurs,
> Ses parfums, ses chansons et ses douces chaleurs![25]

For this flowery ideal attracts him precisely because it is so unlike the contemporary reality:

> Et vous, femmes, hélas! pâles des cierges,
> Que ronge et que nourrit la débauche, et vous, vierges,
> Du vice maternel traînant l'hérédité
> Et toutes les hideurs de la fécondité!

All modern women are thus *femmes damnées* unworthy to be associated with the flowers which connote innocence. They are like the poet's own 'Muse malade' in another poem of this period, tortured by nightmare visions and by 'La folie et l'horreur, froides et taciturnes' (P i 14–15). She, too, being modern ('ton sang chrétien'), lacks the innocent health of antiquity and is thus unable to produce poetry like those

> syllabes antiques
> Où règnent tour à tour le père des chansons,
> Phoebus, et le grand Pan, le seigneur des moissons.

Although the poet claims he 'would like' his muse to be healthy in this way, his invocation is entirely unlike the pro-Hellenist polemic of a Gautier or a Leconte de Lisle. Indeed, the resolution of 'J'aime le souvenir . . . ' suggests that Baudelaire soon saw the incompatibility between this ideal and his own subversion of the poetics of innocence.[26] The passage in which he 'allows' that beauty can be found in modern life plainly gives aesthetic priority to a beauty more complex than that of idyllic nostalgia. The beauty found in the 'races maladives' of modern life has a special quality ('comme qui dirait des beautés de langueur') not characteristic of innocent antiquity, an adult creative power ('ces inventions de nos muses tardives') denied to 'la jeunesse . . . insouciante / Comme . . . les fleurs'. This statement has important implications for Baudelaire's own poetry, not least in its rejection of two kinds of aesthetic simplification. He will be satisfied neither with a Romanticism which unironically idealizes modern life, nor with a Hellenism which can find beauty and value only in antiquity.

Several related poems probably of this period show Baudelaire experimenting with other ways to resolve the tension between antiquity and modernity. In *La Géante*, for example, he conceives a primitive world without the harmonious balance and simplicity of idyll, since the young giantess is one of the 'enfants monstrueux' produced by an unruly 'Nature en sa verve puissante' (P i 22). As if to emphasize that she is unlike the 'jeunesse . . . insouciante' of flowery idyll, the poet ironically uses the verb 'fleurir' to describe her growth:

> J'eusse aimé voir son corps fleurir avec son âme
> Et grandir librement dans ses terribles jeux.
>
> (P i 22–3.)

This creature flowers into an animal innocence of a very equivocal kind, to become an emblem of paradoxical beauty and strength in a non-modern context. In *L'Idéal*, on the other hand, the poet rejects the unironic sentimentalism he sees in certain types of modern beauty:

> Je laisse à Gavarni, poète des chloroses,
> Son troupeau gazouillant des beautés d'hôpital,
> Car je ne puis trouver parmi ces pâles roses
> Une fleur qui ressemble à mon rouge idéal.
>
> (P i 22.)

Once again Baudelaire uses flower imagery to express an aesthetic point, again distinguishing (here in a version of the flower code) between a simplistic form of beauty and a more synthetic one. Both Lady Macbeth and Michelangelo's *Night* are figures whose beauty is a '*résultante* des contraires', since the former is a 'Rêve d'Eschyle éclos au climat des autans' while the latter is at the same time peaceful and disturbingly giant-like, and both paradoxically associate womanhood with violence. Baudelaire is here reaching for an aesthetic ideal more satisfactory than either nostalgic pastoral or sentimentalized modern *mal du siècle*. The 'rouge idéal' he seeks must be, unlike the pale flowers of any kind of simplification, a flower of strong and unsettling paradox. Without the paradox, after all, 'mon idéal n'eût pas été complet'.

By 1846, the term 'l'idéal' was an important one for Baudelaire. He uses it throughout his *Salon* of that year in his strenuous discussion of imaginative perfection in the plastic arts.[27] Although from its origins in neo-classical art theory 'le beau idéal' was defined by reference to the formal perfection of Greek sculpture or Raphael's painting, Baudelaire does not hesitate to re-define it. Thus he argues that Rembrandt, not Raphael, is the real 'idéaliste' (P ii 421) and praises David's *Marat* because, 'cruel comme la nature, ce tableau a tout le parfum de l'idéal' (P ii 409). In his own search for *l'idéal* in poetic terms, too, Baudelaire works within an established dichotomy to produce a new synthetic view. Thus he can treat the opposition between Hellenism and Romanticism synthetically (Lady Macbeth as a 'Rêve d'Eschyle éclos au climat des autans') or find a dualist structure within Romanticism itself: 'Le romantisme est fils du Nord . . . le Nord souffrant et inquiet se console avec l'imagination' (P ii 421). For the Baudelaire of 1846 *l'idéal* must be a '*résultante* des contraires' and Romanticism could best provide for this. It is itself bi-polar in structure, combining a sickly and troubled character with the consolations of the imagination. The flower of his 'rouge idéal' is a flower of Romanticism in this sense, for both Lady Macbeth and Michelangelo's *Night* combine highly disturbing qualities with picturesque or consoling ones. But Romanticism was also 'l'expression la plus récente, la plus actuelle du beau' (P ii 420) and the *Salon de 1846* defines an aesthetic of the modern, 'une beauté nouvelle et particulière' (P ii 496). Thus the poet's own 'rouge idéal' must also be a modern one, not only paradoxical but as strong and unsettling as real experience. Unlike 'la fausse école romantique en poésie', it must conform to 'l'austère filiation du romantisme, cette expression de la société moderne' (P ii 409).

The poem *Un voyage à Cythère*, probably written at about this time,[28] can be seen as a show-piece for an austere modern aesthetic, not least in its rejection of a sentimental ideal hallowed by Romantic and Hellenist piety. Following his source in Nerval, Baudelaire invokes the traditional connotations of Cythera as a flowery paradise of love.[29]

> Belle île aux myrtes verts, pleine de fleurs écloses,
> Vénérée à jamais par toute nation,
> Où les soupirs des cœurs en adoration
> Roulent comme l'encens sur un jardin de roses.

> (P i 118.)

But the subversive modern reality is 'cette île triste et noire', 'un désert rocailleux' with neither myrtles nor flowers. All the poet perceives is 'un objet singulier', pointedly stated to be not

> un temple aux ombres bocagères
> Où la prêtresse, amoureuse des fleurs,
> Allait . . .

but 'un gibet . . . se détachant en noir, comme un cyprès' to which is attached 'un pendu déjà mûr'. The sacralization of love (figured by myrtles and flowers) gives way to a reality in which the only tree is a gibbet, the only flower a rotting corpse. In demythologizing Cythera, the poet has replaced idealization by unpleasant truth, and now concludes the process by providing a bitterly personal interpretation for the *allégorie*: 'un gibet symbolique où pendait mon image!' The poem's subject is thus himself identified with the decomposing corpse whose own wrongdoing ('tes infâmes cultes') and that of others ('ses bourreaux') has brought him to this state. Instead of the expected flowers of the idealized island of love, he has discovered the terrible personal truth about his own degradation through the flesh. The poet has used two connotations of traditional flower imagery (perfection and transience) to confront idealist illusions with a reality not merely modern but personal. Baudelaire's Romanticism will not be merely the 'expression de la société moderne' but a way for the poet to present himself as uniquely self-revealing.[30] This is a new psychological realism, so extreme that irony about false idealization turns into a self-hatred from which the poet cries out to be delivered.

This poem comments on the tradition of pastoral and idyllic floral landscape by only allowing reality to the desert, gibbet, and corpse which represent contemporary personal experience. There are suggestions elsewhere, too, that Baudelaire found it useful to define his own modern and personal poetics in relation to the idyllic tradition. Thus the poet of *La Béatrice*, abandoned to self-loathing in a desert landscape, is mocked by demons as the parody of a poet because he wants to

> intéresser au chant de ses douleurs
> Les aigles, les grillons, les ruisseaux et les fleurs.

Even in the no man's land of modern experience, the poet feels the attraction of the Romantic or elegiac pastoral about which (as about the traditional idealization of women) this poem is so bitterly ironical.

The poet of *A celle qui est trop gaie* makes a related point:

> Quelquefois dans un beau jardin
> Où je traînais mon atonie,
> J'ai senti, comme une ironie,
> Le soleil déchirer mon sein;
>
> Et le printemps et la verdure
> Ont tant humilié mon cœur,
> Que j'ai puni sur une fleur
> L'insolence de la Nature.[31]

Pastoral elegy could find pathos in confronting a poet's 'atonie' (or his 'douleurs') with natural perfection, but these lines insist on the poet's humiliation and his revenge. He is happier presenting himself as the urban poet who looks out at the city 'pour composer chastement mes églogues' and treats the landscape of idyll only as a mid-winter's dream:

> Alors je rêverai des horizons bleuâtres,
> Des jardins, des jets d'eau pleurant dans les albâtres,
> Des baisers, des oiseaux chantant soir et matin,
> Et tout ce que l'Idylle a de plus enfantin.

(P i 82.)

In such poems the perfections of idyllic nature are never perceived without ironic qualification of some kind, whether as fantasy, nostalgia, aesthetic rival, or false idealization. It is as if the poet of modern personal experience must be by definition not only ironic but urban. In the early poem *Le Soleil* Baudelaire had sought a way for the urban poet to reconcile idyllic tradition and urban experience. The sun makes no distinction between country and city, consoling and ennobling them both:

> Ce père nourricier, ennemi de chloroses,
> Éveille dans les champs les vers comme les roses; . . .
>
> Et commande aux moissons de croître et de mûrir
> Dans le cœur immortel qui toujours veut fleurir!
>
> Quand, ainsi qu'un poète, il descend dans les villes,
> Il ennoblit le sort des choses les plus viles.

(P i 83.)

Unlike the sun, the poet can only know urban life, and moreover the sun itself has an ambiguous effect in the countryside, since it awakens worms as well as roses. The poet can neither ignore 'les choses les plus viles' of urban life, nor pretend that sunlit flowery idyll can be celebrated honestly by 'nos muses tardives'.

The intention to treat urban life is still implicit in the announcement of *Les Limbes* in 1850 as a volume 'destiné à représenter les agitations et les mélancolies de la jeunesse moderne'.[32] And the typical poems of this period certainly treat 'les choses les plus viles', sometimes in an explicitly urban setting (like the Prostitution of *Le Crépuscule du soir*, which 'remue au sein de la cité de fange / Comme un ver'), but more often in the no man's land of modern 'agitations' and 'mélancolies':

> Il me conduit ainsi, loin du regard de Dieu,
> Haletant et brisé de fatigue, au milieu
> Des plaines de l'Ennui, profondes et désertes.

> (P i 111.)

This is a place neither urban nor idyllic. It is a flowerless landscape reflecting the psychological state of a modern man unable to seek refuge from his urban experience in any idealization:

> C'est un univers morne à l'horizon plombé,
> Où nagent dans la nuit l'horreur et le blasphème; . . .

> C'est un pays plus nu que la terre polaire;
> — Ni bêtes, ni ruisseaux, ni verdure, ni bois!

> (P i 32.)

It is a place of death ('Je suis un cimetière abhorré de la lune') or of death-in-life:

> Désormais tu n'es plus, ô matière vivante!
> Qu'un granit entouré d'une vague épouvante,
> Assoupi dans le fond d'un Sahara brumeux.

> (P i 73.)

Such deserts of *Ennui* have nothing 'pour éblouir la vue tremblante des enfants ou pour caresser leur oreille paresseuse', unlike the 'puérile utopie' about which Baudelaire was so scathing in 1851.[33] Their only remnants of flowery nature are dead mementoes of urban sentimentality, as in the *Spleen* quoted above ('Je suis un vieux

boudoir plein de roses fanées') or in *Le Léthé*, where the poet
wants to

> respirer, comme une fleur flétrie,
> Le doux relent de mon amour défunt.

> Je veux dormir! dormir plutôt que vivre!

> (P i 155–6.)

Even when espousing an anti-individualist poetics in his article on
Pierre Dupont, he insisted that idyllic escapism was less acceptable
than 'la plainte de cette individualité maladive, qui, du fond d'un
cercueil fictif, s'évertuait à intéresser une société à ses mélancolies
irrémédiables'.[34] For it was some such flowerless netherworld, 'les
limbes insondées de la tristesse',[35] that had become for the Baudelaire of 1851 the landscape which best represented his own
'individualité maladive'.

These anti-pastoral landscapes are flowerless because the 'mélancolies irrémédiables' which they represent absolutely preclude any
of the consolations of idealization. Thus is confirmed the association
between flowers and idealization on which so much of Baudelaire's
earlier poetics of anti-idealization had relied. During his first decade
the poet had made use of several distinct rhetorical strategies of
negation and in all of them the idealizing implications of flower
imagery were subverted or inverted. Early in the decade he had used
flower images to represent the subversive new beauty to be found
in circumstances of degradation. When developing a Romantic
aesthetic of modernity in the years around 1846, he had used flower
imagery to evoke the new 'rouge idéal' of a beauty uniting opposites.
And in *Un voyage à Cythère* and later poems he had adumbrated
a modern aesthetic of self-degradation by negating the idealizing
implications of flowery idyll. In all these cases the poet is concerned
in some sense with negation, whether he is ironizing about accepted
pieties, flatly rejecting them, or presenting a personal sense of self-
hatred or empty melancholy. Appropriately, Baudelaire's treatment
of traditional flower rhetoric (the flower code, flowers of transience,
or flowers of idealization) is boldly and variously ironic in these
poems of his first decade. The flower figures are an image of pieties
to be rejected, a sign of contradiction, or an acknowledged or implied
absence: they are all flowers of negativity, expressions of Baudelaire's
unprecedentedly subversive irony.

iii. *Flowers of synaesthesia and sensual mysticism*

> . . . rêver des jours entiers sur le parfum d'une fleur.
>
> (P i 427.)

But the poet of these 'fleurs singulières' (that 'Prince des Charognes') could also boast 'une foule de choses de moi qui ne sont que musc et que roses' (CP i 173–4). For in other poems of the same period Baudelaire could also use flower figures which are neither ironic nor negative in effect. The exotic tropical nature Baudelaire discovered during his early southern voyage seems to have played some part in the development of this type of imagery. Two of his earliest poems— *A une dame créole* (P i 62–3) and *A une Malabaraise* (P i 173–4)—celebrate women whose beauty is related to the sensual beauty of tropical life, by their appearance, fragrance, and warmth. One resembles her 'pays parfumé que le soleil caresse'; the other, living 'aux pays chauds et bleus' is characterized by 'le parfum de [ses] charmes étranges'. Both are associated with flower figures, the first implicitly because her beauty would make 'germer mille sonnets dans le cœur des poètes' in France, the other because her dreams are imagined as 'pleins de colibris, / Et toujours, comme toi, gracieux et fleuris'. For Baudelaire tropical nature itself soon connotes an exotic beauty which appeals to several areas of experience at once: sight, smell, warmth, and eroticism. Thus in the early poem *Parfum exotique*, the poet can find in it a means of evoking a rich sensual well-being in which synaesthesia becomes an indispensable stylistic device (P i 25–6). Here the woman's fragrance, which transports the poet to a tropical landscape, evokes vegetation by appearance and taste ('Une île paresseuse où la nature donne / Des arbres singuliers et des fruits savoureux'), then by smell ('le parfum des verts tamariniers') to suggest (with reference also to movement and sound) a dreamlike tropical eroticism. This is a sensual synaesthetic heaviness similar to that evoked in the lines in praise of Sainte-Beuve's 'livre voluptueux':

> Les soirs italiens, de molle insouciance, . . .
>
> Quand la sombre Vénus, du haut des balcons noirs,
> Verse des flots de musc de ses frais encensoirs.
>
> (P i 207.)

Written several years after he had travelled 'sous les soleils des zones différentes' these lines suggest that the poet is bringing together adolescent memories and literary influence with his tropical experience, to express a cluster of associations in a single flower figure.

The young Baudelaire knew something of the role flowers had played in recent and contemporary discussions of the analogical relations between the senses. As a model for such relations the synaesthetic flower code had not escaped his attention, for it is gently mocked in the 1845 parody of Houssaye's *Sapho*:

> Comme de ses chansons chaudement amoureuses
> Émane un fort parfum de riches tubéreuses.

> (P ii 4.)

By 1846, however, he could quote with approval the passage in which Hoffmann uses the evocative qualities of particular flowers to illustrate the synaesthetic principle:

une analogie et une réunion intime entre les couleurs, les sons et les parfums. Il me semble que toutes ces choses ont été engendrées par un même rayon de lumière, et qu'elles doivent se réunir dans un merveilleux concert. L'odeur des soucis bruns et rouges produit surtout un effet magique sur ma personne. Elle me fait tomber dans une profonde rêverie, et j'entends alors comme dans le lointain les sons graves et profonds du hautbois.

> (P ii 425–6.)

In the section of the *Salon de 1846* where he quotes this passage from *Kreisleriana*, Baudelaire is concerned to establish a 'théorie de la couleur' as the basis for his theory of painting.[36]. Yet Baudelaire has introduced the quotation by wondering whether 'quelque analogiste a établi solidement une gamme complète des couleurs et des sentiments', a few lines after sketching his own tentative *symbolique des couleurs*.[37] It would seem that he is not concerned here with synaesthetic experience for its own sake, since nothing in his argument corresponds to the 'profonde rêverie' of synaesthetic contemplation in Kreisler's account. Instead, he is interested in the principle of *analogie* which can relate one sense perception not only to another but also to a *sentiment* outside the strictly sensual domain. Hoffmann's flower reference itself supports this interpretation, since 'l'odeur des soucis bruns et rouges' produces not only a musical perception but the feelings characterized by the adjectives 'graves et profonds'. In Baudelaire's context, at least, these flowers must be seen as capable of both synaesthetic and emotional/semantic association, with a suggestive power that mediates between sense perceptions and feeling or meaning.

Hoffmann presents his *soucis* as a privileged case, and implies that for him synaesthetic *rêverie* comes more typically in dream, semi-wakefulness, or 'lorsque j'entends de la musique' (P ii 425). Where Baudelaire makes use of synaesthesia in his early poetry, he begins with the sense of smell:

> Comme d'autres esprits voguent sur la musique,
> Le mien, ô mon amour! nage sur ton parfum.
>
> *(La Chevelure*, P i 26.)

But in this poem, as in *Parfum exotique*, the process of synaesthetic association is inseparable from an evocation of emotion and thought, and the operative 'parfum' is 'chargé de nonchaloir'.[38] The parts of the sonnet *Correspondances* most likely to have been written at about this time (1844–7) give a similar interpretation to Hoffmann's principle of *analogie*.[38] The second quatrain announces the synaesthetic principle ('les parfums, les couleurs et les sons se répondent'), while in the tercets 'les parfums' illustrate not only synaesthetic association but emotional/intellectual evocation as well. Indeed, by dividing them into two groups, the poet implies that his priority is to outline a non-synaesthetic *symbolique des parfums*. The 'parfums' of the first type do suggest relations with other senses: touch ('frais comme des chairs d'enfant'), sound ('doux comme les hautbois'), and colour ('verts comme les prairies'), but they are defined as a group by the innocence characterizing these associations. Those of the second group (the 'parfums . . . corrompus') are defined by their qualities of rich expansiveness, and the poet only refers to synaes-thesia as the vehicle for their emotional/intellectual associations, for they 'chantent les transports de l'esprit et des sens'. Again Baudelaire is less concerned with synaesthesia in itself than with the principle of *analogie*, here as a model for the expansion of emotional and intellectual experience. The rhetoric of the *symbolique des parfums* recalls both Hoffmann's *soucis* and the flower-code, but differs from them in several important respects. It not only presents an opposition between innocent and non-innocent ('corrumpus') but also subverts expectations by attributing greater rhetorical power to the second group. Baudelaire's version of the *langage des parfums* contains an implicit criticism of the pieties of flower sentimentality, while itself based on earlier and contemporary speculation about nature's 'confuses paroles' in which the *langage des fleurs* had an important place.

In these lines the consideration of synaesthetic principle grows into a celebration of 'l'expansion des choses infinies' and 'les transports de l'esprit et des sens' which uses language redolent of both sensuality and mysticism. In the *Kreisleriana* quotation synaesthesia is associated with dream, semi-wakefulness, or 'une profonde rêverie', and in the tropical poems with a dreamlike sensual 'expansion' and 'transport'. Baudelaire was discovering that synaesthetic experience was well adapted to the rhetorical purpose of evoking a privileged consciousness at the margin of everyday life. This was a function it had often had in the Romantic celebration of such moments, usually presented in terms of participation in nature and love, and typically with reference to flowers. Baudelaire himself translated one evocation of this kind in *Le Jeune Enchanteur*:

Musique, lumière, étoiles, les sons répandus dans l'air du soir, le balancement d'une rose, le parfum de son calice, les formes vagues qui flottent là-bas dans les nuages, tout ce qui touche mon cœur, flatte mes sens, égaye mon œil, me ramène instantanément vers elle.[40]

As in many such passages, the atmosphere is charged with sensuality and mysticism, both attenuated by sentimentality. It is the atmosphere of one of Baudelaire's most remarkable poems of this period, *Harmonie du soir*:[41]

Voici venir les temps où vibrant sur sa tige
Chaque fleur s'évapore ainsi qu'un encensoir;
Les sons et les parfums tournent dans l'air du soir.

(P i 47.)

These flowers are perceived by several senses at once, even seeming to produce sound as they secrete fragrance: it is as if 'les sons et les parfums' are both breathed out by the swaying flowers to swirl in the evening air. This 'harmonie' has overtones too of both love and mysticism, for the flowers tremble and faint like sentimental belles, but also shimmer and dematerialize in a mystical haze.[42] The fourth line refers again to sentimental sensuality ('valse') and to mystical trance ('vertige'), but it also projects a marked emotional colouring over the whole ('mélancolique' and 'langoureux') and thus makes explicit the connotations of melancholic *langueur* already implicit in the verbs ('s'évapore' and 'tournent'). The dreamlike melancholy is a free-floating emotional atmosphere, itself an aspect of the 'harmonie' produced by the flowers. It is this non-personal emotion, not linked with first-person subjectivity before the last line of the poem, which goes on to provide the emotional content of the remaining three stanzas. The flower *harmonie* is 'triste et beau', and the sense of despair grows throughout the rest of the poem, so that the harmonious stasis of the opening comes to seem threatened by destruction. The tension is only resolved by the restoration of emotional harmony (now fixed in the first-person subject) in the final invocation of mystical sentimentality. The woman's memory becomes an emblem of centralization (the flower-shaped 'ostensoir') recalling and contrasting with the initial image of flower-vaporization.[43]

The flower *harmonie* evoked here is a 'merveilleux concert' like Kreisler's, and is probably also indebted to a passage from Hoffmann's *Le Chat Murr*.[44] It recalls too the procedure of contemporary synaesthetic flower pieces (George Sand's in *Consuelo* or Méry's in *Les Fleurs animées*, for example) where, as in the *Chat Murr* passage, the flowers themselves seem to produce the synaesthetic atmosphere. Indeed, in his use of sensual and mystical connotations Baudelaire seems to owe less to Hoffmann than to such pieces, for in them flowers sing of 'beautés idéales et mystérieuses' (Méry) and 'harmonies idéales' (Sand), or express 'd'enivrantes pensées d'amour' (Karr). Even more significantly, Baudelaire has here found a poetic style which can combine an ambiguous emotional suggestiveness with a sense of autonomous musicality evoked by considerable repetition of sound and phrase. It is as if the poet had in mind, when composing this *harmonie* of free-floating sensual perceptions and emotions, the claims made for the mysterious expressive 'harmonies idéales' of floral synaesthesia—emotion-filled yet mystically impersonal. Here, in any case, the 'mystères de la poésie' (Sand) are not merely celebrated but demonstrated.

It cannot be proved that Baudelaire knew Sand's text, or Méry's or Karr's.[45] In any case the creation of a new allusive language in *Harmonie du soir* to express sentimental mysticism and dreamlike *langueur* is a singular achievement of the fertile years before 1850, and exceptional even in the corpus of his own work. Yet several of the few other poems which are stylistically comparable also contain reference to flowers,[46] and this suggests that the flowers of mysticism did indeed play a formative role in the development of this kind of language in his poetry. Baudelaire was certainly aware of the rhetorical suggestiveness of any reference to flowers which implies a world beyond normal experience. In *Du vin et du haschisch* (1851) he ends the section on Paganini's Spanish guitarist with a series of questions relying on a mystical pathos not unlike that of *Harmonie du soir*: 'Et maintenant où est-il? Quel soleil a contemplé ses derniers rêves? . . . Où sont les parfums enivrants des fleurs disparues? Où sont les couleurs féeriques des anciens soleils couchants?' (P i 386). The flowers are an image of a sensual experience existing almost mystically in the imagination.[47] Flowers have an equally suggestive function in *Tristesses de la lune*, where the poet compares the moon to a beautiful woman half-falling asleep:

> Mourante, elle se livre aux longues pâmoisons,
> Et promène ses yeux sur les visions blanches
> Qui montent dans l'azur comme des floraisons.
>
> (P i 65.)

Here suggestions of eroticism ('pâmoisons') and mysticism ('visions') are presented together, and the flower simile ('floraisons') intensifies both. The poem *La Mort des amants* (published 1851) follows a not dissimilar pattern:

> Nous aurons des lits pleins d'odeurs légères,
> Des divans profonds comme des tombeaux;
> Et de grandes fleurs dans des jardinières,
> Écloses pour nous sous des cieux plus beaux.[48]

Sentimental eroticism is heightened by the pathos of the lovers' deaths in a setting characterized as 'mystique', and by the anticipation of the absolute plenitude of their love beyond death. This mystical state is prefigured by the exotic beautiful elsewhere in which the flowers have already bloomed 'pour nous', and they become almost a sacrament of the mystical consummation of love in death.[49] By their connotations of love, their exotic origin, and their full-blown state, they resume in themselves the thematic development of the poem. But the ambiguous allusiveness of the flower image (with the support of alliteration in the 1857 version) also helps to create the dreamlike suggestiveness which characterizes the language of the poem. As in *Harmonie du soir*, the flower imagery here makes a determinative contribution to a suggestive poetic style, to such an extent that Baudelaire would seem to be providing stylistic proof

of the mysterious rhetorical powers claimed for flowers by others
before him.

The poem *L'Invitation au voyage*, written several years later,[50]
provides explicit evidence that Baudelaire was aware of such speculation about the mystical *langage des fleurs*. The poet first expresses
love for the woman he is asking to travel with him to an exotic and
almost mystical country which will fittingly mirror her beauty:

> Là, tout n'est qu'ordre et beauté,
> Luxe, calme et volupté.

> (P i 53.)

Then once more flowers are invoked in a context of love and mystical
perfection, and the poet characterizes the room where the lovers
would live:

> Les plus rares fleurs
> Mêlant leurs odeurs
> Aux vagues senteurs de l'ambre,
> Les riches plafonds,
> Les miroirs profonds,
> La splendeur orientale,
> Tout y parlerait
> A l'âme en secret
> Sa douce langue natale.

The flowers' rareness indicates refinement and privilege, but they
also appear to have mysterious powers—even (since 'mêlant' implies
their agency) those of active intervention. They seem to orchestrate
the other parts of the room to provide a harmony of mingled sense-
impressions, and thus express the communion between the self and
material things which would exist in the ideal country the poet
imagines. 'Là-bas', their language would symbolize and effect the
perfect relationship between material world and spiritual self, a privileged communion which is at the same time the birthright of the
human psyche: 'Sa douce langue natale'. The child in *Bénédiction*
knows the same language ('il joue avec le vent, cause avec le nuage')
and the poet of *Élévation* declares that the man is fortunate indeed

> Qui plane sur la vie, et comprend sans effort
> Le langage des fleurs et des choses muettes.

> (P i 10.)

In all three poems, knowledge of this language is seen as a sensual delight and a mystical privilege ironically unrealizable or unrecoverable in the real adult world: for Baudelaire this ironic truth is inescapable, as it does not seem to have been for others who speak of the mystical *langage des fleurs*. Significantly, Baudelaire also differs from almost all his predecessors and contemporaries by not merely celebrating this language but imaginatively appropriating it in his own poetic language. The suggestive evocation of an ideal of mystical-sensual experience in *L'Invitation au voyage* (as perhaps too its prosodic musicality) is certainly indebted to Romantic mystical flower theory.

In his development as a poet, Baudelaire had discovered not only the associative suggestiveness of flowers (in synaesthetic or metaphorical *analogie*) but also their rhetorical use in evoking a consciousness at once heightened and dreamlike, mystical and sensual. It is not remarkable that this poet of the 1840s and 1850s should have made some use of the flowers of sensual mysticism or *harmonie*: it would be surprising if he had not. Baudelaire is exceptional only in his creative appropriation of them in the formation of a poetic style which realizes the aspirations of several generations of literary flower theorists. His advantage over them was perhaps his ironic awareness that if poetry does not make flowers speak or sing in harmony, they will remain silent. For having spent much time developing his unprecedented flowers of negativity, he knew very well the limits of flower idealization.

iv. *Flowers of the Muses*

> A un blasphème, j'opposerai des élancements vers le Ciel, à une obscénité, des fleurs platoniques.
>
> (P i 195.)

Baudelaire had not, for all that, neglected the traditional flower figure standing for artistic or literary beauty or poetry itself: the ancient flowers of the muses or the Ronsardic 'poëme est une fleur'. Although he accepts this figure from the first as a commonplace, describing some of his poems as 'des fleurs' in a letter of 1841 and poetry itself as 'une fleur' several years later (as reported by· Houssaye), he seems unwilling to apply it to his own work without qualification. Thus, the poems are 'des fleurs . . . singulières' and poetry 'une fleur rarissime, qu'il faut respirer, cueillir et effeuiller soi-même dans la religion de la fière solitude'.[51] Similar restrictions apply in *La Mort des artistes* (1842–3?) to his use of an image which implies the traditional figure. Here the context evokes the extreme difficulties of artistic creation, which cause such despair to some artists that they

> N'ont plus qu'un seul espoir qui souvent les console.
> C'est que la mort, planant comme un soleil nouveau,
> Fera s'épanouir les fleurs de leur cerveau.[52]

The flowers of the Muses become an ironic image for the tragic frustration of the artist, since they are dreams in the mind never aesthetically realized in life. At the same time they are flowers of mystical pathos, blossoming only under the black sun of death. These are *fleurs du mal* at once mystical and ironical, evoking a beauty indestructible as an ideal but wellnigh unrealizable in real conditions. This figure identifies an important aspect of the rhetoric of degradation elaborated elsewhere in the early works. For the poet cannot create beauty out of degradation unless he is productive, as the poet makes clear in *Le Mauvais Moine*:

> Rien n'embellit les murs de ce cloître odieux.
>
> Ô moine fainéant! quand saurai-je donc faire
> Du spectacle vivant de ma triste misère
> Le travail de mes mains et l'amour de mes yeux?

> (P i 16.)

The dignity of the artistic enterprise envisaged here is tragically unrealized, but it is not unlike that affirmed by the flower image closing *La Mort des artistes*: in both cases the ideal of beauty is the (ironic) consolation for the degradation of unproductivity. Several years later Baudelaire returns to these themes in *Le Guignon* (1849–51), at the same time relating them to the public's indifference to the poet. The title and the quatrains evoke the frustration caused by the difficulty of creation and the poet's lack of recognition, both made more unbearable by the approach of death. In the tercets the metaphors of jewel and flower represent not only the unacknowledged achievements of the poet but also his own unrealized creative potential:

> — Maint joyau dort enseveli
> Dans les ténèbres et l'oubli,
> Bien loin des poiches et des sondes;

Mainte fleur épanche à regret
Son parfum doux comme un secret
Dans les solitudes profondes.

(P i 17.)

By their hiddenness and their relation to the poet's 'cimetière isolé'
they have the status of dead things, just as the poet is 'dead' for
the public and his creative possibilities 'dead' unless realized. Yet
jewel and flower are at the same time figures for the mystical survival
of the possibility of beauty despite the poet's unproductiveness,
public indifference, or the poet's death: indeed they display their
beauty all the more proudly because it is hidden from undiscerning
public or discouraged poet. These ambiguities are confirmed by the
juxtaposition of the two metaphors: the jewel suggesting indestruc-
tibility, the flower ephemerality. Yet the flower is itself not only
vulnerable but absolute, projecting 'son parfum doux comme un
secret' in an eternal present tense. Here again the metaphor celebrates
beauty as an ideal beyond frustration and vulnerability, by attributing
both ironical and mystical senses to 'les diamants et les fleurs de la
muse' (P ii 333).

Baudelaire treats a similar theme in *La Rançon* (1847–51?),
adopting an ironically sententious structure owing something
to a Christian-based 'socialisme mitigé'.[53] He states that man
must work to cultivate 'l'Art' and 'l'Amour' as if they were two
fields:

> Pour obtenir la moindre rose,
> Pour extorquer quelques épis,
> Des pleurs salés de son front gris
> Sans cesse il faut qu'il les arrose.

These lines point to the difficulty of producing any flowers or grain,
and hence to the major irony of the poem. The suffering inherent
in the work is necessary 'pour payer sa rançon' but will not of itself
propitiate 'le juge' on the day of reckoning:

> Il faudra lui montrer ses granges
> Pleines de moissons, et des fleurs
> Dont les formes et les couleurs
> Gagnent le suffrage des Anges.

(P i 173.)

Artistic and charitable work is required to produce abundant harvests and mystically beautiful flowers, yet the bitterest effort only produces grain and flowers pathetic in amount and quality. In this poem Baudelaire implicitly rejects his own facile anti-utilitarianism of 1846, when he had claimed to take pleasure in seeing 'un républicain' attacked because such a man is 'un ennemi des roses et des parfums, un fanatique des ustensiles' (P ii 490). Now he insists no less firmly on the importance of art, while also acknowledging the selfless work of the humanitarian. But in 'un monde où l'action n'est pas la sœur du rêve' (P i 122), neither social action nor artistic creation fulfil their aspirations. Once more the flowers of art mediate ironically between the ideal and the realizable.

In a pattern now firmly established, Baudelaire has recourse to the flower metaphor once again when he returns ('dépolitiqué' after the events of 1851) to the problem of productivity in *L'Ennemi* (published in June 1855). In this poem the garden is an allegory of the poet's creative powers, now unproductive after the ravages of his stormy youth. Although in 'l'automne des idées' he should be producing mature fruit, the poet is obliged to re-order the 'terres inondées' to make further production possible, but with no certainty that growth will result:

> Et qui sait si les fleurs nouvelles que je rêve
> Trouveront dans ce sol lavé comme une grève
> Le mystique aliment qui ferait leur vigueur?

Once more the flowers of art are subject to ironical limitation, dreams in the mind which will only blossom if nourished by a 'mystique aliment' in the garden. The poet's work must feed on some mysterious element in his creative psyche before it can grow, and this process of self-consumption is related to that of the last three lines:

> — Ô douleur! ô douleur! Le Temps mange la vie,
> Et l'obscur Ennemi qui nous ronge le cœur
> Du sang que nous perdons croît et se fortifie!

> (P i 16.)

Just as time and unproductiveness consume life, growing as they feed off the poet, so too will his work (if he can provide the strength it needs) consume his very substance as its 'mystique aliment'. But the flowers of poetry, once endangered by the poet's youth and now by the uncertainty of his future, will prove his strength even as they consume it. These flowers of art grow out of his self-sacrifice, and the poet who dreams of them shows once more that for him the enterprise of poetry combines self-degradation with high dignity.

As an allegory of the creative self this poem has considerable confessional substance, suggesting that for Baudelaire this was a period of significant reflection about his creative past and future. It was very likely written either shortly before or soon after Baudelaire chose the definitive title for his collection of poems, some time in late 1854 or early 1855.[54] The circumstances of this choice are reported by Asselineau:

Dieu sait s'il en fut longuement question! Celui qui donna le titre définitif, *Fleurs du mal*, c'est Hippolyte Babou, je m'en souviens très-bien, un soir au café Lemblin, après une longue enquête sur le sujet.[55]

This was by no means Babou's first use of a flower oxymoron of this extreme type, since seven years before he had congratulated Balzac on his evocation of the poetry of evil in a similar formula: 'vous seul pouvez cueillir, au bord du précipice, ces jolies fleurs vénéneuses poussées sur du fumier'.[56] In 1850, besides, he had described the poems in Lemer's anthology *Poètes de l'amour* (including Baudelaire's own poem *Lesbos*) as 'efflorescences maladives', when attacking the 'dépravation vulgaire' of the 'pauvres artistes manqués' who had contributed them. Babou's sensitivity in registering (whether in praise or blame) the morally subversive tendencies in contemporary writing must have been an advantage in his literary friendship with Baudelaire after 1851. It enabled him to recognize that the 'caractère frappant de nouveauté poétique' in his colleague's work was no mere vulgar depravity but a commitment to create poetic beauty out of degradation deeply experienced and pondered: 'une voix de poète, où se révèle l'âme qui lutte, qui sent et qui pense. Quand l'âme soufre [*sic*] la voix est plus belle.'[57] Thus the title Babou proposed to Baudelaire was an epigrammatic critical accolade. It was also, surely, an acknowledgement of the frequent appearance in Baudelaire's poetry of flower imagery, particularly of an oxymoronic type used by Babou himself. But Babou was not the only man in the Café Lemblin for whom the title embodied Baudelaire's poetic originality and his predilection for subversive flower imagery. Asselineau, Monselet, and all those who joined in the 'longue enquête sur le sujet' must have approved the title. And Baudelaire himself seems to have adopted it on the spot.

II. Les Fleurs du Mal

i. *The 'titre calembour'*

Jamais il ne pourra représenter les péchés sous forme de fleurs.

(CP ii 83.)

Simply as an oxymoron, *Les Fleurs du Mal* corresponds to Baudelaire's conviction that 'plus un titre est singulier, meilleur il est', or his requirement that titles should be either 'mystérieux' or 'pétards'.[58] But his is also a 'titre calembour', *mystérieux* to the extent that it has several meanings which play ambiguously against one another. Even the first element, 'les Fleurs', is only apparently disingenuous. By itself, this reference to a hallowed tradition seems a noble commonplace, not inappropriate to Baudelaire's conception of the 'Grand style (rien de plus beau que le lieu commun)'.[59] Yet even the traditional substantive is equivocal in meaning, as reference to its revived popularity in flower titles of the period reminds us.[60] '(Les) Fleurs' often of course stood simply for 'poems', usually with a qualifying epithet to indicate their character (thus in 1853 there are 'Fleurs du panier' and 'Fleurs d'automne') and sometimes forming a light oxymoron (in 1852 'Les Fleurs ignorées', and in 1853 'Fleurs de tristesse'). And the strict sense of anthology, as a selection of the most beautiful poems or literary *morceaux*, is still in use in titles of 1853 like 'La Guirlande de fleurs' or 'Les Fleurs de l'éloquence'. Variants of this are found in the titles of small devotional works frequently produced at the mid-century in provincial *bien-pensant* circles, which like the keepsake genre blended literary and popular-sentimental elements. Some of these are latter-day *florilegia*, edifying selections of writings or anecdotes of the past such as 'Les Fleurs de la morale en action' (1852) or 'Fleurs des Saints' (1855). Others are simply presented as anthologies: 'Fleurs choisies dans les litanies de la sainte Vierge' (1853) or 'Les Fleurs de mai' (1855). More noteworthy are those in which the noun 'Fleurs' implies not merely poems or *morceaux choisis* but the Christian idealization of grace and virtue: 'Fleurs du paradis' (1854) or 'Fleurs du désert, ou Hymnes à Marie' (1853). These titles evoke the religious beauty and importance of their contents and promise examples of grace and incitements to virtue and devotion. They also recall the flowers of church decoration and of traditional religious language. The devotional work *Les Fleurs* (1854) idealizes flowers and calls the Church a 'paradis terrestre', 'un vrai parterre . . . où les belles fleurs des vertus exhalent l'odeur d'un parfum divin'.[61] Thus, some titles could suggest exalted devotional meanings for '(Les) Fleurs', while others promise edifying illustrations, or a selection of the best and most beautiful of a kind. In others again, whether devotional or not, the title indicates a collection of poems which are themselves the *fleurs des Muses*.

Commonplace it may be, but the noun *Fleurs* is already ambiguous in these contemporary titles, and when Baudelaire articulates it with *le Mal* it becomes even more semantically *mystérieux*. Since it heads a collection of poems, the title certainly indicates that these are poems related to evil. This unprecedented claim implies a subversive intent (in itself *pétard*) in relation to the traditional associations between literature and *le Bien*, and suggests that the poems do not belong to 'les provinces les plus fleuries du domaine poétique',[62] where the literary flowers are those of virtue. But since the title ironically recalls as well the devotional works which might generically be called *Les Fleurs du Bien*, it can be taken to identify not merely poems of/about evil, but poems which praise the mystical beauties and graces of evil. This interpretation generates subversive irony about the flower idealization of the moral/religious domain. It suggests at least that evil can be as attractive as good (the view of the cynical dandy?) and at most that the author is a confirmed Satanist.[63] If, however, the title follows the *florilegium* pattern and has the less extreme sense of 'edifying illustrations of evil', the expression may be read as having either a satanistic intent or a more virtuous one. In the latter case the poems become *exempla* of evil chosen for the reader's instruction by the author-moralist—a reading supported by the introductory poem *Au Lecteur*, with its list of vices.[64] The title has a similar sense if the flower reference is understood in terms of the flower code: as a *symbolique des fleurs du mal* in which each flower represents a different vice or sin, or even as an ironical *langage des fleurs* in which the flowers speak not of ideals but of the various evils of the real world.[65] This interpretation is one of several explicitly sanctioned by Baudelaire himself, in his efforts between 1859 and 1866 to obtain a frontispiece which would 'représenter les péchés sous forme de fleurs' for editions of his poems.[66] In this and other ways Baudelaire sought to correct the 'malentendu fort bizarre' (in part certainly caused by his *pétard* title) which had led to the trial of 1857 and the wider dissemination of his reputation as 'le Prince des Charognes'. Yet he had been aware before publication that 'ce misérable dictionnaire de mélancolie et de crime' could 'légitimer les réactions de la morale',[67] and the title certainly implies that evil has beauties of its own. Indeed Baudelaire must have appreciated its ability both to evoke the beauties of evil ('le vice est séduisant, il faut le peindre séduisant') and to safeguard the moral aspect of literary dignity ('mais il traîne avec lui des maladies et des douleurs morales singulières') and his concept of 'l'unité intégrale' of art.[68]

Indeed, the title has other possible senses which confirm that he intended an integral reading of it. *Le Mal* is itself ambiguous for it does not denote moral-metaphysical evil or 'crime' alone. It can also signify 'mélancolie' and 'maladies et . . . douleurs' of various types, as is clear from the parallel term *fleurs maladives* in the *dédicace* to Gautier. This not only validates the moralist sense (vice leading to 'maladies et . . . douleurs morales') but suggests a most significant aesthetic point deriving from the ambiguity of 'du' in the title. If these are not flowers having the qualities of evil but rather flowers created out of *Le Mal* (in its various senses), they become emblematic trophies of an art which can transform unlikely material of whatever sort into beauty. Thus the poet is like an alchemist since he creates aesthetic (and moral?) value from repugnant and unlovely things, or like a horticulturalist producing *fleurs* by nourishing them with *fumier*.[69] This interpretation of the title claims a dignity for the poet which is primarily aesthetic but also has other implications. If Baudelaire has journeyed beyond poetry's 'privinces les plus fleuries', it is not just because these are already over-cultivated but because the cultivation of *fleurs du bien* is banal and excessively easy: 'Il m'a paru plaisant, et d'autant plus agréable que la tâche était difficile, d'extraire la *beauté* du Mal' (P i 181). The poet's efforts to avoid the banality of conventional idealization lead him to take up an aesthetic challenge all the more worthwhile because of its difficulty. But the task of extracting beauty from *le Mal* is more momentous than the distiller's or the miner's, since it involves nothing less than redefining the relationship between the aesthetic and the psychological and moral orders. Amongst the possible a priori senses of the title this is the most inclusive and ambitious. For here the poet becomes an aesthetic and moral hero creating in difficult conditions an unprecedented kind of poetic beauty related in a new way to moral and psychological reality.

ii. *Flowers and the 'esthétique du Mal':*

> Les charmes de l'horreur n'enivrent que les forts!
>
> (P i 97.)

In itself, Baudelaire's title can give rise to a number of plausible interpretations, and the poet's own explicit reference to several of these is confirmation that only a non-reductive or plural reading can adequately render the title's complexity. The title of course takes on its full sense in relation to the poems composing the volume in its several editions. But any determination of its significance for Baudelaire's poetics must take some account not only of his poetic practice (and especially the use of flower imagery) but also of his poetic theory, in the whole body of his work both before and after 1855.

As an oxymoron linking flowers with negativity, the title undoubtedly calls attention to the various rhetorical uses of anti-idealization in the poetry written before 1855. There too, flowers (traditionally associated with idealization, beauty, and poetry) had been associated in various ways with negativity. These flowers now become the emblems of an aesthetic programme apparently extended to the whole volume, an aesthetic in which negativity or *le Mal* will have a central place.

In *Au Lecteur*, the poem placed first in order from the first appearance of the title in 1855, Baudelaire highlights the importance of *le Mal* by presenting an extreme neo-Jansenist view of a humanity given entirely to sin, either actively committing crimes or passively projecting them. By inviting the reader to recognize this world as his own the poet disarms moralizing reactions through his insistence that any idealizing morality (any *fleurs du bien*) would be irrelevant to such a world. Yet this vision of a humanity controlled by sin, however often it recurs throughout Baudelaire's work, is equally often accompanied by a sense of human suffering. Thus in 1855 the poem following *Au Lecteur* was *Réversibilité*, drawing attention to 'la honte, les remords, les sanglots, les ennuis, / Et les vagues terreurs . . . P i 14), and in 1857 *Bénédiction*, with its insistence on the centrality of 'la souffrance' and 'la douleur' (at least for the poet). Indeed, in 'ce misérable dictionnaire de mélancolie et de crime' (P i 187) sin and suffering shade into one another as the two subtly related forms of *le Mal*, the *malum acti* and *malum poeni* of medieval theology. The central concept of *l'ennui*, for example, is both the worst of vices (*Au Lecteur*) and the worst of sufferings (the *Spleen* poems).[70] The poem *Le Voyage* gathers up both aspects of *le Mal* into its overall vision of a world characterized by sin ('Le spectacle ennuyeux de l'immortel péché' — P i 132) and suffering ('une oasis d'horreur dans un désert d'ennui' — P i 133). By placing this poem at the end of the 1861 volume, Baudelaire recalls *Au Lecteur* and provides an even more programmatic justification for the anti-idealizing nature of his poetics: any flower-like idealization (whether moral, psychological, or aesthetic) must be seen against the dark background of *le Mal* as generalized sin and suffering. If, as Baudelaire insists in 1855, 'Le beau est toujours bizarre', strange indeed must be the beauties of a poetry growing out of the vision of a world dominated by *le Mal*, beauties very different from a 'beau banal'.[71]

This *esthétique du Mal* can be seen creatively at work in the numerous poems about women from all periods of the poet's career. From the beginning (as in the poem about Sara) he often presented women—in negative terms which inverted the traditional and Romantic idealization of them—as associated in some way with sin and suffering. This characterization is at its most extreme with the prostitutes and lesbians of the early poems, and with the woman who torments the poet/lover, the 'Femme impure', 'reine des péchés', 'reine des cruelles', or 'démon sans pitié' of the first cycle of love poems.[72] Yet the most strident illustrations of this tendency to link women with *le Mal* are most often accompanied by an equally marked insistence on the woman's beauty or attractiveness. This dichotomy is given full extension as a paradox in an early poem:

> Et je chéris, ô bête implacable et cruelle!
> Jusqu'à cette froideur par où tu m'es plus belle!
>
> (P i 27.)

In this characterization woman is a 'Bizarre déité' indeed, an oxymoron of beauty and cruelty (a *fleur du Mal*) accentuating at the same time aesthetic idealization and moral/psychological negativity.

In strong contrast, the woman of the second love cycle[73] appears to be presented as idealized not only in aesthetic terms but also in moral and psychological ones. She is 'l'Ange gardien, la Muse et la Madone', characterized not only by *beauté* but also by 'gaieté', 'bonté', 'santé', and 'bonheur'.[74] Yet even this paragon of idealization only has meaning in the context of sin and suffering, for a poet who is a 'pauvre âme solitaire' liable (without her) to fall into any 'piège' or 'péché grave'.[75] It is because of this difference between them that she can make available for the poet the possibility of idealization, appropriately expressed in a flower image:

> Que diras-tu, mon cœur, cœur autrefois flétri,
> A la très belle, à la très bonne, à la très chère,
> Dont le regard t'a soudain refleuri?

> (P i 43.)

Yet this contrast between ideal woman and experienced reality can give rise to a much more negative reaction. Thus in *A celle qui est trop gaie* (P i 57) he sees her happiness as a reproach ('comme une ironie') to his own 'atonie', and remembers humiliation turning into revenge 'sur une fleur'. His fantasized revenge against the woman results from the realization that such a flower-like ideal can only ironically co-exist with his consciousness of *le Mal*.

Moreover several of the poems in this cycle insist that this ideal figure must not be over-idealized. The poem *Réversibilité* (P i 44–5) poses a series of questions (reproaches?) about her distance from the world of sin and suffering. And in his 1861 edition Baudelaire began the second cycle with a poem which overtly denounces the woman as a *mensonge* to the extent that she appears to deny the truth that 'vivre est un mal'.[76] Here the poet claims the right to 's'enivrer d'un *mensonge*': the woman's ideal qualities are beautiful flower-like illusions, cherished because they provide a means of escaping from the experienced reality of *le Mal*.[77]

The woman of the third cycle of love poems is a mysterious and changeable combination of affirmative and negative qualities, 'Alternativement tendre, rêveur, cruel'.[78] Sometimes she recalls the woman of the first cycle, in that the poet finds in her the same possibilities of oxymoron:

> Ô femme dangereuse, ô séduisants climats!
> Adorerai-je aussi ta neige et vos frimas,
> Et saurai-je tirer de l'implacable hiver
> Des plaisirs plus aigus que la glace et le fer?

> (P i 50.)

Elsewhere she is asked to provide consolation for the poet:

Vous êtes un beau ciel d'automne, clair et rose!

(*Causeries*, P i 56.)

Amante ou sœur, soyez la douceur éphémère
D'un glorieux automne ou d'un soleil couchant.

(*Chant d'automne*, P i 57.)

But in none of these poems is she a figure capable of giving the poet any real hope. Whether this woman is seen as a wintry climate in which the poet can find pleasure (or beauty), or as an autumnal consolation which cannot in fact console him, her beauty in either case is dialectically related to negativity. Here, as in the first two love cycles, the poet uses female beauty to investigate how attempts at idealization (especially aesthetic ones) can be related to *le Mal* which dominates his experience. Together, the three cycles show that beauty and *le Mal* are each too various for their relationship to be a simple one.

In a series of poems on women written between 1858 and 1861, Baudelaire's investigations of his *esthétique du Mal* remained as central as before the adoption of the title *Les Fleurs du Mal* and the publication of the first edition, but were now associated even more explicitly with flower imagery. These poems make clear he was still unwilling to reduce this aesthetic to a single principle, and indeed wished to insist that the concept of the *fleurs du Mal* must contain contradictions. In *Sonnet d'automne* (1859) the Faustian poet refuses to tell 'Marguerite' his 'secret infernal' or his 'noire légende', and then makes an ambiguous plea:

Aimons-nous doucement. L'Amour dans sa guérite,
Ténébreux, embusqué, bande son arc fatal.
Je connais les engins de son vieil arsenal:

Crime, horreur et folie! — Ô pâle marguerite!
Comme moi n'es-tu pas un soleil automnal,
Ô ma si blanche, ô ma si froide Marguerite?

(P i 65.)

The poet pleads for a consoling autumnal love with this 'pâle marguerite' despite his knowledge of love's devastating effects. She is a flower (a pearl!) by her beauty and because she represents the hope of consolation; yet the epithet 'pâle' indicates that she cannot console strongly—perhaps because, being no longer young, she also knows love's sufferings. The juxtaposed exclamations opening the second tercet only emphasize the irony of seeking consolation in this flower, yet autumnal love and beauty are at once fatal and desirable. These contradictions are no doubt the poet's own 'secret infernal': the attraction of woman's beauty is irresistible but dangerous. Yet Baudelaire is interested less in statements about men and women than in the relationship between beauty and *le Mal*. Two poems from the same year (and the same manuscript) reinforce this point by their parallel structure. In *A une Madone* P i 58-9) the altar and the statue the poet imagines constructing for his 'Madone' will be built 'au fond de ma détresse', from elements of his own suffering love. This is an allegory of the poet's habitual attempts at idealization, and the last section represents an equally typical attack on it. Having built the statue to the woman the poet will plant in her heart the knives of the seven deadly sins: no such 'autel fleuri' to beauty (l. 30), even if built devotedly out of suffering, can be immune to human destructiveness. In *Le Masque* (P i 23-4) the female 'statue allégorique' is also presented first as an idealization of beauty 'promettant le bonheur', but then seen only as a mask for 'la véritable tête, la sincère face' of 'la Douleur'. She is a 'beauté parfaite' suffering the 'mal mystérieux' of life itself, ' — comme nous!' Together these two allegories show that beauty (like an idealized woman) is an ideal that cannot be isolated from the realities of sin and suffering, a *fleur du Mal*.

Yet Baudelaire had never considered this tragic paradox sufficient by itself to account for the relations between beauty and *le Mal*, as he reminds us in *L'Amour du mensonge* (1860). Here the poet presents a beautiful woman whose 'front pâle' is 'embelli par un morbide attrait'. He seeks to find the meaning of her curious beauty in a series of questions:

> Es-tu le fruit d'automne aux saveurs souveraines?
> Es-tu vase funèbre attendant quelques pleurs,
> Parfum qui fait rêver aux oasis lointaines,
> Oreiller caressant, ou corbeille de fleurs?

> (P i 99.)

Although her beauty primarily suggests consolation, it is morbid too—not just 'fruit d'automne' and 'corbeille de fleurs' but 'vase funèbre' as well. But, although at first hoping that the woman does have some moral or psychological secret (whether consoling or morbid), he ends by celebrating her beauty as sufficient in itself:

> Mais ne suffit-il pas que tu sois l'apparence,
> Pour réjouir un cœur qui fuit la vérité?
> Qu'importe ta bêtise ou ton indifférence?
> Masque ou décor, salut! J'adore ta beauté.

> (P i 99.)

It is as if the *mensonge* of her beauty is more important than the truth of *le Mal*. And the poet is consistent with himself when he suggests that such an aesthetic absolute must be an ambiguous beauty, a flower-like consolation but one 'attendant quelques pleurs'. In the poem *Madrigal triste* (1861) he again insists that beauty is only intensified by sadness:

> Sois belle! et sois triste! Les pleurs
> Ajoutent un charme au visage,
> Comme le fleuve au paysage:
> L'orage rajeunit les fleurs.

> (P i 137-8.)

This woman is most beautiful in suffering; it is her awareness of 'l'horreur', 'l'angoisse' and 'les sanglots' which, by answering to the poet's own more extreme knowledge of 'l'Enfer' and 'l'irrésistible Dégoût', makes her beauty more attractive. In the same way, flowers are most beautiful in (or after) a storm, and the comparison implies that this is a general aesthetic point. The poet who had adopted his flower title six years before writing this poem is here emphasizing an essential (and constant) element of his poetics. The point is not merely that (as in *A une Madone* or *Le Masque*) aesthetic idealization cannot honestly be dissociated from *le Mal*, but that beauty indeed gains aesthetic power from being associated with it.[79]

For some *fleurs du Mal* are not merely beautiful despite (or in contrast to) *le Mal*, but all the more beautiful because of it. The latter point had been from the first an important element in his self-discovery as a poet in practice and in theory. He had given in the 1846 *Maximes* a justification of 'le goût de l'horrible' and in 1856 had defended Poe's 'amour de l'horrible pour l'horrible'.[80] The trial of 1857 had forcefully raised the question of his own reputation as a poet of 'l'horrible', and he seems to have been uneasy about this.[81]

Yet in 1859 he published a poem which strongly emphasized this aspect of his poetics. This was *Danse macabre*, which presents 'un grand squelette féminin tout prêt à partir pour une fête' (a concept suggested by Christophe's figurine) in a description evoking at once beauty and horror.[82] The skeletal woman's sense of her own beauty as a 'coquette maigre aux airs extravagants' is reinforced by reference to flowers: she is carrying a 'gros bouquet', wearing 'un soulier pomponné, joli comme une fleur', and her skull is 'de fleurs artistement coiffé'. At the same time her import as an image of death is equally clear, and the poet relies considerably on the evocation of horror appropriate to the medieval *danse macabre* of the title: the 'danseurs' at the 'fête' are blind to the approach of death. Yet Baudelaire is not concerned to moralize but to 'expliquer le plaisir subtil contenu dans cette figurine' (P ii 679), establishing an ambiguous relationship between beauty and *le Mal*. Thus he juxtaposes coquetry ('sottise'), lubricity ('fautes'), and the reality of death, so that the figurine has the 'charme d'un néant follement attifé'. These ironies are already inherent in 'L'élégance sans nom de l'humaine armature', and it is finally this beauty that is celebrated—a beauty (at once plastic and evocative of horror) which corresponds to the poet's 'goût le plus cher'. At the centre of this complex poem is an aesthetic motto (presented as such in the *Salon* commentary): 'Les charmes de l'horreur n'enivrent que les forts!' (P i 97; P ii 679). Others are unable to see beauty here because they seek a more banal erotic beauty, or because their nausea blinds them to it. For Baudelaire this beauty, like the flowers which decorate it, can only gain in 'charmes' from its horror. The charms of this beauty are, like the 'fleurs magnifiques engraissées par la destruction' of the late prose poem *Le Tir et le cimetière*,[83] a species of *fleurs du Mal* in which aesthetic idealization triumphantly uses *le Mal* for its own enrichment.

This is no doubt the most extreme version of the poet's *esthétique du Mal*.[84] It is all the more striking in this poem because of the ambiguity of the concept of *l'horreur*. This latter includes the connotations of the skeleton itself (the 'antique douleur' of death) along with the traditional sense of the foolish blindness of a 'risible Humanité'. But *l'horreur* has an additional meaning supplied by the references to lubricity ('L'enfer allumé dans ton cœur') and thus takes on all the Baudelairian senses of *le Mal*—sin, foolishness, suffering, and death. The beauty which is strengthened by association with *le Mal* in all these senses must be a powerful force indeed. Nor was Baudelaire in any doubt about the wider significance of this point for his aesthetics. He makes use of it, for example, in defence of Poe's 'amour de l'horrible', when he shows that the latter's characters (typically suffering in horror or sickness) are all the more fully realized for being presented 'sur des fonds violâtres et verdâtres où se révèlent la phosphorescence de la pourriture et la senteur de l'orage'.[85] He is more explicit in his defense of Guy's paintings illustrating prostitutes, where he sees nothing to incite prurience but 'rien que l'art pur, c'est-à-dire la beauté particulière du mal, le beau dans l'horrible'.[86] Whether in poetry, fiction, or painting, art can present 'les charmes de l'horreur', 'la phosphorescence de la pourriture', or 'le beau dans l'horrible'.[87]

Indeed this extreme paradox of aesthetics is the *cas limite* which guarantees the possibility of an 'art pur':

> Tu marches sur des morts, Beauté, dont tu te moques;
> De tes bijoux l'Horreur n'est pas le moins charmant.

> (*Hymne à la Beauté*, 1860, P i 25.)

It is because beauty retains its qualities (or even finds them enhanced) when associated with death or 'l'Horreur' that it can be seen to be independent of moral and psychological valuation:

> Viens-tu du ciel profond ou sors-tu de l'abîme,
> Ô Beauté? ton regard, infernal ou divin,
> Verse confusément le bienfait et le crime . . .

> Que tu viennes du ciel ou de l'enfer, qu'importe,
> Ô Beauté!

Baudelaire no doubt placed this poem immediately before the three love cycles in the 1861 edition in order to emphasize the structural similarity between his treatment of this Beauty (personified as female) and the beauty of woman, in her infernal and divine aspects. For the same concept is implicit in the love cycles. There too, as in *Hymne à la Beauté*, beauty can never be isolated from *le Mal* which dominates all human activity, but must at the same time be welcomed as the only value as strong as *le Mal* itself, powerful enough to make 'l'univers moins hideux et les instants moins lourds'. It would seem, indeed, that *la Beauté* and *le Mal* are the two necessary poles of Baudelairian aesthetics: both are in some sense absolute and neither

can ever exclude the other. Beauty can be found anywhere (even in
le Mal), yet *le Mal* can never be evaded. It is in terms of this paradox
(in itself an important sense of the title) that Baudelaire defines his
own theory of aesthetic autonomy.[88] Because it has to acknowledge
le Mal, art cannot be divorced from 'les conditions de la vie',
and thus cannot commit the errors of 'l'école de *l'art pour l'art*'
which 'en excluant la morale, et souvent même la passion, était
nécessairement stérile'.[89] But since beauty is by no means always
associated with *le Bien*, art must at the same time reject 'la grande
hérésie poétique des temps modernes . . . l'idée d'utilité directe'.[90]
Those who refuse to acknowledge *le Mal* are 'marmoréens et anti-
humains':[91] Baudelaire will give us not cold marble but *fleurs du
Mal* growing out of human life itself. Those who want art to serve
le Bien rather than beauty are trying to attach 'de lourds légumes
à des arbustes de delectation'.[92] Baudelaire will more appropriately
give us flowers, for any didacticism in poetry 'repousse les diamants
et les fleurs de la muse'.[93] Poetry cannot ignore 'les conditions de
la vie', but 'elle n'a pas la vérité pour objet, elle n'a qu'Elle-même'.
The aesthetics of the *fleurs du Mal* is a fully realistic one as well
as an aesthetics of 'l'art pur'.

But it is undeniably an *esthétique du Mal*, as his notebook
'définition du Beau, de mon Beau' reminds us:

C'est quelque chose d'ardent et de triste . . .   — Je ne prétends pas que
la Joie ne puisse pas s'associer avec la Beauté, mais je dis que . . . la
Mélancolie en est pour ainsi dire l'illustre compagne, à ce point que je ne
conçois guère (mon cerveau serait-il un miroir ensorcelé?) un type de Beauté
où il n'y ait du *Malheur*.[94]

In any beauty dominated by joy there could be little place for that
consciousness of *le Mal* which is indispensable in his aesthetics. The
rest of the passage suggests that this consciousness must play a very
important part indeed, since human beauty is always characterized by

une ardeur, un désir de vivre, associé avec une amertume refluante, comme
venant de privation ou de désespérance . . . des besoins spirituels, des
ambitions ténébreusement refoulées, — l'idée d'une puissance grondante,
et sans emploi . . .

Thus he concludes that 'le plus parfait type de Beauté virile est *Satan,*
—à la manière de Milton', since this figure too is pre-eminently
conscious of bitter deprivation and frustration. It is with this
understanding that the *Épigraphe* composed for a later edition places

the volume under the patronage of Satan, whose example it reflects. No 'Lecteur paisible et bucolique, / Sobre et naïf homme de bien' can understand 'ce livre saturnien, / Orgiaque et mélancolique' (P i 137). Its *fleurs du Mal* are utterly unlike the innocent flowers of pastoral, and the non-bucolic consciousness which can appreciate them will know 'les gouffres', as an 'Âme curieuse qui [souffre] / Et [va] cherchant [son] paradis'. For this 'satanic' tormented consciousness, suffering is only increased by the frustrated awareness of an unattainable paradise. It is thus a self-consciousness structured by its own (satanic) 'rhétorique' of frustration, depending on an alternation between 'gouffres' and 'paradis', *Spleen* and *Idéal*, and never achieving fulfilment:

> Emporte-moi, wagon! enlève-moi, frégate!
> Loin! loin! ici la boue est faite de nos pleurs! . . .
>
> Comme vous êtes loin, paradis parfumé!
>
>   (*Moesta et errabunda*, P i 63.)

This is a rhetoric of irony, for each flowery paradise turns into the mud of suffering so that even the thought of such impossible idealizations is further torment, 'comme une ironie' (P i 157). Satan is 'le rusé doyen' of this rhetoric because better than any he knows 'l'ironie, cette vengeance du vaincu' (P ii 168). The poet, like Satan, is

> Un de ces grands abandonnés
> Au rire éternel condamnés
> Et qui ne peuvent plus sourire!
>
>   (*L'Héautontimorouménos*, P i 79.)

In his endless frustration the poet ('Grace à la vorace ironie') is his own torturer, reduced to tormenting self-contemplation:

> Tête-à-tête sombre et limpide
> Qu'un cœur devenu son miroir!
>
>   (*L'Irrémédiable*, P i 80.)

This is the psychological prison of the *Spleen* poems—a frustrated self-awareness made up of boredom, melancholy, dead memory, nihilism, and despair, with only an occasional illusory hope of escape ('l'Espoir, / Vaincu, pleure'—P i 75). This state of suffering is figured, then, as hell, military defeat, madhouse, torture-chamber, 'miroir ensorcelé', prison, and, in several poems, as a flowerless Sahara of the mind. But the poet's own self-awareness is, after all, the subjective reflection of a world objectively dominated by Satan and *le Mal*, as other poems remind us. Thus *Duellum* insists that interpersonal relations are also marked by frustration and reciprocal torment, for here two lovers destroy each other in a dry savage landscape like hell itself, its only flowers bitterly ironic emblems of mutual destruction: 'Et leur peau fleurira l'aridité des ronces' (P i 36). In these extreme conditions it is the ironic consciousness (in the objective world as well as the subjective) which makes the poetic enterprise possible:

> Puits de Vérité, clair et noir,
> Où tremble une étoile livide,
>
> Un phare ironique, infernal,
> Flambeau des grâces sataniques
> Soulagement et gloire uniques,
> — La conscience dans le Mal!
>
> (*L'Irrémédiable*, P i 80.)

Whether the 'Verité' to be confronted is that of the self or of the world, the poet must find in *l'horrible* the graces of satanic irony— *fleurs du Mal* in a domain not graced by any other kind.

It is by a similar ironic procedure that modern life becomes a fit subject for poetry. For Baudelaire sees modern life as dominated in a special way by the satanic consciousness: 'il semble que cette part infernale de l'homme, que l'homme prend plaisir à s'expliquer à lui-même, augmente journellement, comme si le Diable s'amusait à la grossir.'[95] Confronted by modern life a poet can like Banville (according to Baudelaire in 1861) refuse 'de se pencher sur ces marécages de sang, sur ces abîmes de boue', thereby deliberately creating a poetry neither satanic nor ironic but reflecting 'un retour très volontaire vers l'état paradisiaque'. For the poet who, like Baudelaire himself, intends to 'descendre des régions éthéréennes' into modern reality, a different procedure is required: 'De la laideur et de la sottise il fera naître un nouveau genre d'enchantements' (P ii 166–7). In some verses probably intended to serve as epilogue for the 1861 edition, Baudelaire claims to have followed the same procedure in his confrontation as a poet with contemporary Paris: 'Tu m'as donné ta boue et j'en ai fait de l'or' (P i 192). By this strong affirmation of his alchemical powers the poet differs triumphantly from the narrator of *Le Mauvais Vitrier* (1862) who is unable to obtain coloured glass ('des vitres magiques, des vitres de paradis') which would recreate modern life as 'la vie en beau' (P i 285). The emblem of the latter's frustrated perversity (his 'humeur' is 'hystérique' or 'satanique') is the 'pot de fleurs' which smashes the merchant's unmagical glass. The flowers of Baudelaire's title, on the other hand, are his own emblems for a poetry of gold and enchantment successfully created out of the 'boue' and 'laideur' of modern life. This is one model of the creative act for the poet who treats modern reality, but another is found in the more definitive (but still unfinished) *Épilogue* for the 1861 volume:

> Le cœur content, je suis monté sur la montagne
> D'où l'on peut contempler la ville en son ampleur,
> Hôpital, lupanar, purgatoire, enfer, bagne,
>
> Où toute énormité fleurit comme une fleur.

> (P i 191.)

Every enormity which flourishes in the modern city is here seen as beautiful in itself, blossoming out of suffering and corruption with the autonomous beauty of the horrible. Here poetic creativity is seen as a process of celebration ('Je voulais m'enivrer de l'énorme catin, / Dont le charme infernal me rajeunit sans cesse') rather than one of transformation ('tu m'as donné ta boue et j'en ai fait de l'or'). Yet both processes presuppose an ironic consciousness — a satanic one able to confront the horrors of modernity without flinching, but one capable as well of either finding or creating 'grâces sataniques' in the midst of the horror. The Satan who is 'le rusé doyen' of rhetoric presides over Baudelaire's ironic poetry of modern life, and over both its major strategies. Whether the *fleurs du Mal* are poetic transformations of *le Mal* or poetic celebrations of it, they are beauties belonging appropriately to 'l'art moderne' with its 'tendance essentiellement démoniaque' (P i 168).

For Baudelaire, then, the ironic consciousness shapes the poet's relationship to modernity, but also the whole of his personal experience (notably in matters of love) in the world of *le Mal*. Time and again he expresses these ironic perceptions in the image of *fleurs du Mal* or in formulations which imply it (particularly flower imagery in various negative contexts): indeed it is plain that commitment to his oxymoronic title helped him at many points to articulate his ironic vision. In a similar way, his treatment of the image of the 'fleurs de la muse' (P ii 333) had always been controlled by irony, to emphasize the difficulty and frustration experienced in producing poetry. In the series of poems on this subject written before 1855 he had indeed suggested in various ways that the flowers of beauty only gain in mystic beauty from the poet's suffering and degradation. The poet appears to be rejecting the optimistic side of this paradox in a poem of 1859, *Le Squelette laboureur*, in which he takes up again the pessimism of *La Rançon* (written ten or so years earlier) only to intensify it. Where the earlier poem presented creative work as a field resistant to the artist's efforts to 'obtenir la moindre rose', the poem of 1859 shows (in a *transposition d'art*) skeletons at work in a bare field:

> Et que, sempiternellement,
> Hélas! il nous faudra peut-être
>
> Dans quelque pays inconnu
> Écorcher la terre revêche
> Et pousser une lourde bêche
> Sous notre pied sanglant et nu?

> (P i 94.)

This vision of endless labour for some unflowerlike profitless 'moisson étrange' (l. 17) expresses poignantly Baudelaire's sense of his own difficulties as an artist cultivating ungrateful ground. This was very likely reinforced not only by his own experience of being misunderstood and undervalued as an artist, but also by his (wholehearted?) conviction of working in a period less propitious for poetry than the preceding Romantic one. Thus in *Le Coucher du soleil romantique* (1862) the high days of Romanticism are presented as an idyllic sunlit landscape ('fleur, source, sillon'), whilst the literary present is a deadly dark *marécage* typified by 'Des crapauds imprévus et de froids limaçons' rather than flowers.[96] Yet during this period and amidst his own frustrations, Baudelaire produced poetic *fleurs* despite (and no doubt because of) these limitations.

This is certainly an important sense of the title *Les Fleurs du Mal*, and the poet no doubt had it in mind when describing in similar metaphors the artistic life-work of several of his contemporaries.

When considering Poe's works against the background of 'l'orage permanent de sa vie', he states that 'ces éblouissantes végétations étaient le produit d'une terre volcanisée'.[97] He describes Delacroix's character in terms which suggest a similar relation of art to life: 'On eût dit un cratère de volcan artistement coiffé par des bouquets de fleurs.'[98] And he presents the actor Rouvière in a similar way:

Voilà une vie agitée et tordue, comme ces arbres, — le grenadier, par exemple, — noueux, perplexes dans leur croissance, qui donnent des fruits compliqués et savoureux, et dont les orgueilleuses et rouges floraisons ont l'air de raconter l'histoire d'une sève longtemps comprimée.[99]

For Baudelaire, it was no doubt the most triumphant irony of all that his own amazing flowers had grown out of a life devastated by suffering, shaped and twisted by frustration.

By calling his volume *Les Fleurs du Mal*, Baudelaire had claimed a central place in his poetics for this irony of poetic production: the title was to stand as an emblem of his poetic achievement. But by adopting his title he had at the same time admitted and confirmed the significance in his pre-1855 poetry of a flower imagery constantly used to subvert idealization. He had also drawn attention to the subject-matter of many of the poems composing the volume, now explicitly claimed as literary 'flowers' concerned with *le Mal*. He had thus adopted as a programme that significant aspect of his poetics dependent on an *esthétique du Mal*. This was a poetics aptly summarized by the oxymoron of the title (beauty/ *le Mal*) since it was shaped by the relations between the aesthetic absolute of beauty and the moral and psychological absolute of *le Mal*. It was everywhere informed by the ironic consciousness resulting from the disjunction of conventional associations between beauty, goodness, and happiness, a consciousness aptly reflecting the modern poet's experience of life. By committing himself to this title Baudelaire defined himself as a poet suffering, celebrating, and transforming his experience to produce triumphant flowers of modern beauty. And his commitment to the title undeniably helped him to articulate this poetics more fully in the years after 1855.

iii. *The 'langage des fleurs' and the 'correspondances'*

C'est là, n'est-ce pas, dans ce beau pays si calme et si rêveur, qu'il faudrait aller vivre et fleurir?

(P i 303.)

Although Baudelaire's title calls attention to the highly significant ironical concerns of his work, it does not appear to be related explicitly in the same way to the other major aspect of his poetics.[100] Yet after choosing his title in 1855 the poet continued to explore the *harmonies* of synaesthesia and sensual mysticism central to earlier poems like *Harmonie du soir* and *L'Invitation au voyage*. These poems appear to have very little to do with ironic modernity and evoke instead a privileged consciousness on the margin of everyday life. It would seem indeed that Baudelaire associated synaesthetic perception especially with such marginal moments of intense perception, and several references between 1851 and 1855 confirm this. Thus when describing the second phase of the experience of *haschisch* in 1851 he notes:

Les objets extérieurs . . . se révèlent à vous sous des formes inconnues jusque-là . . . Les équivoques les plus singulières, les transpositions d'idées les plus inexplicables ont lieu. Les sons ont une couleur, les couleurs ont une musique . . . Les proportions du temps et de l'être sont dérangées par la multitude innombrable et par l'intensité des sensations et des idées. On vit plusieurs vies d'homme en l'espace d'une heure.[101]

Here synaesthesia is one aspect of an extreme dislocation of the normal conditions of perception. In *Tout entière*, probably dating from 1852–4, the poet celebrates a synaesthetic experience inspired by the perfect *harmonie* of the woman's physical presence:

> 'Ô métamorphose mystique
> De tous mes sens fondus en un!
> Son haleine fait la musique,
> Comme sa voix fait le parfum!'
>
> (P i 42.)

The intensity of this mystical union of the senses makes it quite unlike ordinary experience. So too with Baudelaire's evocation in 1855 of the 'harmonies nouvelles' experienced in discovering a new country:

ces odeurs . . . ces fleurs mystérieuses dont la couleur profonde entre dans l'œil despotiquement, pendant que leur forme taquine le regard, ces fruits dont le goût trompe et déplace les sens, et révèle au palais des idées qui appartiennent à l'odorat . . . toute cette vitalité inconnue . . . quelques milliers d'idées et de sensations . . . [102]

In this passage, as in those quoted above, Baudelaire evokes the

transpositions from one sense to another in order to characterize a marginal and privileged consciousness of great intensity.

In other texts of the same period, however, he speaks of this heightened form of consciousness in another way. When claiming in 1852 that adolescents are capable of a special perception forgotten by adults he writes: 'C'est alors que les objets enfoncent profondément leurs empreintes dans l'esprit tendre et facile; c'est alors que les couleurs sont voyantes, et que les sons parlent une langue mystérieuse.'[103] In this intensified awareness of objects, colours, and sounds, there is no explicit transposition of the senses, but instead an insistence that here sense impressions take on mysterious meaning. The same process is more extensively described in a paragraph on Delacroix in the 1855 *Exposition* article:

Edgar Poe dit . . . que le résultat de l'opium pour les sens est de revêtir la nature entière d'un intérêt surnaturel qui donne à chaque objet un sens plus profond, plus volontaire, plus despotique. Sans avoir recours à l'opium, qui n'a connu ces admirables heures, véritables fêtes du cerveau, où les sens plus attentifs perçoivent des sensations plus retentissantes, où le ciel d'un azur plus transparent s'enfonce comme un abîme plus infini, où les sons tintent musicalement, où les couleurs parlent, où les parfums racontent des mondes d'idées? Eh bien, la peinture de Delacroix me paraît la traduction de ces beaux jours de l'esprit. Elle est revêtue d'intensité et sa splendeur est privilégiée. Comme la nature perçue par des nerfs ultra-sensibles, elle révèle le surnaturalisme.[104]

The experience described here owes its intensity to the discovery (through the senses) of special significance in the things of the material world. This text recalls the passages evoking synaesthesia in that in both cases the senses are principal agents of the intensity of the moments described: nature provides sense impressions which either reveal their likeness to each other or to meanings and feelings in the observer. The material world is no longer perceived as static and inanimate, for aspects of it are discovered to relate to each other or to human understanding or feeling in unexpected ways. As Baudelaire puts it in a passage of 1856, 'La nature dite inanimée participe de la nature des êtres vivants, et, comme eux, frissonne d'un frisson surnaturel et galvanique.'[105] Here, as in the previous passage, the writer gives a new and particular sense to the term *surnaturel* as he names a mode of perception which provides for the initiate a special mode of participation in the life of nature.[106]

The Baudelaire of the mid-forties had habitually presented syn-aesthetic association in the context of the evocation of meaning and feeling, and seen *analogie* as the principle of both. A decade later his growing interest in the experience of the *surnaturel* seems to have encouraged him to provide a wider context for the two types of sense *analogie*. It is in the *Exposition* article of 1855 that he mentions for the first time the concepts of *analogie universelle* and *correspondances*, and it was probably in this period too that he composed the first quatrain of the sonnet *Correspondances*:[107]

> La Nature est un temple où de vivants piliers
> Laissent parfois sortir de confuses paroles;
> L'homme y passe à travers des forêts de symboles
> Qui l'observent avec des regards familiers.

(P i 11.)

These lines present a model familiar to us from Baudelaire's evocations of *surnaturalisme*, and may legitimately be interpreted in these terms.[108] For here too 'la nature dite inanimée' reveals itself at certain moments ('parfois') in a special relation to the observer: privileged to participate in nature by means of the senses, he perceives sounds as 'paroles', sights as 'symboles'. Aspects of the material world are perceived as having intellectual or emotional significance, thus revealing *correspondances* between the things of nature and human affectivity and establishing the possibility of an *analogie universelle* between every aspect of nature and an equivalent human thought or feeling. The second quatrain, however, introduces the other type of *analogie*:

> Comme de longs échos qui de loin se confondent
> Dans une ténébreuse et profonde unité,
> Vaste comme la nuit et comme la clarté,
> Les parfums, les couleurs et les sons se répondent.

When nature co-operates with the observer in the experience of *surnaturalisme* it also reveals the reciprocal relations between various aspects of the material world. The implication that these *correspondances* are independent of the observer only enhances the sense of mystery here, and the context remains that of 'L'homme' who can, 'parfois', enter into this mystery. The tercets confirm this by illustrating (in terms of *parfums*) the two processes of *analogie* which characterize *surnaturalisme* for the observer: the smells are discovered to have *correspondances* both in other sense impressions and in thoughts or feelings. The two types of *correspondances*—synaesthetic and symbolic—are complementary aspects of 'l'immense analogie universelle' in which the experience of the *surnaturel* allows the observer to participate.[109]

In the 1857 and subsequent editions, the sonnet *Correspondances* is placed immediately after these lines:

> [Heureux celui . . .]
> — Qui plane sur la vie, et comprend sans effort
> Le langage des fleurs et des choses muettes!
>
> (P i 10.)

In the poem *Élévation* these lines sum up the poet's aspiration towards a privileged awareness like that associated with *surnaturalisme*, thus suggesting that the poem following them will be concerned with the same awareness. Even more significantly, these lines strongly indicate that the following poem will explain the nature of 'le langage des fleurs et des choses muettes'. The flower language had, of course, been associated for over fifty years with the idea of intense participation in the life of nature, often in contexts which strongly recall the Baudelairian *surnaturel*. At the same time it had also been closely related, in dozens of literary and paraliterary forms, with the concept of *analogie*, and hence characterized as both synaesthetic and symbolic. It was thus a highly apt model for Baudelaire's interest in privileged participation in nature through *analogie*, and may even have had a determinative influence on his expression of this.[110] By 1857, in any case, he could acknowledge by the juxtaposition of these two poems that his approach to the *correspondances* was similar to that implied by the concept of the flower language. For if *le langage des fleurs* was a well-known emblem for the synaesthetic and symbolic codes of nature, it could stand as a model for all the *correspondances* in nature—*le langage des choses muettes*.

The poem *L'Invitation au voyage* was probably written in late 1854 or early 1855, at a time in the poet's career when his interest in *le surnaturel* was undeniable.[111] Appropriately, the poem's evocation of a mysterious sensual awareness of material things is made possible by the synaesthetic *langage des fleurs*, a model for the soul's 'douce langue natale'. In the prose poem of the same title probably written within the next year, the poet again evokes the experience of the *surnaturel*, filled by 'la multiplication des sensations' and marked by 'une plus profonde et plus significative solennité'.[112] Visual impressions are experienced as 'une symphonie muette et mystérieuse' and 'un parfum singulier' seems 'comme l'âme de l'appartement'—illustrations of a heightened awareness of material things. But the most significant manifestation of the *surnaturel*, in this poem which gives complex expression to it, is a flower image. In this dream of travelling with a woman to a country 'où tout vous ressemble' the 'pays singulier' is Holland, known for its 'savantes et délicates végétations'. It is a country where the 'alchimistes de l'horticulture' have sought to improve on nature by creating new types of flowers. By transforming material flowers according to their 'fantaisie', imagining flowers like the 'tulipe noire' or the 'dahlia bleu', such horticulturalists suggest a process the poet too can follow.[113] Through the experience of *surnaturalisme*, material things and ordinary life become significant growths of the imagination. Here are no ordinary flowers but the 'Fleur impossible, tulipe retrouvée, allégorique dahlia', the woman whose significance is that of the country as a whole; the 'pays singulier' of *surnaturalisme* is her 'analogie', her 'correspondance'.[114] This is a complex image related to the symbolic aspect of 'le langage des fleurs et des choses muettes'. For here the material world gains a new relation with thought and feeling, as woman, flower, and 'pays singulier' take on the significance of the *surnaturel* itself.

As 'allégorique dahlia' this flower recalls the symbolic flower-code, and the allegorical meaning of this 'Fleur impossible, tulipe retrouvée' is the very possibility of idealization. It is a figure for that special perception which enables us to find in material things 'la multiplication des sensations' and find 'la jouissance positive' in moments set apart from the ordinary. At the same time it is a figure for the power of the imagination which actively transforms nature:

C'est l'imagination qui a enseigné à l'homme le sens moral de la couleur, du contour, du son et du parfum. Elle a créé, au commencement du monde, l'analogie et la métaphore. Elle décompose toute la création, et, avec les matériaux amassés et disposés suivant des règles dont on ne peut trouver l'origine que dans le plus profond de l'âme, elle crée un monde nouveau.[115]

The imagination can create a new perception in which (in the words of the prose poem) 'la Nature . . . est réformée par le rêve, où elle est corrigée, embellie, refondue' (P i 302). The imagination which thus produces an idealized version of the material world is inseparable from the experience of the *surnaturel*, which is accessible to anyone, and can be enjoyed in very various contexts.[116] Yet it is especially akin to artistic creativity, because the artist can evoke its use at will, creating 'par l'exercice assidu de la volonté et la noblesse permanente de l'intention . . . un vrai jardin de beauté'.[117] The vocation of the poet involves choosing to use the 'douce langue natale' of the imagination by an act of will, entering purposefully into 'les rapports intimes et secrets des choses, les correspondances et les analogies' (P ii 329). By choosing to understand 'le langage des fleurs et des choses muettes' he is able to create the 'Fleur impossible', the 'vrai jardin de beauté' of nature corrected and idealized so that it becomes art.

Baudelaire's *surnaturalisme* is not pantheism, and his flower language is clearly not a religion of 'légumes sanctifiés'.[118] And it has no explicitly transcendental function either: the meanings of the 'allégorique dahlia' and the *correspondances* are not found beyond this world, but rather outside (or 'above') normal experience in privileged imaginative awareness. Yet for Baudelaire the *langage des fleurs* is a figure for the human (and especially the poetic) imagination, a 'faculté quasi-divine' (P ii 329) serving to 'reform' nature or idealize it. And the 'fleurs miraculeuses' of idealization are so unlike those of ordinary experience that it becomes possible to see how Baudelaire could write in 1857 (no doubt under pressure from the Poe text he was translating):

C'est cet admirable, cet immortel instinct du Beau qui nous fait considérer la terre et ses spectacles comme un aperçu, comme une correspondance du Ciel . . . C'est à la fois par la poésie et *à travers* la poésie . . . que l'âme entrevoit les splendeurs situées derrière le tombeau.[119]

Elsewhere Baudelaire habitually speaks of the poetic imagination in terms less reminiscent of transcendental mysticism. But even so, his poetics of the *surnaturel* can seem disquietingly inconsistent with the rest of his work. A critic like Walter Benjamin sees a clear disjunction: 'the notion of the *correspondances* . . . stands side by side and unconnected with the notion of "modern beauty"'.[120] Enid Starkie raises a related problem about Baudelaire's title, aware as she is of the idealizing tendencies in his poetry: 'This title . . . suggests only one aspect of his work'.[121] The flowers of the *surnaturel* can seem like very different growths from the *fleurs du Mal* of modern beauty, or of Baudelaire's title.

iv. An integrated poetics: 'fleurs du Mal'
and flowers of the 'correspondances'

> [Une] parfaite idéalisation, qu'il était impossible de ne pas
> supposer vivante, possible, réelle.
>
> (P i 321.)

Baudelaire chose his title in late 1854 or early 1855, and probably
wrote the poem *L'Invitation au voyage* during this period; the prose
poem was very likely written after the adoption of the title. It may
be for this reason (rather than because of its prose genre) that this
version insists so much on the conditions limiting the *surnaturel*.
Indeed, in a period when he was highly conscious both of
surnaturalisme and of his new title *Les Fleurs du Mal*, he could hardly
avoid pointing out the vulnerability of the idealized flowers of the
imagination:

Des rêves! toujours des rêves! et plus l'âme est ambitieuse et délicate, plus
les rêves l'éloignent du possible . . . Vivrons-nous jamais, passerons-nous
jamais dans ce tableau qu'a peint mon esprit, ce tableau qui te ressemble?

> (P i 303.)

For the idealization realized by art is, after all, as unlike real life
as the 'Fleur impossible' is unlike nature. The perfect flower can
seem 'allégorique', its meaning the *Idéal*, but it can in the end only
mean impossibility: only irony remains as the flower either loses all
allegorical significance or becomes an emblem of *le Mal* which makes
idealization impossible. It is a new species of *fleur du Mal*, an
idealized flower of imaginative *analogie* to which 'corresponds' a
negative meaning.[122] The prose *Invitation* thus brings together
explicitly for the first time the two aspects of his poetics — ironic
modernity (here given form in a resolutely modern and ironic
genre)[123] and the sensual 'mysticism' of the *correspondances*. It
would seem that his adherence to the new title committed Baudelaire
to investigating the contrasting aspects of his work in a new way,
and to discovering how they were related to each other.

Certainly, when discussing the theory of *correspondances* in his
critical writing from 1855 onwards, Baudelaire was concerned to
consider it in relation to *le Mal*. This was the case when, within
months (or weeks) of choosing his title, he published his first
discursive statement on the *analogie universelle* in the article on the
1855 *Exposition*:

Quoiqu'il y ait dans la nature des plantes plus ou moins saintes, des formes plus ou moins spirituelles, des animaux plus ou moins sacrés, et qu'il soit légitime de conclure, d'après les instigations de l'immense analogie universelle, que certaines nations — vastes animaux dont l'organisme est adéquat à leur milieu — aient été préparées et éduquées par la Providence pour un but déterminé, but plus ou moins élevé, plus ou moins rapproché du ciel, — je ne veux pas faire ici autre chose qu'affirmer leur *égale* utilité aux yeux de CELUI qui est indéfinissable, et le miraculeux secours qu'elles se prêtent dans l'harmonie de l'univers.

(P ii 575.)

Ostensibly a plea for a tolerant cosmopolitanism, this passage sets out a complex theory of reciprocal relations. There is an *analogie* between plants, forms, animals, and nations, but at the same time each of these categories contains entities which are ranged on a scale of relative moral (or spiritual) goodness and yet equally contribute to 'l'harmonie de l'univers'. By stating that plants (for example) do not all have the same positive moral connotations, Baudelaire is here implicitly distancing himself from those mystical celebrations of nature which assume that all plants 'correspond' without differentiation to the spiritual realm. Since one might conclude that humanity (like the nations) can embody a range of moral qualities analogous to the same range in (say) plants, Baudelaire is here further implying the possibility of a *symbolique des plantes* in which different plants might 'correspond' to specific human types (or even to specific human feelings) arranged on a scale of moral valuation. This would closely parallel the *symbolique des parfums* illustrated in the tercets of *Correspondances*, with its scale of human feelings ranging from innocence to corruption. Whether this sonnet was composed in its final form before or soon after the writing of the 1855 article, it indicates the same concern not to restrict 'l'harmonie de l'univers' to a celebration of undifferentiated universal goodness.

In his letter to Alphonse Toussenel of 21 January 1856, Baudelaire discusses precisely this issue. He agrees with the *fouriériste* that '*l'imagination* est la plus *scientifique* des facultés, parce que seule elle comprend *l'analogie universelle*, ou ce qu'une religion mystique appelle la *correspondance*' (CP i 335–7). He criticizes him however for a pervasive optimism ('Qu'est-ce que c'est que l'homme naturellement bon?') which derives from 'la grande hérésie moderne . . . la doctrine *artificielle*, substituée à la doctrine naturelle, — je veux dire la suppression de l'idée du *péché originel*'. The problem thus posed is whether the natural world can be undifferentiatedly good if it is linked by *analogie* with sinful man, and Baudelaire offers a speculation of his own:

à propos de *péché originel*, et de *forme moulée sur l'idée*, j'ai pensé bien souvent que les bêtes malfaisantes et dégoûtantes n'étaient peut-être que la vivification, corporification, éclosion à la vie matérielle, des *mauvaises pensées* de l'homme — Aussi la *nature* entière participe du péché originel.

This is a radical critique indeed of optimistic harmony doctrines, implying that every negative human thought finds not merely an *analogie*, but an embodiment in some form of nature.

Baudelaire was not so extreme in the application of such thinking to the theory of poetry over the next few years, but equally committed to reconciling the *correspondances* and *le Mal*. In his article on Gautier of 1859 he praises the latter's 'immense intelligence innée de la *correspondance* et du symbolisme universels, ce répertoire de toute métaphore,' and shows how the poet makes this knowledge serve the language of poetry:

C'est alors que la couleur parle, comme une voix profonde et vibrante; que les monuments se dressent et font saillie sur l'espace profond; que les animaux et les plantes, représentants du laid et du mal, articulent leur grimace non équivoque; que le parfum provoque la pensée et le souvenir correspondants; que la passion murmure ou rugit son langage éternellement semblable.

(P ii 117–18.)

The *correspondances* are of course associated with intensity of experience, but now include *analogies* with negative connotations, like the plants which are 'représentants du laid et du mal'. This is a 'langage des fleurs et des choses muettes' which is also a *langage des fleurs du Mal*. Here, and in an equally important passage in his article on Victor Hugo (1861), the notion of the *correspondances* has become an inclusive theory which allows poetic language not merely to render

les plaisirs les plus directs [que l'âme humaine] tire de la nature visible, mais encore les sensations les plus fugitives, les plus compliquées, les plus morales (je dis exprès sensations morales) qui nous sont transmises par l'être visible, par la nature inanimée, ou dite inanimée; non seulement, la figure d'un être extérieur à l'homme, végétal ou minéral, mais aussi sa physionomie, son regard, sa tristesse, sa douceur, sa joie éclatante, sa haine répulsive, son enchantement ou son horreur; enfin, en d'autres termes, tout ce qu'il y a d'humain dans n'importe quoi, et aussi tout ce qu'il y a de divin, de sacré ou de diabolique.

(P ii 132.)

Just as the appearance of 'un être . . . végétal' can evoke 'sensations morales' (affirmative or not), so every phenomenon of nature (whether *fleur du Bien* or *fleur du Mal*) can evoke some aspect of human feeling, from the 'divine' to the 'satanic'.[124] Poets like Gautier and Hugo understand the *langage des fleurs* in all its moral and psychological differentiations, and only thus become able to speak a poetic language which acknowledges both the external world and morally various human reality. For Baudelaire, this must be a language in which flower figures, like every other metaphor, can fully express both 'enchantement' and 'horreur'.

When thinking about poetic theory between 1855 and 1861, Baudelaire was clearly aware that it must take full account of both aspects of his own poetics. Aware too of the numerous flower images in his poetry associated not just with *surnaturalisme* but with ironic modernity, he had within five or six years after adopting his title set up a theory which gave some account both of the flowers of 'enchantement' (those of *Harmonie du soir* or *L'Invitation au voyage*) and the flowers of 'horreur' (those of *Une martyre, Voyage à Cythère*, or *Danse macabre*) in his poetry. Yet the volume is not called *Les Fleurs du Bien et du Mal*. It can be argued that Baudelaire chose a one-sided title in order to emphasize the unprecedented irony of his poetry.[125] However, since in itself the term *fleurs* suggests idealization (as Baudelaire knew with the whole of Western tradition) and the intensity of *surnaturalisme* (as he knew with Romantic tradition), the title's double formulation is best seen as evoking both *surnaturalisme* and irony. The poet's commitment to his title as a full expression of his mature 'bi-polar' poetics could well have suggested the statement made in his notebook late in his career (perhaps in 1859):

Deux qualités littéraires fondamentales: surnaturalisme et ironie.
Coup d'œil individuel, aspect dans lequel se tiennent les choses devant l'écrivain, puis tournure d'esprit satanique.[126]

The poet looks at the world in a special way and understands how the things in it relate to each other and to him: this is the *surnaturel* familiar from many texts related to sensual mysticism or *correspondances*. Yet this understanding cannot exclude the satanic awareness of *le Mal* in the human world, and hence the ability of the natural world to reflect this by *analogie* or metaphor. Baudelaire had always known that without the ironic consciousness poetry risked giving an inadequate and banal account of (modern) moral and psychological reality. By the end of two decades of writing (five or so years after choosing his title) he had reconciled this view with his interest in *analogie* and the *correspondances* in an integrated poetic theory in which 'surnaturalisme' and 'ironie' had a necessary part, each complementing the other.[127]

Appropriately, Baudelaire's preoccupation with the complementarity of these two qualities is reflected in his creative work in this last period, between 1859 and his death. In several poems of this period (grouped together in the 1861 edition) Baudelaire gives a particularly dark account of the relationship between *surnaturalisme* and *ironie*. All these poems grow out of a pessimism like that of *Le Goût du néant* (1859), a sense of loss subverting the *correspondances*: 'Le Printemps adorable a perdu son odeur!' (P i 76). Now without the pluri-sensual enchantment of a flowery *surnaturel*, the poet only desires the *néant* of resignation and death. In *Obsession* (1860) he again seeks nothingness, and rails against a natural world which cannot provide it:

> Comme tu me plairais, ô nuit! sans ces étoiles
> Dont la lumière parle un langage connu!
> Car je cherche le vide, et le noir, et le nu!

> (P i 75.)

The *correspondances* themselves have become threatening ironic presences, and even 'les ténèbres' of a starless night would turn out to be 'des toiles'

> Où vivent, jaillissant de mon œil par milliers,
> Des êtres disparus aux regards familiers

> (P i 76.)

Total darkness would offer no escape from these 'regards familiers' (which recall the same words in *Correspondances* describing the symbolic aspect of nature) and nature's *correspondances* win an ironic triumph. In *Alchimie de la douleur* (1860) the poet becomes 'le plus triste des alchimistes', whose ironic powers subvert nature's meanings:

> Par toi je change l'or en fer
> Et le paradis en enfer;
> Dans le suaire des nuages
>
> Je découvre un cadavre cher
> Et sur les célestes rivages
> Je bâtis de grands sarcophages.
>
> (P i 77.)

This process turns the 'Vie et splendeur' of nature into human 'douleur', yet it represents a special kind of creative achievement, as the active verbs imply ('je change', 'je découvre', 'je bâtis'). In *Horreur sympathique* (1860) the same claim is expressed, for there the mournful skies and clouds find their ironic *analogie* in the 'orgueil' and 'rêves' of a proud poet exiled from his 'paradis' to 'l'Enfer où mon cœur se plaît' (P i 78). The poet whose irony makes him 'un faux accord / Dans la divine symphonie' (P i 78) can turn 'splendeur' into 'douleur' or 'horreur' into ironic pleasure. In all these poems he shows that ironic horror can overwhelm *surnaturalisme* without destroying its structures, and that even in these conditions the poet finds a creative language.

The poet can, through similar unusual uses of the *correspondances*, find unexpected meanings not only in nature but also in the modern city.[128] Paris is thus a 'cité pleine de rêves' in which 'tout pour moi devient allégorie' or where 'tout, même l'horreur, tourne aux enchantements'.[129] In *Rêve parisien* (1860), however, Paris is transformed in dream into a 'terrible paysage' made up only of metal, marble, and water, a city silent and sunless, but where 'ces prodiges . . . brillaient d'un feu personnel!', bright with an ambiguous *surnaturalisme*:

> C'étaient des pierres inouïes
> Et des flots magiques; c'étaient
> D'immenses glaces éblouies
> Par tout ce qu'elles réflétaient!
>
> (P i 102.)

Indeed this *paysage* is a figure for the power of the imagination to reorganize, 'reform', or idealize the external world by an act of will: the poet is 'Architecte de ses féeries'. He even banishes flowers (along with the whole of 'le végétal irrégulier') and abolishes (by a 'terrible nouveauté!') the sense of hearing, thereby destroying both conditions of the *langage des fleurs* . . . The poet who has rearranged the urban landscape at will (creating a parody of both city and natural world) has thus carried out the ironic operation of changing the very conditions of *l'analogie universelle*. Yet the final irony is that the poet's 'volonté' belongs only in dream, as the poet wakes powerless in an all too real city.

The *paysage* in this dream represents a *surnaturel* which might be called artificial: it is understood to be 'above nature' yet dissolves when confronted with real life. In this sense it recalls Baudelaire's words on the *paradis artificiel* of drug-taking:

Ce seigneur visible de la nature visible (je parle de l'homme) a donc voulu créer le paradis par la pharmacie, par les boissons fermentées, semblable à un maniaque qui remplacerait des meubles solides et des jardins véritables par des décors peints sur toile et montés sur châssis. C'est dans cette dépravation du sens de l'infini que gît, selon moi, la raison de tous les excès coupables . . . [130]

The desire to replace the real flowers of nature with those of an artificial paradise is perhaps a 'dépravation', but it is linked with the 'sens de l'infini'. This passage well expresses Baudelaire's ambiguity about drug-taking, on which he wrote extensively during this period. But he is equally equivocal about the possibility of any escape into an 'Idéal artificiel' which claims to compete with the real world. In *Le Voyage* (1860) 'Le Lotus parfumé' is offered to those who, tired of the horror of life, want to 's'enivrer de la douceur étrange / De cette après-midi qui n'a jamais de fin' (P i 133), in a tempting *infini* which is neither death nor life. This paradise is delusive and the same topos is used in *Le Joueur généreux* (also conceived in 1860) to characterize a paradoxical hell chosen by people escaping life because of their 'horreur de l'ennui' and their 'désir immortel de se sentir vivre' (P i 325). These people seek a delusory *surnaturel* in the desire to change the moral and psychological conditions of life, not unlike others who practise magic or sorcery because they 'veulent, en opérant sur la matière . . . conquérir une domination interdite à l'homme' (P i 439). The desire to escape from human reality is as understandable as the attempt to change the natural world, for both are enterprises suggested by the *sens de l'infini*. And both promise a release from limitations, in the same way as *l'âme du vin* promises 'la poésie / Qui jaillira vers Dieu comme une rare fleur!'[131] Yet such promises are after all a 'dépravation du sens de l'infini', for neither dreams, drug-taking, escapism, magic, nor wine can legitimately or lastingly offer the infinite. There are implications here for poetry itself. It too embodies the quest for *l'Idéal* (itself a rare flower pushing upwards toward *l'infini*), but it cannot in the end flout the conditions imposed by natural and human reality. It must be 'l'infini dans le fini', for it is both 'ce qui n'est complètement vrai que dans un autre monde' and 'ce qu'il y a de plus réel'.[132]

The prose poem *La Chambre double* is clearly an allegorical presentation of these principles. It first describes a dreamlike room, 'une chambre véritablement spirituelle' where:

Les meubles ont l'air de rêver; on les dirait doués d'une vie somnambulique, comme le végétal et le minéral. Les étoffes parlent une langue muette, comme les fleurs, comme les ciels, comme les soleils couchants.
. . . Ici, tout a la suffisante clarté et la délicieuse obscurité de l'harmonie.

                                                        (P i 280–2.)

This is a hyperbolical *surnaturalisme* at home in intimacy: the 'langue muette' of the surroundings is a domesticated *langage des fleurs* and cosmic 'harmonie' is manifested on a small scale. Material things seem quietly alive, communicating half-understood meanings and feelings to the poet, and their *harmonie* is completed by a sensuous perfume and the presence of love, a woman who is 'la souveraine des rêves'. The experience is sensual and mysterious, a 'vie suprême' in which 'le temps a disparu; c'est l'Éternité qui règne, une éternité de délices!' Baudelaire gives us here his fullest expression of the *Idéal*, an idealization in every way of human experience and material reality. But this *infini*, however fully experienced, is subject to the limitations of the *fini*. The *surnaturel* dissolves in a moment, as the sleazy or banal realities of existence overwhelm perception; time, memory, and *ennui* return, an ironic critique of the *Idéal*. The structure of the experience (like that of the room) remains, although now filled with 'dégoût' instead of 'délices'; an 'hideux vieillard' replaces the woman, the furniture is filthy and tattered, the smell 'le ranci de la désolation'. The *langage des fleurs*, with its idealized meanings, is replaced by a *langage du mal*, a discourse composed 'de Souvenirs, de Regrets, de Spasmes, de Peurs, d'Angoisses, de Cauchemars, de Colères et de Névroses'. In each case the structures of poetic language are identical: *analogie* links material things with human experience, whether they are perceived as *Idéal* or reality, *enchantement* or *horreur*.

For Baudelaire the structures of experience are the structures of poetic language: both follow the rules of *analogie* and both encompass *surnaturalisme* and *ironie*. This point is well illustrated in the prose poem *Les Bienfaits de la lune* (1863), a subtle study of experience structured as reciprocity (*correspondances*) and contrast (*ironie*), expressed in an equivalent poetic discourse. The child-woman marked by the moon as an appropriate lover for the poet (fellow *lunatique*) is fated to love what the moon loves:

ce que j'aime et ce qui m'aime: l'eau, les nuages, le silence et la nuit; la mer immense et verte; l'eau informe et multiforme; le lieu où tu ne seras pas; l'amant que tu ne connaîtras pas; les fleurs monstrueuses; les parfums qui font délirer; les chats qui se pâment sur les pianos et qui gémissent comme les femmes, d'une voix rauque et douce!

(P i 341.)

The evocation of the two lovers' involuntary *Idéal* suggests *enchantement* but also *horreur*, for they are doomed to frustration in their relations with nature and each other. This is a world of sensuality and mystery but it is tinged with ironic melancholy; *surnaturalisme* and *ironie* are here subtly blended, like the flowers which are 'monstrueuses' or 'les fleurs sinistres qui ressemblent aux encensoirs d'une religion inconnue'. Appropriately the rhetorical *fleurs* expressing this experience are all related either to *analogie* or to oxymoron. Moonlight is directly compared with other aspects of nature ('comme une atmosphère phosphorique'), personified ('Divinité', 'marraine'), and associated with the lovers by various natural and human 'moon-like' qualities. At the same time the text is traversed by figures of contrast and oxymoron: 'un poison lumineux', 'l'eau informe et multiforme', 'nourrice empoisonneuse'. Like the 'fleurs sinistres', the stylistic features of this poem grow out of *surnaturalisme* and *ironie*, the 'deux qualités littéraires fondamentales'.

In the notebook page where he names these qualities together, the poet further characterizes *le surnaturel* in these words: 'Le surnaturel comprend la couleur générale et l'accent, c'est-à-dire intensité, sonorité, limpidité, vibrativité, profondeur et retentissement dans l'espace et dans le temps' (P i 658). The privileged consciousness of the *surnaturel*, its *correspondances* intensifying and idealizing perception, suggesting a rich and evocative poetic language like *le langage des fleurs* . . . Yet in Baudelaire's poetic language, qualities like 'couleur' and 'intensité' are by no means confined to contexts evoking the *Idéal*: they characterize not just *La Chambre double* but other texts of this period like *Les Bienfaits de la lune* and even *Alchimie de la douleur* and *Horreur sympathique*. How could it be otherwise, since in all these texts *surnaturalisme* and *ironie* work together to produce an 'intensité' of poetic effect? The *correspondances* may evoke enchantment or (by ironic reversal) horror instead (*La Chambre double*); they may be coloured by irony to produce a suggestive blend of enchantment and horror (*Les Bienfaits de la lune*); they may turn the enchantment of nature into the horror of the ironic consciousness (*Alchimie de la douleur*); or they may transform horror into ironic enchantment (Horreur sympathique). The poetic process begins in the poet's experience of the outside world ('l'aspect dans lequel les choses se tiennent devant l'écrivain') and his relationship to it ('coup d'œil individuel'): out of this experience comes *analogie*, on the model of the *langage des fleurs*. But the experience is also filtered through the ironic consciousness ('puis tournure d'esprit satanique') which (at least implicitly) inverts the values provided by *analogie*, on the model of the *fleurs du Mal*. The poetic language is structured in the same way—by *analogie* (whether of unironic resemblance, ironic similarity, or ironic dissimilarity) and by irony (whether implicit or explicit).[133] Together the flowers of the *correspondances* and the *fleurs du Mal* provide the model for Baudelaire's poetic language. This is the intense and resonant language of a modern poet: 'Qu'est-ce que l'art pur suivant la conception moderne? C'est créer une magie suggestive contenant à la fois l'objet et le sujet, le monde extérieur à l'artiste et l'artiste lui-même.'[134] The poet who practises the 'opérations magiques, sorcellerie évocatoire'[135] linking the material world with meanings and feelings (especially ironic ones) produces a poetic language of 'intensité, sonorité, limpidité, vibrativité, profondeur'. It is modern because, like Romanticism and the *langage des fleurs*, it gives importance to both the external and the subjective, and to the intense relationship between them. Baudelaire's language is modern in a special way because, like the *fleurs du Mal*, it expresses not banal undifferentiated goodness or sentiment but a new ironic consciousness in relation to the external world. For him, *le langage des fleurs* is indeed the *langage des fleurs du Mal*.

In his last few years of work in the early sixties, then, Baudelaire gave full expression to the inclusive poetic theory he had developed since choosing the title *Les Fleurs du Mal*. This theory, elaborated

mostly in critical writing and prose poems (and a few poems included
in later editions of the poetry)[136] may seem only marginally relevant
to that volume itself: a large number of the poems in the 1857 edition
were, after all, composed before 1855. Yet it is legitimate to find
Baudelaire's mature theory prefigured in his earlier poetry, and even
to read the whole volume in the light of it. If in fact the poem
Correspondances was composed entirely in the mid-forties (as some
have argued), then the poet already possessed the main elements of
an integrated poetics at that date. Some lines of 1845 by his friend
Prarond might suggest knowledge of Baudelaire's poem (or at least
some related notions) at that early date;

> Tout est beau, tout est bon sous les arbres, nos temples,
> Et, cependant qu'ainsi tu rêves et contemples,
> Les vices, les serpents au sifflement moqueur,
> Grouillent dans ton cerveau, poète, et dans ton cœur.[137]

Confronting the beauties of nature, the poet remains ironically aware
of *le Mal* in himself: here is the germ of Baudelaire's title and of
his mature theory. But even if this speculation is not convincing,
many poems before 1855 show that Baudelaire was at least partially
in possession of the theory later made explicit. At the beginning of
his career, the poem about Sara centres on an ironic reversal of
analogie by which the woman's (objective) unattractiveness becomes
a subjective flower of beauty for the poet. A similar process is found
in *Une charogne* and *Une martyre*, while in *Voyage à Cythère* an
imagined flowery landscape finds its ironic *analogie* in the punitive
reality of the island. Indeed, everywhere in the early poems
Baudelaire's mature theory can be seen to be implicit. It is most
strikingly prefigured, however, in his use of flower imagery before
1855: the flowers of nature could stand as an *analogie* both for
various types of moral and psychological negativity and for a sensual
mysticism or an impossible idealization. By choosing his flower title
the poet consciously confirmed the importance of both these types
of flower imagery, as of the intermediate third type which presents
literary flowers as mystical but ironic growths. The arrangement of
the poems in the 1857 edition makes clear his awareness of the
importance of these flowers in his poetics: the first four poems after
Au lecteur exhibit the first two types of flower imagery and the
volume closes with *La mort des artistes*, with its morbid flowers of
creativity.[138] The changes of order in the 1861 edition indicate no

weakening in his commitment to the 'flower poetics', but rather a desire to point up certain aspects of it (notably the notion of modern beauty) more unmistakably.[139] Remarkably, Baudelaire was able to use a title invented by someone else (and half-way through his career) to make sense of his whole poetic enterprise. It not only led him to articulate an integrated poetics, but revealed in retrospect the unitive principle of his early poetry—that the flowers of creativity, of irony, and of *surnaturalisme* all bloom together.

Baudelaire's extensive poetic use of the structures of the mystical flower language was unprecedented, and the ironic fleurs du Mal were his own invention: *a fortiori*, his integrated flower poetics reveals how strenuously aware he was of the 'sorcellerie évocatoire' of his art. This was a supremely conscious and deliberate artist, as he reminds us in the prose poem *Le Fou et le Vénus* written in 1862–3. Here an all-perceiving narrative voice describes a sunlit 'vaste parc' where

L'extase universelle des choses ne s'exprime par aucun bruit . . .

On dirait qu'une lumière toujours croissante fait de plus en plus étinceler les objets; que les fleurs excitées brûlent du désir de rivaliser avec l'azur du ciel par l'énergie de leurs couleurs, et que la chaleur, rendant visibles les parfums, les fait monter vers l'astre comme des fumées.

(P i 283.)

Once more the landscape of the *surnaturel* evokes the possibility of idealization, and the flowers are figures for the desire to compete with *l'Idéal*. Conscious of his habitual modes, the poet ironically overturns these idealizing *correspondances*: 'Cependant, dans cette jouissance universelle, j'ai aperçu un être affligé.' This is 'un de ces bouffons volontaires', a clown suffering from the impossibility of achieving his *Idéal*. Like the 'fleurs excitées' of the *surnaturel* he is a figure for the necessary tension between *Spleen* and *Idéal*, ironic frustration and creative achievement.[140] The narrator who observes both garden and clown knows well the necessity of both *surnaturel* and *ironie*, flowers and frustration. He is the poet of *Les Fleurs du Mal*, here an eye/I observing his own creative awareness and insisting on his own sense of poetic purpose: both *fleurs* and clown are 'volontaires'.

The prose poem *Une mort Héroïque* also contains three figures for the conscious artist: one of these is a clown with the indispensable creative marks of 'l'art, l'effort, la volonté'. In his last performance, observed by artist-king and artist-narrator, the clown produces 'une parfaite idéalisation' especially admired by these two observers aware of the death awaiting him, which gives him 'une auréole . . . où se mêlaient, dans un étrange amalgame, les rayons de l'Art et la gloire du Martyre' (P i 321). This poetic halo, like the 'couronne mystique' of the poet of *Bénédiction*, is an emblem of both the triumphant achievements of great art and the sufferings they demand. The clown's idealization is 'parfaite' because it combines 'la magie du luxe étalé' with 'l'intérêt moral et mystérieux' of suffering and death: only art combining *surnaturalisme* and *ironie* can 'voiler les terreurs du gouffre'. Triply conscious of the nature of his art, Baudelaire insists that only creative *fleurs du Mal* can defy the final *mal*, death itself.

With his almost religious conception of high art, Baudelaire never forgets the importance of the poet's consciousness, deliberation, and *volonté*. But the poet's intention, pursued through all the *Mal* inherent in creativity and life itself, was to produce the 'parfaite idéalisation', the 'ivresse', the 'sorcellerie évocatoire' of his art. In the prose poem dedicated to Franz Liszt he presents the thyrsus, a stick entwined with flowers, as an emblem of art:

— Le bâton, c'est votre volonté, droite, ferme et inébranlable; les fleurs, c'est la promenade de votre fantaisie autour de votre volonté; c'est l'élément féminin exécutant autour du mâle ses prestigieuses pirouettes. Ligne droite et ligne arabesque, intention et expression, roideur de la volonté, sinuosité du verbe, unité du but, variété des moyens, amalgame tout-puissant et indivisible du génie.

(*Le Thyrse*, 1863, P i 336.)

In his own pursuit of 'expression', Baudelaire discovered, invented, and perfected a variety of means. But it was perhaps in his use of flower imagery over twenty years, and in the integrated flower poetics of his maturity, that Baudelaire most clearly showed how purposefully he could deploy the 'sinuosité du verbe'. In an article of 1861 he finds for Marceline Desbordes-Valmore's poetry of suffering an appropriately floral comparison: 'Des massifs de fleurs représentent les abondantes expressions du sentiment. . . . Les fleurs se penchent vaincues . . . ' (P ii 149). His own rather different poetry—at once imaginative and purposeful, magically evocative and rigorously intelligent—is well represented in the words of *Le Thyrse*:

Ne dirait-on pas que toutes ces corolles délicates, tous ces calices, explosion de senteurs et de couleurs, exécutent un mystique fandango autour du bâton hiératique?[141]

Baudelaire's flowers prove indeed to be the one indispensable emblem of the poetics of the author of *Les Fleurs du Mal*, 'chantre de la Volupté et de l'Angoisse éternelles'.

4

FLOWER POETICS
OF OTHER TYPES,
1840–1870

Baudelaire's work was written and published in the three middle decades of the century (1840–68), a period in which poetry was characterized both by continuity with Romanticism and by reaction against it. Baudelaire was not alone in his elaboration of a personal poetics out of the theory and practice of the earlier movement, nor was he the only poet to adapt the Romantic 'culte des fleurs' for his own literary purposes. In the middle of this period Gérard de Nerval developed a poetics as remarkable as Baudelaire's although in full continuity with Romanticism. It was during this period too that poets like Gautier, Banville, and Leconte de Lisle elaborated a conception of poetry which, by the time it was consecrated in *Le Parnasse contemporain* in 1866, seemed to propose a clearly post-Romantic orientation for poetry. And in their different ways both Nerval and the Parnassians gave, like Baudelaire, considerable importance to the flower figure in their poetry and poetics.

I. The Flowers of Nerval's Poetics

i. *Flowers of 'le Rêve' and the goddess*

Nerval's major work was published in the early fifties, but he had been young in the high days of Romanticism. In his youth in the late twenties and early thirties, he had been as aware as any of his contemporaries of the traditions which served as sources for Romantic flower imagery, whether literary or mystical. In a poem of 1830 he is already experimenting with the concept of nature's harmony:

> Le papillon, fleur sans tige . . .
>
> Dans la nature infinie
>   Harmonie
> Entre la plante et l'oiseau?[1]

But Nerval's early poetry more usually combines Romantic grace with imitation of the literary models he presented in 'Les poètes du XVIᵉ siècle' in 1830, and his Ronsardian *odelettes* are marked by a flower imagery contributing lyrical grace-notes to the themes of spring, nature, and love.

Among the lessons to be learnt from sixteenth century poetry was its resourceful use of the flowers of transience, and Gérard did not fail to note this in his article. While pointing out the conventional nature of the 'espèce de syllogisme' employed by Ronsard in a poem like 'Mignonne, allons voir si la rose . . . ', he insists that 'la mise en œuvre en a fait un des morceaux les plus frais et les plus gracieux de notre poésie légère' (L 953–4). Thus it is scarcely surprising to find Nerval himself later taking up the challenge of turning the *carpe diem* with grace and economy, in a song written in 1846 for the libretto of *Les Monténégrins*:

> Les belles choses
> N'ont qu'un printemps;
> Semons de roses
> Les pas du temps.[2]

In another theatrical text several years later he again uses this conceit (adding a reference to 'l'horloge des fleurs'):

> Les heures sont des fleurs l'une après l'autre écloses
> Dans l'éternel hymen de la nuit et du jour;
> Il faut donc les cueillir comme on cueille les roses
> Et ne les donner qu'à l'amour.[3]

The *carpe diem* formula, taken up by Gérard at these various stages of his career, evokes the perfection and vulnerability of flowers in order to contrast woman's beauty and the possibilities of love with loss and death. It is a syllogism moving from a pessimistic aphorism to an optimistic imperative which assumes that 'Le Dieu du monde / C'est le plaisir', and for Gérard it was already by the eighteen-forties no doubt ironic in its implications.[4] The writer of the letters of *Un Roman à faire* (1842) has already adopted his characteristic posture of 'souffrance' caused by the uncertainty of love and even hesitates to express his love in a letter:

La pensée se glace en se traduisant en phrases, et les plus douces émotions de l'amour ressemblent à des plantes desséchées, que l'on presse entre des feuillets, afin de les conserver mieux. — Songer! . . . que ce peut être par là qu'on vous juge et que l'on peut jouer sur un morceau de papier son avenir et son bonheur, sa vie et sa mort! Non! non! je . . . garde les belles fleurs de mon amour, qui ne veulent plus s'épanouir que près de vous et sous vos yeux![5]

This is an equivocal gallantry, for it is his own life and death which are in question rather than the woman's: it is the flowers of his own love which are vulnerable, and particularly so when committed to paper. The writer thus draws attention to the impossibility of rendering the experience of love in writing while paradoxically expressing its intensity: the vulnerable flowers are also 'belles'. Whether or not this letter originated as a 'real' letter to Jenny Colon or any other woman, this text makes clear (with the other letters of *Un Roman à faire* and their subsequent textual history) that for Gérard the rhetoric of love and its flowers is a matter of life or death.

Similar concerns are implicit in *Les Cydalises*, an important poem of the late eighteen-forties which implies another transformation of the *carpe diem* theme;

> Où sont nos amoureuses?
> Elles sont au tombeau:
> Elles sont plus heureuses,
> Dans un séjour plus beau!
>
> Elles sont près des anges,
> Dans le fond du ciel bleu,
> Et chantent les louanges
> De la mère de Dieu![6]

The women once loved in this life have indeed proved vulnerable to death, but whatever their status as women/flowers in life ('blanche fiancée' 'jeune vierge en fleur', or 'Amante délaissée / Que flétrit la douleur') they are happier in death. Where the *carpe diem* seeks to turn woman's vulnerability to death to male advantage, this poem transforms men's experience of loss into an assertion of women's transcendent invulnerability. At the same time the women's salvation is a consolation for the poet, and it is even suggested that his own salvation might depend on his earlier contact with them ('L'Éternité profonde / Souriait dans vos yeux . . . '). Elsewhere indeed Gérard can imagine his own death as associated with love of a woman ('ma plus grande envie ne peut être que de mourir pour vous') and as itself a consoling female figure ('la mort . . . m'apparaît, couronnée de roses pâles') offering him not 'le plaisir, mais le calme éternel'.[7] It is as if his own salvation is mysteriously linked with the assumption of 'les Cydalises' into heaven, where they (like the poet) celebrate an idealized female figure, for they 'chantent les louanges / De la mère de Dieu!'.

For Gérard, indeed, romantic idealization of woman legitimizes (and is in turn confirmed by) the celebration of a transcendental female figure like 'la mère de Dieu'. His account of his youth in *Sylvie* (1853–4) places this tendency in the historical context of the *bohème* of the high Romantic period: 'Vue de près, la femme réelle révoltait notre ingénuité; il fallait qu'elle apparût reine ou déesse, et surtout n'en pas approcher.'[8] And he associates this idealization with the Romantic enthusiasm for poetry and love ('nous étions ivres de poésie et d'amour') in terms which invoke a female divinity: 'l'homme matériel aspirait au bouquet de roses qui devait le régénérer par les mains de la belle Isis.' These flowers of Isis (regenerative counterparts of the transient flowers of the *carpe diem*) belong to a syncretic figure representing all aspects of idealized femininity and divinity, and Nerval quotes in 1845 the passage in Apuleius in which Isis defines herself as such a figure: 'moi, dont l'univers a adoré sous mille formes l'unique et toute-puissante divinité' (*Isis* (1845), L 657). This is a goddess capable of giving salvation to her devotees even in death, for

dès que tu auras franchi le sombre bord, tu ne cesseras encore de m'adorer, soit dans les ténèbres de l'Achéron ou dans les Champs-Élysées; et si, par l'observation de mon culte et par une inviolable chasteté, tu mérites bien de moi, tu sauras que je puis seule prolonger ta vie spirituelle au-delà des bornes marquées.

The 'pâles roses' of death are mysteriously like Isis' roses of regeneration, just as the 'Cydalises' (whose flower-like beauty is transient yet eternal) themselves partake of the salvific femininity of which Isis is for Nerval the supreme type.

For all that, the women of *Les Filles du feu* (1854) are by no means undifferentiated from one another. In the short play *Corilla* (1839), the earliest piece included in the volume, the heroine has the power to offer or refuse Fabio's 'bonheur': 'Un mot d'elle va réaliser mon rêve, ou le faire envoler pour toujours' (L 664). As operatic prima donna Corilla is a distant 'reine' with 'une grâce divine' (by turns becoming 'toutes ces héroïnes que j'adorais en elle') and her agreeing to meet him is like the condescension of a goddess ('elle descend vers moi'). Thus when she comes to him disguised as a humble *bouquetière* he fails to recognize her: 'Tu es, toi, la fleur sauvage des champs: mais qui pourrait se tromper entre vous deux?' (L 677). It is as all too human 'femme réelle' that she invokes a version of the *carpe diem*: 'Puisque vous ne voulez pas de mes fleurs, je les jetterai dans la mer en passant; demain elles seraient fanées.' Here, expressed in comic theatrical form, is the basis of a typological differentiation of femininity which Gérard developed further in *Octavie* (first called *L'Illusion* in 1845). The various female figures of this tale are distinguished from one another by a complex series of resemblances and differences. Thus Octavie, the young English girl marked by her 'douceur' and 'candeur de vierge', is a 'fille des eaux', while the Italian woman is seductive and frightening, 'un peu sorcière ou bohémienne', and associated with volcanic fire. So too Octavie is like the goddess Isis since she enacts her rites but unlike her as a 'femme réelle', while the 'sorcière' is seen by the narrator as a 'bizarre illusion' like and unlike his idealized (and rejecting) 'amour fatal' in Paris. Moreover, the 'sorcière' is related in an equally ambiguous way both to the 'figure de sainte Rosalie, couronnée de roses violettes' who protects her, and to the figure of 'La mort . . . couronnée de roses pâles' who welcomes the narrator in his suicidal despair at having betrayed his absent ideal love (L 639–47). This text evokes different aspects of womanhood in a complex rhetoric of water and fire, north and south, purity and seduction, sanctity and sorcery, rejection and acceptance, violet and pale roses. The range of female qualities is at the same time a rhetoric combining hope and despair about the possibility of a love corresponding to the protagonist's ideal.

The more extensive prose work *Sylvie* reformulates many of the same elements in a schema of female types again expressing the themes of love, rejection, and transience. Here again we find a woman seen by the protagonist as 'reine ou déesse' and 'une image que je poursuis' (L 591–3), the Parisian actress Aurélie. But in his concern to 'fixer mon idéal' (L 622) Nerval makes use in this text of the resources of memory, so that his love for the actress is seen to have had 'son germe dans le souvenir d'Adrienne, fleur de la nuit éclose à la pâle clarté de la lune, fantôme rose et blond glissant sur l'herbe verte à demi baignée de blanches vapeurs' (L 597). Yet Adrienne had soon left ordinary country life to become a nun ('Aimer une religieuse sous la forme d'une actrice!') and memory directs the narrator to the more accessible Sylvie, a simple village girl whose 'amoureux' he had been in youth: 'Elle existe, elle, bonne et pure de cœur sans doute. Je revois sa fenêtre où le pampre s'enlace au rosier . . . Elle m'attend encore . . . ' (L 597). If Adrienne is a star-like flower of the night in his memory, Sylvie is a more ordinary flower of nature, and a deleted passage presents a youthful memory in similar terms:

deux figures se combattaient dans mon esprit: l'une semblait descendre des étoiles et l'autre monter de la terre. La dernière disait: Je suis simple et fraîche comme les fleurs des champs: l'autre: je suis noble et pure comme les beautés immortelles conçues dans le sein de Dieu.

(L 910.)

That flower references have a mnemonic function in this tale is confirmed when the narrator's decision to revisit Sylvie and the region of his youth becomes a journey of the memory signalled by some roadside flowers:

Plus loin que Louvres est un chemin bordé de pommiers dont j'ai vu bien des fois les fleurs éclater dans la nuit comme les étoiles de la terre . . . — Pendant que la voiture monte les côtes, recomposons les souvenirs du temps où j'y venais si souvent.

(L 599.)

Indeed the domain of youthful memory is an innocent paradise, a 'pays où fleurissait encore l'idylle antique' (L 624), in which the youth's mock wedding with Sylvie is associated with flower folk-song, 'ces strophes . . . amoureuses et fleuries comme le cantique de l'Ecclésiaste' (L 607). Yet a memory of the nun Adrienne acting in a masque, 'transfigurée' as an angel triumphant despite 'les débris du monde détruit' (L 608), suggests that even the past was not all flowery idyll. His visit to Sylvie indicates that the past cannot be recaptured ('Les fleurs de la chevelure de Sylvie se penchaient . . . le bouquet de son corsage s'effeuillait' (L 610)) and even the landscape is imbued with a sense of loss, just as the lake at Ermenonville is 'étoilé de fleurs éphémères' (L 614). Sylvie's final (delayed) revelation that Adrienne had died in the convent years before thus confirms the sense that for the narrator the present survives 'sur les débris du monde détruit'. The flower figures deployed throughout are seen to have been signs of the vulnerability of illusion:

Ermenonville, pays où fleurissait encore l'idylle antique . . . tu as perdu ta seule étoile, qui chatoyait pour moi d'un double éclat. Tour à tour rose et bleu comme l'astre trompeur d'Aldebaran, c'était Adrienne ou Sylvie, — c'était les deux moitiés d'un seul amour. L'une était l'idéal sublime, l'autre la douce réalité.

(L 624.)

These women are both equally flowers and stars, now lost to him and leaving behind a heaven and earth entirely disenchanted. Yet like the 'Cydalises' of the earlier poems, these 'flambeaux éteints' and vulnerable flowers somehow survive the narrator's initiation into loss. As with the initiates of Eleusis celebrating the great goddess, he has passed 'les bornes du non-sens et de l'absurdité: la raison pour moi, c'était de conquérir et de fixer mon idéal' (L 622). Like the water, fire, and roses of *Octavie*, the flowers and stars of *Sylvie* are figures for Nerval's celebration of ideal love as an 'image que je poursuis' (a fiction!) that is beyond reason and reality, and for his construction of a myth of salvation made possible by writing.

For Nerval the pursuit of ideal love is like a quest for salvation: the use of religious terms pervades his discussion of love. Yet this is much more than an idealized 'culte des dames': when he spoke of 'l'homme matériel' aspiring after 'le bouquet de roses qui devait le régénérer', Gérard had in mind an individual regeneration with cosmic implications. This mystical vision is implicit in his treatment of the doctrine of cosmic harmony in *Vers dorés* (1845/1854). The poem immediately adopts the tone of a polemic against the free thought of 'l'homme matériel' not interested in the realm of the spirit:

> Homme, libre penseur! te crois-tu seul pensant
> Dans ce monde où la vie éclate en toute chose?
> Des forces que tu tiens ta liberté dispose,
> Mais de tous tes conseils l'univers est absent.[9]

The consonantal and syntactical violence of these lines rejects any view of human life which ignores the life of nature. Nerval's description of the three realms of nature emphasizes not their beneficent harmony or communication with each other and with man but rather the autonomous life of each realm (the animal's 'esprit agissant', the flower's 'âme', and the metal's 'mystère d'amour'), polemically upending the usual *échelle* which places minerals lowest in the scale. Nature's life is not without beneficent qualities ('une âme à la nature éclose', 'un mystère d'amour', 'un pur esprit') but its meaning is more hidden ('Souvent dans l'être obscur habite un Dieu caché') than revealed: even if 'A la matière même un verbe est attaché', nature's meaning seems scarcely accessible and anyway unpredictable. Nature is here disquietingly independent of man, and possibly dangerous: 'Respecte . . . ', 'tout sur ton être est puissant', 'Crains . . . un regard qui t'épie' 'quelque usage impie'. This is a natural world in which man must dispose of his spiritual freedom in fear and trembling, and its *langage des fleurs* speaks of salvation and damnation.

In *Aurélia*,[10] the document which sums up so much of his mature thought, Nerval insists on the importance of nature for human destiny. In an esoteric vision the narrator learns that the *épreuves* of each human life have eternal implications for nature and for all humanity (L 766). This universal solidarity is expressed by multiples of the number seven, a mystery to be accepted without analysis ('Autant vaudrait demander compte à la fleur du nombre de ses pétales ou des divisions de sa corolle') but which links matter with human activity ('le bien et le mal') across time and space. Besides, man's relations to nature can only be understood in terms of the mother goddess presiding over them. Thus it was 'Une déesse rayonnante' who first 'guidait . . . l'évolution rapide des humains' (L 777), and the result of the Fall was that 'Partout mourait, pleurait, languissait l'image souffrante de la Mère éternelle' (L 779). Her sufferings are sympathetically related to nature's vulnerability ('Les bocages que j'avais vus si verts ne portaient plus que de pâles fleurs et des feuillages flétris') as well as humanity's: 'Au pied des arbres frappés de mort et de stérilité . . . on voyait . . . se flétrir des enfants et des jeunes femmes énervés et sans couleur' (L 778). This suffering recalls the narrator's experience as the mourner of Aurélia, on one occasion wanting to join her in death 'à cette heure, et au milieu des arbres, des treilles et des fleurs d'automne' (L 781). A moment like this takes on its full meaning in relation to the apocalyptic vision of the 'dame qui me guidait', enfolding in her arm 'une longue tige de rose trémière':

elle se mit à grandir sous un clair rayon de lumière, de telle sorte que peu à peu le jardin prenait sa forme, et les parterres et les arbres devenaient les rosaces et les festons de ses vêtements; tandis que sa figure et ses bras imprimaient leurs contours aux nuages pourprés du ciel. Je la perdais ainsi de vue à mesure qu'elle se transfigurait, car elle semblait s'évanouir dans

sa propre grandeur. 'Oh! ne fuis pas! m'écriai-je . . . car la nature meurt
avec toi!'
   . . . je vis que le jardin avait pris l'aspect d'un cimetière. Des voix disaient:
'L'Univers est dans la nuit!'

(L 772.)

This is a cosmic vision of female (and floral!) vulnerability which
emphasizes nature's dependence on the goddess, and the narrator's
dependence on both for his salvation.

The second part of *Aurélia* opens with the narrator reflecting not
only on the loss of Aurelia but also on the threat of spiritual
perdition. Yet in a 'vision merveilleuse' the goddess makes him a
promise which reveals the purpose of his spiritual initiation:

'Je suis la même que Marie, la même que ta mère, la même aussi que sous
toutes les formes tu as toujours aimée. A chacune de tes épreuves, j'ai quitté
l'un des masques dont je voile mes traits, et bientôt tu me verras telle que
je suis . . . '

(L 805.)

Now sure that his sufferings are the 'épreuves de l'initiation sacrée'
(L 810), he can achieve mystical awareness of his oneness with nature
and its harmonies:

des découpures de feuilles, des couleurs, des odeurs et des sons, je voyais
ressortir des harmonies jusqu'alors inconnues. 'Comment, me disais-je, ai-
je pu exister si longtemps hors de la nature et sans m'identifier à elle? Tout
vit, tout agit, tout se correspond; les rayons magnétiques émanés de moi-
même ou des autres traversent sans obstacle la chaîne infinie des choses
créées; c'est un réseau transparent qui couvre le monde, et dont les fils déliés
se communiquent de proche en proche aux planètes et aux étoiles. Captif
en ce moment sur la terre, je m'entretiens avec le chœur des astres, qui prend
part à mes joies et à mes douleurs!'

(L 810.)

This sense of participation in nature (from flowers to stars!) is
significantly different from the fearful warnings of *Vers dorés*: yet
here too the awareness of nature's life raises the question of salvation
or damnation. For if man is related with everything in nature his
thoughts and actions take on cosmic significance:

rien n'est impuissant dans l'univers: un atome peut tout dissoudre, un atome
peut tout sauver!

Ô terreur! voilà l'éternelle distinction du bon et du mauvais.

(L 811.)

Fearing that he is himself 'à jamais classé parmi les malheureux', he appeals to 'l'éternelle Isis, la mère et l'épouse sacrée' and receives the assurance of salvation: 'je me sentais revivre en elle'. The work ends with the same 'divinité de mes rêves', now figured as a star, announcing that 'l'épreuve . . . est venue à son terme'. She explains that he is now free of the 'anciennes illusions' which allowed him to think that 'la Vierge sainte' could die, as in the earlier vision of the woman with the 'rose trémière' engulfed in the death of nature. For salvation means believing that neither the woman, nor nature and its flowers, can finally die. During his initiation he has participated in the meaning of the universe and learnt that its flowers and stars speak of both salvation and damnation. Now he has achieved a vision of the triumphant invulnerability of the flower-like and star-like goddess for whom 'les feuillages et les fleurs s'élevaient sur la trace de ses pas' (L 736). In the quest for salvation, as in the pursuit of love, he has been able to 'passer les bornes du non-sens et de l'absurdité' and thus triumphantly to 'fixer [son] idéal'.

It is this love and worship of the divine femininity presiding over the individual's and nature's life which is evoked in the first two stanzas of the sonnet *Artémis*.[11] The second quatrain announces the necessity of love in an imperative maxim addressed (in the *vous* form after the *tu* of the previous line) to woman, goddess, and poet: 'Aimez qui vous aima du berceau dans la bière' (L 702). This calls on the divine femininity who manifests herself both as woman and goddess to love the suitor/worshipper who loved her in her earthly form throughout her lifetime. But his own love for her must also last a lifetime (from *his* birth to *his* death) since woman and goddess have always mystically loved him, and now do so as one female figure: 'Celle que j'aimai seul m'aime encor tendrement'. His love for the woman seemed unrequited ('j'aimai seul') and ended by death ('j'aimai'), yet he loved her more truly than other suitors ('j'aimai seul') and now affirms that his love is (and always was) returned, in a mode at once mystical and tender. The next line emphasizes that the goddess who received the beloved woman (and will receive him) in death 'couronnée de roses' is indeed identical with the earthly woman: 'C'est la mort — ou la morte . . . ' His love for her is 'délice' and 'tourment' because it has involved the lover's *épreuves* of doubt and loss as well as joy, and the worshipper's fear of damnation as well as hope of salvation. This woman's rose is more than a figure for sentimental love or piety, for 'La rose qu'elle tient, c'est la *Rose trémière*'. She is the goddess who presides over nature as well as over humanity: her '*Rose trémière*' recalls the shared vulnerability of women, men, and the flowers of nature ('ô tourment!') but also their regeneration ('Ô délice!'), for this is a transcendental *Rose* (capitalized and italicized) symbolizing the goddess's power. With its many flowers on a single stem, this flower is a figure for the plural identity of the goddess herself, reflected in nature's fertile multiplicity but also variously embodied (as Artémis, Isis, etc.) in religious thought and successively embodied in human women.[12] It thus becomes an emblem for the vision evoked in the first quatrain:

> La Treizième revient . . . C'est encor la première;
> Et c'est toujours la seule, — ou c'est le seul moment;
> Car es-tu reine, ô toi! la première ou dernière?

The cyclical movement of the *ballet des heures* reflects the recurrence of death and regeneration in nature, like the flowers 'l'une après l'autre écloses / Dans l'éternel hymen de la nuit et du jour'. But it also attributes regenerative powers to the goddess in the eternal 'seul moment' of the poet's vision of love and mystical reality. He cannot distinguish between successive manifestations of her since she is always 'la seule', and will remain uniquely herself throughout his experience of time and nature: just as the *Rose* is the salvific archetype of the vulnerable flowers of nature, so Artémis is the 'type éternel' redeeming the poet's experience of 'des femmes diverses'.[13] A deleted title for this sonnet was 'Artémis ou le Rêve et la Vie', for the poet is here seeking once more to 'fixer [son] idéal' and make his 'Rêve' preside victoriously over life.

ii. Flowers of 'la Vie' and poetry

In these various texts of poetry and prose Nerval seeks to present his 'idéal' or 'Rêve' as a vision of salvation in relation to which he himself must be receptive: like the flowers or stars of nature, woman and the goddess are here perceived as powerful presences outside himself whose blessing he desires. Yet in order to receive the grace and love they represent he must prove himself worthy by undergoing the sufferings of initiation, and his survival through these *épreuves* requires an active sense of purpose. Elsewhere in his work, in fact, the writer developed a rhetoric of his own suffering yet purposeful nature to express his perception of his own active role in the construction of the 'Rêve' of his art. Where the salvific myth of grace and love starts from an appreciation of women and nature, this rhetoric of the poet's self begins with the rejection of a supreme father or male God. On this apparently psychological basis Nerval constructs a theory of the artist indispensable to the spiritual and literary synthesis of his most remarkable last texts. Indeed the flower rhetoric of the latter cannot be understood without some awareness of the poet's earlier creative use of this *hantise du père* in contexts where fire imagery is more common than that of flowers.

In *Le Christ aux Oliviers* (1844/1853/1854) the rejection of the father is implicit in the epigraph ('Dieu est mort! . . . vous n'avez plus de père!') and leads to scepticism not only about Christianity but about the possibility of any meaning in a God-less world: 'nul esprit n'existe en ces immensités' (L 706). Instead of the eye of God there is an empty socket like a black sun ('une orbite / Vaste, noire et sans fond'), and every aspect of nature is now seen as controlled only by 'Froide Nécessité!'. The Christ who makes this realization is thus the 'éternelle victime' in a new sense, a poet or 'fou' sacrificing himself in a meaningless world, yet sublime in his courage in facing the empty truth: he becomes the new 'dieu' (or 'démon') replacing the father God.

Nerval was to develop similar themes in the other poems of *Les Chimères*.[14] Thus *Horus* (1854) takes up the theme of the dying God ('le dieu Kneph'), here rejected by his wife Isis in favour of Horus, who is her son by Osiris and a pupil of Hermes. While Kneph is a god of destructive volcanoes vomiting icy fire, Isis is a goddess of water, rainbows, and regeneration: her son represents 'l'esprit nouveau' which rejects the old patriarchal order (Christianity) for a new world in which nature (Isis) and mystery (Hermes) are honoured. In *Delfica* (1854) the desire for the return of the pagan gods (displaced by the Judaeo-Christian father God) is explicit. The poem invokes Apollo and his oracles in its title and other references, and announces:

> Ils reviendront ces dieux que tu pleures toujours!
> Le temps va ramener l'ordre des anciens jours.

(L 701.)

In this hopeful context volcanic fire represents the hope of change ('La terre a tressailli d'un souffle prophétique'), and evocation of the Mediterranean expresses nostalgia for the oracular mystery of a non-patriarchal religion here represented by Apollo the god of art. This sonnet is closely related to *Myrtho* (1854), equally marked by the nostalgia for the south and for paganism. Here too volcanic fire suggests imminent change ('Je sais pourquoi là-bas le volcan s'est rouvert . . . ') and here the poet explicitly associates the return of the old gods with his own art: 'Car la muse m'a fait l'un des fils de la Grèce' (L 696). The landscape of the Posilippo links the theme of fire (it is 'de mille feux brillant') with that of poetry ('les rameaux du laurier de Virgile'), and the poem finally joins Christian northern modernity and pagan South in a symbolic (flower-code) union: 'le pâle Hortensia s'unit au Myrte vert!'

This is a poet defining himself as a 'fils de la Grèce', devotee of nature, fire, and mystery, rather than as an obedient son of the father God, seen as dead, cold, or destructive. In *Antéros*, indeed, he presents himself explicitly as a rebel against Jehovah 'le dieu vainqueur', following Satan 'le vengeur' and his 'race' of rebels rejected by Jehovah/Zeus and fighting on with 'tête indomptée' and 'rage au cœur' (L 699). They resemble the Prometheus of *La Pandora* (1854) who in his concern for men stole 'le feu du ciel' from Jupiter, and suffered his punishment (L 745-6). Here is a figure implacably opposed to the father God and suffering *épreuves* as a consequence: the fire which he steals is a sign of the new order, of destruction and creativity. It is like the volcanic fire in *Delfica* and *Myrtho* signalling the replacement of Jehovah's reign by a pagan pantheon embracing the mysteries of nature and the goddess, the new reign of creativity for which Antéros, 'protégeant tout seul' his mother the earth, must undergo the initiation of the underworld ('plonge trois fois dans les eaux du Cocyte'). The poet's rebellion against the Father results in suffering which may be irremediable but is courageous, purposeful, and creative.

Nerval's most extended treatment of this personal myth of the poet is found in the 'Histoire de la Reine du Matin et de Soliman Prince des Génies' (1850) included in *Voyage en Orient* (1851). The artist-figure here is Adoniram, chief architect and metal-founder of Soliman's temple in Jerusalem, a man whose 'audacieux génie le plaçait au-dessus des hommes . . . Il participait de l'esprit de lumière et du génie des ténèbres!' (LV 567-8) King Soliman worships

Jehovah's 'tyrannie jalouse' and is himself jealous of the artist 'qui soumet les éléments et dompte la nature': he comments bitterly that 'Il n'est pas encore vainqueur . . . Adonaï seul est tout-puissant!' (LV 617) It is during the visit of the 'reine de Saba', Balkis, that Adoniram learns the truth about his nature. In a vision, Tubal-Kain reveals that they are both of the ancient race of rebels descended from 'Eblis, l'ange de lumière' (LV 626). It is a race hated by God, since 'ce Dieu jaloux a toujours repoussé le génie inventif et fécond' (LV 627), but it is also the race of men 'issus de l'élément du feu', whose creativity is more important than their suffering. By contrast Soliman, the 'fidèle serviteur d'Adonaï', is of the descent of Adam 'pétri du limon' (LV 626), and it is on this spiritual difference between the two races that the rest of the story depends. Thus Adoniram is accepted by the prophetic bird as the suitor of the queen (where Soliman had been refused) because he recognizes her as one of his race: 'esprit de lumière, ma sœur, mon épouse, enfin, je vous ai trouvée! Seuls sur la terre vous et moi, nous commandons à ce messager ailé des génies du feu dont nous sommes descendus.' (LV 644) The difference between the races even determines the end of the story, and the 'génies du feu' predict the 'perte de Soliman' and a future for the descendants of Adoniram: 'De toi naîtra une souche de rois qui restaureront sur la terre, en face de Jéhovah, le culte négligé du feu, cet élément sacré.' Nerval cannot insist enough on the importance of the cult of fire and the rejection of Jehovah, no doubt because they proclaim the creative purpose that gives meaning to the sufferings of the artist.

For Adoniram, certainly, membership of the race of Cain is primarily important to him as an artist and metal-worker, and the visit to the underworld realm of fire confirms the view of art he has long held. Earlier in the story he tells his pupil not to 'copier les fleurs et les feuillages' of nature 'avec froideur': 'l'art n'est point là: il consiste à créer'. For the real artist must go beyond nature and imagine 'des formes inconnues, des êtres innommés, des incarnations devant lesquelles l'homme a reculé' (LV 571). Thus Adoniram himself 'rêve toujours l'impossible' and 'son cerveau, bouillonnant comme une fournaise, enfantait des monstruosités sublimes' (LV 567). But it is in the underground fire-world at the centre of the earth that he sees a garden where the most nameless dreams of art are realized:

un jardin éclairé des tendres lueurs d'un feu doux, peuplé d'arbres inconnus dont le feuillage, formé de petites langues de flamme, projetait, au lieu d'ombre, des clartés plus vives sur le sol d'émeraude, diapré de fleurs d'une forme bizarre, et de couleurs d'une vivacité surprenante. Écloses du feu intérieur dans le terrain des métaux, ces fleurs en étaient les émanations les plus fluides et les plus pures. Ces végétations arborescentes du métal en fleur rayonnaient comme des pierreries, et exhalaient des parfums d'ambre, de benjoin, de myrrhe et d'encens.

(LV 625.)

Here is a vision of the forms of art as amazing flowers of fire— bizarre forms with unknown properties of light, heat, colour, texture, and smell. It is a vision too of the accomplishment of *le grand œuvre* of alchemy, by which metals become 'flowers' through the application of fire. In this fiery garden Adoniram learns how to complete his artistic enterprise successfully and how to recognize the wise queen Balkis as an 'esprit de lumière'. Adoniram's awareness of himself as a 'fils du feu' makes him able not merely to dream the impossible forms of his art, but to behold them as wonderful flowers of fire and realize his dreams in art and life.

Yet by the dialectical movement habitual to him, Nerval undermines this optimism by the end of the story, for Adoniram is murdered by the jealous king who serves Jehovah. It is no doubt with a similar sense of the limits of the possible that the narrator presents the alchemical vision in *Aurélia*. In a street in his dream he sees a poster bordered with '[des] guirlandes de fleurs si bien représentées et coloriées, qu'elles semblaient naturelles' (L 785). These flowers introduce the alchemical workshop where he watches a worker modelling in clay and fire an unknown animal (like a llama with wings) and pronounces it

ce chef-d'œuvre, où l'on semblait avoir surpris les secrets de la création divine. 'C'est que nous avons ici, me dit-on, le feu primitif qui anima les premiers êtres . . . ' Je vis aussi des travaux d'orfèvrerie où l'on employait deux métaux inconnus sur la terre . . . Les ornements n'étaient ni martelés, ni ciselés, mais se formaient, se coloraient et s'épanouissaient comme les plantes métalliques qu'on fait renaître de certaines mixtions chimiques.

When he asks if men could not be created in the same way in this workshop, he is reminded that the conditions of life cannot be changed:

Ces fleurs qui vous paraissent naturelles, cet animal qui semblera vivre, ne seront que des produits de l'art élevé au plus haut point de nos connaissances, et chacun les jugera ainsi.

(L 786.)

These flowers (like the animal) have been forged in the alchemical fire of creativity which seems like the primal act of 'création divine', but no one could take them for real flowers. The artist who deliberately seeks to realize the 'monstruosités sublimes' of an impossible new creation is setting himself up to defy the creator of the old order of nature. As a 'génie du feu' he can achieve amazing unknown forms and new flowers which seem natural; but no one is deceived, for the conditions of creation remain those governed by the cold destructive God who jealously brooks no rivals. The alchemical 'culte du feu', with its mysteries of recreated nature, is necessarily inimical to the father God who is the Creator.

In this sense, then, God the father represents for Nerval reality's revenge on the rival world of art. When Adoniram has been initiated into the truth about himself and his art by his 'descente aux enfers' (LV 634), and been accepted by Balkis, he must still face death from his jealous rival. The dream visions of *Aurélia* are themselves a descent into 'un souterrain vague qui s'éclaire peu à peu' (L 753). The reference to Orpheus at the opening of the second part ('Eurydice! Eurydice!' — 'Une seconde fois perdue!' (L 788)) shows that here too it is an artist making the 'descente aux enfers' (L 824). The sense of failure in his quest is not only due to loss of the beloved (whom he imagines consummating a 'marriage mystique' with his 'double') but also to his recognition (after the alchemical episode quoted above) of the limits of human creativity. Appropriately, the second part of *Aurélia* opens with a reference to God the father:

Pourquoi donc est-ce la première fois, depuis si longtemps, que je songe à *lui*? Le système fatal qui s'était créé dans mon esprit n'admettait pas cette royauté solitaire.

(L 788.)

His own 'système' is that of Aurélia and the mysteries of love, Isis and the mysteries of nature, and the alchemical mysteries of art. 'Cette royauté solitaire', on the other hand, is the God who controls the real world in which Aurélia is dead, the old gods a literary fiction, and art a delimited sub-world subordinate to the real.

In various passages in the second part of *Aurélia*, Nerval meditates on the possibility of reconciling himself with such a God, with repeated fearful assertions that he is damned and Aurélia along with him. Yet, by the end, this second *descente aux enfers* is revealed to have been one of the *épreuves* imposed by the goddess. The salvation of the close may be seen as bestowed either by a divinity combining the powers of God and goddess, or by a pagan nature-goddess redeeming the protagonist from Christian 'illusions'. But in either case the narrator has become able to proclaim that his 'système' has not prevented salvation. His initiation into the mysteries of dream, love, and nature has passed through trial and doubt to result in a 'mariage mystique' between 'la divinité de mes rêves' and 'cet époux préféré, ce roi de gloire' (whether the latter is himself, God, or both at once). At least in art, Orpheus is triumphant, for his 'système' has become inclusive enough to harmonize the Father's real world with the mysteries of the goddess, 'la Vie' with 'le Rêve'. In the words of one of Nerval's colleagues, 'l'amant d'Eurydice flotte toujours entre le ciel et la terre, entre les étoiles et les fleurs de la prairie'.[15] Following Orpheus, Nerval reconciles 'le ciel et la terre' in *Aurélia*, in a rhetoric which creates out of God's reality the mysterious starry flowers of nature and love, and the fiery flowers of art.

This Orphic rhetoric provides not only the subject but the main imagery of the two most highly wrought sonnets of *Les Chimères*, a title which resumes in itself the necessary tension between the regenerative illusions of art and the reality by which God denies them. In *Artémis*, after celebrating the divine femininity presiding over nature's life and his own destiny, the poet goes on to set out in the first two lines of the tercets the dialectic of 'le Rêve et la Vie':

> Sainte napolitaine aux mains pleines de feux,
> Rose au cœur violet, fleur de sainte Gudule.
>
> (L 702.)

The first two words ('Sainte napolitaine') already announce this, for the noun suggests both the religion of the father God and ideal femininity, while the adjective evokes a southern (pagan) region of fire. This line presents the conflict between God's real world and the fiery pagan mysteries of art, and the following line characterizes it further. The 'Rose au cœur violet' is an epithet for (or emblem of) both the southern saint (Rosalie) and the northern 'sainte Gudule', and for Nerval it focuses their resemblances and differences. In *Octavie* Saint Rosalie's statue, 'couronnée de roses violettes' was associated with sensual love, volcanic fire, and disillusionment, whereas Saint Gudule recalls the northern Octavie in the same story, cold in purity yet associated with Isis by playing her role. Here, as in *Octavie* the poet has recombined the characteristics associated with 'la Vie' (disillusion, coldness) and with 'le Rêve' (fire, love, illusion, Isis), but here he has forged them into a single flower. It is a flower which like the flowers and stars of *Sylvie* can express 'les deux moitiés d'un seul amour', and the poet's homage to different female qualities as manifestations of the same ideal femininity. In this sense it recapitulates a principal theme of the quatrains, just as 'fleur' and 'feux' together evoke the whole range of nature made accessible in the mysteries of the goddess. On the other hand the naming of 'fleur' and 'feux' also expresses (since both are natural phenomena symbolizing aspects of creativity) the terrible rivalry between nature and creativity: the Creator of nature's flowers and the 'feu primitif' denies the artist the freedom to forge a recreated nature of fiery flowers which he defiantly claims. In its context in these lines this 'fleur', which is also the 'Rose au cœur violet', takes up the connotations of the *Rose trémière* (the regenerative beneficence of love and nature) only to colour them with irony.

For the composite 'sainte' is more complex than the goddess/ woman evoked in the quatrains (by the Christian reference alone) and she now stands in an ambiguous relationship to the poet, which becomes even more equivocal in the question of the next line: 'As-tu trouvé ta croix dans le désert des cieux?' This may be a fearful question implying doubt about the earthly beloved's hope of survival after death (has her death proved a cross without resurrection, and can this 'fleur' survive in the 'désert' of death?). Or it may be a fearful question musing on the irony of a death which means regeneration for her while (by reversed attribution) it represents only a 'croix' for her lover, her heaven his 'désert' of loss. But it might also be a sarcastic question directed against the Christian aspect of the composite 'sainte', for '(les) cieux' are deserted and God is dead. In any case the uncertain tone and the Christian vocabulary of this line lead directly into a stronger affirmation:

> Roses blanches, tombez! vous insultez nos dieux,
> Tombez, fantômes blancs, de votre ciel qui brûle.

The white roses are Christian, since they insult the plural gods of paganism (the gods of the poets), and the lines can scarcely be read as anything but a scathing attack on the Christian God and the white

saints of the cold northern religion which is 'désert' rather than
'feux'. Where in the first tercet the poet blended together the
attributes of God and goddess, he now peremptorily separates them
in order to denounce 'votre ciel'. Imperatively he makes God and
his 'saintes' fall from their cold heaven and destroys it with creative
fire ('votre ciel qui brûle'). For the poet can finally only value
the fiery attributes of the southern saint, as the final line (beside
which Nerval wrote 'Rosalie' in the Éluard manuscript) makes clear:
' — La sainte de l'abîme est plus sainte à mes yeux!' This is
the 'sainte' who is (like Balkis) a kindred 'génie du feu' to the
poet, now seen as the almighty patroness of the fiery underworld
('abîme') of creativity: she is 'plus sainte' than God's saints because
she is ranged with the poet against the cold destructiveness of
the real.

By the end of the poem, then, it is as the guarantor of his own
poetic vocation that the poet celebrates the goddess: she is 'plus sainte
à [ses] yeux' because he speaks as a poet. It is as his muse that she
has loved him in the 'abîme' of his life ('du berceau dans la bière'),
has guided him in his *descente aux enfers* and can save him 'dans
les ténèbres de l'Achéron' (in the words of Isis herself). And unlike
God the father, the goddess of the *Rose trémière* can guarantee the
regeneration both of the poet and of his beloved without destroying
the 'feux' or the dark roses of his creativity. The conflict expressed
in the tercets thus ends in a clear victory for the mysterious flowers
of love, nature, and the 'abîme', which alone are life-giving for the
poet. Yet the poem is also a triumphant synthetic achievement
including reality in its very 'système'. For Artemis/Diana is the
goddess not only of the underworld but of chastity, and like Gudule,
Octavie, and other 'roses blanches' recalls the poet chastely devoted
to the lost beloved as a 'veuf', transposing the grief of queen
Arthemisa (Artémise) for her husband Mausolus. The poet does not
deny reality but includes it in his integrated Orphic vision of creativity
('le Rêve') blossoming like a dark fiery rose in the sterile 'désert'
of real experience ('la Vie').

El Desdichado, originally entitled 'Le Destin', relates this vision
more closely to the poet's own destiny. For where *Artémis* answers
the question of the poet's identity ('Es-tu roi, toi le seul ou le dernier
amant?') in terms of the nature and attributes of the divine patroness,
here the poet is primarily concerned to define himself as lover, son,
and poet:

> Je suis le ténébreux, — le veuf, — l'inconsolé,
> Le prince d'Aquitaine à la tour abolie:
> Ma seule *étoile* est morte, — et mon luth constellé
> Porte le *soleil* noir de la *Mélancolie.*
>
> (L 693.)

As a lover he is unhappy (*desdichado*), 'veuf' and 'inconsolé' like the Brisacier of Nerval's *Roman tragique* of 1844 ('le prince ignoré, l'amant mystérieux, le déshérité, le banni de liesse, le beau ténébreux'), and like the character 'Le Destin' in Scarron's *Roman comique* he is unhappy because of 'une *étoile* fugitive qui m'abandonnait seul dans la nuit de ma destinée'.[16] Since his loss of the beloved woman ('Ma seule *étoile* est morte') this star of love has become for him a '*soleil* noir' in death, her memory now radiant with sadness ('la *Mélancolie*'). As a son he feels rejected by his father (*desdichado*), cut off from his inheritance ('la tour abolie'), and without parental consolation ('inconsolé'). But despite this sense of loss and vulnerability he survives ('Je suis'), and is a poet ('mon luth'). As a poet he has Adoniram's 'génie des ténèbres' ('le ténébreux') and like him is of Cainite race proud to be disinherited by the supreme Father who has destroyed the (southern) tower symbolizing his descent as he destroyed the works of Enoch and Adoniram's temple. The title *El Desdichado* is in this sense a boast of noble lineage and the prince-poet's 'luth' blazes with fiery creativity ('constellé') defiantly emblazoned with the fire of the 'abîme' (' le *soleil* noir'). This is the fire ambitious to burn up God's heaven ('votre ciel qui brûle') until God's eye becomes only an 'orbite . . . noire', but the poet like other 'génies du feu' must acknowledge with noble melancholy the cold omnipotence of 'le dieu vainqueur'. Melancholy is therefore a condition of being for this 'déshérité', for whom the only acceptable salvation is one that does not deny that he is 'banni de liesse' by his proud vocation.

All his experience is (and must remain) that of 'la nuit du tombeau', the underground realm of loss, which is also paradoxically that of creative fire. Thus he asks the goddess, 'toi qui m'as consolé', to grant him the salvation appropriate to a poet:

> Rends-moi le Pausilippe et la mer d'Italie,
> La *fleur* qui plaisait tant à mon cœur désolé,
> Et la treille où le pampre à la rose s'allie.

For salvation lies for him in the creative fire and underground *épreuves* of poetry, associated now with the region around Naples which in *Octavie* was the landscape of the temptation of death (welcoming him as Isis) and the recall to life (celebrated by the visit to Isis' temple). Salvation lies therefore in the initiation into the life and creativity beyond loss: 'la *fleur*'. This is a flower deprived of designation (in an *œuvre* where naming is a potent figure of rhetoric) in order to gain all possible meaning, itself a 'tombeau' to be filled with poetic intensity. Like the *Rose trémière* it alludes to the mysterious regeneration of nature and love despite their vulnerability, and like the 'rose au cœur violet' it recalls (by its juxtaposition with the fire implied in the preceding line) the poet's vocation to create fiery flowers in defiance of reality. These senses are also connoted by *l'ancolie* (the flower suggested by rhyme with '*Mélancolie*' and noted by Nerval in the margin of the Éluard manuscript) with its associations of melancholy and mysticism; this flower's normal flower-dictionary sense of *la folie* (another hidden rhyme) provides further commentary on the vocation of the poet. Like the 'rose' lovingly intertwined with the 'pampre', the *fleur* signifies the possibility of mystical union and creative growth through the *épreuves* of 'la nuit du tombeau', through the 'non-sens' and 'absurdité' (*la folie*) of the poet's initiation. Indeed it owes its very brightness to the darkness of suffering and meaninglessness in which it shines, itself an '*étoile* . . . dans la nuit du tombeau' or a '*soleil* noir'. Thus he has already found the salvation he seeks by the very enterprise of defining himself as a lover and poet, and the questions of the next line contain their own answers: 'Suis-je Amour ou Phébus? . . . Lusignan ou Biron?'. For he is both love (despite the apparent loss of it) and creative fire (despite the suffering creativity entails). Like Eros and Lusignan he has won and lost a 'mariage mystique' with a goddess (Eros' Psyche) or a fairy (Lusignan's Melusine); like Biron/Byron he is a rebellious lover/troubadour and like Phoebus/Apollo he is a fiery supreme poet.

These proud rhetorical questions delineate a poet-lover like Orpheus and lead to an unqualified affirmation of the unity of 'le Rêve et la Vie'. First the poet proclaims his 'mariage mystique' with the goddess as an experienced fact of the recent past:

> Mon front est rouge encor du baiser de la reine;
> J'ai rêvé dans la grotte où nage la sirène . . .

These moments of union with manifestations of the goddess have been mystical indeed, and are rewards for the poet's fidelity. Yet his triumphs in the underground realm are finally his own: 'Et j'ai deux fois vainqueur traversé l'Achéron'. More victorious than Orpheus (who returned only once from his *descente aux enfers*) this is a poet whose salvation is his star-figured 'luth' bright with creative power blazing in the darkness. It is his 'lyre' itself which effects the mystical union between poet and transcendental woman, making her finally sigh or cry out the song of the poet's own triumph. In this poem which is his own 'tombeau' Nerval makes the flowers and stars of nature and love sing with his own voice, the 'soupirs' and 'cris' of poetry.

In this way Nerval shows his own proud awareness of the unprecedentedly allusive and intense poetic language of these sonnets 'composés dans [un] état de rêverie *super-naturaliste*'.[17] It is a language of mystical *rêverie* which, beyond 'les bornes du non-sens et de l'absurdité', triumphantly manages to 'fixer [son] idéal'. The poetic prose of the *Mémorables* achieves a similar poetic goal in its expression of Nerval's Orphic ideal. And here too flower and star express the meaning of nature and love which is poetry itself:

Sur les montagnes de l'Himalaya une petite fleur est née — Ne m'oubliez pas! — Le regard chatoyant d'une étoile s'est fixé un instant sur elle, et sa réponse s'est fait entendre dans un doux langage étranger. — *Myosotis*!
   Une perle d'argent brillait dans le sable; une perle d'or étincelait au ciel . . . Le monde était créé.

(L 817.)

On the heights of mystical awareness the star's glance is answered by the flower's language, a language mystical yet tender, strange (*Myosotis*) yet commonplace ('Ne m'oubliez pas'). This is the language of nature's communication with itself (flower and star), yet it is the speech of poetic creation: 'Le monde était créé'. And the world of poetry is the world in which the dreams of love and mysticism ('Chastes amours, divins soupirs!') become real. In this text (perhaps his last), Nerval makes explicit the supreme synthesis achieved in *Aurélia*, the 'mariage mystique' between God and the goddess. The narrator proclaims that the goddess is 'si grande qu'elle pardonne au monde, et si bonne qu'elle m'a pardonné', and, at the moment of supreme realization,

j'ai revu celle que j'avais aimée transfigurée et radieuse. Le ciel s'est ouvert dans toute sa gloire, et j'y ai lu le mot pardon signé du sang de Jésus-Christ.

Une étoile a brillé tout à coup et m'a révélé le secret du monde des mondes. Hosannah! paix à la terre et gloire aux cieux!

(L 819.)

These lines express the amazing psychological and spiritual synthesis towards which Gérard's 'système' seems always to have tended, in a language remarkable for 'le mérite de l'expression'. The whole of nature sings of love in an Orphic language of flowers, stars, and creativity:

l'air vibre, et la lumière brise harmonieusement les fleurs naissantes. Un soupir, un frisson d'amour sort du sein gonflé de la terre, et le chœur des astres se déroule dans l'infini; il s'écarte et revient sur lui-même, se resserre et s'épanouit, et sème au loin les germes d'une création nouvelle.

(L 819.)

So the final flower figure celebrates both mystical and poetic achievement: 'la fleur d'anxoka, la fleur soufrée, — la fleur éclatante du soleil!' (L 820). Here is the realization of that other dream which had long haunted Gérard—that nature and love could be redeemed from transience. It is expressed in his last *carnet* in a mystical variant of the *carpe diem*: 'Les plus belles fleurs ont perdu leur odeur: elles la retrouveront au paradis' (L 863). The flowers of Gérard's literary expression have indeed played an indispensable part in his enterprise of achieving salvation through poetic language.

II. The Hellenist Flowers of Parnassian Poetics

On peut dater d'André Chénier la poésie moderne . . . Un frais souffle venu de la Grèce traversa les imaginations; l'on respira avec délices ces fleurs au parfum enivrant qui auraient trompé les abeilles de l'Hymette . . . Ce retour à l'antiquité, éternellement jeune, fit éclore un nouveau printemps.

(T. Gautier, *Rapport sur le mouvement poétique*, 1868.)[18]

i. Flowers in the development of Hellenist poetics

The period 1840–70 saw the development and maturation of those Hellenizing tendencies in poetry which were called Parnassian after 1866. From the vantage-point of 1868 Gautier could imply that all poetry since Chénier had been in some sense Hellenist. Romantic poetry belies any such assertion, and although Chénier's Hellenizing neo-Classicism had been hailed as an inspiration by the young Romantics, it was never a major influence on their poetry. Yet the pastoral tendencies in Romanticism were fertile ground for any development which enabled poetry to turn away from contemporary life. Chénier himself could define poetry as incompatible with urban society:

> Venez. J'ai fui la ville aux Muses si contraire,
> Et l'écho fatigué des clameurs du vulgaire.
> Sur les pavés poudreux d'un bruyant carrefour
> Les poétiques fleurs n'ont jamais vu le jour.[19]

During the eighteen-twenties and thirties many Romantic poets had expressed the flowery attractions of pastoral evasion, and none more strongly than Vigny:

> Pars courageusement, laisse toutes les villes; . . .
>
> Les grands bois et les champs sont de vastes asiles, . . .
>
> Marche à travers les champs une fleur à la main.[20]

Most Romantic poets agreed that the flowers of nature had a privileged association with the flowers of poetry.

Although this Romantic consensus did not in itself imply any Hellenizing tendency, some writers associated their love of nature with ancient Greece. Lamartine could appear to deny interest in it: 'Que m'importe Agamemnon et son empire? . . . Je voudrais voir seulement la vallée d'Arcadie; j'aime mieux un arbre, une source sous le rocher, un laurier-rose au bord du fleuve . . . que le monument d'un de ces royaumes classiques.'[21] Yet this passage in fact affirms the pastoral option (as against 'empire' or 'royaume') in the landscape of its Classical origins. Musset, in any case, had no hesitation about acclaiming ancient Greece as an ideal alternative to the present:

> Grèce, ô mère des arts, terre d'idolâtrie,
> De mes vœux insensés éternelle patrie,
> J'étais né pour ces temps où les fleurs de ton front
> Couronnaient dans les mers l'azur de l'Hellespont.[22]

These flowers are attributes of Greek art and nature together, as if the ideal landscape must inevitably be associated with artistic beauty. Quinet makes this point explicitly in 1833 when imagining Athens defending itself before God for its love of beauty:

Si je levais les yeux, les étoiles germaient dans mes nuits de printemps; leurs
fleurs embaumées se retournaient vers moi sur leurs tiges d'azur pour me
dire: 'Vois-tu . . . je suis plus belle que toi . . . ' . . . Seigneur, j'étais jalouse
des étoiles . . . Pour vous plaire autant qu'elles, j'ai cueilli dans le marbre
mes guirlandes d'acanthe . . . [23]

Quinet's reference to flower-like stars validates the Greek sense of
beauty by finding in it an almost religious feeling for nature. For
Ménard too Greek culture was closely related to nature:

> La race des héros naissait sur les hauteurs;
> Et les peuples nouveaux descendaient dans les plaines
> Et sous leur pas germaient les hymnes et les fleurs, . . .
>
> L'hyacinthe mêlait ses arômes dans l'air.[24]

Renan was to put the same idea in discursive form in 1853: 'La
mythologie grecque . . . n'est que le reflet des sensations jeunes et
délicates . . . *L'homme primitif voyait la nature avec les yeux de
l'enfant.* A peine séparé de la nature, il conversait avec elle, il lui
parlait et entendait sa voix.[25] By attributing the origins of Hellenic
culture to a knowledge of nature's language (the *langage des fleurs*
. . .), Renan is affirming here the widely held view that Greekness
is a special mode of closeness to nature. And this is apparent even
in the culture's post-history, according to Quinet in 1842: 'Et quand
tout est fini, voyez comment la terre lui est légère! Les fleurs croissent
de toutes parts sur ses ruines. La sérénité s'attache à ses restes.'[26]
The flowers covering Greek ruins are figures for the serene naturalness of a culture which not surprisingly exerts an appeal as a pastoral
alternative to contemporary society.

Gautier's d'Albert had, after all, evoked the Hellenic past as an
alternative to the present: 'Je suis un homme des temps homériques;
— le monde où je vis n'est pas le mien, et je ne comprends rien à
la société qui m'entoure.'[27] Nor was Houssaye in 1852 the last to
make his poetic persona complain of sharing the same 'mal du pays,
car son pays est un autre temps'. Yet around 1840 the Greek
alternative was not self-evidently a viable one. Even Gautier could
doubt the relevance of classical inspiration for present art:

> — Comment la belle Muse antique,
> Droite sous les longs plis de sa blanche tunique,
> Avec ses cheveux noirs en deux flots déroulés
> Comme le firmament de fleurs d'or étoilés, . . .

> Pourrait-elle descendre auprès de moi sur terre?[28]

Yet in 1839 Sainte-Beuve had pronounced on the viability of classical culture with some prescience:

> Paganisme immortel, es-tu mort? On le dit.
> Mais Pan tout bas s'en moque et la Sirène en rit.[29]

In the eclectic literary climate of the early eighteen-forties, however, it was not at all clear how a revived Hellenism was to be assimilated, or which ideological tendency of the period could recuperate it to best advantage. Was it to be allied, for example, with *l'art social* or with *l'art pour l'art*, with pantheism, Fourierism, or even Christianity?

This ideological ambiguity is illustrated in the work of two writers early associated with Hellenism: Laprade (whose first poetry appeared under titles like *Éleusis* and *Psyché*) and Banville (who called his 1842 volume *Les Cariatides*). Both present themselves as pastoralists, Laprade claiming that the poet is a 'géant à l'étroit dans les villes' and Banville advising him to turn to nature:

> Eh bien! mêle ta vie à la verte forêt! . . .
> Cueille la fleur agreste au bord du précipice.[30]

They both use Hellenism as a model for communion with nature. Laprade can claim that

> Le monde est plein de Dieux cachés sous mille noms;
> C'est ce chœur qui nous parle et que nous comprenons.

Yet he is unwilling to give the Greek gods any metaphysical status:

> Vers l'Olympe désert ne tourne plus les yeux,
> Regarde dans ton cœur, c'est là que sont les Dieux!
> Cueille les fleurs et l'or pour vêtir ces idoles.[31]

Banville fears that the Greek gods of nature have departed ('Nature, où sont tes Dieux?') but is determined to bring them back:

> Viens! ceux qu'on a crus morts, nous les retrouverons! . . .
> Et celle-là surtout, vierge délicieuse,
> Qui fait grandir, aimer, naître, sourdre, germer,
> Fleurir, tout ce qui vit et vient tout embaumer.[32]

At the same time, both poets combine the cult of antiquity with

Fourier's social optimism. Thus Laprade ends *Éleusis* with a Utopian appeal:

> Un monde va s'ouvrir tout peuplé d'harmonies . . .
>
> Marchez vers l'orient en troupes fraternelles;
> Pour un hôte nouveau cueillez des fleurs nouvelles.[33]

By 1846 Banville too could envisage the *harmonies* of nature and Hellenism revived in a modern Fourierist *Harmonie*. The poet seeks to 'Reconquérir la joie perdue' by singing 'sous les divins noms que la Grèce leur a trouvés, la Beauté, la Force et l'Amour',[34] so that

> Tout ce qu'on pleura,
> Dévouement, liberté, génie,
> Tout refleurira
> Pour le règne de l'Harmonie.[35]

For Banville too the flowers of Fourierist optimism, no less than those of pastoral or pantheism, are compatible with the nostalgia for Hellenism.

The young Leconte de Lisle was equally eclectic, yet he early revealed a psychological bias of his own. Thus while still connected with Romantic liberal catholicism he could praise 'Chaque fleuron divin de l'empire du beau' while announcing his stoicism: 'le rêveur sacré . . . Jette un dernier sourire en face du tombeau'.[36] He presents nature as the pastoral embodiment of this stoical idealism in another early poem:

> Les larges nénuphars, les lianes errantes,
> Blancs archipels, flottaient enlacés sur les eaux,
> Et dans leurs profondeurs vives et transparentes
> Brillait un autre ciel où nageaient les oiseaux.[37]

This setting is starkly contrasted with the suffering of the human world, however, for the dead man near the fountain ('libre des maux soufferts') is seen as irrelevant to nature and its flowers:

> Sur les blancs nénuphars l'oiseau ployait ses ailes
> . . . sans penser aux morts . . .

This poet's concern with psychological detachment (already an extreme form of the pastoral enterprise) was compatible with his adopting both Fourierism and Hellenism together in 1845. Thus he hails Fourier in an ode of 1846 ('un monde a germé dans ta tête,

/ Un monde a fleuri dans ton cœur') and salutes Hellenism along
with Fourierist doctrine in *L'Idylle antique*:

> Brises des mois fleuris, brises harmonieuses,
> . . . versez-nous toujours la grâce et l'harmonie,
> Doux concerts de l'Antiquité![38]

Here once more the poet has used flower imagery to signal an
idealizing refusal of the present reality, now in the name of a better
Hellenist past and an equally harmonious Utopian future. And for
him, as for Laprade and Banville, Hellenism had its part to play
in the eclectic search for a flowery alternative to present society, this
desire to 'gravir l'âpre montagne où fleurit l'idéal'.[39]

Hellenism was certainly capable of being adapted to other currents
of thought, whether escapist or meliorist, stoical, pantheistic, or
Utopian. Like them it embodied a flower-like ideal *harmonie*
contrasting with the present, and in itself the concept of *harmonie*
only invited ideological synthesis. But for writers concerned to
produce 'l'art serein qui crée un ciel nouveau' (in Laprade's phrase
of 1840), Hellenism had a special virtue. It could provide a version
of *harmonie* which emphasized serenity, proportion, and formal
order — qualities as relevant to aesthetic as to ideological consider-
ations. Louis Ménard later summarized these values as 'La notion
divine particulière à la Grèce . . . l'idée de la loi, c'est-à-dire
de l'ordre, de la proportion, de l'harmonie.'[40] And Nerval noted in
1845 how starkly these qualities contrast with general experience:
'Le ciel mythologique rayonnait d'un trop pur éclat, il était d'une
beauté trop précise et trop nette, il respirait trop le bonheur,
l'abondance et la sérénité, pour s'imposer longtemps au monde agité
et souffrant.'[41] Such formal qualities could indeed be hailed as a
means of salvation from confusion or disorder, as when Louis de
Ronchaud in 1840 praised 'la forme . . . sans laquelle tout est
chaos'.[42] And Gautier, notably, had insisted in *Mademoiselle de
Maupin* that formal beauty was to be appreciated in itself as a source
of happiness: 'J'adore sur toutes choses la beauté de la forme; — la
beauté pour moi, c'est la Divinité visible, c'est le bonheur palpable,
c'est le ciel descendu sur la terre.[43] He had, too, memorably associated formal beauty with Greek art, in many passages of the same
work tending towards a manifesto of Hellenist formalism: 'Je conçois
parfaitement le fol enthousiasme des Grecs pour la beauté'.[44] Other
currents of aesthetic thought during the decade of the eighteen-thirties

supported this formalism. Kantian aesthetics and the diffuse polemic about *l'art pour l'art* had popularized *le beau* and *la forme* as values which could be considered apart from other aspects of art.[45] So too academic discussion of *le beau idéal* was making increasing reference to Greek sculpture, and the practical example of artists like David d'Angers and Ingres had encouraged an appreciation of Greek plastic values.[46] By the late thirties aesthetic opinion was as ready to welcome the formal order and serenity of Greek art as ideological thought was eager to appropriate Greek ideal *harmonie*.

Flower imagery was to play a significant part in the growing appreciation of Greek formal beauty. In 1835 G. Planche defined the attributes of beauty in somewhat Kantian terms but with reference to flowers and Greek art: 'Quels sont les éléments de la beauté elle-même? . . . l'ordre et le mouvement réunis . . . La beauté du Parthénon et la beauté du dahlia se composent des mêmes éléments.'[47] But poets soon began to relate Greek beauty of form to the flowers of pastoral serenity, even in the apparently un-pastoral context of sculpture. Thus Hugo in *Au statuaire David* (1840) insists on the need for purity of form in terms which relate Greek sculpture to pastoral florality:

> Il faut que, Vénus chaste, elle sorte de l'onde,
> Semant au loin la vie et l'amour sur le monde,
> Et faisant autour d'elle, en son superbe essor, . . .
>
> De toute herbe une fleur, de tout œil une étoile![48]

And Gautier makes an even more explicit parallel between Greek sculpture and the pastoral refusal of political life:

> Vos discours sont très-beaux, mais j'aime mieux des roses.
> Les antiques Vénus, aux gracieuses poses,
> Que l'on voit, étalant leur sainte nudité,
> Réaliser en marbre un rêve de beauté,
> Ont plus fait, à mon sens, pour le bonheur du monde,
> Que tous ces vains travaux où votre orgueil se fonde; . . .
>
> Le lis ne file pas et ne travaille pas;
> Il lui suffit d'avoir la blancheur éclatante.[49]

Just as roses and the lily are emblems of pastoral, so classical sculpture is the plastic realization of a 'rêve de beauté' also contrasting with the real world. Banville too relates Greek sculpture to pastorality in *Prosopopée d'une Vénus*, where a statue of Venus is given words decrying present society and its art:

> En ce temps où la fleur se cache sous les herbes,
> Nul ne sait le secret de nos formes superbes,
> Nul ne sait revêtir quelque rêve éclatant
> De contours gracieux, et dans son cœur n'entend
> L'harmonie imposante et la sainte musique
> Où chantent les accords de la beauté physique![50]

Here the *harmonie* of beautiful plastic form is also that of a flowery Greek world unlike the present, and Laprade invokes a similar vision when addressing the Belvedere Apollo in *Éleusis* (1841):

> Tout fleurit sur tes pas! Tu fais croître et transformes,
> Ô dieu de l'harmonie, ô roi des belles formes! . . .
>
> Et sur ce monde neuf, planant en souverain,
> Tu jettes sur ton œuvre un œil fier et serein.[51]

In all these passages Greek sculpture represents the flowering of beautiful form and naturalness together, the *harmonie* of plastic beauty and psychological serenity, and the aesthetic realization of a dream of ideal otherness. Indeed here the forms of Greek sculpture are a continuation of pastoral by other means, and the flower figure serves as emblem both of their superlative beauty and of their difference from contemporary reality.

For all that, the question of precisely how a programmatic formalism was related to the struggling and suffering of real life was not to be easily resolved. Not all Greek sculpture, after all, represented Venus or Apollo, and a statue like that of Niobe suffering the loss of her children could scarcely stand for an ideal alternative to present troubles. Gautier presents this statue in 1838 as a 'fantôme de marbre' and a 'symbole muet de l'humaine misère', and the poem distances human suffering by concentrating on the marble 'symbole' itself.[52] This was one resolution of the problematic relation between formalism and disordered emotion. But it was not the one Laprade had in mind when he wrote these lines in 1840:

> Rêve de marbres grecs et de tableaux romains . . .
>
> Poursuis la couleur nette et la forme finie,
> Va dorer ta statue au soleil d'Ionie,

Apprends des maîtres grecs les secrets du contour
Sans fermer ton oreille aux maîtres de l'amour,
Fais ton livre émouvant mais de style sévère,
Beau vase athénien, plein de fleurs du Calvaire.[53]

Laprade is here suggesting that the main lesson of Greek formalism is an aesthetic one relating only to the severe stylistic control of an emotive content perhaps entirely un-Greek — emotionally stirring, Romantic, or 'Christian'. Amédée René suggested in 1841 yet another strategy:

Niobé! Niobé! la grande désolée . . .

Comme tu sais souffrir! comme tu portes, ô reine,
Des extrêmes douleurs l'impassible fierté!
Et comme tu maintiens la forme souveraine
Qui t'enveloppe encor de sa divinité . . .

Ô Sphinx de la souffrance, impénétrable et beau,
Que rend si fièrement la sévère camée,
Ou ce marbre éclatant, froid comme le tombeau![54]

This Niobe is no longer a 'symbole muet': the severe control of formalism is now given psychological extension and the detached formal beauty of the 'marbre éclatant' expresses the moral and emotional detachment of 'l'impassible fierté'. Did Hellenist formalism, which promised an art above ideology and beyond emotion, necessarily imply a stoical bias of its own?

The very title of Banville's first volume *Les Cariatides*, as well as its title poem,[55] seem to promise aesthetic and emotional detachment. The poem insists on the formal beauty of the Caryatids: they are 'filles de Paros' created by 'le sage ciseleur' as part of a 'monument' with 'radieuses lignes'. They are, too, crowned with 'acanthe en fleurs', and graciously welcoming to the birds and winds of nature. At the same time they are figures of stoic endurance, suffering from the sun's rays without lowering their gaze, and never bending their 'têtes fraternelles'. Yet their emotional detachment remains in some sense within the aesthetic realm, for unlike suffering humanity they are not exposed to 'l'injustice et la haine', and from their height they witness the procession of those who cannot avoid such suffering. These are 'les héros et les Dieux de l'amour', legendary representatives of frustration and the emotions, all suffering because they

seek 'un lys dans les tempêtes'. The poem which began by celebrating
the beauty and endurance of the Caryatids ends with the celebration
of 'ces martyrs', who deserve crowns of 'myrte' and 'laurier'. It is
as if the poet wishes to grant to suffering humanity the aesthetic
status which preserves the Caryatids from real suffering. The poem
A Vénus de Milo follows a not dissimilar pattern, for here as in the
title poem Greek sculpture is associated with the aestheticizing of
life, just as throughout the volume a diffuse Hellenism is everywhere
accompanied by a general pastoral florality.

Banville's next volume, *Les Stalactites*, published in 1846, illustrates the same tendencies more consistently. For example *La
symphonie de la neige* (dated January 1844) is a confident display
of aesthetic detachment. It starts with a décor of snow, which
the poet prefers even to a pastoral 'printemps des oiseaux et des
fleurs':

> Mais moi, j'aime à songer devant cette harmonie,
> Et toutes les blancheurs des rêves anciens
> Mettent d'accord leurs voix pour une symphonie.[56]

The whiteness of snow (the absence of colour and life) prompts
withdrawal into a detached dream *harmonie* in which reality is
replaced by a *symphonie* of literary motifs evoking whiteness — 'les
Anges', 'les nuages', 'des cygnes', 'Ces filles de la Grèce', white
'dames' and 'cavaliers', and finally a white Romantic heroine:

> Mais ces pâles amours de fleurs et de sculptures,
> Dont je mène en chantant le chœur étiolé,
> Sont encore à mes yeux moins blanches et moins pures
> Que votre âme sereine, o Lys inviolé![57]

Hellenism thus contributes to this poem not merely some of its motifs
but the formalist model for an art beyond life, a poem so detached
that finally its only subject is the 'chœur étiolé' of lilies and whiteness.
In *A Olympio* (dated May 1845) Banville celebrates his now confident
formalism by saluting his poetic creations as both flowers of spring-
like beauty and living statues:

> Vous vivrez, ô mes fils! et comme d'un jeune arbre
>   On secouerait les fleurs,
> Moi je ferai couleur avec mon doigt de marbre
>   Votre sang et vos pleurs.

> Comme une floraison par le printemps hâtée,
> Par l'effort de mon bras
> Tu sortiras du bloc, ô jeune Galatée!
> Et tu me souriras![58]

Once more flowers and sculptures serve as emblems of his poetry, the two tropes together now indeed summarizing Banville's poetics.

Thus the poem 'Sculpteur, cherche avec soin . . .' which stands like a manifesto at the end of *Les Stalactites*, does not fail to invoke these figures. It begins with an insistence on formal beauty, here again seen as incompatible with the disorders of the emotions:

> Sculpteur, cherche avec soin, en attendant l'extase,
> Un marbre sans défaut pour en faire un beau vase;
> Cherche longtemps sa forme et n'y retrace pas
> D'amours mystérieux ni de divins combats.[59]

There follows a list of Greek heroes and gods as cameo illustrations of troubled emotion, even including 'Artémis, / Surprise au sein des eaux dans sa blancheur de lys'. Such disordered feeling must be excluded from a creation of ideal beauty and order:

> Qu'autour du vase pur, trop beau pour la Bacchante,
> La verveine mêlée à des feuilles d'acanthe
> Fleurisse, et que plus bas des vierges lentement
> S'avancent . . .

The formal purity of the sculpted vase is such that it triumphantly flowers into beauty (the verb 'Fleurisse' is significantly placed to maximize this effect). It is the serene detachment of a beauty flowering beyond real experience, a 'cold pastoral' only achieving aesthetic status by consciously excluding the vicissitudes of life.

The poem which Banville was to place at the head of *Les Stalactites* could serve as a show-piece for the poetics of 'cold pastoral':

> Dans les grottes sans fin brillent les Stalactites.
>
> Du cyprès gigantesque aux fleurs les plus petites,
> Un clair jardin s'accroche au rocher spongieux,
> Lys de glace, roseaux, lianes, clématites.
>
> Des thyrses pâlissants, bouquets prestigieux,
> Naissent . . . [60]

For here are white 'sculptures' isolated from life, cold ideal flowers

of beauty, natural growths bright with aesthetic ideality. But by their
origins they can be seen, too, as figures for controlled stoical
suffering:

> Pour installer ce rare et flamboyant décor . . .
>
> Il a fallu les pleurs des Soirs et des Aurores.
>
> Car, toi pour qui le roc orna ces floraisons
> De rose, de safran, et d'azur constellées,
> Tu le sais, Poésie, ange de nos raisons,
>
> Ces caprices divins sont des larmes gelées!

Here at the end of the poem Banville insists that a poetics of detached
formal beauty cannot define itself without reference to suffering.
These sculpted stalactites or 'floraisons' are finally 'larmes gelées':
the detachment of aesthetic formalism is akin to the stoical awareness
of *lacrimae rerum*. Yet Banville is primarily concerned in these poems
(despite the Fourierist preface of the volume) with the 'rare et
flamboyant décor' which can offer an alternative to contemporary
life.

It was during this period too that Leconte de Lisle was exploring
the same questions in relation to Hellenism and Fourierism. It was
scarcely surprising that this young poet should choose the Venus de
Milo as the subject of a poem, published in March 1846 in the
Fourierist journal *La Phalange*. He begins by hailing the statue in
terms now familiar:

> Salut, marbre sacré, rayonnant de génie,
> Déesse irrésistible au port victorieux,
> Pure comme un éclair et comme une harmonie,
> Ô Vénus, ô beauté, blanche mère des dieux![61]

The vocabulary might be Banville's ('marbre . . . rayonnant', 'Pure',
'harmonie', 'beauté', 'blanche') and even the inhabitual attention
paid to Venus as goddess is subordinate to the statue's aesthetic
interest. The early stanzas claim that the goddess of the statue cannot
be characterized as any one of the humanly-based personae of Venus
(as virginal 'Aphrodite', seductive 'Cythérée', and so on) because
she includes all these types in a manifestation beyond human likeness:

> Non, Déesse! — Semblable à la fleur intégrale
> En qui règnent l'éclat, l'arôme et la couleur,
> Tu contiens leurs beautés dans ta beauté royale.

She is a mystical *harmonie* of beauties, recalling the *harmonie* of
the music or language of flowers, or Fourier's Utopian *Harmonie*
integrating nature and humanity. The flower reference relates her
as well to the pastoral ideal alternative to present experience, and
the poem emphasizes this point:

> Et tu n'as point connu le trouble et la douleur!
>
> Du bonheur impassible, ô symbole adorable,
> Calme comme la mer en sa sérénité,
> Nul sanglot n'a brisé ton sein inaltérable,
> Jamais les pleurs maudits n'ont terni ta beauté!

She is 'impassible' not through any stoical endurance but because
she is beyond human experience by her divinity, her Greekness, and
(above all) her aesthetic status as a beautiful form. The poet expresses
admiration for the Greek sculptors whose 'main a pétri cette forme
immortelle' and prays to the goddess for help with his own poetry:

> Que je n'étouffe pas sur les autels de l'âme
> La forme, chère aux dieux, la fleur de leurs amours.

The goddess herself is both harmonious 'fleur intégrale' and sculp-
tural 'forme immortelle', the superlative model for the 'fleur' of
poetic form. And, like the goddess, this poetry will be a 'fleur' and
a 'harmonie' beyond human experience, unconcerned with 'le trouble
et la douleur'. Flowers, sculpture, and *harmonie* once more stand
for a poetic art uniting purity of form with emotional detachment.
These figures are by 1846 indispensable to the new Hellenist poetics.

This poem of 1846 is perhaps the most uncompromising and
consistent manifesto of Greek formalism, yet it outlines an aesthetic
position with ideological extension. The last stanza includes the
prayer that the goddess/statue should become 'la divine maîtresse'
of humanity: a restored Greek aesthetic *harmonie* is seen to promise
a new *harmonie* for society, a Fourierist Utopia beyond 'le trouble
et la douleur'. The poet invoked this escapist and meliorist ideal
again two months later in *Églogue harmonienne*, in which Greek
beauty ('Pulchra', 'la forme enchanteresse') is called the 'Rayon des
jours anciens qui [dore] l'avenir'.[62] Yet in this poem Christianity
('Casta') is also invoked as a hope for the future. Just as he
had presented the Venus de Milo as a 'fleur intégrale' har-
moniously including many beauties, so now he envisages a hopeful
synthesis of Christianity and Hellenism in a harmonious 'double

rayonnement'. However, this poem perhaps owes less to such ideological syncretism than to a poetic temperament attracted to aesthetic and emotional detachment. For the 'beauté' of Greek formalism and the 'sainte pudeur' of Christianity represent respectively the artistic and psychological forms of that *impassibilité* which the poet had attributed to the Venus de Milo and was to attribute to Niobe in a poem published in January 1847.[63] The latter is clearly more concerned with stoicism ('sérénité') and aesthetic Hellenism ('blancheur divine') than with optimistic syncretism.

By July 1847 his treatment of a similar subject in Hypatie confirms this tendency. The learned Alexandrian woman killed by Christians for her pagan beliefs is presented as 'Ignorante des maux et des crimes humains', like a flower in her beauty and her detachment:

> Comme un jeune lotus croissant sous l'œil des sages,
> Tu grandis, transparente en ta virginité,
> Tant les dieux avaient fait, chaste fleur des vieux âges,
> Resplendir ton génie à travers ta beauté.[64]

It is by these flower-like attributes that she becomes a model for the poet:

> Dors! mais vivante en lui, chante au cœur du poète
> L'hymne mélodieux de la sainte beauté!
>
> Elle seule survit, seule elle est éternelle.

Here is a Hellenism significant above all because it stands for aesthetic values, unlike the Christianity which replaced it:

> Car l'impure laideur est la reine du monde,
> Et nous avons perdu le chemin de Paros!

In the defence of 'Paros' the artist rejects not only 'laideur' but Christianity, and like Hypatie must seek beauty with serenity.

It was this version of Hellenism that other young Greek enthusiasts like Louis Ménard and Thalès Bernard greeted in 1847 as legitimate: Bernard recognized the poem *A Vénus de Milo* as an important Hellenist statement while disallowing its Fourierist elements.[65] Whether influenced by such men or rather following a poetic and temperamental logic of his own, Leconte de Lisle was in any case now committed to a doctrine of aesthetic Hellenism and withdrawal which discouraged syncretism. It was in this spirit that he composed further Greek poems and collected them with the earlier ones in the

1852 *Poèmes antiques*. So here he excises Utopian references from *Vénus de Milo* and reduces them in *Niobé*. He also gives *Églogue harmonienne* a new non-Fourierist title (*Chant alterné*) and adds revisions which cancel the poem's syncretist optimism. The revised poem suggests that the two voices express an aesthetic rather than an ideological synthesis: beauty is now a 'fleur étincelante et féconde', while 'chastity' has

> la tige d'or et les odeurs divines
> Et le mystique éclat de l'éternelle fleur.[66]

For this poet, art itself depends on the integration of the flower of beauty with the flower of mystical withdrawal, and the 1852 preface insists on 'l'impersonnalité et la neutralité' of his poetry.[67]

Leconte de Lisle's opposition to ideological syncretism was to form, in fact, the intellectual framework of much of his work in the eighteen-fifties and beyond, for this relies on the principle that racial mythologies are discrete systems which reveal differences in culture rather than similarities. Yet his poetic temperament tended to subvert this principle and *Bhagavat* (published in the 1852 volume) exemplifies how, despite close attention to a particular landscape and philosophy (in this case Indian), the poet's values remain constant. Thus the Brahman sages who reject the 'vaines rumeurs de l'homme et des cités' have opted for an 'inaction surhumaine' in a landscape of flowery serenity:

> Des larges nymphéas contemplant les calices
> Ils goûtaient, absorbés, de muettes délices. . . .
>
> Et sur les fleurs de pourpre et sur les lys d'argent, . . .
>
> Dans la forêt touffue, aux longues échappées,
> Les abeilles vibraient, d'un rayon d'or frappées.
>
> Telle la vie immense, auguste, palpitait;
> Rêvait, étincelait, soupirait et chantait;
> Tels, les germes éclos et les formes à naître
> Brisaient ou soulevaient le sein large de l'Être.[68]

In their search for final enlightenment they seek to be dissolved into 'le lotus à cent feuilles, / Bienheureux Bhagavat'. The god is described in a series of floral metaphors and holds in his hand 'le nymphéa sacré': by him the sages are united to 'l'Essence première, / . . . / Abîme de néant et de réalité'.[69] Flowers here characterize

both the serenely beautiful landscape and the calm plenitude of
withdrawal from life. Even with a non-Greek subject and setting,
Leconte de Lisle remained the poet who had first learned confidence
in his art as a Hellenist, the poet whose Hellenism was a commitment
to flower-like pastoral detachment and flower-like beauty of form.

Before publishing *Émaux et Camées* in 1852, Gautier had already
considerably influenced the development of the new aestheticizing
tendencies, especially through *Mademoiselle de Maupin*. In the late
thirties he had continued to advocate both the aesthetic significance
of Hellenism and the flower-like pastoral detachment of all art.
After Hugo's pronouncement in 1840 on the poet's social function,
Gautier's position remained unchanged in a poem of 1841:

> J'aime d'un fol amour les monts fiers et sublimes! . . .
>
> Rien qui rappelle l'homme et le travail maudit. . . .
>
> Ils ne rapportent rien et ne sont pas utiles;
> Ils n'ont que leur beauté, je le sais, c'est bien peu;
> Mais, moi, je les préfère aux champs gras et fertiles.[70]

So in another mountain poem of the same period (published in 1845)
he turns away from the view of Spain ('comme un panorama')
towards the beauty of 'les pics étincelants, / Tout argentés de neige'
and then towards a small mountain flower:

> Mais, avant toute chose,
> J'aime, au cœur du rocher,
> La petite fleur rose,
> La fleur qu'il faut chercher.[71]

Like the mountains with their 'crête pure', this flower is an emblem
of the distance between beauty and ordinary life. Recalling the useless
flowers of the 1835 preface or the pastoral flowers of the poem of
1838, it adumbrates a self-sufficient art making no concessions to
society.

Most of the poems of *Émaux et Camées* (1852) were composed
during the political and social turbulence following the revolution
of 1848, but the verse preface (finished in May 1852) adheres to the
poet's long-held position. He invokes the example of Goethe, who
had turned away from the upheavals of the Napoleonic wars toward
oriental poetry and imitated the latter in a poetic work of his own,
a 'Fraîche oasis où l'art respire'. Gautier claims that just as Goethe

> s'isolait des choses
> Et d'Hafiz effeuillait les roses,
>
> Sans prendre garde à l'ouragan
> Qui fouettait mes vitres fermées,
> Moi, j'ai fait *Émaux et Camées.*[72]

The poetry he is presenting will, like that of Hafiz and Goethe, be flower-like in its indifference to turbulent modern society, but also (presumably) in its fresh and delicate beauty. And the well-known advocate of *l'art pour l'art* is indeed introducing here a poetry which is charming and intimate, with the restraints of scale suggested by the title.

These qualities are immediately evident in three of the first poems to be published (in January 1849), pieces which were to set the tone of the volume as a whole. One of these is *Le Poème de la femme*, with a subtitle ('Marbre de Paros') promising a serene Greek formalism. Yet it shows us, in fact, a modern woman 'en train de montrer ses trésors'; she arrives dressed 'en grand apparat' trailing 'un flot de velours nacarat' and is soon seen to be wearing a 'chemise' which is 'un nuage de batiste'. It is on to this background of delicate modernity that the poet projects a series of high aesthetic comparisons. The woman has come to 'lire un poëme, / Le poëme de son beau corps', and she is a fit subject for Greek artists:

> Pour Apelle ou pour Cléomène,
> Elle semblait, marbre de chair,
> En Vénus Anadyomène
> Poser nue au bord de la mer.

She is an 'hymne à la beauté' in the high Hellenist manner, yet the poem casually passes on to other aesthetic comparisons. Now 'lasse d'art antique', the woman poses on a rug as 'la sultane du sérail' or 'l'odalisque d'Ingres', and settles dreamily on cushions as if 'morte du volupté', while the poet pretends to mourn her death:

> Que les violettes de Parme,
> Au lieu des tristes fleurs des morts
> Où chaque perle est une larme,
> Pleurent en bouquets sur son corps.

Here high aesthetic criteria are playfully juxtaposed with fashionable Parma violets, just as in the poem as a whole the Hellenist evocation

of marble and flowers (of ideal beauty and escapism) is confronted
with the modernity of a *demi-mondaine*. Yet this modernity has a
charming plastic beauty itself quite distinct from the modern world
of disordered emotion and political upheaval. The poem is doubly
isolated from 'le trouble et la douleur', by its aesthetic (including
Hellenist) references and by its intimate modern beauty.

The title of the poem *Symphonie en blanc majeur* announces a
poetic *harmonie* of whiteness and an exercise in formalist detachment. The poem is indeed a series of variations on the theme of
whiteness, interweaving literary allusions with references to white
things in private life (woman's clothing, ivory piano keys) and in
nature ('les camélias blancs', doves, stalactites, snow, and ice). But
Greek sculpture is not forgotten:

> Paros au grain éblouissant, . . .
>
> Le marbre blanc, chair froide et pâle,
> Où vivent les divinités.

Flowers and marble are even presented together:

> L'aubépine de mai qui plie
> Sous les blancs frimas de ses fleurs;
> L'albâtre où la mélancolie
> Aime à retrouver ses pâleurs.

These examples of whiteness are all related by colour but subtly
contrasting in texture, a harmonious evocation of physical things
set apart from the rest of experience by their cold whiteness but
foregrounded in their visual and tactile sensuousness. For here too
Gautier conciliates a detached aesthetic realm with the charms of
present experience, and the poem is a tribute to the 'implacable
blancheur' of a modern woman. Once more the poet celebrates a
plastic beauty which mediates between aesthetic detachment and
sensuous present experience, yet remains isolated from the disorders
of modern life.

He affirms the same values in *Affinités secrètes*, again with reference to whiteness, Hellenism, marble, and flowers. The poem opens
by describing two marble blocks in a Greek temple, two pearls
recalling Venus, two roses of Granada, and two Venetian doves.
These are beautiful plastic objects distanced by being set back in the
past, but already evoking intimacy since sentimental 'affinités' are
ascribed to each pair. Even when stressing their mutability the text

is an enumeration of beautiful things:'

> Marbre, perle, rose, colombe,
> Tout se dissout, tout se détruit;
> La perle fond, le marbre tombe,
> La fleur se fane et l'oiseau fuit.

Indeed the pantheism announced in the poem's subtitle ('Madrigal panthéiste') serves to recuperate the plastic charm of these 'formes' for the present, since their destruction is followed by 'de lentes métamorphoses' so that finally

> les molécules fidèles
> Se cherchent et s'aiment encore.

Thus the marble and the flowers (like the pearls and doves) recreate sensuous 'affinités' in the present, reborn in the relationship of 'deux jeunes amants'. Here again Gautier has used Hellenist escapism (as he uses the concepts of mutability and pantheism) in the service of an intimate sensuousness of the present moment.

The other poems collected in the 1852 volume (and those added to it until 1872) all manifest an intimate modernity usually related in similar ways to aesthetic motifs and criteria. These are often Hellenist ones, as in *Fantaisies d'hiver*:

> La Vénus Anadyomène
> Est en pelisse à capuchon;
> Flore, que la brise malmène,
> Plonge ses mains dans son manchon.

But whether Hellenist or not, these aesthetic references perform two poetic functions at once. While the high aesthetic values are relativized by juxtaposition with present sensuousness, they also serve as an aesthetic frame for it. The result is aesthetic detachment on a reduced scale, and the intimacy of a present moment isolated by subtle aesthetic means—a poetics of *émaux et camées*.

Gautier is here proposing a new poetics for *l'art pour l'art*. It is like Hellenist formalism in that it is intended as an alternative to the disorder of life but also by its emphasis on plastic beauty and aesthetic values. Banville could salute Gautier in 1856 for his aesthetic detachment and his formalism: Gautier, he says is (like a pastoralist) a 'poète oiseleur' following his 'pur/Caprice', but he is also a 'ciseleur', a 'bon ouvrier' in poetic form. Gautier's reply of the following year (*L'Art*) insists on the rewarding difficulty of working within a constraining form:

> Oui, l'œuvre sort plus belle
> D'une forme au travail
> Rebelle,
> Vers, marbre, onyx, émail.

Like Banville he associates poetry with sculpture, but he notes at the same time the virtues of a restrained aesthetic scale ('onyx', 'émail'). For Gautier's specific contribution to the new poetic orientation was indeed the intimate subtlety of his art. Thus when treating one of the high Hellenist themes in his *Bûchers et tombeaux* of 1858, his rhetorical and ideological constraint is characteristic:

> Le squelette était invisible
> Au temps heureux de l'Art païen; . . .

> Entre les fleurs et les acanthes,
> Dans le marbre joyeusement,
> Amours, aegipans et baccantes
> Dansaient autour du monument; . . .

> Et l'art versait son harmonie
> Sur la tristesse du tombeau. . . .

> Reviens, reviens, bel art antique,
> De ton paros étincelant
> Couvrir ce squelette gothique.

Gautier's manner is underplayed, subtle, and charming, and by presenting ideological exposition in terms of plastic sensuousness it admirably complements his theme. Yet these lines propose a recognizable Hellenism: here is the habitual rejection of Christianity, ugliness, and suffering in favour of a happy Greek aestheticism, once more associated with marble, flowers, and *harmonie*. When this poem was included along with *L'Art* in the augmented second edition of 1858, Gautier's volume demonstrated that an intimate modern poetry could also find a model in the 'bel art antique'.

By 1852 Banville, Leconte de Lisle, and Gautier had between them proposed a new conception of poetry defined to a large extent with reference to Hellenism, and they continued to illustrate it in various ways in poetry produced over the next twenty years or so. Part of Hellenism's attraction was its ability to provide topoi representing an alternative to contemporary life:

Ô chévrier! ce bois est cher aux Pièrides.
Point de houx épineux ni de ronces arides;
A travers l'hyacinthe et le souchet épais
Une source sacrée y germe et coule en paix. . . .

Au nom des Muses! viens sous l'ombre fraîche et noire![73]

Hellenist reference could evoke a poetic space outside urban society and the present time, and flower figures contributed to this same pastoral effect: indeed the Hellenist flower was a double emblem of pastoral otherness. But Hellenism also provided for these poets a criterion of plastic beauty by its association with the detached beauty of Greek sculpture. Hellenist beauty contrasted with the ugliness of modern civilization, and was thus a sufficient poetic subject in itself. Moreover, imitation of its formal values seemed to ensure an art which would (like Greek art itself) confirm its supreme importance by outlasting its society: the artist who achieves an 'onyx poli' is a 'vainqueur de l'oubli'.[74] Hellenism could thus imply that the poet was not merely isolated from his society but superior to it by his evocation and creation of beauty. And here too the flower figure (traditional emblem of poetry and of superlative beauty) was supremely convenient for the Hellenist project:

Et l'Olympe entier, d'amour transporté,
Salua la fleur avec la beauté.[75]

The Hellenist flower was an emblem not only of withdrawal into pastoral ideality but of the artistic achievement which could turn escapism into triumph.

The Hellenist model of psychological withdrawal and supreme detached beauty proved a creative one in non-Greek contexts as well. Thus the *coupe* of Banville's title poem in *Le Sang de la coupe* (1857) is a thing of plastic beauty (a 'verre entouré de fleurs') from which the lover-poet resignedly drinks the dregs of life and love. Beauty is here associated with a form of detachment from life, just as Leconte de Lisle in many of his non-Greek poems after 1852 was to associate the static visual beauty of landscape (whether Northern, tropical, or oriental) with a mood of resignation or doomed rebellion. In such contexts flowers can serve as emblems of ideal detachment, and Banville whimsically imagines an ideal alternative world in which all would be transparency:

> On verrait d'ici luire au pays du Japon
> Une fleur écarlate! . . .

> Les routes n'auraient plus que des fleurs d'angsoka
> Et de larges tulipes.[76]

The exotic beauty of these flowers represents a refusal of reality, while for Leconte de Lisle the beauty of flowers is more often associated with an *impassible* resignation (as with the Egyptian roses of *Néréfou-Ra* or the tropical flowers of the jungle poems). These beautiful flowers have a similar function to those of Hellenism, just as the poetry in which they occur shows the wider poetic relevance of Hellenist aesthetic detachment.

ii. Flowers and Parnassian poetry

After the political upheavals of 1848–52 and the establishment of the Second Empire, many felt the need to consider anew exactly how poetry and society were related. With their uncompromising answer to this question, the three major Hellenist poets gained in readership during the rest of the decade. But it was only after 1860 that their model for poetry began to exert general influence, and then on the new generation of young poets. Glatigny was the first of these, with his volume *Les Vignes folles* of 1860, and in the title poem (dedicated to Banville) he defines his poetry in relation to Hellenism. His poetic monument is no Greek temple but a 'pauvre édifice nain' not built of 'marbre de Paros', yet

> J'ai planté sur le seuil un vivace églantier
> Qui jette à tous les vents ses roses odorantes . . .

> Quelques jasmins aussi, de rouges amarantes.[77]

Modestly aware of the flower-decorated marble-like form to which Hellenist poetry aspires, Glatigny clearly owes as much to Banville as to his own

> Muse au beau front,
> Impassible figure aux ondoyantes lignes.

But Gautier's sensual modernity is also detectable, as in the address to a modern woman in *Aurora*:

> Je t'aime et je t'adore, ô corps harmonieux
> Où vivent les contours des antiques statues,

> Marbre fort et serein . . .
> Que m'importe la fleur de la virginité.[78]

Marble, flowers, and *harmonie* are figures which between them define the Hellenist aesthetic of Gautier and Banville, and Glatigny's use of the same figures reveals the extent of his indebtedness.

Within the next few years the poetics of these major Hellenists was to become known to many other young poets, and to be discussed in their cafés, salons, and reviews.[79] They were also to discover Leconte de Lisle, especially after the publication in 1862 of the *Poésies barbares*. Léon Valade registers something of the effect of this volume in a poem of 1863:

> Las du chœur énervé des modernes guitares, . . .
>
> Le poète écœuré remonte aux temps barbares, . . .
>
> Où, dans la fauve horreur des flores exotiques,
> Parmi les jaguars prompts qui rôdent à pas lents,
> Va s'enivrer, la nuit, de parfums violents.[80]

Or in the poem *Midi*, borrowing more than a title from the master:

> Midi, volcan fécond, roule sa lave blanche. . . .
>
> Pas d'ombre: la couleur de toutes parts ruisselle.
> L'eau devient de l'argent, la fleur une étincelle; . . .
>
> Et je demeure là sans parole et sans geste.[81]

And the volume in which these imitations occur shows a considerable indebtedness to properly Hellenist poetry.[82] A poem by Albert Mérat of the same period illustrates the possibility of crossing the tropical genre with a Hellenist one, with the aid of the flower imagery common to both:

> Le ciel sourit; le sol jase; la rose est folle:
> A l'hymen du soleil elle tend sa corolle;
> Et l'antique Vénus est éparse dans l'air.[83]

So too in an early sonnet by José-Maria de Heredia, *Le Lis* (1863), the lily first appears virginally Hellenic and then responds to a heavy Lislean atmosphere:

> Tel, au brûlant baiser de la brise égarée
> Où flotte de pollen amoureux, s'enflammant
> Le lis sème dans l'air sa poussière dorée![84]

These poets show the unmistakable influence of the Hellenist masters.

Indeed the influence of the older poets clearly involved not only plastic elements but psychological *impassibilité* as well. Mérat in 1864–5 presents *Les Avalanches* as both implacable and beautiful:

> Dans la sérénité lointaine de l'azur
> L'immortelle blancheur des neiges étincelle,
> Magnifique et sculptée ainsi qu'un marbre pur.[85]

Heredia in *L'Héliotrope* (1862) describes the plastic beauty of the sunflower and envies its exposure to the unfeeling sun:

> Enfin, toute flétrie, elle demande l'ombre;
> Mais le Dieu, la criblant de ses flèches sans nombre,
> Lui verse sans pitié son implacable jour.
>
> C'est après ce destin que soupire mon âme.[86]

Catulle Mendès combines flowers and sculpture with personal suffering:

> Amoureuse des roses
> Et des œillets naissants
>   Descends
> Dans mon cœur, si tu l'oses,
>
> Dans mon cœur dévasté,
> Ô vivante statue
>   Vêtue
> De ta seule beauté![87]

Elsewhere he insists, though, that 'sanglots humains' are unknown to the Muse: 'le trouble est banni des âmes qu'elle hante'. Whatever the inconsistencies of these poets, they had clearly learned from their elders both the figural lexicon of Hellenism and its concern with *impassibilité*: understandably they became known before 1866 as both *formistes* and *impassibles*.

The young poets had certainly discovered that the flower figure was indispensable to Greek-inspired formalism. Some lines from Glatigny's 1864 volume show that he understood this:

> Les fleurs que nous cueillons ne sont pas éphémères; . . .
>
> Car nous savons donner un corps à nos Chimères
> Et sculpter nos héros dans les blocs résistants.[88]

Sully Prudhomme is equally aware of it in *Les Marbres* of January 1866:

> Le marbre blanc, ce lis des pierres! . . .
>
> Il est le seul qui montre unie
> La matière au pur idéal![89]

And Armand Silvestre, in the prologue to *Sonnets Païens*, addresses a 'corps féminin' as a work of art and calls her 'fleur du rêve païen', 'marbre fait chair' and 'L'impérissable en sa splendeur altière'.[90] The young poets' unanimity on the flower-like attributes of Hellenist beauty undeniably made a primary contribution to their self-awareness as a literary group.

These poets were essential members of the group which met in the 'entresol du Parnasse' at Lemerre's bookshop, and which was responsible for *Le Parnasse contemporain*, appearing in instalments from March to June 1866 and then in book form later in the same year.[91] The volume places first contributions by Gautier, Banville, and Leconte de Lisle, between them the masters of the new group's poetics. One of Gautier's poems (*La Marguerite*) might be a comment on the literary assumptions shared by many of the contributors, as it speaks of the Chinese tradition of writing while looking at flowers:

> La vue et le parfum de ces fleurs favorites, . . .
>
> Inspirent aux lettrés, dans les formes prescrites,
> Sur un même sujet des chants toujours divers.

> (p. 5.)

His own 'bouquet de vers épanouis' is itself a variation on the subject of poetic flowers to which most of the other 'Parnassians' paid some tribute. Banville contributed a long Hellenist poem (*L'Exil des Dieux*), a lament for the passing of the Greek gods well summarized in the words of Aphrodite:

> Ce doux enivrement des êtres, ce baiser
> Des choses, qui toujours voltigeait sur tes lèvres,
> Ce grand courant de joie et d'amour, tu t'en sèvres!
> Ils ne fleuriront plus tes pensers, enchantés
> Par l'éblouissement des blanches nudités.
> Donc subis la laideur et la douleur. Expie.

> (pp. 11–12.)

This is a convincing restatement of the flower-like appeal of Hellenist nature mysticism, and one of Leconte de Lisle's contributions is an equally fine illustration of a different aspect of Parnassian poetics. This poem, once more using a beautiful static décor as a background to psychological withdrawal, is *La Vérandah*:

> Au tintement de l'eau dans les porphyres roux
> Les rosiers de l'Iran mêlent leurs frais murmures, . . .
>
> Sous les treillis d'argent de la vérandah close,
> Dans l'air tiède embaumé de l'odeur des jasmins, . . .
>
> La Persane royale, immobile, repose.

> (pp. 18–19.)

The poem culminates indeed in total immobility, as the garden falls silent ('Les rosiers de l'Iran ont cessé leurs murmures') in sympathy with the queen's drugged unconsciousness. Formal elements in the poem (circularity, repetition) accentuate the tranquil static quality of both setting and subject, achieving in an exemplary way this poet's ideal of impassive beauty and emotional withdrawal.

Amongst the poets represented in the volume, very few do not make some use of flower figures, or pay some tribute to Hellenism or to *impassibilité*. Some indeed use such references to define their own poetics by distancing themselves (slightly) from assumptions known to be shared. One of these is L.-X. de Ricard:

> Que les rimeurs de pastorales
> Alternent en stances égales
> Les gloires des fleurs et des cieux;
>
> Moi, je chante un hymne candide
> A l'amour . . .

> (*Le Printemps*, p. 115.)

Many of the minor poets, like Armand Renaud, manage little more than a confusion of fashionable motifs:

> Échanson, couronne mon verre
> De fleurs aux arômes divers.
> Boire en silence est trop sévère:
> Prends ta lyre et dis-moi des vers. . . .
>
> En ce monde tout est futile.

> (*Ivresse douce*, p. 211.)

Others raise imitation almost to the level of art, like Mendès with his Lislean orientalism:

> Le grand Lotus, berceau des trois Mondes, s'élève,
> Doux comme le soleil des jours d'automne, et blanc! . . .
> Il verse la candeur et la limpidité
> De l'aube dans l'effroi de la nuit qui s'achève.
>
> (*Le Mystère du Lotus*, p. 52.)

But some attain effects not only fashionable but poetical, like the splendid final line of François Coppée's *Le Lys*: 'Noble et pur, un grand lys se meurt dans une coupe' (p. 277). The volume also contains early work by several major new poets, including Verlaine and Mallarmé: amongst them too was Heredia, the most important of those who were to remain committed to the assumptions of the 1866 group. Several of his contributions (placed between Banville and Leconte de Lisle) have Hellenist subjects. But *Fleurs de feu* evokes stoical survival in a landscape now 'immobile' and silent, long after the 'Chaos' of primeval volcanic fire:

> Pourtant, dernier effort de l'antique incendie, . . .
>   on voit . . .
> Sur la tige de fer qui d'un seul jet s'élance
> S'épanouir la fleur des cactus embrasés.
>
> (p. 13.)

This is a proud fiery flower, its blossoming a heroic attainment of beauty in difficult conditions. It is an emblem for the aesthetic beauty and moral *impassibilité* which were to define Heredia's poetics over almost three decades as he prepared the single volume representing his achievement (*Les Trophées*, 1893), itself originally to be called *Fleurs de feu*.

The first Parnassian volume (a second was to follow in 1871, a third in 1876) was indeed, as Gautier noted in 1868, a 'bouquet printanier' which 'représente assez justement l'état actuel de la poésie'.[92] But the view of poetry it canonized was unmistakably that which had been developed over the last three decades in association with Hellenist formalism.[93] It envisaged a poetry refusing the disorder of the world in order to contemplate beauty or even its own formal qualities, a poetry supremely aware of its own aesthetic status. In the development of this poetics the Hellenist dream had played a central role: as Sainte-Beuve noted, the 'grâce incomparable' of Greece understandably had a flower-like appeal for 'la pensée fatiguée par notre civilisation moderne et par notre vie compliquée'.[94] But in this project the flower figure was indispensable too, for like Greek art it evoked both superlative beauty and an ideal contrasting with 'le monde agité et souffrant'. While Baudelaire's and Nerval's flowers both served (in their respective ways) a poetry transforming life into art, the flowers of the Parnassian muses served an art seeking independence from reality.

5

THE FLOWERS OF
SYMBOLIST POETICS

I. Flowers and the Beginnings of a New Poetics

i. Baudelairian flowers in a Parnassian context

The poetics of Symbolism were developed to a large extent under
the dual influence of Baudelaire and of Parnassian values, and had
their beginnings in the decade of Baudelaire's last years and the
triumph of Hellenist formalism. In the eighteen-sixties young poets
could hardly fail to be influenced by the theory and practice of
Banville, Leconte de Lisle, and Gautier. But a few of them attempted
at the same time to assimilate Baudelaire (despite a general lack
of interest in his work) and such poets often reveal Baudelaire's
influence by alluding in an otherwise Parnassian context to his
distinctive flowers of oxymoron or negativity. As early as 1859
Henri Cantel was attempting in *Le Mal et le Beau* to account for
Baudelaire's flower-title in terms of formalism:

> J'ai respiré tes Fleurs du Mal, ces roses pâles,
> Émeraudes d'amour, douloureuses opales,
> Que tailla ta main vive avec un art nouveau.[1]

Glatigny attempted in *Les Vignes folles* (1860) to integrate Baudelairian allusions with Hellenist *impassibilité*, as in *Les Roses et le vin*:

> Mariez vos parfums, mariez vos couleurs,
> Roses et Vin qui domptez les cruelles douleurs.[2]

Mendès too could show traces of Baudelaire in his generally Hellenist
Philoméla (1863), in lines like these:

> L'enfer qui donne aux lys le poison des ciguës
> A mis en Elle un charme exécrable et vainqueur.[3]

Another of these poets, Léon Dierx, produced poetry more markedly
Baudelairian, with titles like *Le Balcon* and such lines as these:

> Au fond de la mémoire, éclorez-vous, ô fleurs
> Du rêve où s'éteindra l'écho de nos douleurs.[4]

In 1866 *Le Parnasse contemporain* contained Baudelaire's own *Nouvelles Fleurs du Mal*, but few contributions by other poets where his influence was of major significance. The authors of *Le Parnassiculet contemporain* treated Baudelaire's manner as a genre of Parnassian poetry, but parodied his oxymoron and negativity in *Le Convoi de la bien-aimée*:

> Je prendrai ton baiser chaste et délicieux,
> Tes soupirs embaumés, tes serments et tes larmes
> Claires comme un poison qui dort au sein des fleurs.[5]

Gautier himself well appreciated Baudelaire's singularity and noted it when writing in 1868 on the *Parnasse* volume: 'Quelques nouvelles *Fleurs du mal*, de Baudelaire, s'épanouissent bizarrement au milieu de ce bouquet comme des roses noires, et se distinguent au premier flair à leur parfum vertigineux.'[6] He is in no doubt here (as in other significant comments of the same year) about the difference between Baudelairian and Parnassian poetics. Nor was Maurice Rollinat when as a young poet he expressed in some lines of 1868 an *esthétique du mal* clearly in opposition to Parnassian criteria:

> J'aime l'âcre parfum des plantes vénéneuses
> Et les gouffres béants, pentes vertigineuses,
> Enfin difformités, contorsions, laideurs,
> Valent autant pour moi que toutes les splendeurs.[7]

Three young poets during this decade, however, registered an appreciation both of Parnassian poetics and of Baudelaire's singularly different poetic values. Their own first work shows them attempting to assimilate both poetic models, each one soon proposing his own distinctive poetic synthesis; it also shows them relying to a considerable extent on the flower imagery common to both poetic exemplars. In this way Verlaine, Rimbaud, and Mallarmé were preparing the revolutionary flower poetics of Symbolism.

ii. Verlaine

Verlaine was certainly a Parnassian. Indeed in several manifesto poems of 1866 he articulated the new group's poetic assumptions in their most uncompromising form. Thus *Vers dorés* (in the *Parnasse* volume) praises the true poets' 'égoïsme de marbre',[8] while in his own first volume the *Prologue* speaks of their 'fierté sereine' and 'amour du beau', and the *Épilogue* of their Hellenist formalism:

> Nous donc, sculptons avec le ciseau des Pensées
> Le bloc vierge du Beau, Paros immaculé.[9]

Yet Verlaine was already a fervent Baudelairian in 1865, when he wrote on him for Ricard's *L'Art*. He presents the older poet as committed like the Parnassians to 'le Beau pur' but also insists on Baudelaire's 'profonde originalité', his ability to represent 'l'homme physique moderne, tel que l'ont fait les raffinements d'une civilisation excessive, en un mot, le *bilio-nerveux* par excellence'.[10] And Verlaine was clearly invoking Baudelaire when he gave his own collection a title (*Poèmes saturniens*) recalling the older poet, and announced his character as a 'Saturnien': 'Bonne part de malheur, et bonne part de bile' (R 21). Here is a temperament apparently unfitted to the 'fierté sereine' of the Parnassian ideal, and much of the poetry in this volume reveals a certain intellectual and emotional disarray. In *L'Angoisse*, for example, the poet repudiates Nature, 'l'Homme' and 'l'Amour', and even mocks 'l'Art' and '[les] temples grecs', announcing that

> Lasse de vivre, ayant peur de mourir, pareille
> Au brick perdu jouet du flux et du reflux,
> Mon âme pour d'affreux naufrages appareille.
>
> (R 30.)

Taken with the rest of the poem, these lines illustrate in confessional form the passive and restlessly undetermined temperament which, along with Baudelairian and Parnassian influence, was to inform Verlaine's poetry.

His poetic temperament is already exemplified in one of his earliest poems, *Nevermore* (R 27). It treats a remembered moment of love, but sets it in an autumn landscape 'atone' and 'monotone' in atmosphere, yet swept by restless wind ('la bise détone'). The sentimental moment is distanced, moreover, in various ways—by the use of temporal disorientation, marks of impersonality ('fit sa voix', etc.), and repetitive figures of syntax, assonance, and rhyme. At the heart of the poem, too, is a conversation composed of a question ('Quel fut ton plus beau jour?') and a silent response. In this way the first three stanzas evoke the lovers' intimacy with strange indirectness, so that the reference to flowers in the last tercet has an occult and powerful effect:

> Ah! les premières fleurs, qu'elles sont parfumées!
> Et qu'il bruit avec un murmure charmant
> Le premier *oui* qui sort de lèvres bien-aimées!

These are flowers of sentimentality now evoking a mysterious non-determination of time, place, and mood; they are fragrant emblems of innocence and happiness but also (given the poem's title) of transience and *spleen*. And they are figures which gain their effect from a new kind of language, a style owing something both to Baudelairian irony and Parnassian detachment.

Many of Verlaine's poetic experiments at this period seem to derive from the same two models, which taken together correspond so well to a psychological state both restless and disengaged. One of his most original early pieces, *Mon Rêve familier* (R 29), gives exemplary expression to this 'rêve étrange et pénétrant', while the dream woman also recalls precedents like Baudelaire's 'Fleur impossible' (in the prose poem *L'Invitation au voyage*) and statuesque Parnassian indifference ('Son regard est pareil au regard des statues'). And in *Après trois ans* (R 27) the poet provides a minimal anecdotal framework for a similar psychological state. The narrator is returning to a garden he knew three years earlier, and neither the circumstances nor the feelings of present or past are further made explicit. His observation that 'J'ai tout revu' suggests that whatever the disorientation and transience outside the garden, within it nothing has changed:

> Les roses comme avant palpitent; comme avant,
> Les grands lys orgueilleux se balancent au vent.

Poised between serenity and restlessness these flowers hint at expectancy, but the final lines register only a subtle blend of sad transience and reassuring lack of change:

> Même j'ai retrouvé debout la Velléda
> Dont le plâtre s'écaille au bout de l'avenue,
> — Grêle, parmi l'odeur fade du réséda.

The indeterminacy of this mood is summed up in the adjective 'grêle' (ambiguous as to grammatical function and meaning), yet like the dilapidated statue it has overtones of an unspecified distress, a distanced *spleen*. This is the mood which finally permeates the garden with the smell of reseda, a fragrance not only flowery but 'fade' (indeterminate and sad). For Verlaine flowers (as both sight and smell) can evoke emotional disengagement and *spleen*, serenity and implied disorientation: they are figures easily adaptable to the new language he was developing from his two exemplars.

The poem *Un Dahlia* (R 47), suggests Verlaine's wry awareness of the pressure of Baudelairian and Parnassian precedents, and indeed 'the anxiety of influence' (in Harold Bloom's phrase). He addresses the flower in terms recalling Baudelaire's *La Beauté*:

> Courtisane au sein dur, à l'œil opaque et brun . . .
>
> Et tu trônes, Idole insensible à l'encens.

This flower is a 'courtisane' cruelly rejecting love, reminiscent also of Parnassian models. The flower's 'grand torse reluit ainsi qu'un marbre neuf' and although it has 'aucun/Arôme' there are 'impeccables accords' in its 'beauté sereine'. Yet the poem has an equivocal relation with its Baudelairian and Parnassian exemplars, and the last lines even hint at parody of them:

> — Ainsi le Dahlia, roi vêtu de splendeur,
> Élève sans orgueil sa tête sans odeur,
> Irritant au milieu des jasmins agaçants!

Verlaine seems to be satirizing here the *culte des fleurs* itself, for this *blason* of the dahlia is no flower-dictionary encomium. Where in the traditional flower language 'Chaque fleur dit un mot du livre de nature', this dahlia has no 'meaning' (or a contradictory one: 'vêtu de splendeur' and 'sans orgueil') just as it has no smell and either gender. The poet's final irritation is a reaction against the whole tradition of fixed meaning as much as against his particular poetic models.

Yet these models were indispensable to him as he found new ways of fixing indeterminacy of meaning in poetic language, as he did notably in some of the *Paysages tristes*. Parnassian influence is seen at its most unassimilated in the poem *L'Heure du Berger* (R 40), where a misty landscape at sunset suggests psychological withdrawal ('les fleurs des eaux referment leurs corolles') and then the finality of a white star amidst blackness ('Blanche, Vénus émerge, et c'est la Nuit'). In *Promenade sentimentale* there is a similar landscape:

> Le couchant dardait ses rayons suprêmes
> Et le vent berçait les nénuphars blêmes;
> Les grands nénuphars entre les roseaux
> Tristement luisaient sur les calmes eaux.

Here aspects of the landscape itself (water lilies which are pale and sad) express the same psychological state as the protagonist's ('Moi j'errais tout seul, promenant ma plaie'), and the resigned sadness of both has Baudelairian and Parnassian precedents. Indeed the 'nénuphars blêmes' are in their sadness and paleness correlatives not only of the protagonist's feelings but of the incantatory effect produced by the poem's stylistic features: syntactical parallelism, constant *enjambement*, a long synthetic sentence, and thematic circularity. The poetic discourse which begins and ends with sad pale 'nénuphars' embodies sadness and paleness in a new *langage des fleurs*, like the traditional one both mysterious and expressive, but here only expressive of its own mysterious *spleen*.

As a sunset flower-piece hinting at the language of flowers, Verlaine's poem recalls Baudelaire's *Harmonie du soir*, and another poem in the same section, *Crépuscule du soir mystique* (R 37), is even closer to this model. Here, as in the Baudelaire poem, the sunset mood is that of memory as well as sadness:

> Le Souvenir avec le Crépuscule
> Rougeoie et tremble à l'ardent horizon
> De l'Espérance en flamme qui recule
> Et s'agrandit . . .

In this poem too the flowers are presented not only visually (here as a metaphor for the mixed colours of the sunset) but as *parfums*:

> ainsi qu'une cloison
> Mystérieuse où mainte floraison
> — Dahlia, lys, tulipe et renoncule —
> S'élance autour d'un trellis, et circule
> Parmi la maladive exhalaison .
> De parfums lourds et chauds, dont le poison
> — Dahlia, lys, tulipe et renoncule —
> Noyant mes sens, mon âme et ma raison,
> Mêle dans une immense pâmoison
> Le Souvenir avec le Crépuscule.

The synaesthetic *harmonie* of flowers in the Baudelaire poem results

in a 'langoureux vertige', but the 'parfums' of Verlaine's flowers are an all-pervasive atmosphere subverting meaning and threatening consciousness. These are not only flowers of psychological withdrawal but *fleurs du mal* evoking a dangerous 'pâmoison', a poisoned *spleen*: Verlaine's language here passes beyond the suggestive *langage des fleurs* into a 'mystical' but sinister semi-consciousness. This is realized stylistically in a discourse beyond fixed meaning, using only two rhymes, continuous *enjambement*, a single long sentence, repetend lines, semantic circularity, and a dream-like present tense. Here perhaps more than in any other of the stylistic experiments of his first volume, Verlaine exemplifies his poetics of troubled indeterminacy, his personal adaptation of Baudelairian disorientation and Parnassian detachment.

This was the poetics which was to serve him in much of his later work, including *Fêtes galantes* (1868). For at the centre of this escapist world of restless *commedia dell'arte* and Watteauesque nonchalance is the psychological state characterized by expressions like 'rêver', 'sangloter d'extase', 'cette heure dont la fuite / Tournoie' or 'de ton cœur endormi / Chasse à jamais tout dessein' (R 83, 91, 96). This is the state evoked in the 'Mystiques barcarolles, / Romances sans paroles' of the poem *A Clymène*, with its synaesthetic *correspondances*: 'ta voix, étrange / Vision', 'la candeur / De ton odeur' (R 92). It is the principle of indeterminacy which also governs the tone and style of many of the poems of *Romances sans paroles* (1874), as in the first of the *Ariettes oubliées*—

> C'est l'extase langoureuse,
> C'est la fatigue amoureuse,
>
> (R 147.)

—or the second of the same series:

> Et mon âme et mon cœur en délires
> Ne sont plus qu'une espèce d'œil double
> Où tremblote à travers un jour trouble
> L'ariette, hélas! de toutes lyres!
>
> (R 148.)

If the poet's evocation of this state often relies in this way on *correspondances* between the senses, it does not do so in order to discover meaningful analogies but to characterize a realm beyond any such fixed meaning. Verlaine can indeed associate this topos with flowers, as in *Crépuscule du soir mystique*, or in lines from the play *Les Uns et les autres* (written in 1871):

> Comparable à ces fleurs d'été que nous voyons
> Tourner vers le soleil leur fidèle corolle
> Lors je tombe en extase et reste sans parole,
> Sans vie et sans pensée, éperdu, fou, hagard.

(R 287.)

But this reference to flowers, like the reference to the *correspondances*, only serves to emphasize the differences between the Romantic (or even Baudelairian) *langage des fleurs* and Verlaine's own evocation of a state beyond consciousness. His own language is a discourse beyond fixed meaning and analogy, mysterious and entirely self-sustaining. It is as if Verlaine has 'Hellenized' the Baudelairian flower language of the *correspondances* by exiling it altogether from the world of meaning and the senses.

In another aspect of his work, Verlaine had drawn other lessons from Baudelairian ironic realism, as some lines from *La Bonne Chanson* demonstrate:

> Le bruit des cabarets, la fange des trottoirs, . . .

> Bitume défoncé, ruisseaux comblant l'égout,
> Voilà ma route — avec le paradis au bout.

(R 127.)

Such realist evocations are for Verlaine, however, flowerless. Even after his meeting with Rimbaud, he made no attempt to imitate the younger poet in his flower poetics of visionary realism, despite the understanding of this suggested in *Crimen Amoris*:

> Or le plus beau d'entre tous ces mauvais anges
> Avait seize ans sous sa couronne de fleurs. . . .
> 'Oh! je serai celui-là qui créera Dieu!'

(R 324.)

On the contrary, Verlaine's later flower imagery is very often that of the traditional religious symbolism of salvation and sacrifice, as in *Conseil falot* (1874): 'C'est d'être des fleurs, / Au champ du martyre' (R 317). Yet in one extraordinary poem, written soon after his fight with Rimbaud, his imprisonment and conversion, he brings together sensual mysticism with allusions to his own situation, poised indeterminately between Rimbaldian sensuality and Christian spiritual discipline:

> Parfums, couleurs, systèmes, lois!
> Les mots ont peur comme des poules.
> La chair sanglote sur la croix. . . .
>
> Cieux bruns où nagent nos desseins,
> Fleurs qui n'êtes pas le calice.

> (R 227.)

By its oblique and lapidary style, however, this language is as indeterminate and impersonal as any of his earlier *romances sans paroles*, and the urgent tone only contributes further to its troubled mystery. Here is a disorientated language of 'parfums', 'couleurs', and 'fleurs', as ironic as Baudelaire and as non-realist as Hellenism, yet neither expressing meaning nor invoking escape. Like so much of Verlaine's poetry it is indeed 'De la musique avant toute chose' (R 261).

iii. Rimbaud

In his letter to Banville dated 24 May 1870, the fifteen-year-old Rimbaud announced his poetic vocation:

> Que si je vous envoie quelques-uns de ces vers, . . . — c'est que j'aime tous les poètes, tous les bons Parnassiens, — puisque le poète est un Parnassien, — épris de la beauté idéale; . . .
> Dans deux ans, dans un an peut-être, je serai à Paris. — Anch'io, messieurs du journal, je serai Parnassien! — je ne sais pas ce que j'ai là, qui veut monter . . . — Je jure, cher maître, d'adorer toujours les deux déesses, Muse et Liberté.[11]

Included in this letter are three poems which show how the young Rimbaud understood the Parnassian Muse and its relation with 'Liberté'. In the long manifesto poem *Credo in unam* (B 40–5) he makes clear that for him this commitment implies a version of Hellenism ('— O Vénus, o Déesse! Je regrette les temps de l'antique jeunesse') and announces his faith in the Goddess of nature and love—Cybele ('Et tout croît et tout monte!') or sea-born Venus ('fleur de chair que la vague parfume'). And this flower-like goddess of sensuality and nature represents a Hellenism opposed to Christianity:

> Je crois en toi! je crois en toi! Divine mère,
> Aphrodite marine! — Oh! la route est amère
> Depuis que l'autre Dieu nous attelle à sa croix;
> Chair, Marbre, Fleur, Vénus, c'est en toi que je crois!

This is a Hellenism of marble and flowers, no 'cold pastoral' but a sensuous Utopia:

> Le grand ciel est ouvert! Les mystères sont morts
> Devant l'Homme, debout, qui croise ses bras forts
> Dans l'immense splendeur de la riche nature!

With all its ideological implications, this poet's alternative world of 'splendeur idéale' remains a recognizable version of poetic Hellenism, as its floral apotheosis confirms:

> Kallipyge la blanche et le petit Éros
> Effleureront, couverts de la neige des roses,
> Les femmes et les fleurs sous leurs beaux pieds écloses!

Here, as throughout the poem, the flowers are figures for a poetic vision of sensuous freedom in nature (recalling the freeing *harmonie* of the Hellenist/Utopian *langage des fleurs*): the Venus of this flowery Hellenism is both 'Muse' and patroness of 'Liberté'.

Rimbaud's adherence to this version of Parnassian poetics was no doubt dictated by his own restlessly vital temperament, as this is revealed in another of the poems sent to Banville, *Sensation* (B 39):

> l'amour infini me montera dans l'âme,
> Et j'irai loin, bien loin, comme un bohémien,
> Par la Nature, — heureux comme avec une femme.

These lines are phrased in terms of personal intention (with six verbs in the first-person future within eight lines), and express the same eagerness for sensation as the sensuously Parnassian *Credo in unam*. Yet he was also capable of assimilating another aspect of Parnassian poetics, for in *Ophélie* (B 46–7), the third of the poems sent to Banville, he presents a distant withdrawn figure in a serenely isolated natural setting:

> Sur l'onde calme et noire où dorment les étoiles
> La blanche Ophélia flotte comme un grand lys, . . .

Les Nénuphars froissés soupirent autour d'elle; . . .
— Un chant mystérieux tombe des astres d'or.

Here is a pale flower-like 'lys' floating among 'nénuphars' and serenaded by dream-like stellar harmonies — a representative of cold beauty ('belle comme la neige') in the supreme detachment of death. She is of course a figure for the poet (with her 'grand front rêveur' and the 'romance' she murmurs to nature) and indeed an emblem of the poet's difficult vocation. She has died because, inspired by 'l'âpre liberté', she desired to participate in nature ('ton cœur écoutait le chant de la Nature') and in love:

> Ciel! Amour! Liberté! Quel rêve, ô pauvre Folle!
> Tu te fondais à lui comme une neige au feu:
> Tes grandes visions étranglaient ta parole
> — Et l'Infini terrible effara ton œil bleu!

Rimbaud here brings two Parnassian topoi together in contrast: on the one hand the ideal of free sensuous experience in nature and love, and on the other the model of detached beauty isolated from life. Indeed the young poet apparently presents the latter as an ironical comment on the former, as if reflecting on the limits or dangers of the *grandes visions* of sensuous participation. Yet the final resolution of the poem attempts to reconcile the two models, by means of flower imagery:

> — Et le Poète dit qu'au rayon des étoiles
> Tu viens chercher, la nuit, les fleurs que tu cueillis;
> Et qu'il a vu sur l'eau, couchée en ses longs voiles,
> La blanche Ophélia flotter, comme un grand lys.

For 'le Poète' appreciates both the sensuous visionary flowers of the living Ophelia ('les fleurs que tu cueillis') and her lilial beauty in death, and thereby claims privileged knowledge about the relationship between the two: the *langage des fleurs* of Ophelia's visions participates mysteriously in her flower-like detachment. In this doubly Parnassian context Rimbaud affirms his commitment both to visionary sensuousness and to the ideal of poetic beauty, both to 'Liberté' and 'Muse'.

But this poem, with its highly personal resolution of the two aspects of Parnassian poetics, perhaps also demonstrates the

influence of Baudelaire. It brings together, after all, a poetic ideal
and the limiting conditions of reality, a mysterious sensual *langage
des fleurs* and a beautiful flower of death. And in Rimbaud's
subsequent work only one poem was to give clear expression to
Parnassian poetics alone, with no traceable Baudelairian influence.
This was *Tête de faune* (B 85), where the poet uses a Parnassian static
décor to evoke sensuous feeling:

> Dans la feuillée incertaine et fleurie
> De fleurs splendides où le baiser dort,
> Vif et crevant l'exquise broderie,
>
> Un faune effaré montre ses deux yeux
> Et mord les fleurs rouges de ses dents blanches.

The faun here participates intimately in flowery nature (emerging
from among its flowers and even sensuously tasting them) and
the 'fleurs . . . où le baiser dort' are (like the faun) figures for a
heightened relationship between nature and feeling in an unequivo-
cally Parnassian context. Much of Rimbaud's other early work, on
the other hand, clearly shows his awareness of Baudelaire's poetics.
Even the Parnassian *Credo in unam* perhaps owes something to
Baudelaire's 'J'aime le souvenir . . . ', and certainly describes Venus
as 'étrangement belle'. A poem like *Vénus anadyomène*
(B 61) (dated 27 July 1870) is quite explicitly Baudelairian; here is
a woman tattooed with the words 'Clara Venus', repugnantly ugly
and sick, smelling 'Horrible étrangement' and whose 'croupe' is
'Belle hideusement d'un ulcère à l'anus'. Rimbaud's use of
corruscating realism to subvert idealization (here that of the
Parnassian Venus!) shows him intelligently adapting the imaginative
world of the poet of *Les Fleurs du Mal*.

In Rimbaud's next period of development, few of the echoes of
Baudelaire are as anodyne as that of *Le Buffet*: 'les fleurs sèches
/ Dont le parfum se mêle à des parfums de fruits' (B 80). More
usually at this period, Rimbaud shows he has learned from him
that poetry could attack accepted pieties of any kind. Thus in the
poem *Le Mal* (B 73) opposition to the Christian God is expressed
no longer in terms of literary Hellenism but with angry irony ('Il
est un Dieu . . . / Qui dans le bercement des hosannah s'endort').
And in *Les Assis* (B 83–4) the poet finds a strong new language
to attack a less exalted target, the bureaucratic self-sufficiency of
librarians,

> Le sinciput plaqué de hargnosités vagues
> Comme les floraisons lépreuses des vieux murs.

This robust invective seems not only angry about sedentary dullness but satirically playful about poetic style itself, and the ironic flower imagery suggests Baudelairian precedent while surpassing it in wayward metaphorical inventiveness:

> Des fleurs d'encre crachant des pollens en virgule
> Les bercent, le long des calices accroupis
> Tel qu'au fil des glaïeuls le vol des libellules
> — Et leur membre s'agace à des barbes d'épis.

Poetic flower allusions are fancifully combined with realism in this description of sedentary day-dreaming. This is a new language developed to satirize both literary and social pieties, and Rimbaud can even seem (in other poems in this vein) to be parodying his major exemplar Baudelaire, as in the final lines of *Oraison du soir* (B 87):

> Doux comme le Seigneur de cèdre et des hysopes,
> Je pisse vers les cieux bruns, très haut et très loin,
> Avec l'assentiment des grands héliotropes.

But the stylistic and ideological violence of poems like *Les Pauvres à l'église* or *L'Orgie parisienne* owe their ironic realism to the subversive example of Baudelaire, justifying Rimbaud in his desire to find new expressive means for both 'Muse' and 'Liberté'. By the winter of 1870–1 Rimbaud's sense of poetic freedom and his opposition to sedentary conformism evidently found more support in Baudelairian than in Parnassian precedent.

Yet in *Les Poètes de sept ans* (B 95–7), written in late 1870 or early 1871, Rimbaud shows that Parnassian models could still contribute to his developing poetics. The Poem's title suggests generalization about child poets, but the text presents a child characterized so as to explain the poetics finally proposed in it. Here is a boy already longing for freedom from 'obéissance' forced to hide his rebelliousness under 'd'âcres hypocrisies', and already commited to non-conformity in various ways. It is in dreaming, reading, and writing especially that freedom takes shape as an alternative to conditions of dull oppressiveness:

> A sept ans, il faisait des romans, sur la vie
> Du grand désert, où luit la Liberté ravie,

> Forêts, soleils, rives, savanes! — Il s'aidait
> De journaux illustrés . . .

Here an escapist landscape is described as a subject for the imagination, a bright dream of freedom in distant nature. After further
reference to habitual oppression, however, he evokes the escapist
ideal again, in a language embodying more fully its sensuous appeal:

> — Il rêvait la prairie amoureuse, où des houles
> Lumineuses, parfums sains, pubescences d'or,
> Font leur remuement calme et prennent leur essor!

Here is the sensuous nature of *Credo in unam*, evoked in terms of
light, smell, gentle movement, and soaring flight. This is a discourse
not merely denoting free sensation but seeking to realize it in poetic
imagery, and the poet later takes this process even further:

> Il lisait son roman sans cesse médité,
> Pleins de ciels ocreux et de forêts noyées,
> De fleurs de chair aux bois sidérals déployées,
> Vertige, écroulements, déroutes et pitié!

This escapist dream embodies the ideal of freedom in a dislocation
of habitual levels in nature: the skies are like clay, the forests both
drowned and stellar. The flowers which unfold in this alternative
reality are both carnal blossoms and radical growths of the imagination, emblems of sensuousness like Rimbaud's Parnassian Venus
(also a 'fleur de chair') and emblems of an imaginative subversiveness
reminiscent of Baudelaire. They are figures for the need to escape
from oppressive conformism into an ideal sensuous dream world,
and at the same time for a disorientating psychological experience
('Vertige') and a radical act of the liberating imagination ('pitié').
The child's dream or 'roman' is the adolescent Rimbaud's poetics,
now a highly original elaboration of his major literary precedents,
but still committed to both 'Muse' and 'Liberté'.

Rimbaud gave the date 26 May 1871 for this poem which illustrates
his new approach to poetry and provides an 'autobiographical'
aetiology for it. It was in the same month that he produced two
documents which show with what extreme self-awareness he
envisioned his poetic vocation at this stage—the letters addressed
to G. Izambard (13 May) and to P. Demeny (15 May).[12] In the
second and longer letter particularly he attempts an account (almost

incoherent in its youthful intensity) of his poetic vocation as he now understands it, summarized in terms common to both letters: 'Je veux être poète, et je travaille à me rendre *voyant*' and 'JE est un autre' (I). Having recognized that he is 'né poète' (I), the poet must become fully aware of his own consciousness: 'il cherche son âme, il l'inspecte, il la tente, l'apprend' (D). He can thus say 'J'assiste à l'éclosion de ma pensée: je la regarde, je l'écoute' (D), and it is in this sense, first, that the poet recognizes that 'JE est un autre'. But once aware of his 'âme' as an objective phenomenon flowering outside himself, he must cultivate its otherness:

Dès qu'il la sait, il doit la cultiver . . . il s'agit de faire l'âme monstrueuse . . .
Je dis qu'il faut être *voyant*, se faire *voyant*.
Le Poète se fait *voyant* par un long, immense et raisonné *dérèglement* de *tous les sens*. Toutes les formes d'amour, de souffrance, de folie; . . . Ineffable torture . . . où il devient entre tous le grand malade, le grand criminel, le grand maudit, — et le suprême Savant! — Car il arrive à *l'inconnu* . . . et quand, affolé, il finirait par perdre l'intelligence de ses visions, il les a vues!

(D.)

By this willed dislocation (perceptual and psychological) of habitual consciousness, the poet becomes in a second sense 'un autre' to himself and others, passing far beyond ordinary experience into an unknown realm. But he is visionary to a purpose, a Promethean 'voleur de feu' bringing back from 'là-bas' knowledge of the unknown, defining 'la quantité d'inconnu s'éveillant en son temps dans l'âme universelle', and thus 'un multiplicateur de progrès' (D). Rimbaud is envisaging a poetry which withdraws from normal experience only to become more real and more liberating, 'Muse' serving 'Liberté' as never before.

But to make the 'inconnu' available in this way, the poet-*voyant* must 'Trouver une langue', and Rimbaud characterizes the appropriate language thus: 'Cette langue sera de l'âme pour l'âme, résumant tout, parfums, couleurs, de la pensée accrochant la pensée et tirant' (D). This ambitious intention owes much to Baudelaire and to the major Parnassian precursors but is also a revisionist critique of them. Later in the letter to Demeny, Rimbaud declares that Gautier, Leconte de Lisle, and Banville are 'très voyants' but too concerned to 'reprendre l'esprit des choses mortes', while Baudelaire is 'le premier voyant, roi des poètes, *un vrai Dieu*' but diminished by his 'milieu trop artiste' and his 'forme . . . mesquine'.[13]

Rimbaud's language will be, then, not *de l'art pour l'art* but 'de l'âme pour l'âme', for he is a poet committed not to cold plastic Hellenism or Baudelairian aesthetic restraint but to living experience at its most extreme. Rimbaud's will be a language 'résumant tout, parfums, sons, couleurs', like the flowery language of Utopian sensual *harmonie* of his own Parnassian *Credo in unam*, or like the *langage des fleurs* of Baudelaire's synaesthetic sensual mysticism.[14] But where these flower languages evoke escapist sensuousness or mysterious ideal harmony, Rimbaud's will express the super-real visions he has obtained by willed forceful participation in *l'inconnu*, 'la pensée accrochant la pensée et tirant'. This will be neither a discourse of serene detachment nor even of *surnaturalisme et ironie*, but the powerful expression of a radically new vision—'du nouveau, idées et formes' (D).

This was the ambitious new poetics the young poet articulated again in a poem he wrote a few months later (it is dated 14 July 1871) and sent to Banville the following month: *Ce qu'on dit au poète à propos de fleurs*. This work, written fifteen months or so after his pro-Parnassian declaration to Banville, opens with a scathing attack on Parnassian flower-like detachment:

> Ainsi, toujours, vers l'azur noir
> Où tremble la mer des topazes,
> Fonctionneront dans ton soir
> Les Lys, ces clystères d'extases! . . .
>
> Des Lys! Des lys! On n'en voit pas!
> Et dans ton Vers, tel que les manches
> Des Pécheresses aux doux pas,
> Toujours frissonnent ces fleurs blanches!
>
> (B 115.)

Rimbaud is not merely providing a pastiche of the serene lilies of Banville's poetry, but denouncing the unreality of these poetic flowers (for in the real world 'On n'en voit pas!') These lilies are representative, besides, of the floral monotony of all similar poetry (in which 'La Flore est diverse à peu près / Comme des bouchons de carafes') for 'Roses', 'Lotos bleus', and 'Hélianthes' are all

> Vieilles verdures, vieux galons!
> Ô croquignoles végétales!
> Fleurs fantasques des vieux Salons! . . .

— Tas d'œufs frits dans de vieux chapeaux,
Lys, Açokas, Lilas et Roses!

These are the monotonous unreal flowers of literary convention,
emblems of a lifeless formalist poetry:

> L'Ode Açoka cadre avec le
> Strophe en fenêtre de lorette;
> Et de lourds papillons d'éclat
> Fientent sur la Pâquerette.
>
> (B 116.)

Here, as throughout the poem, Rimbaud's linguistic exuberance and
his derisive versification contribute to a serious didactic purpose,
which is to insist on the need for a poetry open to realities beyond
floral formalism:

> — En somme, une Fleur, Romarin
> Ou Lys, vive ou morte, vaut-elle
> Un excrément d'oiseau marin?
> Vaut-elle un seul pleur de chandelle?
>
> (B 117.)

But it must also be a poetry in which habitual associations are
dislocated and recombined in a disorientating new language:

> Trouve, aux abords du Bois qui dort,
> Les fleurs, pareilles à des mufles,
> D'où bavent des pommades d'or
> Sur les cheveux sombres des Buffles!
>
> Trouve, aux prés fous, où sur le Bleu
> Tremble l'argent des pubescences,
> Des calices pleins d'Œufs de feu
> Qui cuisent parmi les essences!
>
> Trouve des Chardons cotonneux
> Dont dix ânes aux yeux de braises
> Travaillent à filer les nœuds!
> Trouve des Fleurs qui soient des chaises!
>
> Oui, trouve au cœur des noirs filons
> Des fleurs presque pierres, — fameuses! —
> Qui vers leurs durs ovaires blonds
> Aient des amygdales gemmeuses!
>
> (B 118.)

These stanzas are a virtuoso illustration of the new poetry Rimbaud envisions, in which flowers no longer serve lifeless convention but contribute to a prodigious synthesis—including references to philosophy, medicine, fairy tale and domestic life (with a matching lexical eclecticism), and confusing the three realms of nature together. The flowers of Rimbaud's new visionary language are indeed poetic growths unknown to reality, but they blossom organically out of a new ordering of phenomena—literary, intellectual, natural, physiological, and perceptual. They become figures for a poetry beginning in reality and conventional knowledge but ending in the expression of the unknown:

> De tes noirs Poèmes — Jongleur!
> Blancs, verts, et rouges dioptriques,
> Que s'évadent d'étranges fleurs
> Et des papillons électriques!

> (B 120.)

Strange flowers indeed, poetic and supernatural yet affirming reality, amazingly imaginative yet based in modern experience (like electricity or chairs). The poet has repudiated Parnassian unreality to create a poetic meta-world of his own, and has assimilated Baudelaire's realistically ironic *surnaturalisme* only to surpass it in subversive strangeness.

This is the poet of *Voyelles* (also written in the summer of 1871), who can create from his personal attribution of colours to particular vowels a poetic language both referential and enigmatically visionary. In order to make explicit the 'naissances latentes' in each coloured vowel he produces an associative sequence for each one, with the list for 'E blanc' perhaps the simplest of these, a series of items exemplifying whiteness:

> . . . E, candeurs des vapeurs et des tentes,
> Lances des glaciers fiers, rois blancs, frissons d'ombelles.

Here are white things from various fields of experience, each implying equivalent psychological connotations (candour, pride, sublimity, innocence) but together composing a *symphonie en blanc* recalling Banville or Gautier. Yet the 'lances' and 'tentes' have warlike overtones, and this is only one of five sequences: the black series preceding it (with its flies and 'puanteurs cruelles') and the red one following it (with its 'sang craché') here frame Parnassian detachment in a context of psychological extremes. The sequence for 'U vert' follows a somewhat different pattern:

> U, cycles, vibrements divins des mers virides,
> Paix des pâtis semés d'animaux, paix des rides
> Que l'alchimie imprime aux grands fronts studieux.

The first and last units in this series have no explicit colour associations: the noun 'cycles' (probably suggested by the tuning-fork shape of the letter U) and the 'paix des rides' (linked semantically with the 'Paix' of green pastures). So too in the last sequence the 'suprême Clairon' is suggested either by association with the colour blue (the blue of empty sky suggesting the Last Judgement?), with the shape of the letter 'O' (like the mouth of a trumpet), or with the finality implied by O/Omega. But the semantic connotations of this sequence are all related to the idea of fulfilment, and the poem ends with the mystical or sensual apotheosis of the 'rayon violet de Ses Yeux!'. The associative procedures of this poem are based on *analogie* and thus recall the flower dictionary, which could find 'meaning' in the shape or colour of flowers just as Rimbaud here finds it in the shape or colour of vowels: the five sequences indeed compose a vowel dictionary, a *langage des voyelles*.[15] The conventional flower language had provided a synaesthetic and connotative illustration of *l'analogie universelle* on a small scale. So too Rimbaud's short poem ranges through varied sense-perceptions (smell, sound, movement, shape, texture), various semantic connotations (cruelty, serenity, passion, peace, fulfilment), and different realms of experience (from flies and oceans to the human world and 'Silences traversés des Mondes et des Anges'). Yet this poet's *correspondances* do not illustrate the *profonde unité* of the world experienced (as they do for Baudelaire). Instead the disparate elements of experience presented here are only unified by the poem's analogical structure, as if the experience of the *'dérèglement de tous les sens'* or of 'l'inconnu' were being expressed by a poetic language 'résumant tout, parfums, sons, couleurs'. The poet-*voyant* here provides his own subversive commentary on the flower-language, as well as his own revisionist multi-coloured *symphonie*.

It is clear that Rimbaud conceived the enterprise of the poet as a dangerous exploration of the unknown, promising not so much mystical unity as radical disorientation. He articulated this conception in another way in *Le Bateau ivre*, written just before his meeting with Verlaine in September 1871. Here he insists once more on the necessary withdrawal from conventional experience, using the figure of a boat sailing down-river to the sea, soon liberated from all constraints and running free and alone on the sea without rudder or anchor:

> Et dès lors je me suis baigné dans le Poème
> De la Mer, infusé d'astres et lactescent,
> Dévorant les azurs verts; où, flottaison blême
> Et ravie, un noyé pensif parfois descend.

This experience of free sensuousness offers participation in several levels of nature at once (the sea surface, the sky above, and the depths) and in an oxymoronic synthesis of the emotions ('les rousseurs amères de l'amour!'). It offers a visionary perception of a nature both mystically beautiful and frighteningly unfamiliar:

> Et j'ai vu quelquefois ce que l'homme a cru voir!
> J'ai vu le soleil bas, taché d'horreurs mystiques.

Such visions can associate sea-phosphorescence with eyes or with the life-sap of vegetation:

> Baiser montant aux yeux des mers avec lenteurs,
> La circulation des sèves inouïes.

Or they can mingle flowers with human and animal life:

> J'ai heurté, savez-vous, d'incroyables Florides
> Mêlant aux fleurs des yeux de panthères à peaux
> D'homme! . . .

> (B 129.)

These animal-human flowers are beautiful but threatening, just as the visionary experience is often violent and dislocating ('hystériques', 'écroulements', 'échouages hideux'). But elsewhere flowers are associated with moments of consolation ('Des écumes de fleurs ont bercé mes dérades') and tender oneness:

> La mer dont le sanglot faisait mon roulis doux
> Montait vers moi ses fleurs d'ombre aux ventouses jaunes
> Et je restais, ainsi qu'une femme à genoux.

> (B 130.)

Thus the participation in the 'Poème / De la Mer' offers flowers of various types, unfamiliar synthetic growths like a

confiture exquise aux bons poètes,
Des lichens de soleil et des morves d'azur.

(B 130.)

Indeed these flowers of sea, sky, and 'd'incroyables Florides' are
typical figures of *l'inconnu* itself—*d'étranges fleurs* unstable in their
emotional connotations and capable of association with any aspect
of nature. Like the visionary voyage itself, the flower imagery here
associates together sea, sky, and underwater depths, as well as
emotions of triumph, violence, and tenderness, in a unitive experience. Yet for the perceiving subject this is an experience finally
overwhelming ('martyr', 'bateau perdu', 'planche folle') because of
the contradictions it contains:

Les Aubes sont navrantes.
Toute lune est atroce et tout soleil amer:
L'âcre amour m'a gonflé de torpeurs enivrantes.

(B 131.)

The antitheses here insist that the visionary experience is self-
destructive ('Ô que j'aille à la mer') although the last two stanzas
show that the *voyant* refuses to return to habitual adult social experience. This is an experience structured by contradiction (both desirable
and impossible), like the synthetic oxymoronic flowers of its *visions*.
Rimbaud is here expressing both confidence in his own visionary
power and awareness of its limitations and difficulties: the flowers
of his poetics are post-Parnassian free beautiful growths beyond
normal experience and post-Baudelairian ironic flowers of negativity.

Few of Rimbaud's verse poems written after his meeting with
Verlaine have the visionary power of *Le Bateau ivre*. Several of them,
however, reformulate its themes, structure, and flower imagery, while
testifying by their versification and obliqueness to Verlaine's influence. Thus in *Comédie de la soif* he calls on myth or literature to
provide visionary experience for him ('Anciens exilés chers, / Dites-
moi la mer') but then realizes

Non, plus ces boissons pures,
Ces fleurs d'eau pour verres;
Légendes ni figures
Ne me désaltèrent.

(B 152.)

The paper flowers of literature (floating only in the glass of domestic experience) can no longer satisfy his thirst for sensuous life, and the poem ends with his desire to

> Expirer en ces violettes humides,
> Dont les aurores chargent ces forêts.

(B 154.)

In *Chanson de la plus haute tour* he again expresses a 'soif malsaine' for experience in terms of flower imagery:

> Ainsi la Prairie
> A l'oubli livrée
> Grandie et fleurie
> D'encens et d'ivraies.

(B 158.)

So too in *Âge d'or* he juxtaposes intellectual activity ('mille questions' leading only to 'ivresse et folie') with a spontaneity welcoming and flower-like:

> Reconnais ce tour
> Si gai, si facile:
> Ce n'est qu'onde, flore,
> Et c'est ta famille!

(B 162.)

And in *Fêtes de la faim* he contrasts his thirst ('C'est le malheur') with floral sensuous intimacy:

> Au sein du sillon je cueille
> La doucette et la violette.

(B 170.)

These flowers are emblems of unitive fullness of experience but also of dissatisfaction, and in *Mémoire* the floral image of fulfilment ('le souci d'eau — ta foi conjugale, ô l'Épouse!') becomes one of disillusioned frustration:

> Jouet de cet œil d'eau morne, je n'y puis prendre,
> ô canot immobile! oh! bras trop courts! ni l'une
> ni l'autre fleur: ni la jaune qui m'importune,
> là; ni la bleue, amie à l'eau couleur de cendre.

(B 178.)

There is here too a new despair about the passage of time ('Les roses des roseaux dès longtemps dévorées!') which emphasizes the urgency and the difficulty of achieving the unitive vision.

The double aspect of the flower image finds a parallel in the two sets of prose poems, for the overall disillusionment of *Une saison en enfer* is flowerless, while the *Illuminations* are bright with the flowers of desire and vision. In *Après le déluge* they evoke a primeval innocence restored by the cleansing of the Flood: 'Oh! les pierres précieuses qui se cachaient, — les fleurs qui regardaient déjà' (B 253). Like the precious stones (mystically hidden in the earth), the flowers go on representing wholeness and innocence whatever the subsequent history of the world, and the prose poem alludes to them in similar terms after a fanciful description of the world's adulthood: '— oh! les pierres précieuses s'enfouissant, et les fleurs ouvertes!' They are figures for a oneness of vision like that of childhood, in which (as in *Enfance*) 'les fleurs de rêve tintent, éclatent, éclairent' or 'Des fleurs magiques bourdonnaient' (B 255–6). They propose a fresh participation in the very life of nature, as in *Aube*: 'La première entreprise fut, dans le sentier déjà empli de frais et blêmes éclats, une fleur qui me dit son nom' (B 284). The flower which speaks to the poet promises him (as did the Romantic and Baudelairian *langage des fleurs*) a vision of unitive experience: yet Rimbaud is not conventionally passive before this relevation since it is also an *entreprise* actively undertaken, and soon 'je levai un à un les voiles' (B 284). The floral vision of the prose poem *Fleurs* provides a fine illustration (*illumination*!) of his active poetic agency:

— je vois la digitale s'ouvrir sur un tapis de filigranes d'argent, d'yeux et de chevelures.
    Des pièces d'or jaune semées sur l'agate, des piliers d'acajou supportant un dôme d'émeraudes, des bouquets de satin blanc et de fines verges de rubis entourent la rose d'eau.

(B 285.)

Here indeed is the typical Rimbaldian enterprise. The evocation of the flowers of nature demonstrates its visionary quality in terms of the active human imagination — 'digitale' and 'rose d'eau' in a context of precious stones and beautiful human things ('yeux', 'chevelure', 'satin'), and all arranged as if by human hand. For Rimbaud as poet, the flowers of nature serve finally to justify a visionary splendour which is all his own, a revelation of beauty only given because it has been strongly sought: 'Tels qu'un dieu aux énormes yeux bleus et aux formes de neige, la mer et le ciel attirent aux terrasses de marbre la foule des jeunes et fortes roses' (B 285). His *langage des fleurs* is explicitly that of the all-powerful poet who, like a blue-eyed white god, or like the sea and the sky, can fill the human imagination with the vigorous flowers of nature. This is a vision more ambitious than Parnassian marble-and-flowers, and a flower language transforming Baudelairian paradox. Despite his final disillusionment and literary silence, Rimbaud had undeniably (as he states in *Adieu*) 'essayé d'inventer de nouvelles fleurs, . . . de nouvelles langues'.[16]

iv. Mallarmé

Mallarmé had already written a certain amount of verse before he assimilated the influence of Baudelaire, Gautier, or Banville.[17] Yet in the poetry of his school years, heavily influenced by Hugo and Lamartine, he had already made considerable use of flower imagery. In a poem written as school-work in 1859 (*La Prière d'une mère*), flowers have the conventional connotations of child-like innocence and piety: 'Reçois nos lys, fleurs de l'enfance!' (M 13). He used flower figures more personally in other more confessional poems of 1859, several of which refer to deaths of those close to him — his sister Maria died in 1857 (ten years after the death of his mother) and his young friend Harriet in July 1859. In one of these the poet first laments his sister as a flower now lost to him ('Hier c'était la fleur aux feuilles d'or'), then gains reassurance that she is rejoicing in a flowery eternity ('Et sa voix répondit d'où naît la violette: . . . / "Aujourd'hui c'est le ciel"') (GM 131). In the poem on the death of Harriet, however, he attacks both God and nature for their ironic unconcern with his own loss:

> Tu ris! et comme toi rit l'heureux univers. . . .
>
> La fleur sous le zéphyr que sa senteur parfume
> Berce le papillon, qui, riant, sur l'écume
> Se mire au flot d'azur, écoute son doux chant.
>
> (M 9.)

The same disillusioned irony informs the short poem *A Dieu*:

> As-tu placé dans nos ténèbres
> L'astre pour nous en priver?

> Veux-tu changer en fleurs funèbres
> Le lilas . . . ?

(GM 143.)

Indeed in the strongly ideological *Pan* he rejects Christianity for a pantheist *harmonie* which seems to guarantee a flowery ideal beyond disillusionment:

> ce mot:
> 'Je t'aime! . . .' que tout dit, fleurs grandes aux petites,
> Roses aux astres, la nuit; vague aux roseaux, le jour!

(GM 176.)

This ideal is represented in another way by the concept of survival after death, once more explicitly in the school *narration* (probably revised several years later) called 'Ce que disent les trois cigognes'. Contemplating the rose he associates with his daughter Deborah, Nick Parrit muses that 'Tout n'est pas mort' since the rose is 'une dernière illusion' whose colour and smell 'mêlent l'espérance au souvenir'. He then witnesses Deborah dancing before him and scattering flowers:

> Des lys! des lilas! des verveines!
> Des fleurs! que j'en jette à mains pleines!
> Roses berçant des chants rêveurs.[18]

She is an ideal combining illusion and hope with memory, as do some lines written in November 1859:

> Souviens-toi! Dieu nous mit une lueur sainte,
> Le souvenir — qui fait que notre cœur devient
> Un éden, où l'absent parmi les fleurs revient.[19]

Other poems of the same year suggest, though, that the adolescent's sense of lost innocence was not associated merely with mourning. Thus in *Aveu* in February he was already lamenting the passing of 'l'âge d'or',

> Où je croyais aux anges
> A l'aile étoilée, où les fleurs
> Disaient des mots étranges
>
> A mon cœur! . . .

(GM 127–8.)

Disillusioning experience has silenced such innocent flower language and perhaps poetry as well, for in the past 'je rêvais, ma lyre / Sur mon sein!' (GM 127). So too in May he claims that 'la débauche' has made him 'Une fleur sans parfum, un cœur sans poésie' (GM 141), and even insists in November that any mourning he undertakes must be for his own state:

C'est moi dont le cœur froid se revêt d'un linceul!
Moi . . . qui rêve à l'azur, les deux pieds dans la fange.

(GM 143.)

This is an adolescent poet using his 'lyre' or 'poésie' to express the ironic contradiction between flower-like innocence and his own state of mourning and disillusionment. Indeed these early poems habitually evoke an ideal of innocence—whether accessible in nature or ironically attainable, resurrected by memory or irrevocably lost—set up in antithesis to a strong awareness of negativity, death, or disillusionment.

The poet who could deploy conventional flower imagery in this way was well prepared to appreciate *Les Fleurs du Mal*, and by 1861 or 1862 was reformulating his own habitual antitheses in explicitly Baudelairian terms:

J'ai cherché l'Infini qui fait que l'homme pèche,
Et n'ai trouvé qu'un Gouffre ennemi du sommeil.

(M 14.)

For here 'l'Infini' is a 'rêve fier' like his earlier floral ideal, and the flowerless 'Gouffre' of real experience is 'hérissé d'âpres ronces'. He could see in Baudelaire a poet undergoing all possible disillusionment, and in the Baudelairian *Le Guignon* (1862) imagines ill-fated poets subject to every ironic misfortune:

Grâce à *lui*, s'ils s'en vont tenter un sein fané
Avec des fleurs, partout l'impureté s'allume,
Des limaces naîtront sur leur bouquet damné.

(M 1411.)

But in the same poem he also characterizes a quite different class of poets—proud 'mendiants d'azur' who are Promethean without suffering, and 'consolés étant majestueux'—very likely including poets like Banville and Leconte de Lisle as well as Hugo and

Lamartine. It seems indeed that he was reflecting at this stage on what type of poet he should become. Thus although he can describe Emmanuel Des Essarts (not dismissively) as a poet too engaged with life to 'cueillir des bouquets en chemin', he personally refuses such realism ('Un poëte qui polke avec un habit noir') in terms which suggest a high Parnassian vocation ('Pailletés d'astres, fous d'azur').[20] And in his article in *L'Artiste* of 15 September 1862 ('L'Art pour tous', M 257–60) he presents the poet as an 'adorateur du beau inaccessible au vulgaire' and argues that since 'Toute chose sacrée . . . s'enveloppe de mystère' the poet must keep his distance from the public. He is horrified that *Les Fleurs du Mal* are printed and bought like any cheap novel, and dreams of a literature withdrawn in mystery: 'Ô fermoirs d'or des vieux missels! ô hiéroglyphes inviolés des rouleaux de papyrus!'. Here is a poet presenting Baudelaire as a high criterion for poetry and at the same time calling for a more-than-Parnassian isolation from life. His own work of the next few years (including poems published in the 1866 *Parnasse* volume) was to follow both these patterns.

The poem *Apparition* (1862–4) shows him beginning to integrate both Baudelairian and Hellenist language and themes with the concerns of his own earlier poetry. For here personal dejection is expressed in Baudelairian terms:

> Ma songerie aimant à me martyriser
> S'enivrait savamment du parfum de tristesse . . .
>
> J'errais donc, l'œil rivé sur le pavé vieilli.
>
> (M 30.)

But the setting is less urban than pastoral, an evocation of sad cold beauty with 'séraphins en pleurs / Rêvant . . . dans le calme des fleurs / Vaporeuses' and 'l'azur des corolles'. And the 'apparition' who represents a flowery ideal alternative to his *spleen* is like 'la fée au chapeau de clarté' of his childhood,

> laissant toujours de ses mains mal fermées
> Neiger de blancs bouquets d'étoiles parfumées.
>
> (M 30.)

She is a *symphonie en blanc* evoking death but resurrecting memory, and her white flowers recall Banville and Baudelaire as much as his own earlier ideal of innocence. In *Vere Novo* (1862), the first of a series of poems concerned with the problems of creativity, his sadness is caused by the ironic challenge of the floral ideal:

> Le printemps maladif a chassé tristement
> L'hiver, saison de l'art serein, l'hiver lucide.
>
> (M 34.)

For nature in spring with its 'champs où la sève immense se pavane' is an embodiment of all the potency which the poet (himself 'maladif' and 'triste') would wish for his art, and its flowery beauty ('parfums d'arbres' and 'lilas') only makes him despair of his 'rêve vague et beau'. The end of the poem does not resolve the irony, for the poet remains waiting 'que mon ennui s'élève', while nature's beauty still defies him to rival it:

> — Cependant l'Azur rit sur la haie et l'éveil
> De tant d'oiseaux en fleur gazouillant au soleil.

This poem is Baudelairian in its thematic content (the difficulty of poetic creation), its psychological structure (*spleen et idéal*) and some of its vocabulary. Yet it is structured as a series of reformulations of a single antithesis (already contained in the words 'printemps maladif') and thus takes on a static quality suggesting Hellenist models as well as Baudelaire's *spleen* poems. Mallarmé articulated the same psychological antithesis in *L'Azur* (1864):

> De l'éternel azur la sereine ironie
> Accable, belle indolemment comme les fleurs,
> Le poète impuissant qui maudit son génie
> A travers le désert stérile des Douleurs.
>
> (M 37/M 1432.)

In this poem the ironic contraction between 'l'Azur' and the poet's 'ennui' is enacted as a more spacious psychological drama of attempted flight and ultimate defeat, recalling not only Baudelaire but even Lislean pessimism-amidst-beauty. But Mallarmé is already searching here for a new indirectness of syntax to express the ironies of accepting the challenge of ideal beauty. In this enterprise flowers play an important part, for they represent an ideal both innocent and ironic: rejoicing 'indolemment' in a beauty beyond ordinary experience, they are emblems of the poet's aesthetic ideal and reminders of his own poetic indolence, doubly representative of the poet's mysterious vocation.

The poem *Les Fenêtres* (1863) is equally concerned with the creative
enterprise. The opening narrative section describes a sick man who drags
himself to the windows eager to look out ('d'azur bleu vorace') and then

> Voit des galères d'or, belles comme des cygnes,
> Sur un fleuve de pourpre et de parfums dormir
> En berçant l'éclair fauve et riche de leurs lignes
> Dans un grand nonchaloir chargé de souvenir!

> (M 32–3.)

This escapist ideal (composed of Parnassian and Baudelairian
beauties) has a correlative in the second part of the poem, which
represents the poet as himself sickened by the 'triste hôpital' of
ordinary material life and eager to escape to windows where

> béni,
> Dans leur verre, lavé d'éternelles rosées,
> Que dore le matin chaste de l'Infini

> Je me mire et me vois ange! et je meurs, et j'aime
> — Que la vitre soit l'art, soit la mysticité —
> A renaître, portant mon rêve en diadème,
> Au ciel antérieur où fleurit la Beauté!

> (M 33.)

In a synthesis of many of his earlier themes (innocence, angel, 'rêve',
memory, and resurrection) Mallarmé here evokes an *azur* in which
beauty can flower. It is an ideal state requiring the poet to turn away
from the world to behold his own reflection, thereby becoming pure
spirit like an angel; by the same token it requires that he die to self
and to the world (in this sense 'l'art' *is* 'la mysticité'). But it also
promises rebirth or resurrection: as art, 'la vitre' proposes creative
transformation of existing poetic ideals (Baudelairian or Hellenist
escapism), and as 'mysticité' it resurrects an Eden of innocent
memory. Mallarmé's flower of beauty is already a complex and
delicate growth, and the poem closes with doubts about the viability
of this poetic ideal in the real world and the dangerous possibility
of escaping into the ideal once and for all. Here perhaps for the first
time Mallarmé shows his awareness of the all-inclusive and unprecedented character of his creative enterprise.

The poet approaches his high poetic vocation in another way in
January 1864, in the poem first entitled *Épilogue*. He declares himself

'Las de l'amer repos' of inactivity and 'plus las sept fois' of frustrating attempts to write new poetry (the 'pacte dur / De creuser par veillée une fosse nouvelle / Dans le terrain avare et froid de ma cervelle'). He is ashamed because he is unworthy of his poetic vocation:

> Une gloire pour qui jadis j'ai fui l'enfance
> Adorable des bois de roses sous l'azur
> Naturel . . .

> (M 35.)

His childhood awareness of flowery nature is an ironic reproach to present uncreativity, and the memory of that Eden-like dawn threateningly evokes the final dawn (associated with the white roses of death) when the poet must account for his talents:

> — Que dire à cette aurore, ô Rêves, visité
> Par les roses, quand, peur de ses roses livides,
> Le vaste cimetière unira les trous vides?

> (M 35/M 1428.)

In response the poet turns away from the frustrations of creativity as he has been conceiving it ('L'Art vorace d'un pays cruel') and proposes instead a strategy of creative withdrawal:

> Imiter le Chinois au cœur limpide et fin
> De qui l'extase pure est de peindre la fin
> Sur ses tasses de neige à la lune ravie
> D'une bizarre fleur qui parfume sa vie
> Transparente, la fleur qu'il a sentie, enfant,
> Au filigrane bleu du songe se greffant.

> (M 36/M 1428.)

This dying flower recalling (resurrecting!) childhood innocence has the power to make the artist's life 'Transparente' as he devotes himself life-denyingly to it alone ('la mort telle avec le seul rêve du sage'): only such single-mindedness will allow him to create, 'serein' and 'distrait', an aesthetic landscape worthy of the pure ideal. The flower of this art of self-denial and mysterious creativity shows the poet a way to rival childhood's 'bois de roses sous l'azur / Naturel', and make some answer to the white roses of mortality.

The poet must thus be totally committed to his enterprise and find beyond frustration and outside life an art which is self-sustaining in its mystery. And here more than in any earlier poem Mallarmé was finding a language appropriate to his poetic ideal, a language itself *transparent*, *serein*, and *distrait*. For here indeed syntactical displacement creates mysterious ambiguity, long sentences and verb-postponement produce a sense of ritual and noble distance, and unexplained figures provide a necessary obscurity. This is a language aspiring to a mysterious otherness in which the flowers of rhetoric imitate the floral ideal of beauty. Mallarmé could find considerable precedent for this in Baudelaire, Gautier, and Banville, as he acknowledges in April 1864 in the prose poems of *Symphonie littéraire* (M 261–5), evoking their poetics to describe his own. His presentation of Baudelaire opens in a sad landscape with 'un ciel livide d'ennui': there are 'Nulles fleurs, à terre, alentour' but a sunset of 'une singulière rougeur' suggests 'une avalanche de roses mauvaises ayant le péché pour parfum'. In this realm 'une amère sensation d'exil' induces a longing for 'la patrie', and the older poet reveals how this longing is satisfied: 'Devant moi se dresse l'apparition du poète savant qui me l'indique en un hymne élancé mystiquement comme un lis.' Mallarmé thus finds in Baudelaire a precedent for the psychological structure and *thématique* of his own poetry, for its mysterious language of *ennui* and mystical *idéal*, and for its ironical and mystical flower imagery. When presenting Gautier as a representative of 'l'Idéal' he imagines a landscape like 'le Paradis', with a sky whose 'azur a encore perdu l'ironie de sa beauté'. This is a condition of restored innocence which calls forth all the resources of the 'être spirituel': — le trésor profond des correspondances, l'accord intime des couleurs, le souvenir du rythme antérieur, et la science mystérieuse du Verbe'. Gautier, then is another model for Mallarmé's new poetic language of mystery, while Banville is invoked as the patron of the more sensual aspects of an ideal uncompromisingly floral: 'il marche en roi à travers l'enchantement édénéen de l'âge d'or, célébrant à jamais la noblesse des rayons et la rougeur des roses, les cygnes et les colombes, et l'éclatante blancheur du lis enfant, — la terre heureuse!' Together Gautier and Banville thus represent an unironic ideal of innocence and the example of all three poets collectively confirms Mallarmé's own aspirations for a poetic language both ironic and idealizing, innocent and sensual, beautiful and mysterious.

For him as for his exemplars this was a language constantly celebrating the poetic significance of flowers, and the poem *Les*

Fleurs (written in March 1864) is yet another floral *art poétique*.[21]
It first presents flowers in their primal non-ironic state, in an Edenic
symphonie of innocence:

> Des avalanches d'or du vieil azur, au jour
> Premier et de la neige éternelle des astres
> Mon Dieu, tu détachas les grands calices pour
> La terre jeune encore et vierge de désastres.
>
> (M 33/M 1424.)

Yet the list of flowers which follows reveals an ironic contrast
between the ideal purity first attributed to them and other poetic
connotations. The 'glaïeul' is 'fauve', the 'laurier' recalls 'âmes
exilées' and its blushing colour suggests injured innocence ('la pudeur
des aurores foulées'). Mallarmé recalls the flower dictionary here
only to adapt it to his own purposes (the usual 'meaning' of the
laurier-rose is *Gloire*) and goes on to characterize the sensuality of
the rose as threatening:

> Et, pareille à la chair de la femme, la rose
> Cruelle, Hérodiade en fleur du jardin clair,
> Celle qu'un sang farouche et radieux arrose!
>
> (M 34.)

In the midst of the immaculate 'jardin clair', the rose's sensuality
blossoms into sadism, and its shining blood-redness evokes both
radiance and death. This flower, like all the others, participates by
its origins in primal brightness and eternal innocence, yet it also
partakes in sensuality and destruction. The next stanza characterizes
the lily

> Et tu fis la blancheur sanglotante des lys
> Qui roulant sur des mers de soupirs qu'elle effleure
> A travers l'encens bleu des horizons pâlis
> Monte rêveusement vers la lune qui pleure!

In a world in which floral beauty can imply death, the lily in its white
purity (still announcing the original innocence) also becomes an ironic
flower, since now innocence must necessarily be 'sanglotante'. But
it is only in such a world that the ideal takes on its full value in an
antithetical structure: the lily is all the more sadly white for its
contrast with the rose. Besides, only in such a world does the yearning

for the ideal have any meaning, and this stanza therefore alludes repeatedly to the desire for it ('soupirs', and 'l'encens bleu', 'horizons', 'Monte rêveusement'). This is a world in which sad whiteness ('blancheur sanglotante') yearns for sad whiteness ('la lune qui pleure'), a world of sorrowful *correspondances*, beauty and irony together. Thus the poet can celebrate a state of affairs which makes possible a poetry of antithesis:

> Ô mon Père, hosannah du profond de nos limbes!
> A jamais hosannah dans l'or des jours sans soirs.

And the apparently anti-Christian sarcasm of the last lines in fact expresses a truth about poetry, as the Aubanel version makes clear:

> Car, n'oubliant personne en ton charmant effort,
> Tu donnas, lui montrant son devoir sans mensonge,
> De fortes fleurs versant comme un parfum la mort
> Au poète ennuyé que l'impuissance ronge.

> (M 1423.)

The poem which began as a floral Hellenist *symphonie* of innocence ends as a celebration of ironic *fleurs du mal*, for only 'de fortes fleurs' breathing the smell of death can truly show the poet his aesthetic duty and turn *impuissance* into creativity. Mallarmé was already committed to a poetry withdrawn from life and mysteriously self-sustaining, but here he insists too on the necessity of irony for his poetry. Indeed in *Les Fleurs* he offers the flower as an exemplary metaphor for the ironic ambiguity of his poetic language. The strong flowers which mean many things at once (innocence and suffering, beauty and death, *spleen et idéal*) typify both the manner and the matter of the poetry he envisages.

Flower imagery had by now played an indispensable part in the development of his poetics, and continued to do so later in 1864 as he advanced further into the mystery of his art. In October he wrote to his friend Cazalis, 'J'ai enfin commencé mon *Hérodiade*. Avec terreur car j'invente une langue qui doit nécessairement jaillir d'une poétique très nouvelle.'[22] He was to work on this project over the next three years, while also working on a parallel project for the *Faune* poem, with an extreme sense of psychological and intellectual crisis. Both the crisis and the new language he envisaged were intimately related to the subject of Hérodiade: 'moi, stérile et crépusculaire, j'ai pris un sujet effrayant, dont les sensations, quand elles sont vives, sont amenées jusqu'à l'atrocité, et si elles flottent, ont l'attitude étrange du mystère'.[23] This is a subject evoking both violence and mystery, like the rose/Hérodiade of the poem *Les Fleurs*. And just as the 'rose/Cruelle' in that poem expressed Mallarmé's antithetical vision at its most *farouche* and *radieux*, so his new subject will be capable of full ironic extension, for its 'sensations' will be alternately violent and quietly mysterious. The blood-red rose of *Les Fleurs* was indeed an emblem of destruction, and appropriately the poet describes his new language as destructive of conventional discourse. His language will ignore the real ('Peindre non la chose, mais l'effet qu'elle produit') and it will suppress 'mots' and 'paroles' in favour of 'intentions' and 'sensations'. It will, too, do away with rational structure, only concerned to 'noter des impressions très fugitives [qui] . . . se suivent comme dans une symphonie'. It will be a language destroying 'meaning', referentiality, and discursive rationality—a language of sensations musically arranged, a symphony of ironic self-awareness beyond meaning and the real world. It will be the invention of a poet who has learned much from his precedents but now creates his own unprecedented *symphonie* of ideality and *langage des fleurs du mal*.

From the start the text presents Hérodiade as poised between life and death ('Tu vis! ou vois-je ici l'ombre d'une princesse?') and flower-like in her ambiguity: the words 'les pâles lys qui sont en moi' suggest both ideality and suffering, beauty and death. Like the beauty of the floral ideal, she is (if alive) vulnerable to destruction and (if dead) invulnerable like a beautiful apparition beyond the world of the senses:

> un baiser me tûrait
> Si la beauté n'était la mort . . .
>
> (M 44.)

The deathly ideality of her 'pâles lys' resembles that of the 'parfums' offered by the nurse, since the perfume's 'vertu funèbre' is 'l'essence ravie aux vieillesses de roses'. Yet these 'roses' have too many connotations of sensuality, and Hérodiade therefore rejects them as an 'ivresse' endangering her own antithetical status:

> Je veux que mes cheveux qui ne sont pas des fleurs
> A répandre l'oubli des humaines douleurs, . . .

Conservent la froideur stérile du métal.

(M 45/M 1445.)

She will reject any use of flowers/perfumes if they are an escapist ideal which excludes suffering, for she wants to remain coldly aware of her own ironic duality. This is the cold consciousness now reflected in the mirror held before her, an 'Eau froide par l'ennui dans [son] cadre gelée'. It is a consciousness sometimes yearning for ideality and lost innocence ('Désolée / Des songes et cherchant mes souvenirs') and sometimes violently disillusioned:

Mais, horreur! des soirs, dans ta sévère fontaine
J'ai de mon rêve épars connu la nudité.

(M 45.)

Concerned only with her own ironic reflection, Hérodiade rejects the nurse's caress as an 'impiété fameuse' and repeatedly refuses to listen to her insinuations about sensual love. The nurse is thus forced to recognize Hérodiade's true nature:

Triste fleur qui croît seule et n'a pas d'autre émoi
Que son ombre dans l'eau vue avec atonie.

(M 46.)

Beautiful like a flower, she is solitary and virginal, coldly distanced both from the world of flowery sensuality and from the flowers of a non-ironic ideal. By choosing the vocation of self-reflection she has become a 'Victime lamentable à son destin offerte', and can now recognize her beauty for what it is:

Oui, c'est pour moi, pour moi, que je fleuris, déserte!
Vous le savez, jardins d'améthyste, enfouis
Sans fin dans de savants abîmes éblouis,
Ors ignorés, gardant votre antique lumière
Sous le sombre sommeil d'une terre première.

(M 47.)

These are the beauties not of sensuality but of the ironic awareness itself, jewels hidden in the depths of consciousness but flowering in bright gardens of dream and memory ('antique lumière', 'terre première'). They are the jewels of self-reflection, bright but cold, figures for a vocation both self-sustaining and destructive of sensual life:

J'aime l'horreur d'être vierge . . .

Toi qui te meurs, toi qui brûles de chasteté,
Nuit blanche de glaçons et de neige cruelle!

(M 47.)

This is a solitary state of innocence and cruelty, life and death, fire
and ice — an ironic beauty reflecting the contradictory conditions of
its existence in 'l'idolâtrie / D'un miroir'.

The scene ends with an explicit expression of these contradictions
in a new form of irony. Hérodiade denies that she is about to die,
again refuses the non-ironic ideal ('l'azur / Séraphique'), but then
expresses a desire for destructive sensuality:

là-bas, sais-tu pas un pays
Où le sinistre ciel ait les regards haïs
De Vénus qui, le soir, brûle dans le feuillage:
J'y voudrais fuir.

(M 48/M 1445.)

She is here rejecting her own earlier rejection of sensuality, thus
destroying the very conditions of her solitary existence, and can
announce: 'Vous mentez, ô fleur nue / De mes lèvres'. Hérodiade has
hitherto celebrated her own ironic beauty in a language of antithesis
and negation, but now pronounces this language itself untrue. The
'fleur nue' of her speech is the negation of a negation, itself a flower
of beauty and destruction. In this nihilistic apotheosis, self-
contradiction issues in something radically new — 'une chose
inconnue' or some mysterious alteration of consciousness:

une enfance sentant parmi les rêveries
Se séparer enfin ses froides pierreries.

(M 48.)

Like *Les Fenêtres*, the *Scène* presents a flowery beauty of life/death
beyond the material world; like *Épilogue* it depicts 'la fin . . . /
D'une bizarre fleur' which is also a beginning. The 'Triste fleur' of
Hérodiade's beauty and the 'fleur nue' of her speech also resemble
the rose/Hérodiade of *Les Fleurs*, in their ironic union of beauty
and negativity. But in the *Scène*, beauty and language flower into
a new poetry of self-destruction and mystery, a poetic flower of
radical indeterminacy and self-negation.

In this work entirely concerned with the conditions of its own existence (or non-existence?) flowers function indistinguishably as imagery, rhetoric, or subject matter. Indeed by its multifunctional and polysemic nature the flower becomes the exemplary figure for a poetry constructed out of self-reference and self-contradiction. This is a poetry in which the conventional relations between language, the world, and the creative self have been deconstructed and reconstructed in new ways, and Mallarmé's 'terreur' is appropriate to his enterprise. Yet the poet was also aware of the significance of his achievement: the flowers which announce self-destruction in the *Scène* could also affirm the triumph of poetry in the various drafts of the *Faune* poem, with flowers once more functioning as a polyvalent emblem of his poetry.[24] As the first version shows, this poem has much in common with the Hérodiade scene, but its imagery and *thématique* are here reformulated and turned (as it were) inside out. Once more a solitary subjectivity (here the faun) is aware of the ironic status of beauty. Here, however, beauty is exteriorized in the voluptuous pastoral setting and at the same time identified with the faun's memory (real or illusory) of a sensual encounter with two naiads ('J'avais des nymphes! / Est-ce un songe?'). The flower imagery grows out of the voluptuous landscape, but becomes a metaphor for the ambiguous status of the sensual memory: when the faun speaks of 'la nudité des roses' he is referring to ideal surroundings but also to sensuality realized as physical nakedness or naked in its unreality. So too the 'glaïeuls séchés . . . / Qu'à l'égal du soleil ma passion saccage' are elements of landscape but also ambiguous signs of desire. The faun is aware that his 'désir torride' may have been an 'illusion de [ses] sens fabuleux', a mere wish-fulfilment imitating nature and inspired by the 'ivresses de la Sève'. So when he questions whether nature's 'lys' were conspiring 'au pudique silence' and remembers the naiads 'fleuries / De la pudeur d'aimer', these are *pudeurs* evoking a physicality at once realized and withheld. Although all these flowers speak of a beautiful voluptuousness both affirmed and denied, the faun's assurance grows, and he recounts the consummation in

> des jardins, haïs par l'ombrage frivole,
> De roses tisonnant d'impudeur au soleil,
> Où notre amour à l'air consumé soit pareil!
>
> (M 1452.)

If 'real' this act is an anti-formulation of Hérodiade's cold mirror-idolatry, and if 'unreal' a sensual re-formulation of it. But in either case it is once more an approach to beauty, here too a beauty ironically aware of the conditions by which poetic truth creates itself. For although the flowers of this sensual discourse recall Hérodiade's 'fleur nue' in their self-contradiction, they speak of a consummation affirming the independent truth of poetry ('Adieu, femmes; duo de vierges quand je vins').

The same sense of affirmation informs the revisions made in subsequent versions, and extends to the flower imagery. For in these versions flower figures refer no longer merely to the landscape and the naiads but to the imaginative subject and to his imaginative act, as if to emphasize the aesthetic autonomy of the floral ideal. Thus in the 'Improvisation' the faun asks

> M'éveillerai-je donc de ma langueur première,
> Droit et seul, sous un flot d'ironique lumière,
> Lys; et parmi vous tous, beau d'ingénuité?

> (M 1457.)

The connotations of creative pride are clear, even if qualified by the term 'ironique' and the ambiguity of 'ingénuité' (innocent pride or withholding modesty?). The *Après-midi* version, however, makes an unqualified affirmation:

> Alors m'éveillerai-je à la ferveur première,
> Droit et seul, sous un flot antique de lumière,
> Lys! et l'un de vous tous pour l'ingénuité.

> (M 51.)

Here is an act of the imagination powerful enough to recreate memory or create independent poetic truth, and its 'ingénuité' is a lilial triumph of ideality beyond irony. This is a strong new use of the flower figure, taken up again in the tribute to the flute found in both later versions:

> Tâche . . . instrument des fuites, ô maligne
> Syrinx, de refleurir aux lacs où tu m'attends.

The flute was the cause of the naiads' flight, but also represents the creative flowering of the imaginative refusal of reality. The *Après-midi* text, moreover, summarizes the whole enterprise in an affirmation of poetic subjectivity:

Aimai-je un rêve?

Mon doute, amas de nuit ancienne, s'achève
En maint rameau subtil, qui, demeuré les vrais
Bois mêmes, prouve, hélas! que bien seul je m'offrais
Pour triomphe la faute idéale de roses.

The *impuissance* of imaginative doubt has now realized itself in a
subtlety of poetic landscape which competes even with nature, in
a rivalry which only reinforces the independence (but also the solitude) of the imagining subject. For in this independence he has
committed a strong imaginative act which can triumphantly lay hold
of rose-like sensuality, in a verbal world rivalling, by a great irony
('la faute'), that of nature. Here Mallarmé-as-faun affirms, through
irony yet beyond it, the triumphant floral ideality of his art.

These are the themes which he reformulates specifically in terms
of poethood in the 1873 *Toast Funèbre* (M 54–5) in honour of
Gautier, whom he hails as the 'emblème' of all poets in his life and
in death. For unlike the non-poet mortal who in death leaves 'la
Terre' for 'le néant' of the 'mots qu'il n'a pas dits', the poet has
already during his lifetime transformed the flowers of nature into
the mysteries of language, in words that survive:

Le Maître, par un œil profond, a, sur ses pas,
Apaisé de l'éden l'inquiète merveille
Dont le frisson final, dans sa voix seule, éveille
Pour la Rose et le Lys le mystère d'un nom.

(M 55.)

By accomplishing the high vocation of rivalling nature ('le devoir
/ Idéal que nous font les jardins de cet astre') he has created self-
sustaining flowers of language surviving beyond transience ('ces
fleurs dont nulle ne se fane') in bright Edenic ideality 'parmi l'heure
et le rayon du jour!' These flowers ('pourpre ivre et grand calice
clair') are, like the poet's tomb, a 'beau monument' ironically
triumphing over silence and darkness: they represent the poet's
victory (ironic, impersonal, and ideal) over reality itself. Mallarmé
has indeed 'coupé les racines chargées de terre de [ses] fleurs'.[25]

v. The eighteen-seventies: the new poetics and other poets

In the decade from the early sixties to the early seventies Verlaine,
Rimbaud, and Mallarmé had each elaborated a new poetics and

language, each making significant use of the flower rhetoric inherited from Baudelaire and the major Parnassian precursors. In their various ways all three assimilated the floral ideal of Hellenism or the flowery *correspondances* of Baudelaire's sensual mysticism, which provided precedents for a poetry self-contemplating and withdrawn and for a style mysteriously self-sustaining. All of them were, besides, indebted in different ways to Baudelaire's ironic *fleurs du mal* as models for a poetry evoking the tension between the ideal and the real world and for a language reliant on irony and antithesis. Indeed for Rimbaud and Mallarmé (and to a lesser extent for Verlaine) the floral tropology of the earlier poets was clearly a determinative influence in the development of their personal poetics and language.

These poets had developed independently, despite a limited area of mutual influence and interaction. Yet they had more in common than their indebtedness to Baudelaire and the major Hellenists, for together they represent a radical new approach to poetry. Verlaine had developed a subtle indirect style evoking a state of indeterminacy beyond normal consciousness, or an ambiguous impersonal modernity. Rimbaud had invented a language combining elements of normal experience in a visionary new synthesis. Mallarmé had constructed a discourse ironically self-negating yet triumphantly autonomous in its mystery. In fact each of these poets had in his own way realigned the relations between poetic language, the imaginative subject, and the world, calling into question not only preceding literary convention but the habits of Cartesian rationality. They had thereby created a language of unprecedented subtlety and obscurity, uncompromisingly poetic by its differences from the conventional languages of society and literature. This was a momentous literary development, which cannot be attributed to any single cause. In one sense it was no doubt the culmination, however, of the two opposing tendencies which had orientated the French literary enterprise from the beginning of Romanticism — on the one hand idealist (pastoral) escapism and on the other the concern with (urban) realism — most recently typified by the Hellenists and Baudelaire. In this sense it was appropriate that the flowers of the new language should mark literary continuity and change simultaneously, by signalling poetry's differences from life as well as a new awareness of its ironic relations with reality.

Amidst the general Parnassian orthodoxy of the eighteen-seventies, only a few young poets shared the interest shown by Verlaine, Rimbaud, and Mallarmé in Baudelaire's poetics. Yet, significantly, the most enterprising of these reveal in their work not only a heightened awareness of the tensions between escapist idealism and real experience, but a corresponding use of flower imagery. One of these was Charles Cros, whose collection *Le Coffret de santal* shows he had assimilated the influence not only of the *Parnasse* and Baudelaire but of his friend Verlaine as well. It reveals a poetry juxtaposing high poetic suggestiveness with a vague domestic *spleen*, as the *Préface* announces:

> Bibelots d'emplois incertains
> Fleurs mortes aux seins des almées, . . .
>
> Pastels effacés, dur camées,
> Fioles encore parfumées,
> Bijoux, chiffons, hochets, pantins,
> Quel encombrement dans ce coffre![26]

At times he evokes a floral ideal, as in *Scherzo*:

> Sourires, fleurs, baisers, essences, . . .
>
> Illuminez ma fantaisie,
> Jonchez mon chemin idéal,
> Et versez-moi votre ambroisie,
> Longs regards, lys, lèvres, santal!
>
> (FW 85.)

Elsewhere his ironic realism can suggest parody of Baudelaire or Parnassian models, as in *Conclusion*:

> Les âmes dont j'aurais besoin
> Et les étoiles sont trop loin.
> Je vais mourir soûl, dans un coin.
>
> (FW 67.)

And in *Rose et muguets* his rhymes for 'la rose' turn the piece into a parody of high poetic evocation ('arrose', 'morose', 'pose', 'chose', 'glose', etc.). Cros is proud to be counted among the 'Dompteurs familiers des Muses hautaines' (FW 48), thus invoking the tension in his work between the poetic ideal and a more personal (or jocular) reality:

> Avec les fleurs, avec les femmes,
> Avec l'absinthe, avec le feu,
> On peut se divertir un peu.
>
> (FW 67.)

These are the flowers of an ideal reformulated in terms of café modernity.

In the early seventies the young Germain Nouveau began producing work in a similar vein, influenced by Verlaine and Cros himself. In an early poem he is already registering an un-Lislean visionary realism:

> Midi. C'est dans la cour; j'écris: un fumier glousse,
> Un chien jappe, un frelon rit, deux scieurs de long
> Font un grincement brun sous un grincement blond
> Et c'est une harmonie étrange et pourtant douce.[27]

In *Les Hôtesses* (1874) he adopts an appropriately Baudelairian tone to express disillusionment with the flowery ideal and readiness for death:

> Dérobe-nous, tes fils sont las, surtout des roses,
> Pas de tout, certe, et vieux d'aller et d'espérer;
> Donne, ô Mort, ton sommeil aux sombres amauroses.

(W 376.)

He uses a similar formula at the end of *L'Âme indifférente* (1875) after evoking an indifference reminiscent of Verlaine's:

> Mon âme, Hélas — morte aux roses! —
> Ne réfléchit plus les choses.

(W 388.)

And in *Les Colombes* too he uses the flower figure as the ironic signal of psychological indeterminacy:

> Ni tout noirs, ni tout verts, couleur
> D'espérance jamais en fleur,
> Les ifs balancent des colombes,
> Et cela réjouit les tombes.

(W 405.)

For Nouveau too the flower has its part to play in a language often unstable in tone, a strange modern *harmonie* of idealization and denial.

A similar language is found in a much more extreme form in the poetry of *Les Amours jaunes* (1873), written by Tristan Corbière in complete independence of the Parisian literary milieu. He is wilfully destructive of high poetic seriousness:

Poète — Après? . . . Il faut *la chose*:
Le Parnasse en escalier, . . .

Le Naïf '*voudrait que la rose*
Dondé! fût encore au rosier!'

(FW 706.)

Aware of the importance of the flower figure for poetry, Corbière singles out the rose as a flagrant example of banal idealization, and then attacks:

Rose, rose d'amour vannée,
Jamais fanée,
Le rouge-fin est ta couleur,
Ô fausse-fleur! . . .

Grise l'amour de ton haleine,
Vapeur malsaine,
Vent de pastille-du-sérail,
Hanté par l'ail!

(FW 724.)

He can even demythologize 'les myosotis, ces fleurs d'oubliettes':

Ici reviendra la fleurette blême
Dont les renouveaux sont toujours passés.

(FW 851.)

Corbière's verbal and psychological acerbity is directed at all (not merely floral) idealization, as the coupled sonnets *Duel aux camélias* (FW 737) and *Fleur d'art* (FW 738) demonstrate. In the first (perhaps recalling Baudelaire's *Duellum*) he presents a harsh landscape in which duellists are preparing to fight:

Un monsieur en linge arrangeait sa manche;
Blanc, il me semblait un gros camélia;
Une autre fleur rose était sur la branche.

The language expressing the spectator's view of the fight is an extraordinary juxtaposition of flowers and realist violence:

— Je vois rouge . . . Ah oui! c'est juste: on s'égorge —
. . . Un camélia blanc — là — comme Sa gorge . . .
Un camélia jaune, — ici — tout mâché . . .

The last tercet suggests that the speaker is himself a protagonist:

> Amour mort, tombé de ma boutonnière.
> — A moi, plaie ouverte et fleur printanière!
> Camélia vivant, de sang panaché!

In this poem the ideal flowers of love are ironically wounded by love's realities, but the second poem subjects even these ironized flowers to searing ridicule:

> Oui — Quel art jaloux dans Ta fine histoire!
> Quels bibelots chers! — Un bout de sonnet,
> Un cœur gravé dans ta manière noire.

He is scathing too about the conceit of the *boutonnière*:

> — Encor ta manière —
> C'est du sang en fleur. Souvenir coquet.

In this parody of his own *fleur d'art*, he is rejecting the idealizing devices of poetry as mere rhetoric, while at the same time refusing any idealization of love:

> Allons, pas de fleurs à notre mémoire! . . .
> Foin du myosotis, vieux sachet d'armoire!

These are the modern self-ironizing flowers of a poetry in which aesthetic or psychological idealization is brutally confronted with the harshness of real experience.

Thus within the dominant Parnassian ambiance of the early and middle seventies, other poets besides Verlaine, Rimbaud, and Mallarmé had integrated Baudelairian ironic realism into a language of their own. They too demonstrate in their own ways the corrosive effect which Baudelairian influence could exert on Parnassian (or any other) conventions of idealization. For collectively all these poets were proposing a dual alternative to Parnassian poetic language. On the one hand their poetry had found ways of representing poetic withdrawal in the very texture of its own language. On the other hand their poetry sought to enfold modern experience in poetic discourse by means of antithesis, irony, and even parody. This was a language in which the flowers of the *idéal* were always ironic, whether in affirmation or denial of the primacy of poetic truth: it was the language of the self-referring flowers of the poetic mystery or the paradoxical flowers of the new ironic realism. And this was

the language the Parisian literary milieu was to discover and acclaim within the next decade.

II. The Flowers of Decadence and 'l'éclosion du Symbolisme'

i. The flowers of decadence

The eventual acceptance of the new post-Baudelairian poetics was closely linked with an increasing appreciation of Baudelaire, and especially with the characterization of him as the exemplary poet of decadence. Aspects of his own work (and even his occasional allusions to the idea of decadence) perhaps invited this association, and the concept was one which had long haunted nineteenth-century sensibility.[28] As early as 1857 Barbey d'Aurevilly had described the poetic talent of the author of *Les Fleurs du Mal* as itself 'une fleur du mal venue dans les serres chaudes d'une Décadence'.[29] In his 1868 comments on recent literary history, Gautier used Baudelaire's title to make the same point:

Les Fleurs du mal sont en effet d'étranges fleurs . . . Elles ont les couleurs métalliques, le feuillage noir ou glauque, les calices bizarrement striés, et le parfum vertigineux de ces fleurs exotiques qu'on ne respire pas sans danger. Elles ont poussé sur l'humus noir des civilisations corrompues.[30]

Gautier's more extensive exposition of this notion in another essay of 1868 was to be determinative for literary history, since it became the *Notice* for the 1868 edition of Baudelaire's works, and henceforth provided an authoritative commentary on them. Here Gautier compared Baudelaire's language with 'la langue marbrée déjà des verdeurs de la décomposition et comme faisandée du bas-empire romain'. And he described the 'style de décadence' (with Baudelaire's style in mind) as a

style ingénieux, compliqué, savant, plein de nuances et de recherches, reculant toujours les bornes de la langue, empruntant à tous les vocabulaires, prenant des couleurs à toutes les palettes, s'efforçant à rendre la pensée dans ce qu'elle a de plus ineffable, et la forme en ses contours les plus vagues et les plus fuyants, écoutant pour les traduire les confidences les plus subtiles de la névrose, les aveux de la passion vieillissante qui se déprave et les hallucinations bizarres de l'idée fixe tournant à la folie. Ce style de décadence est le dernier mot du Verbe sommé de tout exprimer et poussé à l'extrême outrance.[31]

Gautier presents Baudelaire's poetic language as both different from

conventional expression (by its ability to render the ineffable with unprecedented subtlety) and rooted in contemporary experience by its psychological extremism. This is an interpretation of Baudelaire's poetry and flower title which suggests that the flowers of his language are complex literary blossoms growing out of *le Mal* of decadent modernity.

The assessment of Baudelaire's importance as a modern poet was linked, in this interpretation, with the notion that modernity was indeed characterized by 'la névrose', the depravities of 'la passion vieillissante', and 'la folie'. In the eighteen-seventies literary sensibility moved further towards acceptance of this view, influenced no doubt by Parnassian pessimism about society and the Naturalists' interest in degeneracy. In 1879 J.-K. Huysmans (in his Naturalist phase) could hail Baudelaire as a 'prodigieux artiste', and 'l'abstracteur de l'essence et du subtil de nos corruptions, le chantre de ces heures de trouble où la passion qui s'use cherche dans des tentatives impies, l'apaisement des folies charnelles'.[32] So too Barbey d'Aurevilly could repeat more forcefully in 1881 his view of the decadence of contemporary society as represented by Baudelaire's poetry:

la poésie du spleen, des nerfs et du frisson, dans une vieille civilisation, matérialiste et dépravée . . . qui en est à ses derniers râles et à ses dernières pâmoisons . . . Cette poésie phtisique et maladive, d'une époque désespérément décadente . . . [33]

And Paul Bourget argues at length in an essay of 1881 that Baudelaire's sensibility is organically related to contemporary reality. For the three aspects of his poetic temperament — 'mystique, libertin et analyseur' — are 'bien modernes, et plus moderne aussi est leur réunion'. Indeed Baudelaire is so imbued with the modern 'esprit de négation de la vie' and 'croyance à la banqueroute de la nature' that he can be called 'l'homme de la décadence' and even 'un théoricien de décadence'.[34] For the generation of the early eighties, Bourget is rephrasing Gautier's presentation of Baudelaire's *fleurs du mal* as flowers of decadence.

Significantly, these two articles of 1881 both note that Baudelaire is gaining a following, and the literary *bohème* around 1880 certainly took considerable interest in Baudelaire and the idea of decadence. This is exemplified by the popularity in such circles of Maurice Rollinat, whose poetry invoked melancholy, neurosis, and negation in explicitly Baudelairian terms, as in the poem *L'Hypocondriaque*:

> Enténébrant l'azur, le soleil et les roses,
> Tuant tout, poésie, arômes et couleurs,
> L'ennui cache à mes yeux la vision des choses.[35]

This is a heavy atmosphere synthesizing various elements reminiscent of *Les Fleurs du Mal*, as if Rollinat were seeking to illustrate the decadent tendencies of Baudelairian influence. In *Les Roses* he evokes flowers which are emblems of world-weary *ennui* and suggest neurotic instability as well:

> Dans l'air comme embrasé par une chaleur d'âtre
> Elles ont un arôme aussi lourd qu'ennuyé,
> Et par un crépuscule orageux et mouillé
> La blanche devient jaune, et la jaune, verdâtre.[36]

Although Rollinat's long-awaited volume (finally called *Les Névroses*) was not well received on publication in 1883, its title and earlier reputation are indicative of a general receptiveness to Baudelaire and to decadent trends. Another important figure in this literary milieu was Émile Goudeau, whose volume *Les Fleurs du bitume* (1882) claims Baudelairian affinities by its title, and illustrates in many of its poems the main decadent topos — the realist depiction of modern Paris (emphasizing libertinage and *ennui*) with constant comparison to ancient Rome.[37] Jean Lorrain, another member of this literary group, gave striking expression to the theme of Roman decadence in a poem of July 1882 (*Bathylle*), where the flower figure is again associated with world-weary sensuality. It describes an effeminate dancer entertaining sailors:

> Et tandis qu'il effeuille en fuyant brins à brins
> Des roses, comme un lys entr'ouvrant ses pétales,
> Sa tunique s'écarte aux rondeurs de ses reins. . . .
>
> Il partage à chacun son bouquet de cythise.[38]

Thus by 1882 the new sensibility could be characterized in these circles not merely in terms of Baudelaire and decadent Parisian realities but by reference to the historical precedent of decadent Rome, in each case appropriately associated with the flower figure.

It was in mid-1882 that Verlaine returned to Paris, and, although almost unknown to the younger generation (despite the publication of *Sagesse* in 1881), began publishing poetry in their reviews. It was in Vanier's *Paris moderne* in November 1882 that he published *Art poétique*, written eight years earlier. This poem (with its almost self-parodic invocation of 'la chanson grise, / Où l'Indécis au Précis se joint') was to achieve a new notoriety for Verlaine when Charles Morice attacked it in his article 'Boileau-Verlaine' for preaching 'l'obscurité voulue'.[39] But it was in *Langueur* (published in *Le Chat Noir* of 26 May 1883) that Verlaine showed his understanding of the new sensibility, while at the same time demonstrating its affinities with his own post-Baudelairian poetics:

> Je suis l'Empire à la fin de la décadence, . . .
> L'âme seulette a mal au cœur d'un ennui dense
> Là-bas on dit qu'il est de longs combats sanglants.
> Ô n'y pouvoir, étant si faible aux vœux si lents,
> Ô n'y vouloir fleurir un peu cette existence!

> (R 314.)

Here is a poem which easily adapts the topos of Roman decadence (including reference to Bathylle) to Verlainian *ennui* and psychological indeterminacy, and makes typical negative use of the verb 'fleurir'. Verlaine's most important contribution to the new sensibility was, however, his series on 'Les Poètes maudits', published (in the review in which Morice had attacked him, now called *Lutèce*) between August and December 1883. These are studies of Corbière, Rimbaud, and Mallarmé, in which Verlaine gives extensive quotations from their work (either unpublished or inaccessible) and praises them without reserve.[40] These three essays, published in book form in early 1884 by Vanier, assured Verlaine's reputation amongst Parisian *littérateurs* while at the same time revealing the three poets to them. So a milieu already permeated by Baudelairian influence gained some idea of the major figures in the post-Baudelairian revolution in poetics—all *poètes maudits* whose literary flowers grew out of *le Mal* of their existence.

Another major contribution to the new sensibility was J.-K. Huysmans's *A Rebours* (published in May 1884), a work not only committed to Baudelaire and the post-Baudelairians but at the same time the supreme expression of the idea of decadence.[41] Its hero Jean Floressas des Esseintes is the last of a decadent aristocratic line: hypersensitive yet world-weary, he seeks to escape from 'la sottise humaine' by constructing for himself 'une thébaïde raffinée' (H 9) where in isolation he can cultivate every last refinement of sensation.

In search of unusual experience, he has the shell of a tortoise inlaid with jewels in a flower pattern and enjoys the imaginative excitement of foreign travel without leaving Paris. By transforming the banality of the expected into the thrill of paradox, Des Esseintes seeks to discover 'des parfums nouveaux, des fleurs plus larges, des plaisirs inéprouvés' (H 143), and in his post-Baudelairian desire for 'du nouveau' he turns also to pleasures of sensual perception associated with the theory of *correspondances*. Thus he experiments with colours, produces with his 'orgue à bouche' of liqueurs 'des symphonies intérieures', and investigates the 'syntaxe des odeurs' provided by perfumes. In all these experiments nature is made to serve the imagination and the chapter on flowers (VIII) provides a floral metaphor for this enterprise. Des Esseintes had always despised ordinary florist's flowers ('la vulgaire plante') and had come to prefer first hot-house then artificial ones, the work of 'de profonds artistes'. But now 'Après les fleurs factices singeant les véritables fleurs, il voulait des fleurs naturelles imitant les fleurs fausses' (H 118). The new flowers he obtains are magnificent and bizarre 'folies de végétation', all the more beautiful by their paradoxical quality or by 'les magnifiques hideurs de leur gangrène' (H 124). Indeed they are so strikingly unhealthy that they inspire in Des Esseintes a nightmare vision in which 'Tout n'est que syphilis', mysterious natural flowers which by imitating artifice paradoxically suggest the corruption of nature itself.

Whether as nature-imitating-art or nature-as-corruption, these flowers are models for all these attempts to stimulate the imagination in new ways, and they are also emblems for the artistic and literary productions favoured by Des Esseintes. The pictorial art he requires is one of mystery, paradox, and perversity, epitomized by two of Gustave Moreau's pictures. One is the oil painting depicting Salomé as 'la déité symbolique de l'indestructible Luxure, la déesse de l'immortelle Hystérie, la Beauté maudite, . . . la Bête monstrueuse . . .' (H 74). This goddess-like Salomé holds 'le grand lotus' in her hand like a ritual sceptre, while the similar figure in the water-colour *Apparition* is presented as more human ('plus raffinée et plus sauvage') with her 'charme de grande fleur vénérienne'. Whether evoked in terms of mysterious ritual or of venereal nature, these are both flowers of corrupt and paradoxical beauty.

In literature Des Esseintes's taste is defined first by the Latin writers of 'la décadence', but his favourite writers are those moderns

characterized by 'des flores byzantines de cervelle et des déliquescences compliquées de langue' (H 237). Amongst these he gives pride
of place to Baudelaire, because more than any other he had found a
language to 'exprimer l'inexprimable' and 'fixer . . . les états morbides
les plus fuyants' (H 191). Not content to treat human vagaries as
if they were 'floraisons normales plantées dans de la naturelle terre',
Baudelaire has discovered 'les végétations monstrueuses de la pensée'.
The Des Esseintes who thus comments on the poet's *fleurs du mal*
is himself (in Huysmans's allegory of the decadent sensibility) an
extended metaphorical commentary on Baudelaire's floral poetics.
It is thus appropriate that he should note his affinities with the post-
Baudelairian poets. He praises Verlaine for his ability to 'laisser
deviner certains au-delà troublants' and to evoke 'des langueurs' in
his poetry of 'nuance', while he celebrates Corbière's 'énergie
désordonnée' and his 'parfaite obscurité' (H 246–7). In poetry Des
Esseintes is seeking a disorientating language characterized by
subtlety or morbidity, troubling *langueur* or disorder, a language
growing like the 'végétations monstrueuses' of the mind from an
experience extreme, wayward, or marginal. Like Des Esseintes
himself, a poetry of this type exists outside the habitual norms of
naturalness, health, and social expectations.

Fittingly, Des Esseintes treats Mallarmé (whom he prefers to
'classer à part') as a privileged representative of such poetry. While
mentioning *Les Fenêtres*, *Épilogue*, and *L'Azur*, he pays special
attention to the Hérodiade scene and *L'Après-midi d'un faune*. From
the former he quotes eight lines ('Ô miroir! . . . la nudité'), presenting
them as 'bizarres et doux vers' typical of this poet who is 'abrité
de la sottise environnante par son dédain, se complaisant, loin
du monde, aux surprises de l'intellect, aux visions de sa cervelle,
raffinant sur des pensées déjà spécieuses, les greffant de finesses
byzantines' (H 260). From the other poem he quotes the three lines
('Alors m'éveillerai-je . . . l'ingénuité') including 'le monosyllabe
lys!', which he praises for expressing 'allégoriquement en un seul
terme, la passion, l'effervescence, l'état momentané du faune vierge,
affolé de rut' (H 262). Like the mirror in the Hérodiade passage no
doubt, this 'lys' is an example of the stylistic procedure Huysmans
characterizes as typical of Mallarmé's language—his capacity to
'abolir l'énoncé de la comparaison qui s'établissait, toute seule, dans
l'esprit du lecteur, par l'analogie, dès qu'il avait pénétré le symbole'
(H 261). In this language 'le symbole' provides 'par un effet de

similitude, la forme, le parfum, la couleur, la qualité, l'éclat' which are 'les analogies' of the unnamed 'objet' or 'être' which it designates. Mallarmé thus abolishes direct references to the world, and proposes instead a mysterious synaesthetic and symbolic language, a language paradoxical in its self-sustaining complexity and refinement—'une littérature condensée, . . . un sublimé d'art'. And it is after describing Mallarmé's prose poems in similar terms ('le suc concret . . . de la littérature') that Huysmans names him the perfect representative of 'la Décadence d'une littérature' (H 265).

The Des Esseintes who appreciates these writers for their 'flores byzantines de cervelle' and their 'délinquescences compliquées de langue' is the same decadent figure who praises Moreau's flowers of corrupt beauty and the monstrous flowers of nature-imitating-art. He is also the debilitated hypersensitive at last forced by his ill-health to leave his refined retreat and 'rentrer dans la vie commune' (H 282) amidst 'la médiocrité humaine' (H 294). In this sense his imaginative experiments and tastes represent the antithesis of health, reason, society, and nature. Des Esseintes's enterprise suggests that the aesthetic sensibility of decadence which he embodies is a would-be self-sustaining ideal opposed to the very conditions of life, and endangered by them: like his flowers, it is a bizarre natural growth aspiring to the state of art but finally revealing *le Mal* of life itself.

ii. Decadence, Mallarmé and the flowering of Symbolism

Between them, Verlaine and Huysmans had publicized a new poetics and a new sensibility—both strongly associated with Baudelaire and the idea of decadence, but also with an extensive floral tropology. By late 1884 the literary milieu was displaying more interest in the new spirit. Thus Maurice Barrès took up in his review the question of the new Baudelairian sensibility in terms which emphasize its affinities with that of Des Esseintes ('les sensations de Baudelaire et des siens sont . . . les plus excessives'). He suggests too that it leads to a poetry of 'sensations associées' dependent on *cor-respondances* or *analogie* (a new version of the flower language) in Mallarmé, Verlaine, Rimbaud, and Rollinat.[42] The association between post-Baudelairian poetics and the flowers of decadence, besides, was registered in the work of several young poets appearing late in 1884. Charles Vignier's *Tristesses I* is indicative of the new amalgam:

> Roses roses où les rosées
> Roulent leurs gouttes d'argyrose,
> Roses, on les dirait rosées
> Par les fards de l'aurore rose![43]

The same incantatory use of homonyms, assonance, unusual words, and flowers is found in Laurent Tailhade's *Sonnet* of the same period:

> Ô lune pâle qui délie,
> Liliale en le soir berceur,
> Ta lueur d'opale apâlie
> A la douceur d'une âme sœur.[44]

Similar effects are found in one of Moréas's first poems, *Chimaera*:

> J'allumai la clarté mortuaire des lustres
> Au fond de la crypte où se révulse ton œil,
> Et mon rêve cueillit les fleuraisons palustres
> Pour ennoblir ta chair de pâleur et de deuil.[45]

This poetry of ritualized impersonality or morbidity clearly owes much to the major post-Baudelairians and its flowers are also those of the decadence. At least one observer, Jean-Charles Laurent (Louis Marsolleau), found the new trends significant enough to deserve parody, and produced *Les Fleurs blêmes*:

> Rose arrose d'argyrose
> La morose rose rose:
> Oh! l'hymen d'un cyclamen
> Amène un amène amen. . . .
>
> Las! la fleur qui effleure
> L'ultime heure, la meilleure,
> Et pleure; oh! combien subtils
> Les sanglots et les pistils.[46]

This is a parody of the decadent style's subtlety, mystery, morbidity, and paradox, and the accompanying note claims to be exemplifying 'la poésie enfin vraie, celle du transcendentalement intime vertige' (for 'la très niaise humanitairerie musagète se meurt'), thus deftly noting indebtedness to Verlaine, Mallarmé, and Huysmans.

In the second half of 1884 Mallarmé (who had published no poetry of his own since 1876) was working on his own equivocal tribute to the new sensibility—the *Prose (pour Des Esseintes)* published in

January 1885 in *La Revue indépendante*.[47] The title certainly expresses gratitude to Huysmans and admiration for his hero (while the term 'prose' also evokes the 'decadent' Latin of liturgical hymns). The opening exclamation too may be read as a salute to this hyperbolical expression of the post-Baudelairian spirit, acclaiming Des Esseintes as the resurrected embodiment ('sais-tu te lever') of the poet's earlier hopes ('ma mémoire') in Huysmans's hermetic new book ('grimoire'). But this 'Hyperbole!' is also (like the 'lys!' of the earlier poem) a summary statement of Mallarmé's ambitious poetics, an enterprise drawing on all his past experience and knowledge ('mémoire'), now embodied in a mysterious poetic language as inaccessible as a 'grimoire'. This is a language difficult of access in two other ways as well: it is voluntarily isolated from material life ('L'hymne des cœurs spirituels'), and it requires the same patient attention as do 'Atlas' (like maps it outlines an unknown world) or 'herbiers' (it eternizes flowers) or 'rituels' (it celebrates a mystery). This 'hymne' and 'œuvre' recall Des Esseintes and his solitary enterprise, and the first two stanzas thus assume resemblances between poet and decadent.

But the third stanza introduces a contrast with the first two (typographically emphasized in 1885) by presenting the poet's experience not in terms of isolation but of plurality ('Nous fûmes deux, je le maintiens'), and Mallarmé is now unmistakably characterizing his own poetic world. This includes a feminine presence, presented merely as beautiful (maints charmes . . . les tiens') and comfortingly familiar ('sœur'), Eve or Muse present with the poet in a beautiful landscape.[48] This 'paysage' is further characterized in the next two stanzas: it is bright with light ('ce midi') and a place of numerous flowers ('sol des cent iris'), a *locus amoenus* like Eden. Yet it is a domain of indeterminacy and non-intellectual half-consciousness ('ce midi que notre double / Inconscience approfondit') and by characterizing it in this way as both clear and indeterminate the poet raises the question of whether it really exists. This question is simultaneously made explicit: 'L'ère d'autorité se trouble / Lorsque . . . on dit . . . / que . . . son site / . . . / Ne porte pas de nom que cite / L'or de la trompette d'été'. It is possible to deny that this is a place manifesting the golden summer of real-ness; yet the text at the same time questions this negative allegation. It could be proved baseless ('sans nul motif') by the existence of the 'cent iris': 'Ils savent s'il a bien été'. Everything depends on the status of the flowers, and the poet now strongly affirms their existence:

> Oui, dans une île que l'air charge
> De vue et non de visions
> Toute fleur s'étalait plus large
> Sans que nous en devisions.
>
> Telles, immenses, que chacune
> Ordinairement se para
> D'un lucide contour, lacune
> Que des jardins la sépara.

These are flowers which can be seen, not merely envisioned or dreamed, flowers which demonstrate their existence by growing larger and more distinct as they are contemplated in silence by the poet and his companion. It is now made clear that these flowers are related to the process described in the second stanza—the 'patience' by which the poet withdraws from material reality in order to develop his praise of the non-material:

> Gloire du long désir, Idées
> Tout en moi s'exaltait de voir
> La famille des iridées
> Surgir à ce nouveau devoir.

The 'Idées' resulting from the poet's 'patience' or 'long désir' greet these ideal flowers as their lucid counterpart in the domain where the poet wanders with his companion. This is now a world with the clear outline and definition of the real (even the flowers are given their botanical name 'iridées'): it is an island of bright ideality convincingly rivalling nature.

Yet the ninth stanza recalls that the poet's relation with 'cette sœur' is based in non-intellectual indeterminacy: she smiles mysteriously rather than actively looking around her (perhaps without watching the flowers) and the poet once more seeks the communion of their 'double / Inconscience' ('Comme à l'entendre / J'occupe mon antique soin'). At this point the spirit of doubt ('l'Esprit de litige') once more raises questions about the ideal island and its flowers, and once more these are subtly interwoven with affirmation. It is suggested that the island is sometimes unattainable ('Par le flot même qui s'écarte') and its 'rive' an illusory 'jeu monotone' unable to procure 'l'ampleur' or 'l'étonnement' of definite reality ('tout le ciel et la carte / Sans cesse attestés sur mes pas'). Yet at the same time the poet exclaims: 'Oh! sache l'Esprit de litige / . . . / Que de lis multiples la tige / Grandissait trop pour nos raisons / Et non . . . / Que ce pays n'exista pas'. The indeterminacy of the ideal flower island proves not its non-existence but its mysterious powers of evocation: its flowers confuse and surpass ordinary thinking. The 'double / Inconscience' of the poet and his companion is thus a creative indeterminacy appropriate to poetic 'Idées' and demonstrating that they have been fully achieved in their immense floral ideality. It is this realization which dispels any doubts, even for the poet's companion:

> L'enfant abdique son extase
> Et docte déjà par chemins
> Elle dit le mot: Anastase!

She has learnt with the poet that the ideal flowers of poetry can be made to rise up ('Anastase!') in a resurrection of Edenic ideality. But this is an act of the word ('le mot: Anastase!') and it is in the written word that the poet's flowery 'Idées' are realized ('Né pour d'éternels parchemins'), like flowers immortalized in an 'herbier'. Only mortality might threaten this ideal realization, yet death is itself ironized here, since any tomb bearing 'ce nom: Pulchérie!' announces an achieved beauty which is 'caché par le trop grand glaïeul' — protected from death by the floral ideality which is more powerful and immense than reality itself.

The poem thus ends with two hyperbolic exclamations which (recalling the opening 'Hyperbole!') affirm the poet's triumph over the doubts and difficulties accompanying achievement, and over death itself. Unlike Des Esseintes, whose cultivation of the flowers of imaginative paradox ended in failure, the poet is not defeated by 'le trop grand glaïeul' of his ambition but fulfilled in it. Where the perfect decadent was paradoxically defeated by nature (its monstrous flowers emblems of the triumph of *le Mal*), the perfect poet rivals and defeats nature in the immense flowers which are 'le symbole' of his poetry of 'Idées'. Mallarmé's tribute to Des Esseintes is also a critique of his enterprise, affirming that the poetic 'symbole' is viable where the cultivation of decadence is not.

Yet Mallarmé's poem could also be considered a confirmation and justification of Des Esseintes's literary tastes, and for the literary milieu of 1885 the idea of decadence and the poetics of 'le symbole' were not easily differentiated. Together they provided the subject and manner of the most significant work to result immediately from the new publicity: *Les Déliquescences: Poèmes décadents d'Adoré Floupette*, a volume in which H. Beauclair and G. Vicaire create a poetic manifesto through virtuoso parody.[49] In his prefatory 'Vie' of Floupette, his friend Tapora reveals that the young poet has repudiated all earlier literary enthusiasms and is now a *décadent* committed to 'MM. Etienne Arsenal et Bleucoton', for 'Il reste *le Symbole*'. Since this is a post-Baudelairian poetry of decadence and *le Symbole* it is of course a poetry of flowers. The literary café where its poets meet is called 'le Panier fleuri' and Floupette recites there such verses as these:

> Je voudrais être un gaga
> Et que mon cœur naviguât
> Sur la fleur du séringa.

And the poems composing the volume are as diversely floral as their sources. Corbière's derisiveness is a model for much of the parody, and provides many floral touches too:

> Fleur d'opoponax,
> Souvenir d'Anthrax.
>
> (p. 84.)

> Chaste lys! prends en pitié mon Néant! . . .
> Mais je t'aime tant, Canaille de Vierge!
>
> (p. 82.)

There are many traces of Rimbaud, too, and in one poem, *Sonnet libertin*, special reference to his 'grands héliotropes':

> Très dolents, nous ferons d'exquises infamies
> — Avec l'assentiment de ton Callybistris.

Much of the flower imagery recalls Verlaine, as in *Finale*—

> Oh! Cueillons les nénuphars!
> Endormons-nous!
>
> (p. 76.)

— or in *Les Énervés de Jumièges*:

> Passe, en vos yeux morts
> Une fleur de rêve!
>
> (p. 66.)

Mallarmé's language has suggested elaborate flower images like those
of *Cantique*:

> Désespérance morne au seuil du Lys Hymen!
> — Nimbé d'Encens impur j'agonise et je fume, —
> Ô l'Induration lente du Cyclamen!

(p. 80.)

But in many poems there is a seamless interweaving of these
influences, and especially those of Mallarmé and Verlaine, as in
Suavitas:

> L'Adorable Espoir de la Renoncule
> A nimbé mon cœur d'une Hermine d'or. . . .
>
> La candeur du Lys est un crépuscule. . . .
>
> La vie agonise et nous expirons
> Dans la mort suave et pâle des Roses!

(p. 69.)

And Rimbaud, Mallarmé, and Verlaine have all contributed to *Pour
avoir péché* (called *Le Pétunia sauveur* in pre-publication):

> Mon cœur est un Corylopsis du Japon. Rose
> Et pailleté d'or fauve, — à l'instar des serpents,
> Sa rancœur détergeant un relent de Chlorose,
> Fait, dans l'Éther baveux, bramer les Aegypans.
>
> Qu'importe, si je suis le Damné qui jouit?
> Car un Pétunia me fait immarcessible
> Lys! Digitale! Orchis! Moutarde de Louit!

(p. 79.)

As these two poems show, this is a poetry in which flowers are
privileged figures for *spleen* and *idéal*, sensuality and mysticism,
self- negation and salvific withdrawal. They are integrated here (by
force) in a language ranging from the ineffable via the eclectic to
the morbid. This is after all the psychology and style of the
déliquescence, that solvent of all solidities of nature, health, reason,
and reality. Here, in poems with titles like *Idylle symbolique* and
Les Décadents, is a fervent realization of the 'style de décadence'
attributed by Gautier to Baudelaire — 'le dernier mot du Verbe
sommé de tout exprimer'. And this style, as understood in 1885, is

necessarily not only a *langage des fleurs* but a language in which flowers are indeed the privileged model and archetype of the all-expressive 'Verbe'—*la Fleur sommée de tout exprimer*. At the moment of the triumph of the idea of decadence, as Floupette announces that 'Le symbole est venu' (p. 73), it can be said that the Symbol is the Flower, and the Flower is the Symbol.

Yet parody is parody, and even if *Les Déliquescences* presents invaluable evidence about the poetic taste of 1885 it is not in itself the new poetry foreseen by Tapora when he calls Arsenal and Bleucoton 'les deux grands initiateurs de la poésie de l'avenir'. Despite all the bustling activity of the poets of the future in the Parisian literary world of 1885 and 1886, most of their work indeed remained for the future.[50] Only Jules Laforgue's volume *Les Complaintes*, perhaps, suggested the poetic flowering to come. Yet the flurried literary discussion of these two years gave considerable attention to the uneasy relationship between the idea of decadence and the poetics of *le symbole* (in reviews like *Le Décadent*, *La décadence*, and *Le Symboliste*). And it resulted near the end of 1886 in two pronouncements which between them helped to establish a new poetic orthodoxy more *symboliste* than *décadent*.

Thus Moréas, in his article of 18 September in *Le Figaro*, proclaimed that

la poésie symboliste cherche: à vêtir l'Idée d'une forme sensible qui, néanmoins, ne serait pas son but à elle-même, mais qui, tout en servant à exprimer l'Idée, demeurerait sujette. L'Idée, à son tour, ne doit pas se laisser voir privée . . . des analogies extérieures . . . Tous les phénomènes concrets ne sauraient se manifester eux-mêmes: ce sont là des apparences sensibles destinées à représenter leurs affinités ésotériques avec les Idées primordiales . . . Pour la traduction exacte de sa synthèse, il faut au symbolisme un style archétype et complexe . . . [51]

While following Huysmans's definition of Mallarmé's style, Moréas provides here a theory of poetry interesting in its own right. It is conceived within the century-old tradition relating poetic language to the principles of *analogie*, but proposes a revision of it. It assumes that there are indeed *correspondances* linking the natural world and human meaning, but it no longer expects language to mediate between nature (with its 'apparences sensibles') and meaning ('l'Idée'). For now language will refer only to one aspect of the analogical duality—the 'analogies extérieures' of 'l'Idée'—without revealing the 'Idées primordiales' which correspond to them. This is to be a language of sense-evocation serving a hermetic order of 'Idées', a language apparently speaking of the world of the senses but finally occult and self-referring, and thus necessarily complex and obscure in style. Moréas provides here, after all, a plausible account of the procedures of his major exemplars. Had not Verlaine evoked nature as the *analogie* for an *'Idée'* of indeterminacy, and Rimbaud forcefully sought and expressed his own (re)visionary *correspondances*? Had not Mallarmé produced a language self-reflecting enough to negate nature? Certainly all three had developed a poetry in which nature is subordinate to the imaginative subject and to language itself.

They had, indeed, repudiated the model of the conventional *langage des fleurs* in the sense that they no longer expected nature to reveal its meanings to the poet. But in another sense they had adapted it to become the archetype of their own language. For where the traditional flower language spoke of the mysterious *harmonies idéales* of nature, their poetry now speaks of the mysteries of the poet's imagination and of his own language.

Mallarmé expressed this transformation in his own terms in his further contribution to the theory of 'le symbole' of October 1886—his *Avant-dire* to René Ghil's *Traité du Verbe*:

Je dis: une fleur! et, hors de l'oubli où ma voix relègue aucun contour, en tant que quelque chose d'autre que les calices sus, musicalement se lève, idée rieuse ou altière, l'absente de tous bouquets.

(M 857/M 1630.)

For here the only language is that of the poet, who by pronouncing the words 'une fleur!' negates the things of nature ('l'oubli où ma voix relègue aucun contour') or recalls its flowers only as reverse characterizations of his own ('quelque chose d'autre que les calices sus'). The poet's new *langage des fleurs* is the celebration not of nature's *harmonies* but of the mysterious high music by which poetry negates and replaces nature. Besides, Mallarmé's 'fleur' is at once the archetype and the negation of the flowers of decadence, an imaginative elaboration of nature but triumphantly independent of it: it is the privileged model for the sensuous, hermetic, and self-sustaining language of *le Symbole*. By a long tradition flowers had symbolized the superlative beauties of nature and poetry, but now they laughingly announce the supremacy of poetry alone. In this apotheosis and revision of the Romantic tradition, poetry proclaims its autonomy in the symbol of the flower.

CONCLUSION

Fleur hypocrite,
Fleur du silence.

(Rémy de Gourmont, *Litanies de la Rose*, 1892.)

The concepts of Decadence and Symbolism had served in turn to name the new ambitions of poetry, henceforth to exert such powerful influence in literature (and not in France alone). For Decadent intentions may be discerned in later attempts to render contemporary life and modern psychological states in a language ironizing about the troubled relationship between self and reality. Some lines of Laforgue's point to a literary strategy of this type:

Dans les Jardins
De nos instincts,
Allons cueillir
De quoi guérir.[1]

The Symbolist precedent could be claimed, besides, for subsequent writers who turn away from the world towards the self, or towards a self-reflecting language and artistic form. Valéry invoked this process in 1891—

Ô frères, tristes lys, je languis de beauté
Pour m'être désiré dans votre nudité.[2]

—and he was to reformulate it in 1922:

Voir, ô merveille, voir! ma bouche nuancée
Trahir . . . peindre sur l'onde une fleur de pensée.[3]

Many others were to investigate the relations between reality, subjectivity, and art in their own new languages and forms. Indeed the Decadent and Symbolist ambitions of 1885–86 pointed the way to many of the most characteristic literary achievements of the present century. The transformation of poetic theory and practice realized by Baudelaire and the major Symbolists was a precedent for the innovations of Modernism, Surrealism, and much other twentieth-century literary and critical writing. And in this decisive nineteenth-century transformation, floral tropology had undoubtedly played a role of the greatest significance.

The French poets of the nineteenth century made significant use of the flower figure for several reasons. The Romantic poets had taken up floral tropology in the first place for properly literary motives. As they sought to free poetry from the constraints of Classicism (as represented by neo-Classical or Descriptive conventions), they turned towards the poetry of earlier periods and pre-Romantic prose fiction (where they could find extensive floral imagery) or towards esoteric or German writing (in which flowers promised a new relationship with the mysteries of nature). Once established as an important figure in Romantic poetry, the flower soon made a unique contribution to literary development. But another factor in the poets' adoption of flower figures was the great popularity of flowers in nineteenth-century France. Throughout the century French culture was pervaded by a floral sensibility which had its origins in pre-Romanticism but was widely diffused in the popular floral publications of the period. Between 1810 and the eighteen-fifties there grew up a vast paraliterature in praise of flowers, including notably the flower dictionary (first developed as a genre in France). During this period serious writers influenced the development of these popular works and were in turn encouraged to give serious consideration to a floral sensibility so all-pervasive. Until the end of the high Romantic period, indeed, poets shared with their audience the same assumptions about flowers. But after this period the poets' flower imagery can no longer be seen as a reflection of a wider cultural mode, for they now proposed flowers which stood for values quite different from those of popular culture.

For the Romantic period, the flower was an indispensable emblem of nature's beauties and mysteries, and also of several forms of sentimental idealization, including love. But during the very decades when these affirmative associations had become most widely accepted (the eighteen-forties and fifties) they were also being subjected in the new poetry to questioning and revision. Thus at this time the Romantic Nerval came to find in nature's harmonies terrifying risks of damnation and to see the flowers of idealizing love as threatened by reality. So too from the eighteen-forties Baudelaire began subverting the idealizing flowers of love by his modern irony, and even undertook the ironic inversion of the Romantic optimism of nature's *langage des fleurs*. Indeed Nerval and Baudelaire were the last major poets to give central importance to the flowers of nature and love. For from the early forties the Hellenists saw flowers only as an emblem for their refusal of modern life and its emotions (including love). And the major Symbolists, following Baudelaire and the Parnassians, were no longer interested in idealizing either nature or love.

Thus in one sense the history of flower imagery in this period looks like a history of discontinuity and rupture. The age-old tradition associating flowers with affirmative attitudes to nature and love had been broken by poets rejecting at the same time the consensus shared by poets and public about floral tradition in its Romantic form. After Baudelaire and the Parnassians, the flower could no longer promise a meaningful relationship between poet, audience, nature, and love. Yet the flower figure continued to play a role in poetry even after it had lost its power as an emblem of 'présence' (to use Derrida's term). It survived in post-Romantic poetry because by the middle decades of the century the flower had become so essential to the rhetoric of poetics that poets could hardly conceive their enterprise without reference to it.

For this study has demonstrated that during this whole period poets constantly made use of flower rhetoric to express their revisionary relationship with existing literary conventions. Thus the Romantics adapted traditional flower imagery to their own sensibility in the flowers of mysticism and pathos, and found in the *langage des fleurs* a nature more mysterious than that of Descriptive poetry. Baudelaire adapted the sensual-mystical *surnaturalisme* of the language of flowers to his own ironic escapism, while radically revising Romantic idealization in his *fleurs du Mal*, ironic testimonies to the flowering of poetry amidst the difficulties of modern life and consciousness. Nerval adapted the Romantic flowers of idealizing love to his own poetics in which fiery flowers express a neo-Romantic salvation-through-art, integrating *le Rêve* with *la Vie*. The major Parnassians proposed a post-Romantic poetics of flowers and marble to express a pastoral-Hellenist escape from the emotions and suffering of modern life. Finally, the major Symbolist poets variously adapted Parnassian cold flowers and Baudelaire's paradoxical *fleurs du Mal*, while revising the relationship between the *langage des fleurs* and nature, in order to create a new poetics—indeterminate, visionary, or hermatic in its self-reference. From Romanticism to Symbolism, four or more generations had made use of flower rhetoric to express their adherence to a poetic tradition and their elaboration or revision of it. (Indeed at many points flower topoi functioned almost as the 'influence' which caused the productive 'anxiety' of the 'latecomer' poet, to use Bloom's terminology.) Floral tropology was clearly a determinative factor in the development of poetry during this period, as the flower became the one indispensable emblem of poetic continuity and change, the main agent of 'intertextuality' in a poetic tradition progressively more aware of its own unity and self-transformation.

This floral tradition was more than a series of revisions, and there were two major ways in which the flower figure contributed directly to the transformation of poetic theory and practice so generally recognized by the mid-eighties. There was, first, the striking elaboration after 1820 of the most significant of the age-old metaphorical uses of flower imagery. The Romantics inherited from literary tradition the flowers of transience and the superlative flowers of life or spirituality, and invested them with their own characteristic pathos and sentimental mysticism; they also revived the ancient conceit of the flowers of the muses, and appropriated it to their sensibility. Both of these uses were transformed by Baudelaire. His early *fleurs du Mal* were complex negative tropes of his own invention, but had some similarity with the traditional flowers of transience (for Baudelaire *le Mal* ironizes idealization just as transience ironizes blossoming beauty in the traditional figure). At the same time he developed his own flowers of idealizing *surnaturalisme*, and his own version of the flowers of the muses, both of which he made equally subject to ironic modern consciousness. A similar dualism is found in Nerval's use of flower imagery, for this poet postulated his idealizing floral dream of the Goddess with full awareness of the ironic limitations imposed on it by reality. Baudelaire and Nerval both finally resolved dualism, moreover, by integrating ironic reality into a floral synthesis in which poetry celebrates its own triumph. In this way they had each made a resolution only implicit in Romantic tropology, for they had assimilated the dualist flowers of life/death to the flowers of art.

The Parnassians also used the flower figure in a dualist context (here escapist beauty against life and death) but for them flowers were associated only with the Hellenist or exotic dream-world of art set up to exclude the sufferings of life: these are flowers made independent of life or death by their aesthetic status. And the flower figure was further aestheticized by the Symbolist poets, all the more convincingly because they assimilated Baudelairian irony into the very texture of their language. They could therefore make the flower figure serve a poetry ironically aware of life and death yet strongly asserting its own self-reflecting independence, and their flowers participate in a language claiming superiority to ordinary experience by its self-defining difference. These uses of the flower figure from Romanticism to Symbolism therefore reveal a clear development towards a floral art triumphing over all human contingencies. It is as if poets were seeking to combine the flower-connotations of life, death, and art in a supreme synthesis, or as if the tradition of floral tropology were inscribing its own inevitable resolution in their writing. In any case there is no doubt that the flower figure was itself a powerful agent in this elaboration of a poetry triumphantly rivalling, and ironically including, life and death.

But the flower figure contributed in an even more important way to the nineteenth-century transformation of poetry and poetics. The Romantics took over from esoteric tradition and German Romanticism the concept of the *langage des fleurs* as the model for a privileged relationship between the poet and nature's mysteries. For the Romantics this generally implied a special participation in *harmonies* both voluptuous (often synaesthetic) and meaningful, in which nature offered to the poet the means of creating his own privileged poetic language. For the early Romantics the poet was by vocation an initiate in these mysteries, but he was primarily passive in relation to them. In Nerval's account this communion implies salvation or damnation for the participant, while in Fourierist-Utopian versions it is a prefiguration of the universal harmonies of social hope. However, Baudelaire revises this topos in his later synthesis by making the poet not only passively receptive of nature's flowery synaesthetic and symbolic *correspondances* but active in his ironic handling of them: the poet's ironic modern consciousness makes him a powerful agent in the creation of his own poetic *langage des fleurs du Mal*.

In their allusions to the same model the major Symbolists follow Baudelaire by subversively revising it. Thus Verlaine alludes to nature's harmonies only to invoke an indeterminate psychological state, and his own poetic language is ironically empty of nature's meanings. Rimbaud seeks a visionary experience which dis-orders the *correspondances* of nature, and for him its flower language is only a discarded model for his own forcefully disordered language. And Mallarmé finds in the *langage des fleurs* an incitement to rival the beauty and self-sufficiency of nature, challenging him to create the flowers of speech which deny nature's supremacy. In the development from Romanticism to Symbolism, the poet's privileged passivity before nature and its flower language has turned into an assertion of the poet's independent agency and the autonomy of his poetic language.

Here once more it would seem that the poets had developed the implications of the original topos itself. For the Romantic flower language mysteriously promised meaning without finally communicating more than the unsatisfactory 'meanings' of the flower-code or a general sense of ideal harmony or beauty. It was by definition, as Hugo noted, a 'Langue de l'ombre et du mystère, /Qui demande à tous: Que sait-on?', an anti-language paradoxically offering and withholding meaning. Thus later poets could find justification in the convention itself for their elaboration of an ironical version of it (Baudelaire) or the development of their own parallel language of mystery (the Symbolists). It served indeed not only as an incitement to create a language composed of varied elements of meaning and sense-perception, but also as the model for a language expressing paradox and obscurity. It is as if the topos of the *langage des fleurs* were writing its own implications into the very language of the new poetry.

Thus both the principal types of flower rhetoric in French nineteenth-century poetry (connotative flower metaphors and the *langage des fleurs*) were determinative factors in the production of the new poetry—a poetry authoritatively relativizing life, death, and nature by assuming them into its own supreme language. Here is the apotheosis of the literary history of the flower figure, which had always stood for superlative aspects of nature and human life (and their negation) and had long been associated with superlative beauty and art. For the challenge which the flower had always posed to human life and art is here finally answered in the superlatively ambitious poetics of the late nineteenth century: nature's flower is now inscribed in a poetry which fulfils and denies it. Mallarmé is obliged to state that 'la nature a lieu, on n'y ajoutera pas', but he can also claim ('Je dis: une fleur!') that the flower of nature is now relativized by the flower of poetry.

It is clear that the flower rhetoric made a very significant contribution to the transformation of poetics in nineteenth-century France. Indeed, it was perhaps even a necessary condition for the French poetic revolution, and hence for the wider literary innovation influenced by Baudelaire and French Symbolism. The comparative case of English nineteenth-century literature suggests the validity of this hypothesis. For in England flower rhetoric had no significant role in poetics until the general reception of Baudelaire and the Symbolists introduced floral tropology at the same time as it influenced poetics. This demonstrates that those who effected the introduction of French poetics to England (such as Pater, Wilde, and Symons) perceived it to be closely related to the flower figure,[4] and it even suggests that no national literature was able to develop a modern poetics without using the flower rhetoric. Moreover many of the major works of Modernism in France, England, or elsewhere reveal their debt to French Symbolism not least by their florality.[5] Indeed the transformation in the poetic rhetoric of flowers in nineteenth-century France can be seen not only as a prefigurement of modern literary sensibility but as one of the major conditions for its development. This transformation of the flower figure embodied the transition from one literary consciousness to another: for where Romantic flowers had spoken of the mysteries of life and death or of the poet's understanding of nature's language, the flowers of the Symbolists speak of the mysteries of language itself. In the terminology of Jacques Derrida (himself much indebted to Mallarmé) this is a transition from the language of 'présence' to the language of 'différance'. Martin Heidegger expresses a similar modern rejection of the 'metaphysical' status of language in a floral conceit (here reported by Paul Ricœur):

L'évocation de Heidegger est d'autant plus appropriée que la métaphore de l'éclosion s'est imposée à lui, au cœur de sa critique de l'interprétation métaphysique de la métaphore, comme la métaphore de la métaphore: les 'fleurs' de nos mots — 'Worte, wie Blumen' — disent l'existence dans son éclosion.[6]

The floral tropology of the French nineteenth century, and its *langage des fleurs*, made an indispensable (and unjustly neglected) contribution not only to the poetry and poetics of its period but to modern literary culture.

NOTES

CHAPTER 1

1. *Les Fleurs dans notre littérature contemporaine* (Poitiers, L'Horticulture Poitevine, 1896), p. 13.
2. Notably A. de Gubernatis, *La Mythologie des plantes ou les légendes du monde végétal*, 2 vols. (Reinwald, 1878), and C. Joret, *La Rose dans l'antiquité et au moyen âge* (E. Bouillon, 1892).
3. *La Mythologie des plantes*, i, p. xxviii.
4. J. G. Frazer, *The Golden Bough* (3rd edn.), 12 vols. (Macmillan, 1911–15), pt. IV, i, p. 3.
5. M. Eliade, *Patterns of Comparative Religion*, tr. R. Sheed (Sheed and Ward, 1958), p. 324.
6. C. Lévi-Strauss, *La Pensée sauvage* (Plon, 1962), p. 57 *et passim*.
7. See R. Norrman and J. Haarberg, *Nature and Language. A Semiotic Study of Cucurbits in Literature* (Routledge and Kegan Paul, 1980), pp. 154–71.
8. J. Jacobi, *Complex/Archetype/Symbol in the Psychology of C. J. Jung*, tr. R. Mannheim (Routledge and Kegan Paul, 1958), p. 109.
9. S. Freud, *Introductory Lectures on Psychoanalysis*, tr. J. Rivière (Allen and Unwin, 1922), pp. 132–3. G. Bachelard is more pragmatic: 'on pourrait désigner bien des végétaux comme des inducteurs de rêverie particulière . . . Mais la botanique du rêve n'est pas faite' (*L'Air et les songes. Essai sur l'imagination du mouvement* (Corti, 1943), p. 231).
10. But cf. J. Pacotte, *Le Réseau arborescent, schème primordial de la pensée* (Hermann, 1936) and G. Deleuze and F. Guatarri, *Rhizome. Introduction* (Minuit, 1976).
11. N. J. Richardson notes the hymn's cultic links with Eleusis, in *The Homeric Hymn to Demeter* (Clarendon Press, 1974), p. 141.
12. See A. Arber, *The Natural History of Plant Form* (Cambridge UP, 1950), pp. 12–21.
13. *The Oxford Book of Greek Verse in Translation*, ed. T. F. Higham and C. M. Bowra (Clarendon Press, 1938), p. 543. Page references given in text as GT 543.
14. J. J. Wilhelm, *The Cruellest Month. Spring, Nature and Love in Classical and Medieval Lyrics* (Yale UP, 1965), p. 42.
15. C. P. Segal, 'Nature and the World of Man in Greek Literature', *Arion*, vol. 2, pt. 1 (1963), p. 46.
16. R. Harriott, *Poetry and Criticism before Plato* (Methuen, 1969), p. 138.

17. See J. F. d'Alton, *Roman Literary Theory and Criticism* (Longmans Green, 1931), pp. 68–73, and D. A. Russell and N. Winterbottom, *Ancient Literary Criticism* (Clarendon Press, 1972), pp. 413–14, p. 557.

18. Translation from P. Dronke, *Medieval Latin and the Rise of the European Love-Lyric*, 2 vols. (Clarendon Press, 1965), i. 181–2.

19. Isa. 24: 1. The Vulgate, standard text for medieval and later French readers, is here used throughout.

20. Cant. 2: 1–2, 2: 10–12, etc. But this love-dialogue was read as an allegory of the covenant between Jahweh and Israel. In later books, the gentile flower-garland is associated with lechery: cf. Sap. 2:8.

21. Isa. 40: 6–8. The pre-Vulgate Latin speaks of the 'flos foeni', later a common term.

22. Matt. 6: 28, Luc. 12: 27.

23. See J. Chydenius, *The Theory of Medieval Symbolism, Commentationes humanarum litterarum*, XXVII. 2 (1960).

24. *The Oxford Book of Medieval Latin Verse*, ed. F. Raby (Clarendon Press, 1959), p. 369. Page references given in text as ML 369.

25. See M. M. Davy, *Initiation à la symbolique romane* (Flammarion, 1964), pp. 153–5.

26. Many writers (from Augustine on) refer to the emblematic procedure, but they concur more on the need for it than on its results. The 'lesson' of Alan's rose is provided by Isaiah 40: 6–8 and perhaps by Ausonius' rose poem; Walafrid reads the rose as 'martyrs' blood' (by colour analogy, or variation on the 'flos foeni'?).

27. From Isa. 11: 1 — 'Et exgredietur virgo de radice Jesse et flos de radice ascendit'. See P. Dronke, *European Love-Lyric*, i. 184–8.

28. *Carmina Burana*, ed. A. Hilke and C. Schumann (Heidelberg, 1941), pt. ii, no. 78.

29. Bernart de Ventadorn, *Seine Lieder*, ed. C. Appel (Halle, 1915), p. 220.

30. T. P. Harrison and H. J. Leon, *The Pastoral Elegy* (University of Texas, 1939), p. 64.

31. Whatever the aetiology of the 'courtly' flower, there was certainly a revival of enthusiasm for gardens and flowers: see G. Tergit, *Flowers through the Ages*, tr. E. and A. Anderson (O. Wolff, 1961), pp. 51–65.

32. See W. C. Calin, 'Flower Imagery in *Floire et Blancheflor*', *French Studies*, xviii, pt. 2 (1964), pp. 103–11.

33. See E. Langlois, *Origines et sources du Roman de la Rose* (Thorin, 1891), pp. 6–64. From 1323 the 'Jeux floraux' celebrated poetry with flowers.

34. Line numbers refer to the edition of D. Poiron (Garnier-Flammarion, 1974). See J. Fleming, *The Roman de la Rose. A Study in Allegory and Iconography* (Princeton UP, 1969), p. 50 *et passim*.

35. Cf. Albertus Magnus: 'Et nota, quod Christus rosa, Maria rosa, Ecclesia rosa, fidelis anima rosa' (cited in *The Divine Comedy*, translated by C. S. Singleton, 3 vols. (Princeton UP, 1975), vol. iii, pt. 2, p. 511). See also B. Seward, *The Symbolic Rose* (Columbia UP, 1960), pp. 36–52.

36. From Prosper of Aquitaine (fourth century) the *florilegium* was a consistent Western genre. A tenth-century manuscript describes the pious purposes of most ('Hic carpat flores, quis depingat sibi mores'), yet some were purely literary.

37. Cited by D. B. Wilson, *Ronsard, Poet of Nature* (Manchester UP, 1961), p. 11.

38. Quoted ibid., p. 125. Below, the references for Ronsard are given to *Œuvres complètes*, ed. G. Cohen, 2 vols. (NRF/Gallimard (Pléiade), 1950) (as C i 20).

39. See *Ronsard the Poet*, ed. T. Cave (Methuen, 1973), pp. 77, 166–73.

40. J. A. Baïf, *Euvres en rime*, ed. C. Marty-Laveaux, 5 vols. (Geneva, Slatkine Reprints, n.d.), iii. 47. Cf. Ovid: 'Candidior folio nivei, Galatea, ligustri, / floridor pratis' (*Metamorphoses*, xiii. 789 ff.).

41. A. Boase (ed.), *The Poetry of France*, 3 vols. (Methuen, 1964), i. 28.

42. C i 420. See H. Weber, *La Création poétique au XVIe siècle en France de Maurice Scève à Agrippa d'Aubigné* (Nizet, 1955), pp. 341–8.

43. During this period even flower emblematics are made to serve poetic rhetoric: they have lost real didactic point. Thus the close of Ronsard's poem *A la Reine d'Écosse* (L'amour est trompeur . . . / Comme celui qui porte en ses mains closes / Plus de chardons que de lis ni de roses') ironizes the courtly rose and lily.

44. *Épître à Charles Cardinal de Lorraine*, cited by R. J. Clements, *Critical Theory and Practice of the Pléiade* (Harvard UP, 1942), p. 168.

45. Quoted by D. B. Wilson, *Ronsard*, p. 53.

46. Quoted by R. J. Clements, *Critical Theory*, p. 169.

47. See J. Hutton, *The Greek Anthology in France . . . to the year 1800* (Cornell UP, 1946), p. 66.

48. See G. Delley, *L'Assomption de la Nature dans la lyrique française de l'âge baroque* (Berne, Lang, 1969), pp. 129–99.

49. *Œuvres*, ed. A. Adam (Gallimard (Pléiade), 1971), p. 105.

50. Quoted by G. Delley, *L'Assomption de la Nature*, pp. 197–8, 195.

51. See P. Mitchell, *European Flower Painters* (Adam and Charles Black, 1973), and J. Davy de Virville, *Histoire de la botanique en France* (Comité français du VIIIe Congrès International de Botanique, 1954).

52. 'A mon jardinier', *Épître XI* (1696) in Boase, *The Poetry of France*, ii. 52. Boileau specifically links Ronsard with 'la rusticité' in the *Art poétique* (ii. 21–2).

53. See D. Mornet, *Le Sentiment de la Nature en France de J.-J. Rousseau à Bernardin de Saint-Pierre* (Hachette, 1907), *passim*.

54. *Épître à mes vers adressés à la marquise de Pompadour en 1760*, *Œuvres*, 2 vols. (Buisson, 1803), ii. 152.

55. J. Delille, *Les Jardins ou l'art d'embellir les paysages* (Valade, 1782), pp. vii, 1–9. Descriptive poetry clearly had much in common with the English garden, despite Delille's refusal to choose 'entre Kent et Le Nôtre'. See E. Guitton, *Jacques Delille et le poème de la nature de 1750 à 1820* (Klincksieck, 1974), pp. 329–37.

56. *Julie ou la Nouvelle Héloïse*, ed. R. Pomeau (Garnier, 1960), pp. 453–72.

57. *Les Rêveries du promeneur solitaire*, ed. H. Roddier (Garnier, 1960), pp. 103–4.

58. *Du sentiment considéré dans ses rapports avec la littérature et les arts* (Lyon, chez Ballanche et Barret, 1801), p. 40.

59. *Avant-propos* of 1788 (not in 1806 edition) cited in *Paul et Virginie*, ed. P. Trahard (Garnier, 1958) p. xclv. Page references given in text.

60. *Œuvres complètes*, 12 vols. (Garnier, 1939), iii. 65. Page references in text.

61. Chateaubriand notes the rhetorical usefulness of the flower elsewhere: it is 'la fille du matin, le charme du printemps, la source des parfums, la grâce des vierges, l'amour des poètes; elle passe vite comme l'homme mais elle rend doucement ses feuilles à la terre' (ibid., ii. 111).

62. *Stances au bois de Romainville* (1792), cited by W. M. Kerby, *The Life, Diplomatic Career and Literary Activities of N. G. Léonard* (E. Champion, 1925), p. 200.

63. *Œuvres complètes*, ed. C. Walter (Gallimard (Pléiade), 1958), p. 77.

64. *Le Bûcher de la lyre.* (1812), *Œuvres* (Garnier, n.d.), p. 105.

65. *La Gelée d'avril* (1820), cited by G. Charlier, *Le Sentiment de la Nature chez les romantiques français* (Fontemoing, 1912), p. 77.

66. On medieval influence see J. R. Dakyns, *The Middle Ages in French Literature 1851–1900* (Oxford UP, 1973), pp. 1–22, 92–109. On Ronsard, see R. Katz, *Ronsard's French Critics. 1588–1828* (Geneva, Droz, 1966), pp. 148–68. Material from the Greek anthologies (including some Meleager) is found in works like J. Planche's *Cours de littérature grecque, on Recueil des plus beaux passages de tous les auteurs grecs . . .*, 7 vols. (Gauthier, 1827–8).

67. See B. Juden, *Traditions orphiques et tendances mystiques dans le romantisme français (1800–1855)* (Klincksieck, 1971), p. 20.

68. *Hymne de l'autonne* (C i 239–40).

69. *Hermetica*, ed. W. Scott (Clarendon Press, 1924), p. 247. See also A. J. Festugière, *Hermétisme et mystique païenne* (Aubier-Montaigne, 1967), p. 170.

70. *Les Figures hierogliphiques*, in *Trois Traitez de la philosophie naturelle* (G. Farette, 1612), p. 52. Dom A. J. Pernéty, in his *Dictionnaire mytho-hermétique* (Bauche, 1758), links the mythical origins of the rose with the final reddening of the 'matière philosophale' (pp. 441–2), thus explaining alchemical terms like 'rose minérale', 'rose de vie', 'fleurs de la sagesse'.

71. See W. E. Butler, *Magic and the Quabalah* (Aquarian Press, 1964), p. 73.

72. See F. A. Yates, *The Rosicrucian Enlightenment* (Routledge and Kegan Paul, 1972), pp. 47, 65, 221.

73. See A. Viatte, *Les Sources occultes du romantisme*, 2 vols. (Champion, 1928), i. 33 *et passim*.

74. *Concerning Heaven and its Wonders and concerning Hell* (translated by Clowes) (Newbury and Trimen, 1843), pp. 52–3. This work was early translated into French as *Les Merveilles du Ciel et de l'Enfer et des terres planétaires* (1782) and later *Du Ciel et de ses merveilles et de l'enfer* (1850).

75. *L'Homme de Désir* (Lyon, 1790), p. i.

76. *Le Crocodile, ou la guerre du bien et du mal. Poème épico-magique* (1799) (Triades éditions, 1962), p. 42.

77. *Gnostiques de la Révolution. Claude de Saint-Martin*, ed. A. Tanner (Egloff, 1946), pp. 213–14.

78. *Œuvres posthumes*. 2 vols. (Tours, Letourny, 1807), p. 182.

79. A. Fabre d'Olivet, *La Vraie Maçonnerie et la céleste culture*, ed. L. Cellier (PUF, 1952), p. 53, and Ballanche, *Pages choisies*, ed. T. de Visan (Lyon, Masson, 1926), p. 127.

80. A. Viatte quotes this 'importante lettre de Magneval à Sarazin' (13 June 1801), *Les Sources occultes*, i. 216.

81. *Œuvres*, 12 vols. (Geneva, Slatkine Reprints, 1968), iii. 198–9.

82. *Orphée, Œuvres*, 4 vols. (J. Barbezat, 1830), ii. 148.

83. B. Juden establishes affinities between ideas of world-harmony and Orphic developments, *Traditions orphiques*, pp. 99–120, 165–234.

84. *La Contemplation de la Nature* (1764), cited by B. Juden, ibid., p. 119. Later *magnétiseurs* used Bonnet's notion of reciprocal influences: Mesmer himself wrote an *Influence des plantes sur le corps humain* (1766).

85. *Œuvres complètes*, 15 vols. (Méquignon-Marvis, 1820), xiv. 112. The *Harmonies* are arranged like the chain of being, from *végétales* through *humaines* to the *Harmonies du Ciel*. Man understands the whole, and can be 'touché des harmonies mutuelles des végétaux' (xi. 236).

86. *Nuits Élyséennes* (1800), cited by A. Viatte, *Les Sources occultes*, ii. 156.

87. See L. Cellier, *Fabre d'Olivet. Contribution à l'étude des aspects religieux du romantisme* (Nizet, 1972), p. 205, and *La Vraie Maçonnerie . . .*, p. 47.

88. Quoted by A. Viatte, *Les Sources occultes*, ii. 9.

89. 'Premier fragment' (28 May 1808), *Œuvres*, i. 471.

90. *Oberman, lettres publiées par M. . . . Senancour*, 2 vols. (B. Arthaud, 1947), i. 113–14.

91. For the relation of this flower to Senancour's personal flower emblematics, see B. Le Gall, *L'Imaginaire chez Senancour*, 2 vols. (Corti, 1966), i. 117.

92. See R. Gray, *Goethe the Alchemist* (Cambridge UP, 1952), pp. 163–8, 82.

93. See R. Ayrault, *La Genèse du romantisme allemand*, 3 vols. (Aubier-Montaigne, 1961), ii. 558–63.

94. Cited/translated by E. Spenlé, *Novalis. Essai sur l'Idéalisme romantique en Allemagne* (Hachette, 1904), pp. 315–16.

95. *Henri d'Ofterdingen*, édition bilingue, ed. M. Camus (Aubier-Montaigne, 1942), p. 67. Page references given in text.

96. In Spenlé's words, 'la fleur symbolisait à leurs yeux la vie harmonieuse . . . vie de pure rêve' (*Novalis*, p. 315). In Germany the flowers of love poetry (from Goethe to Heine) are less distinctive than the mystical and oneiric flowers of Werner, Tieck, or Brentano.

97. See K. Negus, *E. T. A. Hoffmann's Other World* (Philadelphia, University of Pennsylvania Press, 1965), pp. 53–66.

98. See J. Bousquet, *Thèmes du rêve dans la littérature romantique. France, Angleterre, Allemagne* (Didier, 1974), pp. 101–23, and A. Béguin, *L'Ame romantique et le rêve*, 2 vols. (Cahiers du Sud, 1937), p. 137.

99. *Werke*, ed. Ellonger, 15 vols. (Berlin-Leipzig, n.d.), i. 56.

100. See C. Pichois, *L'Image de Jean-Paul Richter dans les lettres françaises* (Corti, 1963), E. Teichmann, *La Fortune d'Hoffmann en France* (Geneva, Droz, 1961), A. Monchoux, *L'Allemagne devant les lettres françaises de 1814 à 1835* (A. Colin, 1953), and C. Dédéyan, *Gérard de Nerval et l'Allemagne*, 3 vols. (Société de l'enseignement supérieur, 1957–9).

101. *De l'Allemagne*, 2 vols. (Flammarion, 1916–17), i. 170.

102. Ibid., ii. 332.

CHAPTER 2

1. *Œuvres complètes*, p. 516.

2. *Les Trois Règnes de la Nature*, quoted by E. Guitton, *Jacques Delille*, p. 535. The language of botany underwent a major change between 1780 and 1820. Linnaean taxonomy (based on plant sexuality) was an appropriate background for *harmonies végétales* or natural theology (cf. E. Darwin's *The Loves of the Plants*, translated in 1800), but after 1800 the systems of Lamarck, Jussieu, and Candolle (based on morphology) no doubt appealed less to the literary imagination.

3. 'Dictionnaire des termes en usage en botanique', *Lettres sur la botanique* (Club des libraires de France, 1962), p. 217.

4. *Œuvres poétiques*, ed. P. Albouy, 2 vols. (Gallimard (Pléiade), 1964), i. 69. Page references to this edition (as A i 69).

5. *Œuvres poétiques*, ed. M. Bertrand, 2 vols. (Presses universitaires de Grenoble, 1973), i. 99.

6. 'Observations', *Oberman*, i, p. xx.

7. *Nouvel art poétique* (1809), quoted by G. Charlier, *Sentiment de la Nature*, p. 103.

8. *Adieux aux romantiques*, in the *Annales romantiques* of 1825, included in Nodier's *Poésies diverses* (Delongle frères et Ladvocat, 1827), pp. 173–4.

9. *A la critique* (1827), cited in *Le Révélateur d'André Chénier*, ed. A. Ponroy (Châteauroux, Société d'imprimerie du Berry, 1924), p. 34.

10. A. de Vigny, *Œuvres complètes*, ed. F. Baldensperger, 2 vols.

(Gallimard (Pléiade), 1948), i. 65–6, and C. A. de Sainte-Beuve, *Œuvres*, ed. M. Leroy, 2 vols. (Gallimard (Pléiade), 1949), i. 64–71. Reviewing F. Denis' *Scènes de la nature sous les tropiques* (1824), Sainte-Beuve approves of poetic exoticism but warns against a new descriptivism.

11. *Rêves poétiques* (1830), cited by G. Charlier, *Sentiment de la Nature*, p. 323.

12. A. Tastu, *L'Odalisque, Poésies* (Denain, 1826), p. 117. Madame Tastu is here imitating Thomas Moore, as did Desbordes-Valmore.

13. Review of A. Pichot's *Voyage historique et littéraire en Angleterre et en Écosse* (in *Le Globe*, 25 Oct. 1825), *Œuvres*, i. 734–5.

14. *Œuvres poétiques complètes*, ed. M.-F. Guyard (Gallimard (Pléiade), 1963), p. 3. Page references to this edition (as G 3).

15. *Poésies*, p. 271.

16. *Maria, Élégie* (1823), quoted by G. Charlier, *Sentiment de la Nature*, p. 340.

17. Page references below to *Vie, poésies et pensées de Joseph Delorme*, ed. G. Antoine (Nouvelles Éditions Latines, 1956).

18. *Œuvres*, i. 379.

19. *Poésies complètes*, 3 vols., ed. R. Jasinski (Firmin-Didot, 1932), i. 81, 83–4 (preface to *Albertus*, 1832).

20. Ibid., i, p. xx.

21. Preface to *Albertus*, ibid., i. 82.

22. *Mademoiselle de Maupin* (Garnier-Flammarion, 1966), p. 130.

23. Ibid., p. 248.

24. *A un jeune tribun, Poésies complètes*, ii. 114–15.

25. *Mademoiselle de Maupin*, p. 45.

26. Kantian aesthetics have no doubt influenced Gautier here, reaching him via V. Cousin, or more likely via Madame de Staël, whose account of Kant links 'useless' beauty with flowers: 'La nature déploie ses magnificences souvent sans but, souvent avec un luxe que les partisans de l'utilité appelleraient prodigue. Elle semble se plaire à donner plus d'éclat aux fleurs . . . qu'aux végétaux qui servent d'aliment à l'homme. Si l'utile avait le premier rang dans la nature, ne revêtirait-elle pas de plus de charmes les plantes nutritives que les roses, qui ne sont que belles? . . . ce qui sert au maintien de notre vie a moins de dignité que les beautés sans but' (*De l'Allemagne*, ii. 187–8).

27. It is mentioned in her *Letters* (XL), published in 1763 and found in several French translations including Brunot's London edition of 1764.

28. *La Chaumière indienne* (1791) (London, Treutell et Wurtz, 1824), pp. 80–1 and *Œuvres*, xi. 351.

29. 'Sur le langage des fleurs', *Annales des voyages de la géographie et de l'histoire*, ix (1809), pp. 346–58.

30. This language is first noted by the *Dictionnaire de l'Académie française* in 1835: 'En Turquie, on forme avec les fleurs un langage symbolique.'

31. Madame de Genlis, *La Botanique historique et littéraire* (Maradan, 1810); Madame Victorine M(augirard), *Les Fleurs, rêve allégorique* (Buisson, L'Huillier et Renard, 1811); F. Delachénaye, *Abécédaire de Flore ou Langage des fleurs* (Didot l'aîne, 1811).

32. The flower dictionary soon became a recognized genre: see my Bibliography, part III. i, for a full list, and see the end of this chapter on the genre.

33. *A une fleur, Poésies complètes*, ed. M. Allem (Gallimard (Pléiade), 1957), p. 384.

34. *Œuvres*, i. 69.

35. *La Comédie humaine*, gen. ed. P.-G. Castex, 11 vols. (Gallimard (Pléiade), 1976–80), ix. 1054.

36. Gautier comments on the code in the introduction to *Le Selam*, a keepsake of 1830 (quoted by F. Lachèvre, *Bibliographie sommaire des keepsakes*, 2 vols. (Giraud-Badin, 1929), pp. 45–6).

37. *Isabelle* (A. Ledoux, 1833), pp. 98–9.

38. H. de Latouche, *Vers isolés*, in *Le Révélateur d'André Chénier*, ed. A. Ponroy, p. 53.

39. *Adèle* (Renduel, 1820), p. 225.

40. *Œuvres poétiques*, i. 101, 192, 220.

41. *La Comédie humaine*, v. 340. This sonnet (written for Balzac by C. Lassailly) appeared in Balzac's text in 1837, presented as an early Romantic work.

42. *Poésies complètes*, ii. 46.

43. *Œuvres poétiques*, i. 62, 82.

44. *Poésies complètes*, p. 150.

45. T. Gautier, *Mademoiselle de Maupin*, p. 207.

46. *Œuvres poétiques*, i. 108.

47. *Poésies*, p. 160.

48. Hugo, A. i 259; Lamartine, G 49; Desbordes-Valmore, *Œuvres poétiques*, p. 85.

49. *Œuvres poétiques*, i. 90.

50. G 187. Cf. Gautier's variant in *Le Spectre de la rose, Poésies complètes*, ii. 136.

51. *Vie . . . de Joseph Delorme*, p. 91.

52. *La Comédie humaine*, xi. 840, 857.

53. *Poésies complètes*, i. 8.

54. *Poésies complètes*, 2 vols. (Lemerre, 1879), ii. 38.

55. Gautier, *Poésies complètes*, ii. 154 and Vigny, *Œuvres complètes*, p. 65.

56. See J. Gaudon, 'Le Rouge et le Blanc: notes sur *Le Lys dans la vallée*', in *Balzac and the Nineteenth Century*, ed. D. Charlton, J. Gaudon, and A. Pugh (Leicester UP, 1972), pp. 71–8.

57. P. Leroux, 'Du style symbolique' (*Le Globe*, 8 Apr. 1829), quoted by C. Pichois, *L'Image de Jean-Paul Richer . . .*, p. 87. Leroux's article is in part a review of the *Pensées de Jean-Paul*, and his views inspired by the German writer.

58. *Œuvres complètes*, i. 813.
59. *Mademoiselle de Maupin*, p. 149.
60. *Poésies complètes*, p. 378.
61. *De l'Allemagne*, ii. 329. This is part of a paraphrase of Novalis's thought.
62. Anonymous writer (Leroux?) in *Le Globe*, 27 Aug. 1825, quoted by A. J. George, *Lamartine and Romantic Unanimism* (New York, Columbia UP, 1940), pp. 56–7.
63. *L'Idée de Dieu*, G 376. Such figures recall the medieval 'book of nature', as well as esoteric tradition.
64. For Lamartine 'la parole' is 'l'instrument . . . / Qui lit dans la nature et qui bénit pour elle' (G 949), while Hugo advises poets: 'Cherchez dans la nature . . . / Le mot mystérieux que chaque voix bégaye' (A i 805).
65. 'Cours philosophiques' (XXV), *Œuvres*, 3 vols. (Hamman, Société belge de librairie, 1840–1), pp. 420–1.
66. Reported by Sainte-Beuve in an article on T. Jouffroy in *RDM*, 1 Dec. 1833, *Œuvres*, i. 928–9.
67. 'Leçon du 7 fév. 1834 sur la sympathie', *Nouveaux Mélanges philosophiques* (Joubert, 1842), p. 446.
68. *Vie . . . de Joseph Delorme*, p. 150.
69. *A mon ami Leroux, Les Consolations* (1830), *Poésies complètes* (Charpentier, 1840), p. 212.
70. The interest of the literary was solicited by Swedenborgians like G. Oegger (*Essai d'un dictionnaire de la langue de la Nature*, 1831) and E. Richer (*La Nouvelle Jérusalem*, 1832–5), and by *martinistes* like U. Guttinger (*Philosophie religieuse de Saint-Martin*, 1835).
71. *Volupté*, ed. M. Allem (Garnier, 1934), pp. 156–7.
72. *La Comédie humaine*, xi. 779–81.
73. A. Brizeux provides a contemporary explanation of the popularity of this topos: 'Aujourd'hui que tout cœur est triste et que chacun / Doit gémir sur lui-même et sur le mal commun, / . . . nos voix / Se prennent à chanter l'eau, les fleurs et les bois, / Alors c'est un bonheur, quand tout meurt ou chancelle, / De se mêler à l'âme immense, universelle' (*Marie* (1831), *Œuvres complètes*, 2 vols. (M. Lévy, 1860), i. 5–6.
74. *Jocelyn*, X, G 738.
75. 'Journal intime ou le cahier vert', *Œuvres complètes*, ed. B. d'Harcourt, 2 vols. (Les Belles Lettres, 1947), i. 158.
76. *Lélia*, ed. P. Reboul (Garnier, 1960), p. 75.
77. *Mademoiselle de Maupin*, p. 31.
78. Ibid., p. 214.
79. Article on Hoffmann (*Le Globe*, 7 Dec. 1830), *Œuvres*, i. 385.
80. *Que la musique date du seizième siècle* (1837), A i 1101.
81. *A Virgile* (1837), A i 960.
82. *Fonction du poète* (1839), A i 1023.
83. A i 1020, and *Pierres*, ed. H. Guillemin (Genève, Éditions du Milieu du Monde, 1951), p. 195.

84. Cf. H. de la Morvonnais: 'Une langue est partout qui me parle et m'enchante; / . . . / J'entre en communion — communion touchante! / Avec tout ce qui vit' (*La Thébaide des Grèves* (1839), cited by E. Fleury, *H. de la Morvonnais* (H. Champion, 1911), p. 195).

85. 'Les littérateurs contemporains' in *La France littéraire* (1840), new ser., i. 7–8, and *Les Chants d'un prisonnier* (Challemel, 1841), pp. 15, 62, 90.

86. Cited by C. Latreille, *Victor de Laprade* (Lyon, Lardanchet, 1912), p. 85.

87. *Odes et poëmes* (J. Labitte, 1843), pp. 105–8.

88. P. Limayrac, 'La Poésie symbolique et socialiste', in *RDM*, 15 Feb. 1844, quoted by P. Moreau, *Le Romantisme* (del Duca, 1957), pp. 367–8.

89. F. P. Bowman gives a survey of such views in Christian, pantheist, and socialist contexts in Ch. 6 of *Le Christ romantique* (Geneva, Droz, 1973), pp. 195–220.

90. *Sonnets* (A. Gratiot, 1840), no. xxxix.

91. *Œuvres*, ed. H. Lemaître, 2 vols. (Garnier, 1958–66), i. 709. And see Ch. 4. I below.

92. *Les Correspondances*, in *Les Trois Harmonies* (Fellens et Dufour, 1846), pp. 297–8. Constant is better known as Eliphas Lévi.

93. F. P. Bowman points out that doctrines of *harmonie* tend to 'déborder les cloisons étanches; la recherche des harmonies est une pensée en mouvement' (*Le Christ romantique*, p. 218).

94. Voltaire had noted in 1738 that analogies between light and sound suggest that 'toutes les choses dans la nature ont des rapports, que peut-être on découvrira un jour' (cited by B. Juden, *Traditions orphiques*, p. 146).

95. *De l'Allemagne*, ii. 195. For an account of Castel's treatise on the analogies between music and colours (*L'Optique des couleurs*, 1740), and Poncelet's on smell and taste analogies (*Chimie du goût et de l'odorat*, 1755), see Juden, *Traditions orphiques*, p. 146.

96. *Oberman*, i. 164. He recalls Castel in a note: 'Le clavecin des couleurs était ingénieux; celui des odeurs eût intéressé davantage'.

97. Ibid., ii. 80.

98. *Les Fleurs*, pp. 83, 88.

99. 'Souvenirs d'un voyageur étranger' (*Mercure du XIXᵉ siècle*, 1823), reproduced by L. de Wiecklawick (*Alphonse Rabbe dans la mêlée politique et littéraire de la restauration* (Nizet, 1963), pp. 569–74) who wrongly attributes this piece to Rabbe, whereas Senancour expressly claims its authorship in *Isabelle* (p. 98).

100. 'L'Art des parfums' (*L'Ariel*, Apr. 1836), cited by Juden, *Traditions orphiques*, p. 509.

101. *Des couleurs symboliques dans l'antiquité, le moyen âge et les temps modernes* (Treutell et Würtz, 1837), p. 23.

102. Cf. Hoffmann: 'la musique est le langage général de la nature, elle

nous parle en accords merveilleux, mystérieux' (*Kreisleriana, Œuvres complètes*, translated by Loève-Veimars, 19 vols. (Renduel, 1830), xix. 194).

103. *La Comédie humaine*, ix. 1053–7.

104. See Juden, *Traditions orphiques*, p. 508.

105. *La Comédie humaine*, ix. 105.

106. *Le Concert des fleurs* (dated 'Août 1834') appears in Mallefille's collection *Monsieur Corbeau* (M. Lévy, 1859).

107. Ibid., pp. 148–9.

108. *Les Sept Cordes de la lyre* (1834), quoted by B. Juden, *Traditions orphiques*, p. 508.

109. See T. Marix-Spire, *Les Romantiques et la musique. Le Cas George Sand. 1804–1838* (Nouvelles Éditions Latines, 1954), p. 289.

110. *Consuelo, la comtesse de Rudolstadt*, ed. L. Cellier and L. Guichard, 3 vols. (Garnier, 1959), ii. 246, also 228–9.

111. *Voyage autour de mon jardin* (Dumont, 1845), p. 12. Karr was in close contact with the literary milieu, as was Méry (see below).

112. J. J. Grandville, *Les Fleurs animées*, monologue et épilogue par Alphonse Karr, texte par Taxile Delord et le comte Foelix (1846–7), cited from the second edition (G. de Gonet, 1847), p. 169. The preceding passage recalls Castel and *Consuelo* : 'L'harmonie des tons ne répond-elle pas à l'harmonie des couleurs? . . . l'air de cette double harmonie, c'est le parfum'. But Méry also seems to recall Rousseau and Senancour, or Hoffmann, on the personal emblematics of memory: 'Ne vous est-il pas arrivé bien souvent, en écoutant une mélodie, de voir naître en vous le souvenir de certaines fleurs?'.

113. 'Au pays des anémones' (1854), article cited by M. L'Hôpital, *La Notion d'artiste chez George Sand* (Boivin, 1946), p. 277. The documented botanical interests of particular writers cannot in fact be convincingly co-related with their treatment of nature or flowers; Karr claims that almost every poet shows 'par la manière dont il parle . . . des fleurs qu'il n'a jamais pris la peine de les regarder', *Voyage*, p. 21.

114. *Voyage en Orient* (1835), quoted by Y. Boeniger, *Lamartine et le sentiment de la nature* (Nizet et Bastard, 1934), p. 207.

115. Cited by J. Pommier, *La Mystique de Baudelaire* (Les Belles Lettres, 1932), p. 61. Fourier's system is orientated towards the final utopian *Harmonie* which will guarantee 'une analogie beaucoup plus vaste, véritable et universelle, qui transforme les fleurs, les animaux et les minéraux en un immense réseau d'hiéroglyphes et d'énigmes' (quoted by E. Lehouck, *Fourier aujourd'hui* (Denoël, 1966), p. 85).

116. E. Lehouck, *Fourier aujourd'hui*, p. 226.

117. *L'Esprit des bêtes, le monde des oiseaux, ornithologie passionnelle*, 3 vols. (Librairie Phalanstérienne, 1853–5), iii. 332–3. For Fourier the 'périodes limbiques' of a society correspond to 'l'âge du début social et de malheur industriel' (see Pommier, *La Mystique de Baudelaire*, p. 56).

118. A flower manual of 1841 shows this idealization at work, under the entry *Souci*: 'L'emblème des chagrins de l'âme. Cependant on peut modifier cette triste signification. Marié à la rose il n'est que l'expression des peines de l'amour' (*Le Langage des fleurs ou Le Livre du destin* (Gautier, 1841), p. 35).

119. *La Confession d'un enfant du siècle*, ed. M. Allem (Garnier, 1968), p. 72.

120. *Mademoiselle de Maupin*, p. 158. Page references in text.

121. If this is the blue flower of German Romanticism, the context (Maupin's discovery of male chauvinism) is certainly ironic.

122. *Théâtre complet*, ed. M. Allem (Gallimard) (Pléiade), 1962), pp. 89, 91.

123. *Madame Putiphar* (Régine Deforges, 1972), p. 110.

124. *La Comédie humaine*, ii. 857.

125. *Le Cahier vert. Comment les dogmes finissent. Lettres inédites* (Les Presses Françaises, 1961). Renan was to write in 1888 of 'La fleur, langage splendide ou charmant, mais absolument énigmatique, qui semble bien un acte d'adoration de la terre à un amant invisible' (*Feuilles détachées* (Calmann-Lévy, 1892), p. 422).

126. *Nouveaux Mélanges philosophiques*, p. 422.

127. Madame Maugirard, *Les Fleurs* (1811), p. 5; Madame de Genlis, *La Botanique* (1810), p. i; Madame G., *Le Bouquet du sentiment, ou Allégorie des plantes et des coleurs* (Lenormant, Dentu, Janet, 1816), p. 2.

128. L. D., *Le Langage des plantes, des fleurs et des couleurs* . . . (Imp. d'Éverat, 1821), pp. 1–2.

129. H. Hostein, *Flore des dames ou Nouveau Langage des fleurs* (J. Loss, 1839), pp. i, 3, 43.

130. See F. Lachèvre, *Bibliographie sommaire des keepsakes*, pp. 86–96, and my Bibliography, part III.ii.

131. M. Alhoy and J. Rostaing, *Les Fleurs historiques* (Janet, n.d. (1852)), p. 2.

132. *Les Fleurs animées*, p. 3.

133. One of these, by Labie, Commerson, and X. de Montépin, played at the Vaudeville with Marie Daubrun as 'La Pensée' (see *Iconographie de Charles Baudelaire*, C. Pichois and F. Ruchon (Genève, P. Cailler, 1960), p. 130). The other, by Jouhard and Bricet, performed at the Théâtre Beaumarchais, preserves a hint of the album's literary allusiveness, as the naïve Carlo (who has never seen women before) comments on meeting the flower-women: 'Mon précepteur ne me montrait que des fleurs de rhétorique. C'était fort ennuyeux! . . . oh! j'aime bien mieux [ces] fleurs . . .!' (Marchant (1846), p. 5).

134. J. J. Grandville, *Les Étoiles*, texte par Méry (Gonet, 1849), p. 2.

135. Thus C. Pichois claims too much when he assumes that 'Croire à la symbolique des fleurs, cela engage fortement alors [1848] dans le socialisme' (*Baudelaire. Études et témoignages* (Neuchâtel, La Baconnière, 1967), p. 99). One need only consider the bourgeois assumptions of flower manual or keepsake . . .

136. *Les Fleurs* (Lille, Lefort, 1854), p. 25.

137. *L'Esprit des bêtes*, i, pp. ii–iii.

138. A lone voice was to insist in 1857 that the *culte des fleurs* of mid-century culture might have implications no one expected: 'Le grand luxe des fleurs . . . est un indice presque infaillible que le peuple chez lequel on le rencontre approche de sa décadence' (E. A. Carrière, *L'Homme et les choses en 1857*, cited by J.-C. Susini, 'Ce qu'on dit au poète à propos de fleurs . . .', *Bulletin baudelairien* (1979), xiv, Supplément, p. 4.

CHAPTER 3

1. C. Baudelaire, *Œuvres complètes*, ed. C. Pichois, 2 vols. (Gallimard (Pléiade), 1975–6), i. 498. These volumes are cited below as P i and P ii respectively (as P i 498). The letters are quoted from C. Baudelaire, *Correspondance*, ed. C. Pichois, 2 vols. (Gallimard (Pléiade), 1973), cited as CP i and CP ii.

2. Quoted by E. Crépet, *Baudelaire. Étude biographique*, rev. J. Crépet (Messein, 1907), pp. 12–13 n. 2.

3. P i 100. Prarond remembers these two poems among the 'plus vieilles pièces de Baudelaire'. See C. Pichois, *Baudelaire. Études et tèmoignages*, pp. 24–6, for Prarond's lists of early poems.

4. See W. T. Bandy, 'Les morts, les pauvres morts', *RSH* (July–Sept. 1967), pp. 477–80.

5. See E. Starkie, *Baudelaire* (1957 edition) (Pelican Books, 1971), pp. 40–55.

6. From a school-friend's letter (1839?) quoted P i 1229.

7. These expressions from the lines to Sainte-Beuve (P i 206) register the pro-Romantic students' rebellion against academic Classicism.

8. Probably written before June 1841 (see P i 1231 and C. Pichois, *Baudelaire*, p. 27). Even if it was revised later, the poem (built around a single oxymoron) cannot have differed much in any earlier form.

9. See M. Ruff, 'Baudelaire et l'amour', *La Table ronde* (Jan. 1956), cited P i 1231–2.

10. Letter from A. Baudelaire to Aupick (Jan. 1842), cited by Pichois, *Baudelaire*, p. 47, and see E. Crépet, *Baudelaire*, pp. 254–5.

11. See M. Ruff, *L'Esprit du mal et l'esthétique baudelairienne* (A. Colin, 1955). Hugo had justified the artistic use of *le grotesque* in the *Préface de Cromwell* (1827), Sainte-Beuve had been accused of applying 'une théorie du laid' in his *Delorme* (1829), and Borel had almost done so in *Madame Putiphar* (1839). So Gautier could announce in the early forties: 'Il est des cœurs épris du triste amour du laid / . . . / Comme un autre le beau, tu cherches ce qui choque' (*Poésies complètes*, ii. 273).

12. Notably Hugo, whose *Marion de Lorme* (1829) impressed the Baudelaire of 1840 (see L. Cellier, 'Baudelaire et *Marion de Lorme*', in Charlton, Gaudon, and Pugh, *Balzac and the Nineteenth Century*,

pp. 311–20) but was apparently too naïve for the Baudelaire of 1846 (see P ii 477).

13. *Les Mystères de Paris*, 3 vols. (Hallier, 1977), i. 22.

14. The fragment 'Prêtresse de débauche . . .' (P i 209) is explicitly about the lesbian in the modern sense; the proposed title *Les Lesbiennes* doubtless referred to a wider group of *femmes damnées*.

15. In most glossaries *l'hellébore* means 'bel esprit' and *le souci* 'chagrin', while *le laurier-rose* can mean 'gloire' or 'modération'. Using this last meaning, the code signifies moderation overcoming both gaiety and sorrow.

16. The parody, composed by Baudelaire, Banville, Dupont, and Vitu, appeared in *Le Corsaire-Satan* of 24 Nov. 1845 — one month after the first announcement of Baudelaire's title.

17. The poem's verse-form (from the Pléiade or Banville?) and its Jeunes-France excesses point to an early date. The indications in Banville's *Note romantique* and his *Odes funambulesques* commentary (see P i 1059, 1411) suggest 1844–5.

18. See (respectively) the manuals by Madame Leneveux (1832/37), Madame de Latour (1824–44), Madame Maugirard (1810), and *Le Langage des fleurs ou Le Livre du destin* (1841).

19. It too dates from an early period: Prarond claims to have heard it in 1843, and the verse-form and reference to nature confirm this date (see F. Leakey, *Baudelaire and Nature* (Manchester UP, 1969), pp. 21–3).

20. Cf. Banville's less ambitious treatment of graveyards and flowers in 1845:

> Leur âme nous parfume, et la grande Nature,
> Si pleine de raison,
> A fait avec leurs corps tombés en pourriture
> Sa belle floraison.

(*Les Stalactites*, in *Poésies complètes* (Charpentier, 1891), p. 264).

21. See R. Canat, *L'Hellénisme des romantiques*, 3 vols. (Didier, 1951–5), vol. iii especially for 1840–52.

22. On the poetics of Hellenism see Chapter 4.II below.

23. See P i 872, summarizing the interpretations of P.-G. Castex and A. Fongaro.

24. P ii 11. For the association between Greek subjects and pantheistic naturalism, see B. Juden, *Traditions orphiques*, pp. 401–21, 542–54.

25. Cf. A. Houssaye, defending 'les peintres panthéistes' in 1844; 'En effet la nature est encore sainte et belle comme le jour où elle sortit des mains du créateur. Elle est d'autant plus digne de Dieu, qu'elle répand le baume de ses fleurs, l'or de ses moissons . . .', *Revue du Salon de 1844*, cited by D. Kelley (ed.), *Baudelaire, Salon de 1846* (Clarendon Press, 1975), pp. 89–90.

26. It is not certain that Baudelaire conceived the whole poem as a unity

in the early forties, but by 1846 he was indeed thinking about the modernity/antiquity question as in this poem (see P ii 496).

27. See D. Kelley, *Salon de 1846*, pp. 17–40.

28. The poem is based on Nerval's articles in *L'Artiste* in 1844, and Prarond claims to have heard it before 1846.

29. Nerval dreams of 'des rives fleuries' while noting the harsh reality of the modern island: 'Pas un arbre sur la côte que nous avons suivie, pas une rose, hélas!' (cited P i 1070).

30. The poem certainly has wider social reference, since Cythera ('Eldorado banal de tous les vieux garçons') is an element in the widely accepted idealization of love.

31. P i 57. I assume (with A. Feuillerat, *Baudelaire et la Belle aux cheveux d'or* (New Haven, Yale UP, 1941), pp. 28–31) that the poem was written for Marie Daubrun and thus can be dated as early as 1847–8.

32. Advertisement in *Le Magasin des familles*, June 1850 (P i 792–3). With political awareness, the poet is eager to place his own 'individualité maladive' in the wider social context of 'la jeunesse moderne'. The title has socialist (Fourierist) overtones, but does not exclude an aesthetic ideal (cf. Balzac's Frenhofer: 'l'idéal . . . j'irais te chercher dans tes limbes, beauté céleste!', cited P i 796).

33. P ii 26–7. He is attacking 'l'école de *l'art pour l'art*', and the idyllic escapism associated with it (see Chapter 4.II below).

34. P ii 26–7. The allusion is to Sainte-Beuve's *Joseph Delorme*, another 'urban' poet.

35. Expression found in the description (*Salon de 1846*) of Delacroix's painting *Les Femmes d'Alger*: 'son tableau le plus coquet et le plus fleuri. Ce petit poème d'intérieur . . . exhale je ne sais quel parfum de mauvais lieu qui nous guide assez vite vers les limbes insondées de la tristesse' (P ii 440).

36. See D. Kelley, *Salon de 1846*, p. 30.

37. Samuel Cramer's *livre de science* on 'la symbolique des couleurs' (P i 580) would have to be based on a claim like Baudelaire's here: 'il y a des tons gais et folâtres, folâtres et tristes, riches et gais, gais et tristes . . .' (P ii 425). Did Baudelaire know Portal's *Des couleurs symboliques* (which suggests that the flower code originates in the *langue des couleurs*)?

38. F. Leakey shows (*Baudelaire and Nature*, p. 31) that *La Chevelure* very likely dates from the same early period as *Parfum exotique*.

39. Leakey's argument (ibid., pp. 196, 209) for dating the second quatrain and tercets in this period convincingly resolves the classic debate for the present purpose.

40. P i 532. Pichois notes (P i 1408) that the translation does not substantially alter Croly's text in *The Young Enchanter*. Baudelaire's text appeared in February 1846.

41. For dating and context see F. Leakey, 'Pour une étude chronologique des *Fleurs du mal*: Harmonie du soir', *RHLF* (1967), pp. 346–56, and *Baudelaire and Nature*, pp. 82–5.

42. Baudelaire is drawing here on cultural associations between flowers, sentimental love, and religion. The religious significance of flowers was strikingly symbolized in the *Fête-Dieu* with its procession to flower-decked altars (*reposoirs*) on which the flower-shaped *ostensoir* was placed to be honoured by the smoke of the *encensoir* (which Baudelaire here compares to flowers); the devotional work of *Les Fleurs* says that 'La Fête-Dieu est la fête des fleurs' (p. 5).

43. Cf. 'De la vaporisation et de la centralisation du *Moi*. Tout est là' (P i 676).

44. F. Leakey quotes ('Pour une étude . . .', p. 347) the passage from Hoffmann's *Chat Murr* used by Banville as an epigraph in 1846, which may have been a source for Baudelaire here: 'je me promenais dans un jardin délicieux: sous l'épais gazon on voyait des violettes et des roses dont le doux parfum embaumait l'air. Un son doux et harmonieux se faisait entendre, et une tendre clarté éclairait le paysage. Les fleurs semblaient tressaillir de bonheur et exhaler de doux soupirs. Tout à coup, je crus m'apercevoir que j'étais moi-même le chant que j'entendais, et que je mourais'.

45. He certainly knew something of all three writers. He appreciated some aspects of Sand's work (see L. Cellier, 'Baudelaire et George Sand', *RHLF* (Apr.–June 1967), p. 257) and may well have read *Consuelo*. He knew many of Karr's and Méry's friends and must have been aware of *Les Fleurs animées*.

46. Apart from the poems quoted below, perhaps only *Le Balcon*, *Moesta et errabunda*, and *La Vie antérieure* share (in their different ways) the sustained musical suggestiveness of *Harmonie du soir*: all of them have synaesthetic aspects.

47. Conversely, Baudelaire includes a flower reference from Poe's *Berenice* (which he translated in 1851–2) when describing the mystico-sensual use of the imagination under hashish: 'rêver des jours entiers sur le parfum d'une fleur' (P i 427).

48. P i 126, P i 1087. I give the early (1851) version here to show that the 'étranges fleurs sur des étagères' of 1857 are not a retrospective construction from the title *Les Fleurs du Mal*, since strangeness is already implicit here.

49. Cf. an untitled poem of Banville's from the same period, on the same theme:

> Puissent les fleurs de rose aux parfums embaumés
> Sortir de nos deux corps qui se sont tant aimés,
> Et nos âmes fleurir ensemble, et sur nos tombes
> Se becqueter longtemps d'amoureuses colombes.

> (*Poésies complètes*, p. 222)

50. Leakey argues (*Baudelaire and Nature*, p. 241) that it was written in January–March 1855, and Pichois suggests (P i 928) late 1854–early 1855, discounting attempts to date it from 1848.

51. See CP i 88 and P i 1259–60.

52. The text quoted is the earliest version (published 9 April 1851, *Le Messager de l'assemblée*), P i 1091–2. If (as Leakey argues, *Baudelaire and Nature*, p. 19) this poem dates from 1842–3, this is one of the earliest *fleur du mal* figures and the first which is explicitly a flower of art.

53. This is Baudelaire's own description in the manuscript of twelve poems addressed to Gautier (1851–2).

54. The first mention of the new title is in Baudelaire's letter to Victor de Mars of 7 April 1855, in which he announces he is preparing 'un très bel épilogue pour les *Fleurs du mal*' (CP i 312). J. S. Patty ('Baudelaire et Hippolyte Babou', *RHLF* (Apr.–June 1967), pp. 260–72) shows that the title was adopted in the months before this date.

55. E. Crépet, *Baudelaire*, cited by J. S. Patty ('Baudelaire et Hippolyte Babou', p. 262).

56. Cited P i 797.

57. Patty quotes ('Baudelaire et Hippolyte Babou', p. 264) from Babou's review in *L'Athenaeum français* (23 June 1855, p. 534) of the eighteen poems published in *RDM* (1 June 1855), under the title *Les Fleurs du Mal*.

58. See CP i 637 and CP i 378.

59. *Hygiène*, P i 670.

60. See my Bibliography, part III.ii. Such works, particularly numerous in the early eighteen-fifties, must surely have been a factor in Babou's proposal of the title and Baudelaire's acceptance of it.

61. *Les Fleurs*, p. 5. J. Pommier, naming a work of 1874 (*Flore mystique de Saint François de Sales ou La Vie chrétienne sous l'emblème des plantes*), notes that 'Il se peut que l'auteur des "Litanies de Satan" ait vu entre les mains de Madame Aupick quelque volume de ce genre, qui lui aura donné l'idée de prendre le contrepied du symbolisme dévot' (*La Mystique de Baudelaire*, p. 181 n. 76).

62. Project for a 'Préface des Fleurs' (1859?), P i 181. In this section I am concerned with Baudelaire's views only when they confirm possible a priori readings of the title.

63. Or indeed a Hermeticist *blasé* about the world of matter. P. Arnold argues unconvincingly that the flowers of evil are the flowers of matter in the Hermetic sense and that the title's source is in the *Pimandre*, in particular the following passage: 'La Matière . . . qui produit et bourgeonne les imperfections et vices comme fleurs et fruits procédant d'elle' (*Ésotérisme de Baudelaire* (J. Vrin, 1972), pp. 49–50).

64. In the *RDM* of June 1855 this poem was preceded by an epigraph from D'Aubigné's *Les Tragiques* which explicitly claims moral intent, ending 'Mais le vice n'a point pour mère la science / Et la vertu n'est pas fille de l'ignorance'.

65. It is just possible that the title was a conscious attempt to link the poet's second title (*Les Limbes*) with his definitive one, in terms of Fourierist

analogie. For Toussenel had given 'les plantes vénéneuses' the analogical meaning of 'les sociétés limbiques', and Baudelaire had certainly read his major work in 1853–5 (see CP i 335–7).

66. For a full account of these efforts, see C. Pichois and F. Ruchon, *Iconographie* . . ., pp. 100–21 and doc. 108–19. Baudelaire rejected Braquemond's attempt: 'Ces fleurs étaient absurdes. Encore aurait-il fallu consulter les livres sur les analogies, le langage symbolique des Fleurs, etc.'. But he was expecting too much of these dictionaries, as Rops (who next took up the challenge) knew when he resorted to inventing plant 'emblems' unknown to flower manuals, such as *un melon* (Greed), *une cactée* (Anger) etc. Baudelaire had insisted that the plants should appear (as described by Poulet-Malassis) thus: 'Sous le pommier fatal dont le tronc squelette rappelle la déchéance de la race humaine, s'épanouissent *les Sept Péchés Capitaux*, figurés par des plantes aux formes et aux attitudes symboliques . . .'.

67. First version of the *dédicace* to Gautier, P i 187.

68. *Les Drames et les romans honnêtes* (1851), P ii 41. Conversely the title can insist that human evil has a powerful appeal to the imagination despite the horrors of it: 'Les vices de l'homme, si pleins d'horreur qu'on les suppose, contiennent la preuve (quand ce ne serait que leur infinie expansion) de son goût de l'infini' (P i 402).

69. The alchemical process is represented in *Au lecteur* not by Hermes but by *Satan Trismégiste*, who turns will-to-virtue into vice. Baudelaire's title implies an aesthetic Hermes, however (cf. 'Tu m'as donné ta boue et j'en ai fait de l'or', P i 192). The horticultural process seems self-evident, but cf. Jules Sandeau on poison-letters: 'ces fleurs vénéneuses qui croissent et foissonnent dans le fumier des départements' (*Mademoiselle de la Seiglière* (1848) (Nelson, n.d.), p. 205).

70. *L'ennui* is, after all, *le mal du siècle*—a Romanticized version of *accidia*, one of the medieval 'seven deadly sins'. See G. Sagnes, *L'Ennui dans la littérature française de Flaubert à Laforgue* (A. Colin, 1969).

71. *Exposition universelle, 1855, Beaux-Arts*, P ii 578. Baudelaire borrowed this concept of beauty's strangeness from Poe (quoting Bacon) whose *Ligeia* he translated early in 1855. But before writing the article he had already chosen his title and no doubt had it in mind here as well as Poe.

72. P i 27, 28, 34. These poems share a similar value-structure, whether 'inspired' by Sara, Jeanne, someone else, or no one.

73. The poems quoted below from this cycle were sent to Madame Sabatier between Dec. 1852 and May 1854.

74. 'Que diras-tu . . .' (P i 43) and *Réversibilité* (P i 44).

75. 'Que diras-tu . . .' and *Le Flambeau vivant* (P i 44).

76. *Semper eadem* (P i 41).

77. By 1857 Madame Sabatier was no longer 'une divinité' but merely 'femme' (CP i 425). The poet's devotion to her is perhaps illumined (as Pichois suggests) by a comment he makes on Poe: 'Quant aux *petits*

épisodes romanesques y a-t-il lieu de s'étonner qu'un être aussi nerveux, dont la soif du Beau était peut-être le trait principal, ait parfois, avec une ardeur passionnée, cultivé la galanterie, cette fleur volcanique et musquée pour qui le cerveau bouillonnant des poètes est un terrain de prédilection?' (P ii 312).

78. P i 49. The first nine poems in this cycle probably all concern Marie Daubrun, whom the poet describes thus: '*Mlle Daubrun* est une de ces personnes qui sont tantôt bonnes, tantôt mauvaises.' (CP i 294).

79. As the subject of all these poems, 'la femme moderne dans sa manifestation héroïque, dans le sens infernal ou divin' (P ii 594) has proved an excellent means of studying the plurality of relations between beauty and *le Mal.*

80. See P i 548–9 and P ii 317.

81. See P i 193 and CP i 573.

82. The poem (P i 96–8) is quoted and discussed in relation to Christophe's statue in the *Salon de 1859* (P ii 679).

83. P i 351. The prose poem (written in 1863–4) takes up the figure deployed in *Une charogne* twenty years earlier, thus pointing once more to the continuity of Baudelaire's aesthetics of ironic flowers.

84. Perhaps because its aesthetic system was so extreme and unprecedented, this poem became during the poet's lifetime the most widely published of his works (see P i 1028–9).

85. *Edgar Poe, sa vie et ses ouvrages* (1856), P ii 317–18.

86. *Le Peintre de la vie moderne* (1863), P ii 722.

87. In 1865 Baudelaire attacked Jules Janin, in an unfinished article, for stating that happiness was the most suitable emotion for poetry: 'pourquoi donc toujours la joie? Pour vous divertir peut-être. Pourquoi la tristesse n'aurait-elle pas sa beauté? Et l'horreur aussi? Et tout? Et n'importe quoi?' (P ii 237).

88. To speak of Baudelaire's 'theory' of aesthetic autonomy is to assume a great deal, since commentators usually stress the plurality or evolution of his thought on this matter. Yet it is legitimate to the extent that his poetry shows him operating throughout his career within the dialectic of Beauty/*le Mal.* This was stable enough for the title to head a collection of poems written at all periods, and in this sense at least there is an 'architecture secrète' to the work.

89. Both quotations from 1851: *Les Drames et les romans honnêtes*, P ii 41, and *Pierre Dupont* (1), P ii 26.

90. *E. A. Poe, sa vie et ses ouvrages* (1852), P ii 263.

91. Ibid., P ii 263 .

92. Ibid., P i 269.

93. *Notes nouvelles sur Edgar Poe* (1857), P ii 333.

94. *Fusées*, x, 16, P i 657–8.

95. *Réflexions sur quelques-uns de mes contemporains: Théodore de Banville* (1861), P ii 168.

96. P i 149. The printed note claiming (ironically?) that these creatures 'sont les écrivains qui ne sont pas de son école' was written by Baudelaire (P i 1122).
97. Preface to *Histoires extraordinaires* (1854), P ii 291. This image, a version of the poet's first *fleur du mal* in the Latin poem of his schooldays, is taken up not only in the Delacroix passage below but also in the late prose poem *Le Désir de peindre* (1863), where he compares a woman's mouth with 'une superbe fleur éclose dans un terrain volcanique' (P i 340).
98. *L'Œuvre et la vie d'Eugène Delacroix* (1863), P ii 758.
99. *Philibert Rouvière* (1859), P ii 60.
100. Cf. E. Starkie: 'This title, although it suggests only one aspect of his work, has generally been considered to suit the whole collection admirably' (*Baudelaire*, p. 359). The rest of this chapter will claim that this general assumption is justified in terms of Baudelaire's 'flower poetics'.
101. *Du vin et du hachisch* (1851), P i 392–3.
102. *Exposition universelle, 1855, Beaux-arts*, P ii 577.
103. *Edgar Poe, sa vie et ses ouvrages* (1852), P ii 253.
104. P ii 596. This passage is the first to use the terms *surnaturel*, *surnaturalisme* to describe that idealizing mysticism of the senses already evoked in some earlier poems (and in texts related to drug-taking).
105. *Edgar Poe, sa vie et ses ouvrages* (1856), P ii 318.
106. On the poet's earlier uses of the term see F. Leakey, *Baudelaire and Nature*, pp. 179–81. Cf. *Fusées*, xi, 17: 'Dans certains états de l'âme presque surnaturels, la profondeur de la vie se révèle tout entière dans le spectacle qu'on a sous les yeux. Il en devient le symbole' (P i 659).
107. For the dating of the sonnet, the arguments of F. Leakey (*Baudelaire and Nature*, pp. 196, 197, 29) are followed here, as earlier. For Fourier's term *analogie universelle* see P ii 575, and for Swedenborg's term *correspondances* see P ii 577. Baudelaire's interest in universal reciprocal relations certainly predates his first uses of these terms in print, since terms like *harmonie* and *analogie* (used by him in the forties) derive from the same body of thought. But he gives his own sense to them . . .
108. See F. Leakey, *Baudelaire and Nature*, p. 209 *et passim*, and C. Pichois, P i 844.
109. In his own commentary on these two quatrains in *Richard Wagner et Tannhauser à Paris* (1861) Baudelaire insists that the *correspondances* are both synaesthetic and symbolic at the same time: 'ce qui serait vraiment surprenant, c'est que le son *ne pût pas* suggérer la couleur, que les couleurs *ne pussent pas* donner l'idée d'une mélodie, et que le son et la couleur fussent impropres à traduire des idées' (P ii 784).
110. If *Harmonie du soir* dates from the mid-forties (as was assumed above) Baudelaire's interest in the *langage des fleurs* might date from that

period: so might both *Élévation* and *Correspondances*. Interest in both cosmic *harmonie* doctrines and the flower language was equally intense in the forties and fifties. This is why the hunt for precise 'sources' (and dating) here is like looking for a particular straw in a haystack. For all that, the flower-language pieces quoted in the preceding chapter are as likely, 'source pour source', as any others, since Baudelaire's own use of the phrase *le langage des fleurs* is highly significant.

111. The dating of this poem and the related prose poem again follows Leakey (*Baudelaire and Nature*, p. 241, n 3).

112. P i 301–3. But the 1857 version is used here: for variants see P i 1323–4.

113. For discussion of P. Dupont's 'dahlia bleu' and Dumas *père*'s 'tulipe noire', see G. Blin, 'Les Fleurs de l'impossible', *RSH* (July–Sept. 1967), p. 463.

114. This complex trope depends to a great extent on the process already described: through *surnaturalisme*, ordinary flowers of nature become perfect flowers of the *surnaturel* ('ces fleurs miraculeuses') illustrating its two codes, symbolic and synaesthetic. The figure also owes much to the traditional comparison of woman and landscape (see P ii 174), and to the pastoral tradition ('c'est là . . . qu'il faudrait aller vivre et fleurir').

115. *Salon de 1859*, P ii 621. The transforming power of the imagination is already implied in the keyboard metaphor in the 1855 *Exposition* article, in Baudelaire's attack on the type of academic aestheticism 'qui a oublié . . . la forme du végétal' (P ii 577).

116. See F. Leakey, *Baudelaire and Nature*, pp. 186–7.

117. *Le Poème du hachisch* (1857/1860), P i 441.

118. In his letter to F. Desnoyers of 1853 or 1854 (CP i 248) the poet distances himself from the pantheist 'religion nouvelle' of poets like Laprade, mockingly (mis-)quoting the latter ('l'âme des Dieux habite dans les plantes') and seeing in it 'je ne sais quoi de *shocking*'. See F. Leakey, *Baudelaire and Nature*, pp. 122–3, 171–2.

119. *Notes nouvelles sur Edgar Poe* (1857), P ii 334. This is the one passage where Baudelaire seems to assume a Platonic, Martiniste, or Swedenborgian correlation between material and transcendental realities. Since elsewhere he treats the correspondences in terms of experience, the imagination, and metaphor, it seems likely that this passage uses hyperbolical language to emphasize the high value of the *surnaturel*.

120. *Charles Baudelaire: A Lyric Poet in the Era of High Capitalism* (New Left Books, 1973), p. 139.

121. *Baudelaire*, p. 359.

122. In 1861 Baudelaire changed 'Fleur impossible' to 'Fleur incomparable', emphasizing even more ironically its ambiguity as an 'allégorique' emblem — it cannot be compared with reality but is incomparably more beautiful than reality.

123. In the prose poems' dedicatory notice to Houssaye, Baudelaire specifically links the 'prose poétique' of these pieces with 'la fréquentation des villes énormes' (P i 275–6).
124. Everything in the context indicates that the 'divin' and the 'diabolique' are accessible in nature not in any immanent or transcendental way but because they reflect (are available as metaphors for) the human dimension ('le *spirituel*'). The paraphrase of Swedenborg following this passage is used to emphasize that 'tout est hiéroglyphique', and that the poet is 'un traducteur, un déchiffreur'.
125. Thus E. Starkie (*Baudelaire*, p. 359); 'The title's chief value was that it was bound to startle and arouse interest'.
126. *Fusées*, xi, 17, P i 658. For the dating of these notes, see P i 1467–9.
127. But as early as 1855, a few months after choosing his title, Baudelaire was explicitly presenting the two qualities together in a passage on Delacroix's women: 'Qu'elles se distinguent par le charme du crime ou par l'odeur de la sainteté . . . ces femmes malades du cœur ou de l'esprit ont dans les yeux le plombé de la fièvre ou la nitescence anormale et bizarre de leur mal, dans le regard, l'intensité du surnaturalisme' (P ii 594).
128. He saw no real antithesis between city and country at this period: 'Ivresse religieuse des grandes villes. — Panthéisme.' (*Fusées*, ii, 2, P i 651). See F. Leakey, *Baudelaire and Nature*, pp. 160–72.
129. *Les Sept Vieillards* (1859), P i 87; *Le Cygne* (1859–60), P i 86; *Les Petites Vieilles* (1859), P i 89.
130. *Le Poème du hachisch* (1857–60), P i 403. This became the first part of *Les Paradis artificiels* in 1860.
131. *L'Âme du vin*, P i 105. This early poem (published in 1850 and perhaps written before 1843) contained no flower image before the 1857 version. The poet perhaps wanted to make a link between the *paradis* of wine and drugs and the idealizing *fleurs* of his poetry. Pichois notes that flowers were associated commercially with the term 'Paradis artificiels' (P i 1373).
132. The first phrase is quoted from a passage on Delacroix's painting (comparing it with the drug-induced *surnaturel*) in the *Salon de 1859*, P ii 636; the other two from *Puisque réalisme il y a* (1855?), P ii 59.
133. The structuralist critic C. Zilberberg makes the same point: 'Les dénégations de l'espace cosmologique, loin de susciter un espace cosmologique *distinct*, n'aboutissent qu'à informer la noölogie' (*Une lecture des 'Fleurs du Mal'* (Tours, Mame, (Univers sémiotiques) 1972), p. 179.
134. *L'Art philosophique* (1857–60), P ii 598. Although this description might apply in a general sense to all art, for Baudelaire it is a definition of the best Romantic art, rejecting didacticism (as the context makes clear) and giving full importance to the artistic medium ('une magie suggestive'). Cf. P i 398.
135. *Fusées*, xi, 17, P i 658. See also the Gautier article (1859): 'Manier

savamment une langue, c'est pratiquer une espèce de sorcellerie évocatoire' (P ii 117).

136. These include not only the poems named in the preceding section but some of those studied in II.iii—*Sonnet d'automne, L'Amour du mensonge, Madrigal triste,* and *Danse macabre.*

137. Along with J. Pommier, J. Crépet, and G. Blin, M. Ruff is among those who date *Correspondances* in 1845–6: he quotes Prarond's lines from *Ténèbres intérieures* (*L'Esprit du mal,* p. 176).

138. At the close, *La Mort des artistes* identifies all the preceding poems as 'fleurs de son cerveau'. At the opening, *Élévation* and *Correspondances* 'define' *surnaturalisme* and relate it to *ironie,* while *Le Soleil* speaks of the sun awakening 'les vers comme les roses' and the sun/poet who 'ennoblit le sort des choses les plus viles'—an ironic alchemy of *analogie.* The 'architecture secrète' of the whole volume is not an allegorical framework (see P i 798–800), yet all the poems in it form one poetic discourse of (and about) *surnaturalisme, ironie* and creativity, emphasizing each in turn. Corresponding to these three emphases, the three types of flower imagery are figures for the diversity-in-unity which makes the volume more than 'un pur album'. The title emphasizes the unity since it refers to the flowers of irony, the flowers of the *correspondances* (which the sonnet shows capable of 'negative' meanings), and the literary beauty created in suffering.

139. The new section on modern beauty (*Tableaux parisiens*) begins with *Paysage* and *Le Soleil,* both showing *analogie* functioning ironically in an urban context. *Le Voyage* (now the last poem instead of *La Mort des artistes*) insists even more strongly, after inspecting the whole 'échelle fatale' of life, that the final 'hope' of the poet is to find new imaginative flowers beyond death: only there can the ironic *correspondances* really yield 'du nouveau' (a cry of pride and frustration).

140. For discussion of the poet-as-clown see J. Starobinski, 'Sur quelques répondants allégoriques du poète', *RHLF* (Apr.–June 1967).

141. P i 336. In perhaps his very last poem, Baudelaire provides a more elegiac farewell to his art:

> La gerbe épanouie
> En mille fleurs,
> Où Phoebé réjouie
> Met ses couleurs,
> Tombe comme une pluie
> De larges pleurs.

> (*Le Jet d'eau* (1865), P i 160–1.)

CHAPTER 4

1. For his esoteric education see *Les Illuminés* (1852) in *Œuvres,* ed. H. Lemaître, 2 vols. (Garnier, 1958–66), i. 80, and for the poem

see ibid., p. 27. Subsequent references are given to this first volume as L 27.

2. L 38. The song for this *opéra-comique* was later included in *Petits Châteaux de Bohème* as 'Chanson gothique'.

3. *L'Imagier de Harlem ou La Découverte de l'imprimerie*, drame légende . . . de MM. Méry, Gérard de Nerval, et Bernard Lopez, Nlle édition (*Librairie théâtrale*, 1852), pp. 82–3. This was one of several works on which Gérard collaborated with Méry, that tireless propagandist for the *culte des fleurs*.

4. This is a supposition, since Christine Bomboir's important study (*Les Lettres d'amour de Nerval, mythe ou réalité?* (Namur, Presses universitaires de Namur, 1978)) proves conclusively in my view that many of the assumptions made by Gérard's contemporaries (and by critics thereafter) about his love for Jenny Colon are groundless: in fact there is very little evidence about his relations with women. Bomboir's study cannot be ignored, and as J. Guillaume and C. Pichois acknowledge in their *avant-propos* to it, Nerval studies cannot now continue to 'rabaisser une œuvre littéraire à l'étiage de l'anecdote'.

5. *Lettres à Aurélia*, xiii, L 847. This is one of the first six love letters (generally known as the *Lettres à Jenny Colon*, wrongly it would now seem): perhaps begun in the early thirties, this project was revised and added to for the next twenty years.

6. L 32. The term 'Cydalise' (implying great worth or beauty) seems to have originated in the *bohème* of the Doyenné group (see L 8, 10, 34, 876).

7. *Lettres à Aurélia*, L 835–6. This is part of a passage appearing first in *Un roman à faire* (1842), then in *L'Illusion* (1845), then in *Octavie* (1853–4).

8. *Sylvie*, L 591–2. The context of this passage reveals his self-critical awareness of the 'paradoxes platoniques' of this distant worship of women as 'fantômes métaphysiques'.

9. L 709. In the 1845 version (*Pensée antique*), l. 3 has 'ta royauté dispose' and l. 5 'Chaque plante est une âme'; the change to 'ta liberté' and 'chaque fleur' provides greater consistency with Nerval's mature thought about salvation, often expressed in terms of flower imagery. The poem's Pythagorism (signalled by title and epigraph) is mainly based on Delisle de Sales's *De la philosophie de la nature* (1777), as G. Le Breton has shown.

10. As J. Richer shows, this work (or at least its first part) was begun in 1841 and then underwent 'une lente élaboration' (see *Nerval, expérience et création*, 2ᵉ édn. (Hachette, 1970), pp. 418–526).

11. It is legitimate (and for hermeneutic purposes necessary) to consider all Nerval's mature work as one corpus: the writer authorizes this by publishing *Les Chimères* (with *Artémis*) as part of *Les Filles du feu* and mentioning a text like *Aurélia* in his preface to the volume (see L 502).

12. Cf. A. Alan ('Quelques fleurs ésotériques chez Nerval', *L'Herne 37, Gérard de Nerval* (Éditions de l'Herne, 1980), pp. 171–81) whose discussion of this flower scarcely distinguishes it from other Nervalian roses, all seen as signifying 'l'angoisse de mourir et le désir de connaître'. Cf. also B. Juden, who baldly states (*Traditions orphiques*, p. 701): 'Reste dans la *Rose trémière* un symbole de la mère déesse, l'Isis du rêve d'*Aurélia*, et une confirmation de l'expérience initiatique'.

13. In his 'Notes du *Voyage en Orient*' Gérard writes: 'Admirer les mêmes traits dans des femmes diverses. Amoureux d'un type éternel' (*Œuvres*, ii. 798: subsequent page references to this text are cited as LV 798).

14. Only first dates of publication are given for sonnets subsequently cited.

15. E. Pelletan (1845), cited by B. Juden (*Traditions orphiques*, p. 601), whose documentation of Nerval's Orphism is assumed below.

16. L 495, 502. Nerval incorporated his *Roman tragique* (with its reference to Scarron's *Roman comique*) in his preface to *Les Filles du feu* ('A Alexandre Dumas').

17. In his preface ('A Alexandre Dumas') Nerval presents the sonnets of *Les Chimères* as mystically 'obscurs' but truly poetic: 'concédez-moi au moins le mérite de l'expression' (L 503).

18. *Histoire du Romantisme, suivie de notices romantiques et d'une étude sur la poésie française 1830–1868* (Charpentier, 1874), p. 295.

19. *Élégies* (ii), *Œuvres complètes*, p. 56.

20. *La Maison du Berger, Lettre à Éva, Œuvres complètes*, pp. 173–4.

21. Quoted by R. Canat, *La Renaissance de la Grèce antique, 1821–1850* (Hachette, 1912), p. 7.

22. *Les Vœux stériles, Poésies complètes*, pp. 114–15.

23. *Ahasvérus* (1833), cited in R. Canat, *L'Hellénisme des romantiques*, 3 vols. (Didier, 1951–5), vol. ii, *Le Romantisme des Grecs, 1826–1840*, pp. 233–4.

24. *Hellas* (1850?), quoted by F. Desonay, *Le Rêve hellénique chez les poètes parnassiens* (H. Champion, 1928), p. 105.

25. 'Des Religions de l'Antiquité et de leurs derniers historiens', *RDM*, nlle période, 2ᵉ série, ii. 827–8.

26. *Du Génie des religions* (1842), cited by R. Canat, *La Renaissance . . .*, p. 263.

27. *Mademoiselle de Maupin*, p. 201.

28. *Sur un album* (1841), *Poésies complètes*, ii. 220.

29. Quoted by R. Canat, *L'Hellénisme . . .*, iii. 117.

30. *Conseil*, in *Les Cariatides, Les Stalactites, Le Sang de la coupe, Roses de Noël (Poésies complètes)* (Charpentier, 1891), p. 172.

31. *Odes et poëmes* (J. Labitte, 1843), pp. 275, 283.

32. *Erato, Les Cariatides . . .*, pp. 162–3.

33. *Odes et poëmes*, pp. 285–6.

34. Preface to *Les Stalactites, Les Cariatides . . .*, p. 213.

35. *Odelette 56*, quoted by E. Pich, *Leconte de Lisle et sa création poétique* (Lyon, Université Lyon II, 1975), p. 47.

36. Unpublished poem *La Vie et le rêve* (Jan. 1841), cited ibid., p. 24.
37. *La Fontaine des lianes* (later title *La Fontaine aux lianes*), *Œuvres de Leconte de Lisle*, ed. E. Pich, 4 vols. (Les Belles Lettres, 1977–8), ii. 147, 149.
38. *Ode à Fourier*, ibid., iv. 154, and *Les Eolides*, ibid., i. 263. The lines quoted from the latter are found only in the 1846 version, published in *La Phalange* as *L'Idylle antique*.
39. The phrase is Houssaye's, from a letter addressed to *L'Artiste* in 1847, cited by B. Juden, *Traditions orphiques*, p. 577.
40. *Du polythéisme hellénique* (1863), cited by F. Desonay, *Le Rêve hellénique*, p. 82.
41. *Le Temple d'Isis* (in *La Phalange*, 1845), cited by B. Juden, *Traditions orphiques*, p. 564.
42. *Hymne du printemps* (1844), cited by B. Juden, *Traditions orphiques*, p. 715.
43. *Mademoiselle du Maupin*, p. 149.
44. Ibid., p. 151.
45. See D. Kelley, *Salon de 1846*, pp. 87–9.
46. See R. Canat, *L'Hellénisme . . .*, vol. ii, Chapters VI–VIII.
47. 'La Moralité de la poésie', *RDM* (1835), i. 245.
48. *Les Rayons et les ombres* (1840), *Œuvres poétiques*, i. 1070.
49. *Poésies complètes*, ii. 115.
50. *Les Cariatides . . .*, p. 157. The poem is dated 'Février 1841'.
51. *Odes et poëmes*, p. 246.
52. *Poésies complètes*, ii. 91.
53. *Odes et poëmes*, p. 271.
54. *Heures de poésie* (1841), cited by R. Canat, *La Renaissance . . .*, p. 261.
55. *Les Cariatides . . .*, pp. 6–8. The poem did not appear in the original edition, and was only added in the *Poésies complètes* published by Poulet-Malassis in 1857. Yet Banville there dates it 'Juillet 1842' and this, along with the title of the volume, justifies treating the poem as a work of the earlier period.
56. Ibid., p. 260.
57. Ibid., p. 263.
58. Ibid., pp. 272–4.
59. Ibid., p. 275.
60. Ibid., pp. 217–19. Here again the title-related poem, *Décor*, was only added to the volume in the 1857 edition, but since it was there dated 'Décembre 1846' it may legitimately be treated as an illustration of the poetics of the earlier volume.
61. *A Vénus de Milo* (1846 title), *Œuvres*, i. 132. The 1846 version quoted here and below differs in places considerably from the definitive one.
62. Ibid., i. 269–70.
63. *Niobé*, ibid., i. 158–9.
64. Ibid., i. 65–6.
65. See E. Pich, *Leconte de Lisle*, p. 46 *et passim*.

66. *Œuvres*, i. 269–70.
67. Leconte de Lisle, *Articles, Préfaces, Discours*, ed. E. Pich (Les Belles Lettres, 1977), p. 68.
68. *Œuvres*, i. 8–10.
69. Ibid., i. 16, 24–5.
70. *Dans la Sierra (España), Poésies complètes*, ii. 291.
71. *La Petite Fleur rose (España)*, ibid., ii. 268.
72. *Préface, Émaux et Camées*, ed. G. Matoré (Lille, Giard/Geneva, Droz, 1947), p. 3. Quotations below have page references to this edition.
73. Leconte de Lisle, *Symphonie*, *Œuvres*, i. 241.
74. Leconte de Lisle, *Médailles antiques*, ibid., i. 227.
75. *La Rose*, ibid., i. 172.
76. *A Auguste Supersac, Les Cariatides . . .*, p. 175.
77. *Les Vignes folles* (1860), *Œuvres (Poésies complètes)* (Lemerre, 1879), pp. 7–9.
78. Ibid., p. 10.
79. See L. Badesco, *La Génération poétique de 1860. La Jeunesse des deux rives* (Nizet, 1971), *passim*.
80. *A. M. Leconte de Lisle* (1863), *Œuvres (Poésies)* (Lemerre, 1887), p. 31.
81. Ibid., pp. 41–2.
82. See ibid., pp. 99, 161.
83. *Vénus (Sonnets, 1863–64), Poésies (1866–73)* (Lemerre, 1898), p. 28.
84. *Poésies complètes* (Lemerre, 1924), p. 248.
85. *Poésies (1866–73)*, p. 114.
86. *Poésies complètes*, p. 245.
87. *Ariane, (Philoméla*, 1863), *Poésies*, 7 vols. (Ollendorff, 1885), i. 19.
88. *Les Flèches d'or* (1864), *Œuvres (Poésies complètes)*, p. 87.
89. *Poésies (1866–72)* (Lemerre, 1872), p. 104.
90. Poésies (1866–72) (Lemerre, 1880), p. 11.
91. *Le Parnasse contemporain. Recueil de vers nouveaux* (Lemerre, 1866). Page references given in text.
92. *Histoire du Romantisme . . .*, p. 359.
93. It was unmistakable enough to merit the tribute of parody in *Le Parnassiculet contemporain. Receuil de vers nouveaux* (Librairie centrale, J. Lemer, 1867), a parody necessarily saluting the poetics of marble and flowers. Thus the visiting Mandarin notes that 'On imaginait, à leurs vers, qu'ils passent la vie dans des palais de porcelaine, pleins de fleurs, de femmes et d'oiseaux rares, parmi de vastes jardins d'été, où l'eau chante éternellement au fond des vasques de marbre' (p. 10).
94. Cited by F. Desonay (*Le Rêve hellénique*, p. 420), who here runs together comments made by Sainte-Beuve in 1862 and 1870.

CHAPTER 5

1. Quoted by W. T. Bandy and C. Pichois, *Baudelaire devant ses contemporains* (Monaco, Editions du Rocher, 1957), p. 201.
2. *Œuvres (Poésies complètes)*, p. 38.
3. *Le Bénitier, Poésies*, p. 22.
4. *Poésies*, p. 14.
5. *Le Parnassiculet contemporain*, p. 31.
6. *Histoire du Romantisme* . . ., p. 364.
7. M. Rollinat, *Œuvres*, 2 vols. (Minard (Lettres modernes), 1972), i. 68.
8. *Le Parnasse contemporain*, p. 137.
9. *Œuvres poétiques*, ed. J. Robichez (Garnier, 1969), p. 25. Page references given in text (as R 25).
10. Quoted by G. Zayed, *La Formation littéraire de Verlaine* (Nouvelle édition augmentée, Nizet, 1970), p. 237.
11. *Œuvres*, ed. S. Bernard (Garnier, 1960), p. 341. Page references given in text (as B 341).
12. In the text below the former (B 344–6) is designated as I, the latter (B 346–50) as D.
13. Rimbaud does say Baudelaire has the ability to 'inspecter l'invisible et entendre l'inouï' (D), and only finds his 'formes' inadequate (too restrained and 'aesthetic'?).
14. Or indeed like Baudelaire's 'style de décadence' as Gautier describes it in his 1868 article (see below, II.i): Rimbaud may well be alluding to this passage in order to point up his own entirely un-decadent revolutionary vigour.
15. He may even have been influenced by flower dictionaries in a specific sense: Madame Leneveux (1832) gives the 'Emblèmes des couleurs' as: Blanc / innocence, candeur; Noir / mort; Rouge / ardeur; Bleu / amour pur, sagesse; Vert / espérance. Or does this merely show Rimbaud's conventionality in colour association?
16. B 240. The problem of dating is only of marginal importance in this context. Although *Adieu* states that Rimbaud is no longer trying to invent new flowers, *Fleurs* equally clearly shows him doing so. This is not in itself, of course, an indication that *Fleurs* (or the *Illuminations*) was written before *Adieu* (or *Une Saison en enfer*) . . . See C. A. Hackett, *Rimbaud, A Critical Introduction* (Cambridge UP, 1981), pp. 48–9.
17. For Mallarmé's early work see A. Gill, *The Early Mallarmé*, vol. i, *Parentage, Early Years, and Juvenilia* (Clarendon Press, 1979). Like L. Cellier and A. Ayda he shows the young poet much influenced by Hugo and Lamartine, but he differs from them by ascribing less importance to Mallarmé's bereavements during this period. I follow him on this latter point and for quotation of some early poems not included in the Pléiade *Œuvres complètes* (ed. H. Mondor and G. Jean-Aubry (Gallimard, 1945)). Page references to the former are given in the text as GM 10, and to the latter as M 10.

18. Cited by L. Cellier, *Mallarmé ou La Morte qui parle* (PUF, 1959), pp. 188, 190. In her 'enchantement de fleurs' this dancing apparition scatters both the (red?) roses of consoling dreams and white lilies recalling death: she wears 'la couronne de roses blanches qu'ont les jeunes filles dans le cerceuil'. Cellier, followed by J. P. Richard (*L'Univers imaginaire de Mallarmé* (Éditions du Seuil, 1961), pp. 48–9, 78–81), argues that the *symbolique des fleurs* of the mature poet is already evident here. I shall attempt to show that this is no simple flower-code.

19. Cited ibid., p. 24.

20. Review of des Essarts's *Les Poésies parisiennes* (M 256) and the poem *Contre un poète parisien* (M 21).

21. The version of this poem from the Aubanel manuscript is used here (see M 1423–4 for its differences from the 1866 and 1887 versions, which mainly concern the last stanza) because it is very likely the first version, written before Mallarmé began working on *Hérodiade*.

22. *Correspondance*, ed. H. Mondor and L. J. Austin, 7 vols. (Gallimard, 1959–82), i. 137.

23. Ibid., i. 161 (Mar. 1865).

24. I rely here on the dating and texts of the Pléiade editors for the first version, 'Monologue d'un faune', 1865 (M 1450–3) and the second version 'Improvisation d'un faune', 1875 (M 1456–8).

25. *Correspondance*, i. 168.

26. Charles Cros, Tristan Corbière, *Œuvres complètes*, ed. L. Forestier and P.-O. Walzer (Gallimard (Pléiade), 1970), p. 47. Page references for Cros and Corbière are to this edition (as FW 47).

27. Lautréamont, Germain Nouveau, *Œuvres complètes*, ed. P.-O. Walzer (Gallimard (Pléiade), 1970), p. 369. Subsequent page references are to this edition (as W 369).

28. For both these points see A. E. Carter, *The Idea of Decadence in French Literature, 1830–1900* (Toronto UP, 1958), and for the latter alone see K. Swart, *The Sense of Decadence in Nineteenth-Century France* (The Hague, Nijhoff, 1964).

29. Quoted in C. Baudelaire, *Œuvres complètes*, i. 1194.

30. *Histoire du Romantisme . . .*, p. 369.

31. Quoted by A. E. Carter, *Baudelaire et la critique française, 1868–1917* (Columbia, University of South Carolina Press, 1963), p. 27.

32. Cited ibid., p. 49.

33. Cited ibid., p. 50.

34. Cited ibid., pp. 51–3.

35. *Œuvres*, p. 304.

36. Ibid., p. 320.

37. See P. Stephan, *Paul Verlaine and the Decadence 1882–90* (Manchester UP, 1974), pp. 40–1.

38. Cited ibid., p. 41.

39. Cited ibid., pp. 52–3.

40. See N. Richard, *A l'aube du symbolisme* (Nizet, 1961), pp. 105–12.
41. *A Rebours* (Bibliothèque Charpentier, 1910). Page references to this edition (as H 20).
42. 'La Sensation en littérature: la folie de Charles Baudelaire', *Les Taches d'encre*, i, 1 (5 Nov. 1884) and 2 (5 Dec. 1884).
43. *Lutèce* (1 Sept. 1884). Quoted by P. Stephan, *P. Verlaine . . .*, p. 46.
44. *Poèmes élégiaques* (Mercure de France, 1907), p. 92.
45. *Les Syrtes* (1884), *Œuvres* (Mercure de France, 1923), p. 46.
46. *Lutèce* (28 Sept. 1884), cited in N. Richard, *A l'aube du symbolisme*, p. 171.
47. The 1885 version is used here for the title and two other details of punctuation, but is otherwise identical with the definitive one: see M 55–7.
48. The ambiguous identity of this figure poses explicitly the hermeneutic problem represented by the whole poem. In this context a full critical account is not possible, but my paraphrase relies in part on insights from M. Bowie (*Mallarmé and the Art of Being Difficult* (Cambridge UP, 1978)) and J.-P. Richard (who finds in the poem an opposition between 'l'indétermination' and 'la définition consciente', *L'Univers imaginaire de Mallarmé*, p. 401).
49. *Les Déliquescences. Poèmes décadents d'Adoré Floupette*, ed. S. Cigada (Milan, Cisalpino-Goliardica, 1972). Page references given in text.
50. For 1885–6 see K. Cornell, *The Symbolist Movement* (New Haven, Yale University Press, 1951), Chapters IV–V.
51. *Les Premières Armes du symbolisme* (Vanier, 1889), pp. 33–4.

CONCLUSION

1. 'Hamlet', *Moralités légendaires (Œuvres complètes)* (Mercure de France, 1921), p. 43.
2. *Narcisse parle*, *Album de vers anciens* (Gallimard, 1927), p. 31.
3. *Fragment du Narcisse*, *Charmes ou Poèmes*, ed. C. Whiting (University of London, The Athlone Press, 1973), p. 52.
4. See P. Clements, *Canonization of the Subversive: Baudelaire and the English Tradition*. (Princeton UP, 1985).
5. See B. Seward, *The Symbolic Rose*, and M. Paquien, 'La Fonction poétique de la fleur dans l'œuvre de Proust' (unpublished thèse de Maîtrise, Université Lyon II, 1981).
6. P. Ricœur, *La Métaphore vive* (Éditions du Seuil, 1975), p. 392.

BIBLIOGRAPHY

I. Works consulted for Chapter 1

Arber, A., *The Natural History of Plant Form* (Cambridge UP, 1950).

Armstrong, A., *Ronsard and the Age of Gold* (Cambridge UP, 1968).

Ayrault, R., *La Genèse du romantisme allemand*, 3 vols. (Aubier-Montaigne, 1961).

Bachelard, G., *L'Air et les songes. Essai sur l'imagination du mouvement* (Corti, 1943).

Baïf, J. A., *Euvres en rime*, ed. C. Marty-Laveaux, 5 vols. (Geneva, Slatkine Reprints, n.d.).

Ballanche, P.-S., *Œuvres*, 4 vols. (J. Barbezat, 1830).

—— *Pages choisies*, ed. T. de Visan (Lyon, Masson, 1926).

—— *Du sentiment considéré dans ses rapports avec la littérature et les arts* (Lyon, chez Ballanche et Barret, 1801).

Béguin, A., *L'Âme romantique et le rêve*, 2 vols. (Cahiers du Sud, 1937).

Bernard, P., *Œuvres*, 2 vols. (Buisson, 1803).

Bernardin de Saint-Pierre, J. H., *La Chaumière indienne* (London, Treutell et Würtz, 1824).

—— *Œuvres complètes*, 15 vols. (Méquignon-Marvis, 1820).

—— *Paul et Virginie*, ed. P. Trahard (Garnier, 1958).

Bernart de Ventadorn, *Seine Lieder*, ed. C. Appel (Halle, 1915).

Boase, A. (ed.), *The Poetry of France*, 3 vols. (Methuen, 1964).

Bousquet, J., *Thèmes du rêve dans la littérature romantique. France, Angleterre, Allemagne* (Didier, 1974).

Butler, W. E., *Magic and the Quabalah* (Aquarian Press, 1964).

Calin, W. C., 'Flower Imagery in *Floire et Blancheflor*', *French Studies*, xviii, pt. 2 (1964).

Carmina Burana, ed. A. Hilke and C. Schumann (Heidelberg, 1941).

Cave, T. (ed.), *Ronsard the Poet* (Methuen, 1973).

Cellier, L., *Fabre d'Olivet. Contribution à l'étude des aspects religieux du romantisme* (Nizet, 1972).

Charlier, G., *Le Sentiment de la Nature chez les romantiques français, 1760–1830* (Fontemoing, 1912).

Chateaubriand, F.-R. de, *Œuvres complètes*, 12 vols. (Garnier, 1939).

Chénier, A., *Œuvres complètes*, ed. C. Walter (Gallimard (Pléiade), 1958).

Chydenius, J., *The Theory of Medieval Symbolism*, Commentationes humanarum litterarum, XXVII, 2 (1960).

Clements, R. J., *Critical Theory and Practice of the Pléiade* (Harvard UP, 1942).

Curtius, E. R., *European Literature and the Latin Middle Ages*, tr. W. Trask (Routledge and Kegan Paul, 1953).

Dakyns, J. R., *The Middle Ages in French Literature 1851–1900* (Oxford UP, 1973).

d'Alton, J. F., *Roman Literary Theory and Criticism* (Longmans Green, 1931).

Dante Alighieri, *The Divine Comedy*, tr. C. S. Singleton, 3 vols. (Princeton UP, 1975).

Davy, M. M., *Initiation à la symbolique romane* (Flammarion, 1964).

Davy de Virville, J., *Histoire de la botanique en France* (Comité français du VIIIᵉ Congrès International de Botanique, 1954).

Dédéyan, C., *Gérard de Nerval et l'Allemagne*, 3 vols. (Société de l'enseignement supérieur, 1957–9).

Deleuze, G. and Guatarri, F., *Rhizome. Introduction* (Minuit, 1976).

Delille, J., *Les Jardins ou l'art d'embellir les paysages, poème* (Valade, 1782).

—— *Œuvres*, 10 vols. (Furne, 1832–3).

Delley, G., *L'Assomption de la Nature dans la lyrique française de l'âge baroque* (Berne, Lang, 1969).

Dronke, P., *Medieval Latin and the Rise of the European Love-Lyric*, 2 vols. (Clarendon Press, 1965).

Éliade, M., *Patterns of Comparative Religion*, tr. R. Sheed (Sheed and Ward, 1958).

Fabre d'Olivet, A., *La Vraie Maçonnerie et la céleste culture*, ed. L. Cellier (Presses universitaires de France, 1952).

Festugière, A. J., *Hermétisme et mystique païenne* (Aubier-Montaigne, 1967).

Finch, R., *The Sixth Sense. Individualism in French Poetry 1686–1760* (University of Toronto Press, 1966).

Fleming, J., *The Roman de la Rose. A Study in Allegory and Iconography* (Princeton UP, 1969).

Frazer, J. G., *The Golden Bough* (3rd edn.), 12 vols. (Macmillan, 1911–15).

Freud, S., *Introductory Lectures on Psychoanalysis*, tr. J. Rivière (Allen and Unwin, 1922).

Gray, R., *Goethe the Alchemist* (Cambridge UP, 1952).

Gubernatis, A. de, *La Mythologie des plantes ou les légendes du monde végétal*, 2 vols. (Reinwald, 1878).

Guitton, E., *Jacques Delille et le poème de la nature de 1750 à 1820* (Klincksieck, 1974).

Gunn, A. M. F., *The Mirror of Love. A Reinterpretation of the Romance of the Rose* (Lubbock, Texas Technical Press, 1952).

Haggis, D. R. *et al.* (eds.), *The French Renaissance and its Heritage. Essays presented to Alan M. Boase* (Methuen, 1968).

Harriot, R., *Poetry and Criticism before Plato* (Methuen, 1969).

Harrison, T. P. and Leon, H. J. *The Pastoral Elegy* (University of Texas, 1939).

Haywood, B., *Novalis. The Veil of Imagery* (The Hague, Mouton, 1959).

Higham, T. F. and Bowra, C. M. (eds.), *The Oxford Book of Greek Verse in Translation* (Clarendon Press, 1938).

Hoffmann, E. T. A., *Dichtungen und Schriften*, ed. W. Harich, 15 vols. (Weimar, 1924).

—— *Œuvres complètes*, tr. Loève-Veimars, 19 vols. (Renduel, 1830).

—— *Werke*, ed. Ellonger, 15 vols. (Berlin–Leipzig, n.d.).

Hutton, J., *The Greek Anthology in France . . . to the year 1800* (Cornell UP, 1946).

Jacobi, J., *Complex/Archetype/Symbol in the Psychology of C. J. Jung*, tr. R. Mannheim (Routledge and Kegan Paul, 1958).

Joret, C., *La Rose dans l'antiquité et au moyen âge* (E. Bouillon, 1892).

Juden, B., *Traditions orphiques et tendances mystiques dans le romantisme français (1800–1855)* (Klincksieck, 1971).

Jung, C. J., *Collected Works*, 20 vols. (Routledge and Kegan Paul, 1958).

Katz, R., *Ronsard's French Critics. 1588–1828* (Geneva, Droz, 1966).

Kerby, W. M., *The Life, Diplomatic Career and Literary Activities of N. G. Léonard* (E. Champion, 1925).

Langlois, E., *Origines et sources du Roman de la Rose* (Thorin, 1891).

Le Gall, B., *L'Imaginaire chez Senancour*, 2 vols. (Corti, 1966).

Lévi-Strauss, C., *La Pensée sauvage* (Plon, 1962).

McLeod, E., *The Order of the Rose* (Chatto and Windus, 1976).

Malherbe, F. de, *Œuvres*, ed. A. Adam (Gallimard (Pléiade), 1971).

Millevoye, *Œuvres* (Garnier, n.d.).

Mitchell, P., *European Flower Painters* (Adam and Charles Black, 1973).

Monchoux, A., *L'Allemagne devant les lettres françaises de 1814 à 1835* (A. Colin, 1953).

Mornet, D., *Le Sentiment de la Nature en France de J.-J. Rousseau à Bernardin de Saint-Pierre* (Hachette, 1907).

Negus, K., *E. T. A. Hoffmann's Other World* (Philadelphia, University of Pennsylvania Press, 1965).

Nodier, C., *Œuvres*, 12 vols. (Geneva, Slatkine Reprints, 1968).

Norrman, R. and Haarberg, J. *Nature and Language. A Semiotic Study of Cucurbits in Literature* (Routledge and Kegan Paul, 1980).

Novalis, *Henri d'Ofterdingen*, édition bilingue, ed. M. Camus (Aubier-Montaigne, 1942).

Pacotte, J., *Le Réseau aborescent, schème primordial de la pensée* (Hermann, 1936).

Pernéty, A. J., *Dictionnaire mytho-hermétique* (Bauche, 1758).

Pichois, C., *L'Image de Jean-Paul Richter dans les lettres françaises* (Corti, 1963).

Planche, J., *Cours de littérature grecque, ou Recueil des plus beaux passages de tous les auteurs grecs . . .*, 7 vols. (Gauthier, 1827–8).

Raby, F., *The History of Christian Latin Poetry* (Clarendon Press, 1953).

—— (ed.), *The Oxford Book of Medieval Latin Verse* (Clarendon Press, 1959).

Richardson, N. J., *The Homeric Hymn to Demeter* (Clarendon Press, 1974).

Le Roman de la Rose, ed. D. Poiron (Garnier-Flammarion, 1974).

Ronsard, P., *Œuvres complètes*, ed. G. Cohen, 2 vols. (NRF/Gallimard (Pléiade), 1950).

Rousseau, J.-J., *Julie ou la Nouvelle Héloïse*, ed. R. Pomeau (Garnier, 1960).

—— *Lettres sur la botanique* (Club des libraires de France, 1962).

—— *Les Rêveries du promeneur solitaire*, ed. H. Roddier (Garnier, 1960).

Russell, D. A. and Winterbottom, N., *Ancient Literary Criticism* (Clarendon Press, 1972).

Saint-Martin, C. de, *Le Crocodile, ou la guerre du bien et du mal. Poème épico-magique* (Triades éditions, 1962).

—— *L'Homme de désir* (Lyon, 1790).

—— *Œuvres posthumes* 2 vols. (Tours, Letourny, 1807).

—— *Tableau naturel des rapports qui existent entre Dieu, l'homme et l'univers*, 2 vols. (Edinburgh, 1782).

Scott, W. (ed.), *Hermetica* (Clarendon Press, 1924).

Segal, C. P., 'Nature and the World of Man in Greek Literature', *Arion*, vol. 2, pt. 1 (1963).

Senancour, E. P. de, *Oberman, lettres publiées par M. . . . Senancour*, 2 vols. (B. Arthaud, 1947).

Seward, B., *The Symbolic Rose* (Columbia UP, 1960).

Spenlé, E., *Novalis. Essai sur l'idéalisme romantique en Allemagne* (Hachette, 1904).

Staël, G. de, *De l'Allemagne*, 2 vols. (Flammarion, 1916–17).

Swedenborg, E., *Concerning Heaven and its Wonders and concerning Hell*, tr. Clowes (Newbury and Trimen, 1843).

Tanner, A. (ed.), *Gnostiques de la Révolution. Claude de Saint-Martin* (Egloff, 1946).

Teichmann, E., *La Fortune d'Hoffmann en France* (Geneva, Droz, 1961).

Tergit, G., *Flowers through the Ages*, tr. E. and A. Anderson (O. Wolff, 1961).

Trois Traitez de la philosophie naturelle (G. Farette, 1612).

Viatte, A., *Les Sources occultes du romantisme*, 2 vols. (Champion, 1928).

Viaud, G., *Les Fleurs dans notre littérature contemporaine* (Poitiers, L'Horticulture Poitevine, 1896).

Weber, H., *La Création poétique au XVIᵉ siècle en France de Maurice Scève à Agrippa d'Aubigné* (Nizet, 1955).

Webster, T. B. L., *From Mycenae to Homer* (Methuen, 1964).

Wilhelm, J. J., *The Cruellest Month. Spring, Nature and Love in Classical and Medieval Lyrics* (Yale UP, 1965).

Wilson, D. B., *Ronsard, Poet of Nature* (Manchester UP, 1961).

Yates, F. A., *The Rosicrucian Enlightenment* (Routledge and Kegan Paul, 1972).

II. Works consulted after Chapter 1 (excluding paraliterature and flower titles)

i. Primary material

Balzac, H. de, *La Comédie humaine*, gen. ed. P.-G. Castex, 11 vols. (Gallimard (Pléiade), 1976–80).

Banville, T. de, *Les Cariatides, Les Stalactites, Le Sang de la coupe, Roses de Noël (Poésies complètes)* (Charpentier, 1891).

Barrès, M., 'La Sensation en littérature: la folie de Charles Baudelaire', *Les Taches d'Encre*, i, 1 (5 Nov. 1884) and 2 (5 Dec. 1884).

Baudelaire, C., *Correspondance*, ed. C. Pichois, 2 vols. (Gallimard (Pléiade), 1973).

—— *Lettres à sa mère*, ed. J. Crépet (Calmann-Lévy, 1932).

—— *Œuvres complètes*, ed. C. Pichois, 2 vols. (Gallimard (Pléiade), 1975–6).

—— *Salon de 1846*, ed. D. Kelley (Clarendon Press, 1975).

Beauclair, H. and Vicaire, G., *Les Déliquescences. Poèmes décadents d'Adoré Floupette*, ed. S. Cigada (Milan, Cisalpino-Goliardica, 1972).

Bertrand, A., *Gaspard de la Nuit*, ed. J. Palou (Editions du Vieux Colombier, 1962).

Borel, P., *Madame Putiphar* (Régine Deforges, 1972).

Brizeux, A., *Œuvres complètes*, 2 vols. (M. Lévy, 1860).

Constant, A., *Les Trois Harmonies* (Fellens et Dufour, 1846).

Cousin, V., *Œuvres*, 3 vols. (Hamman, Société belge de librairie, 1840–1).

Cros, C. and Corbière, T., *Œuvres complètes*, ed. L. Forestier and P.-O. Walzer (Gallimard (Pléiade), 1970).

Desbordes-Valmore, M., *Œuvres poétiques*, ed. M. Bertrand, 2 vols. (Presses universitaires de Grenoble, 1973).

Dierx, L., *Poésies* (Lemerre, 1872).

Esquiros, A., *Les Chants d'un prisonnier* (Challemel, 1841).

Gautier, T., *Émaux et Camées*, ed. G. Matoré (Lille, Giard/Geneva, Droz, 1947).

—— *Histoire du Romantisme, suivie de notices romantiques et d'une étude sur la poésie française 1830–68* (Charpentier, 1874).

—— *Mademoiselle de Maupin* (Garnier-Flammarion, 1966).

—— *Poésies complètes*, ed. R. Jasinski, 3 vols. (Firmin-Didot, 1932).

Glatigny, A., *Œuvres (Poésies complètes)* (Lemerre, 1879).

Gramont, F. de, *Sonnets* (A. Gratiot, 1840).

Granville, J. J., *Les Étoiles*, texte par Méry (Gonet, 1849).

Guérin, M. de, *Œuvres complètes*, ed. B. d'Harcourt, 2 vols. (Les Belles Lettres, 1947).

Heredia, J.-M. de, *Poésies complètes* (Lemerre, 1924).

Hugo, V., *Œuvres poétiques*, ed. P. Albouy, 2 vols. (Gallimard (Pléiade), 1964).

—— *Pierres*, ed. H. Guillemin (Geneva, Éditions du Milieu du Monde, 1951).

Huysmans, J.-K., *A rebours* (Bibliothèque Charpentier, 1910).

Jouffroy, T., *Le Cahier vert. Comment les dogmes finissent. Lettres inédites* (Les Presses Françaises, 1961).

—— *Nouveaux Mélanges philosophiques* (Joubert, 1842).

Jouhard and Bricet, *Les Fleurs animées* (Marchant, 1846).

Karr, A., *Voyage autour de mon jardin* (Dumont, 1845).

Laforgue, J., *Moralités légendaires (Œuvres complètes)* (Mercure de France, 1921).

Lamartine, A. de, *Œuvres poétiques complètes*, ed. M.-F. Guyard (Gallimard (Pléiade), 1963).

Laprade, V. de, *Odes et poëmes* (J. Labitte, 1843).

Lautréamont and G. Nouveau, *Œuvres complètes*, ed. P.-O. Walzer (Gallimard (Pléiade), 1970).

Leconte de Lisle, *Œuvres*, ed. E. Pich, 4 vols. (Les Belles Lettres, 1977–8).

—— *Articles, Préfaces, Discours*, ed. E. Pich (Les Belles Lettres, 1977).

Mallarmé, S., *Correspondance*, ed. H. Mondor and L. J. Austin, 7 vols. (Gallimard, 1959–82).

—— *Œuvres complètes*, ed. H. Mondor and G. Jean-Aubry (Gallimard (Pléiade), 1945).

Mallefille, F., *Monsieur Corbeau* (M. Lévy, 1859).

Mendès, C., *Poésies*, 7 vols. (Ollendorff, 1885).

Mérat, A., *Poésies (1866–73)* (Lemerre, 1898).

Moréas, J., *Œuvres* (Mercure de France, 1923).

Musset, A. de, *La Confession d'un enfant du siècle*, ed. M. Allem (Garnier, 1968).

—— *Poésies complètes*, ed. M. Allem (Gallimard (Pléiade), 1957).

—— *Théâtre complet*, ed. M. Allem (Gallimard (Pléiade), 1962).

Nerval, Gérard de, *Œuvres*, ed. H. Lemaître, 2 vols. (Garnier, 1958–66).

—— *L'Imagier de Harlem ou La Découverte de l'imprimerie*, drame légende . . . de MM. Méry, Gérard de Nerval, et Bernard Lopez, Nlle édition (Librairie théâtrale, 1852).

Nodier, C., *Adèle* (Renduel, 1820).

—— *Poésies diverses* (Delongle frères et Ladvocat, 1827).

Le Parnasse contemporain. Recueil de vers nouveaux (Lemerre, 1866).

Le Parnassiculet contemporain. Recueil de vers nouveaux (Librairie centrale, J. Lemer, 1867).

Planche, G., 'La Moralité de la poésie', *RDM* (1835), vol. i.

Ponroy, A. (ed.), *Le Révélateur d'André Chénier* (Châteauroux, Société d'imprimerie du Berry, 1924).

Portal, F., *Des couleurs symboliques dans l'antiquité, le moyen âge et les temps modernes* (Treutell et Würtz, 1837).

Les Premières Armes du symbolisme (Vanier, 1889).

Prudhomme, S., *Poésies (1866–72)* (Lemerre, 1872).

Renan, E., *Feuilles détachées* (Calmann-Lévy, 1892).

—— 'Des Religions de l'Antiquité et de leurs derniers historiens', *RDM*, nlle période, 2ᵉ série, vol. ii.

Rimbaud, A., *Œuvres*, ed. S. Bernard (Garnier, 1960).

Rollinat, M., *Œuvres*, 2 vols. (Minard (Lettres modernes), 1972).

Sainte-Beuve, C. A. de, *Œuvres*, ed. M. Leroy, 2 vols. (Gallimard (Pléiade), 1949).

—— *Poésies complètes* (Charpentier, 1840).

—— *Poésies complètes*, 2 vols. (Lemerre, 1879).

—— *Vie, poésies et pensées de Joseph Delorme*, ed. G. Antoine (Nouvelles Éditions Latines, 1956).

—— *Volupté*, ed. M. Allem (Garnier, 1934).

Sand, G., *Consuelo, la comtesse de Rudolstadt*, ed. L. Cellier and L. Guichard, 3 vols. (Garnier, 1959).

—— *Lélia*, ed. P. Reboul (Garnier, 1960).

Sandeau, J., *Mademoiselle de la Seiglière* (Nelson, n.d.).

Senancour, E. P. de, *Isabelle* (A. Ledoux, 1833).

Silvestre, A., *Poésies (1866–72)* (Lemerre, 1880).

Sue, E., *Les Mystères de Paris*, 3 vols. (Hallier, 1977).

Tailhade, L., *Poèmes élégiaques* (Mercure de France, 1907).

Tastu, A., *Poésies* (Denain, 1826).

Toussenel, A., *L'Esprit des bêtes, le monde des oiseaux, ornithologie passionnelle*, 3 vols. (Librairie Phalanstérienne, 1853–5).

Valade, L., *Œuvres (Poésies)* (Lemerre, 1887).

Valéry, P., *Album de vers anciens* (Gallimard, 1927).

—— *Charmes ou Poèmes*, ed. C. Whiting (University of London, The Athlone Press, 1973).

Verlaine, P., *Œuvres poétiques*, ed. J. Robichez (Garnier, 1969).

Vigny, A. de, *Œuvres complètes*, ed. F. Baldensperger, 2 vols. (Gallimard (Pléiade), 1948).

ii. Secondary material

Alan, C., 'Quelques fleurs ésotériques chez Nerval', *L'Herne 37, Gérard de Nerval* (Éditions de l'Herne, 1980).

Arnold, P., *Ésotérisme de Baudelaire* (J. Vrin, 1972).

Badesco, L., *La Génération poétique de 1860. La Jeunesse des deux rives* (Nizet, 1971).

Bandy, W. T. and Pichois, C., *Baudelaire devant ses contemporains* (Monaco, Editions du Rocher, 1957).

Bandy, W. T., 'Les Morts, les pauvres morts', *RSH* (July–Sept. 1967).

Benjamin, W., *Charles Baudelaire: A Lyric Poet in the Era of High Capitalism* (New Left Books, 1973).

Blin, G., 'Les Fleurs de l'impossible', *RSH* (July–Sept. 1967).

Boeniger, Y., *Lamartine et le sentiment de la nature* (Nizet et Bastard, 1934).

Bomboir, C., *Les Lettres d'amour de Nerval, mythe ou réalité?* (Namur, Presses universitaires de Namur, 1978).

Bowie, M., *Mallarmé and the Art of Being Difficult* (Cambridge UP, 1978).

Bowman, F. P., *Le Christ romantique* (Genève, Droz, 1973).

Canat, R., *L'Hellénisme des romantiques*, 3 vols. (Didier, 1951–5).

——— *La Renaissance de la Grèce antique, 1821–1850* (Hachette, 1912).

Carter, A. E., *Baudelaire et la critique française, 1869–1917* (Columbia, University of South Carolina Press, 1963).

——— *The Idea of Decadence in French Literature, 1830–1900* (Toronto UP, 1958).

Castex, P.-G., 'La Beauté, Fleur du Mal', *RSH* (July–Sept. 1959).

Cellier, L., 'Baudelaire et George Sand', *RHLF* (Apr.–June 1967).

——— *Mallarmé ou La Morte qui parle* (Presses universitaires de France, 1959).

Charlton, D., Gaudon, J., and Pugh, A. (eds.), *Balzac and the Nineteenth Century* (Leicester UP, 1972).

Clements, P., *Canonization of the Subversive: Baudelaire and the English Tradition* (forthcoming, Princeton UP).

Cornell, K., *The Symbolist Movement* (New Haven, Yale UP, 1951).

Crépet, E., *Baudelaire. Étude biographique*, rev. J. Crépet (Messein, 1907).

Desonay, F., *Le Rêve hellénique chez les poètes parnassiens* (H. Champion, 1928).

Eggli, E., *Schiller et le romantisme français*, 2 vols. (Gamber, 1927).

Esquiros, A., 'Les Littérateurs contemporains', *La France littéraire* (1840), nlle série, vol. i.

Feuillerat, A., *Baudelaire et la Belle aux cheveux d'or* (New Haven, Yale UP, 1941).

Fleury, E., *Hippolyte de la Morvonnais* (H. Champion, 1911).

Fongaro, A., 'La Beauté, fleur du Mal', *Studi francesi* (1960).

Fuchs, M., *Théodore de Banville* (Moulins, Crepin-Leblond, 1910).

George, A. J., *Lamartine and Romantic Unanimism* (New York, Columbia UP, 1940).

Gill, A., *The Early Mallarmé*, vol. i, *Parentage, Early Years, and Juvenilia* (Clarendon Press, 1979).

Hackett, C. A., *Rimbaud, A Critical Introduction* (Cambridge UP, 1981).

Lachèvre, F. *Bibliographie sommaire des keepsakes*, 2 vols. (Giraud-Badin, 1929).

Latreille, C., *Victor de Laprade* (Lyon, Lardanchet, 1912).

Leakey, F., *Baudelaire and Nature* (Manchester UP, 1969).

——— 'Pour une étude chronologique des *Fleurs du Mal*: Harmonie du soir', *RHLF* (Apr.–June 1967).

Le Breton, G., 'Le pythagorisme de Gérard de Nerval et la source des *Vers dorés*', *La Tour Saint-Jacques*, 13–14 (1958).

Lehouck, E., *Fourier aujourd'hui* (Denoël, 1966).

L'Hôpital, M., *La Notion d'artiste chez George Sand* (Boivin, 1946).

Marix-Spire, T., *Les Romantiques et la musique. Le Cas George Sand. 1804–1838* (Nouvelles Éditions Latines, 1954).

Moreau, P., *Âmes et thèmes romantiques* (Corti, 1965).

—— *Le Romantisme* (del Duca, 1957).

Paquien, M., 'La Fonction poétique de la fleur dans l'œuvre de Proust' (unpublished thèse de Maîtrise, Université Lyon II, 1981).

Patty, J. S., 'Baudelaire et Hippolyte Babou', *RHLF* (Apr.–June 1967).

Pich, E., *Leconte de Lisle et sa création poétique* (Lyon, Université Lyon II, 1975).

Pichois, C., *Baudelaire. Études et témoignages* (Neuchâtel, La Baconnière, 1967).

—— and Ruchon, F. *Iconographie de Charles Baudelaire* (Geneva, P. Cailler, 1960).

Pommier, J., *La Mystique de Baudelaire* (Les Belles Lettres, 1932).

Richard, J.-P., *L'Univers imaginaire de Mallarmé* (Éditions du Seuil, 1961).

Richard, N., *A l'aube du symbolisme* (Nizet, 1961).

Richer, J., *Nerval, expérience et création*, Deuxième édition (Hachette, 1970).

Ricoeur, P., *La Métaphore vive* (Éditions du Seuil, 1975).

Riffaterre, H., *L'Orphisme dans la poésie romantique* (Nizet, 1970).

Ruff, M., *L'Esprit du mal et l'esthétique baudelairienne* (A. Colin, 1955).

Sagnes, G., *L'Ennui dans la littérature française de Flaubert à Laforgue* (A. Colin, 1969).

Starkie, E., *Baudelaire* (1957 edition) (Pelican Books, 1971).

Starobinski, J., 'Sur quelques répondants allégoriques du poète', *RHLF* (Apr.–June 1967).

Stephan, P., *Paul Verlaine and the Decadence, 1882–90* (Manchester UP, 1974).

Susini, J.-C., 'Ce qu'on dit au poète à propos de fleurs . . .', *Bulletin baudelairien* (1979), vol. 14, Supplément.

Swart, K., *The Sense of Decadence in Nineteenth-Century France* (The Hague, Nijhoff, 1964).

Viatte, A., *Le Catholicisme chez les romantiques* (E. de Boccard, 1933).

Wiecklawick, L. de, *Alphonse Rabbe dans la mêlée politique et littéraire de la restauration* (Nizet, 1963).

Zayed, G., *La Formation littéraire de Verlaine* (Nouvelle édition augmentée, Nizet, 1970).

Zilberberg, C., *Une lecture des 'Fleurs du Mal'* (Tours, Mame (Univers sémiotiques), 1972).

III. Paraliterature and titles related to flowers

i: Flower dictionaries

Note. This is a chronological list giving original date of publication, but indications of subsequent editions are added where possible. Since this list depends to some extent on the index supplied by the *Bibliographie de la France* (1810–56), it is much fuller for these years: after 1857 the

Journal de la librairie provides no listing by title alone. Yet it seems that popularity of flower-dictionaries declined after the eighteen-fifties.

Hammer, M., 'Sur le langage des fleurs', *Annales des voyages de la géographie et de l'histoire*, vol. 9 (1809), pp. 346–58. (This article contains a glossary of the Turkish flower code).

Genlis, Madame de, *La Botanique historique et littéraire* (Maradan, 1810).

Maugirard, Madame V., *Les Fleurs, rêve allégorique, dédié à S. M. la Reine Hortense* (Buisson, L'Huillier et Renard, 1811).

Delachénaye, F., *Abécédaire de Flore ou Langage des fleurs* (Didot l'aîné, 1811).

G., Madam, *Le Bouquet du sentiment, ou Allégorie des plantes et des couleurs* (Lenormant, Dentu, Janet, 1816).

Le Langage des fleurs ou les selams de l'Orient (chez Rosa, 1819).

Flore de la botanique des dames (Audot, 1821).

L. D., *Le Langage des plantes, des fleurs et des couleurs ou Dictionnaire complet des plantes, fleurs et couleurs symboliques, donnant leurs véritables significations* (Imp. d'Éverat, 1821).

Troncin, le Docteur, *Langage de Flore, ou Nouvelle Manière de communiquer ses pensées sans se voir, sans se parler, sans s'écrire* (Imp. de Richomme, 1821).

Latour, Madame Charlotte de, *Le Langage des fleurs* (Imp. de Fair, 1824). (This became one of the most popular of these works, with a third edition in 1827 and a sixth in 1844, published by Garnier.)

Les Fleurs et les fruits, Abécédaire et syllabaire, avec de petites leçons tirées de l'Histoire des plantes (Imp. de Casimir, 1825).

Martin, Louis-Aimé, *Le Langage des fleurs* (Bruxelles, Hauman, 1830).

Le Bouquet de Flore (Marcilly, n.d. [1830]).

Leneveux, Madame, *Les Fleurs emblématiques, Étrennes des anniversaires, contenant le langage allégorique des fleurs* (Imp. de Rigoux, 1832). (One of the most popular flower dictionaries, this work was republished under various titles at least five times: a third edition in 1837 was followed by editions in 1848 and 1850 published by Janet.)

Flore galante, ou Langage emblématique des fleurs, contenant la signification symbolique de chaque fleur, son histoire et son origine poétique (Imp. Mme. Huzard, 1838).

Hostein, H., *Flore des dames ou Nouveau Langage des fleurs, précédé d'un cours élémentaire de botanique* (J. Loss, 1839). (There were at least two more editions, in 1841 and 1844.)

Le Langage des fleurs (Imp. de Lacrampe, 1841).

Le Langage des fleurs ou le Livre du destin (Gautier, 1841). (There were at least two more editions, in 1845 and 1850.)

Messire, J., *Le Langage moral des fleurs, etc.* [*sic*] (Tours, Imp. de Pornin, 1844).

Grandville, J. J., *Les Fleurs animées*, monologue et épilogue par Alphonse Karr, texte par Taxile Delord et le comte Foelix (Imp. de J. Claye, n.d.). (This work first appeared in parts between April 1846 and January 1847 and was published in book form at the end of that period by Gonet, with a second edition in the same year: there were several further editions in the eighteen-fifties.)

Lachaume, Jules, *Les Fleurs naturelles, Traité sur l'art de composer les couronnes, les parures, les bouquets, etc., de tous genres, pour bals et soirées, suivi du Langage des fleurs* (Imp. de Plon, 1847).

Fertiault, François, *Le Langage des fleurs, illustré* (Bailly, 1848).

B. R., *Le Langage emblématique des fleurs, d'après leurs propriétés naturelles, leur historique, la consécration ancienne et l'usage, avec la nomenclature des différents sentiments dont chaque fleur est le symbole; suivi de la signification des fleurs et de leur emploi pour l'expression des pensées* (Poissy, Imp. d'Arbieu, 1851). (Editions in 1852 and 1853.)

Riols, J. de, *Le Langage des fleurs* (Guyot, n.d. [1870?]).

ii. Flower titles

Note. This list includes anthologies, devotional works, volumes of poetry, plays, and some keepsakes (to be supplemented by Lachèvre's bibliography) published between 1820 and 1886. Like the preceding list (and for the same reason) it is less full after 1857. The list is arranged chronologically.

Châlons-d'Arge, *Guirlande poétique de Dieudonné, duc de Bordeaux* (Imp. de Béraud, 1820).

Poisson, H., *Florilegium Horatii* (Petit, 1821).

La Corbeille bien assortie, ou Des fleurs pour tous les âges (Denugon, 1821).

Petit Bouquet de famille, ou Recueil de compliments nouveaux (Gratiot, 1821).

La Fleurs des champs, couplets pour la fête de S. M. Charles X (1827).

Les Fleurs, poème mentionné par L'Académie des Jeux Floraux (Tastu, 1829).

Engelvin, J., *Fleurs à Marie* (Leclère, 1834).

Colet, Madame Louise, *Fleurs du midi, poésies* (Dumont, 1836).

Monferrand, A. de, *Fleurs sur une tombe* (Beilin, 1836).

Schmid, *Fleurs de mai* (Audin, 1836).

Kock, P. de, *Les Fleurs et les papillons* (Mevrel, 1837).

Seguin, M.-F., *Fleurs de bruyère* (Desrosiers, 1838).

Mathieu, P. F., *Les Fleurs d'hiver, Prose et poésie* (Troyes, Payn, 1838).

Fleurs de poésies contemporaines (Imp. d'Éverat, 1839).

Orsini, M. l'abbé, *Les Fleurs du Ciel, ou Imitation des saints* (Bailly, 1839).

Bossand, J. B., *Les Églantines, poésies* (Bourg, Bottier, 1840).

Gères, J. de, *Les Premières Fleurs* (Maulde, 1840).

Kien, B., *Fleurs du matin, poésies* (Douai, Crépeaux, 1840).

Magnier, L., *Fleurs des champs, poésies* (Tuzin, 1840).

Perret, J. A., *Bluettes, poésies* (Charolles, Simonin, 1840).

Valchère, Madame C., *Fleurs des champs* (Fontainebleau, Jacquin, 1840).

van Gaver, J., *Fleurs de l'âme, poésies* (Didot, 1840).

B., *Hippolyte et Hyacinthe, Le Paradis des roses, ou le royaume des fleurs* (Pollet, 1841).

Rabion, M. l'abbé, *Fleurs de la poésie française* (Tours, Mame, 1841).

Renaud, l'abbé, *Fleurs de l'éloquence* (Tours, Mame, 1841).

Tampucci, H., *Quelques Fleurs pour une couronne, poésies* (Sainte-Ménéhould, Pognée-Darnauld, 1841).

Fleurs du désert (Moulins, Desrosiers, 1842).

Fleurs et épines, almanach (Saintin, 1842).

Julvécourt, P. de, *Fleurs d'hiver, poésie* (Sceaux, Dépée, 1842).

Pétasse, J., *Fleurs des champs* (Beaûne, Blondeau-Dejussieu, 1842).

Dubois de Thouville, Mademoiselle, *Fleurs de l'amitié, contes aux enfans* (Maulde, 1843).

R., M. l'abbé, *La Fleur de Marie ou les fleurs du mois de mai* (Amiens, Caron-Vitet, 1843).

C., Stéphane, *Fleurs éphémères, poésies* (la Croix-Rousse, Lépagnez, 1843).

Ténint, W., *Fleurs des fèves* (Boulé, 1843).

Les Fleurs parlant au cœur du chrétien (Lyon, Giberton et Brun, 1844).

Lebon, H., *Fleur du ciel, ou Les Merveilles de la charité chrétienne* (Lyon, Rusand, 1844).

Seguin, M.-F., *Fleurs et larmes* (Ambert, Seguin, 1844).

Desplaces, A., *La Couronne d'Ophélie* (Schneider, 1845).

Ducror, F., *Fleurs des alpes, poésies religieuses* (Lyon, Pommet, 1845).

Fleurs des saints ou Choix de narrations édifiantes . . . (Lacrampe, 1845).

Hemet, M. l'abbé, *Fleurs d'Angleterre ou Choix de morceaux de littérature anglaise* (Toulouse, Delsol, 1845).

Lefilleul des Guerrots, *Les Fleurs de la Fête-Dieu* (Rouen, Perron, 1845).

Turquéty, Edouard, *Fleurs à Marie* (Proux, 1845).

Calmel, l'abbé, *Fleurs à Marie, poésies sacrées* (Limoges, Boute, 1846).

Montlouis, R. de, *Les Violettes* (Tours, Pornin, 1846).

Poulain, J., *Les Pervenches* (Boulogne, Delahodde, 1846).

Labie, Commerson et Montépin, *Les Fleurs animées, Vaudeville en un acte* (Marchant, 1846).

Bessède, B., *Les Églantines, poésies* (La Rochelle, Vigny, 1847).

Chambelland, L., *Les Fleurs de la Pologne, ode* (Gratiot, 1847).

Fleurs des pauvres (Bordeaux, Dupuy, 1847).

Fleurs et fruits du précieux sang (Sirou, 1847).

Gransard, Madame A., *La Fleur de la montagne, dédiée aux jeune filles* (Bautruche, 1847).

M., Mademoiselle Julia, *Les Pavots du Parnasse* (Brière, 1847).

Mercx, L. F. de, *Fleurs et fleurettes* (Moulins, Desrosiers, 1847).

Monavon, G., *Jeunes Fleurs, Poésies* (Lyon, Rey, 1847).

Mondelot, *Hyacinthes* (Charpentier, 1847).

Auguste, T., Fleurs d'exil, Poésies (Montpellier, Virengue, 1848).

Esquiros, A., *Fleur du peuple, Poème* (Gerdes, 1848).

Les Fleurs bénies (Moulin, Desrosiers, 1848).

Jouhanneaud, l'abbé P., *Fleur angélique* (Limoges, Barbou, 1848).

d'Helf, Madame, *Les Fleurs sous la neige* (Limoges, Barbou, 1849).

Les Fleurs du peuple et la république au pilori (Lacour, 1849).

Joba, P., *Fleurs fanées, Souvenir d'un ami mourant* (Metz, Verronais, 1849).

Julia, M. l'abbé, *Fleurs à Marie* (Toulouse, Montaubin, 1849).

Martin, N., *Une gerbe, Poésies nouvelles* (Gerdès, 1849).

Maitrias, l'abbé, *Bouquet de fleurs à Marie* (Lille, Lefort, 1849).

Miquelon, F., *Fleurs et ronces, poésies* (Avignon, Jacquet, 1849).

Beuzeville, C., *Fleurs du chemin* (Rouen, Brière, 1850).

C. J., *Les Bouquets du sentiment* (Maison, 1851).

Duplessis, G., *La Fleur des proverbes français* (Passard, 1851).

Fleurs et papillons, Alphabet (Bedelet, 1851).

Fleurs de juin, mois de saint sacrement (Arras, Le Franc, 1851).

Lepelletier, E., *Les Violettes, Poésies* (Garnier, 1851).

Ménard, Madame, *Le Bouquet de roses* (Tours, Mame, 1851).

Poncy, C., *Bouquets de marguerites, poème* (Toulon, Laurent, 1851).

Vautier, L., *Les Fleurs sont mes amours, poésie nouvelle* (Rouen, Lecointe, 1851).

Alhoy, M. et J. Rostaing,, *Les Fleurs historiques* (Janet, n.d. (1852)).

la Bedollière, E. de, *Les Fleurs de la morale en action* (Limoges, Ardant, 1852).

Brizeux, A., *Marie, la fleur d'or* (Garnier, 1852).

Chatelin, E., *Les Fleurs ignorées, poésies* (Beaulé, 1852).

Le Gai, H., *La Fleur des calembours* (Pillet, 1852).

La Moisson des fleurs, choix de poésies (Lille, Lefort, 1852).

Barins, M. de, *La Guirlande de fleurs, contenant lettres, bouquets, compliments (en vers et en prose)* (Lebailly, 1853).

Barthet, A., *Fleurs du panier, poésies* (Gratiot, 1853).

Belly, Madame L., *Les Violettes* (Prève, 1853).

Bonneton, J., *Les Épines de la vie. Stances* (Lacour, 1853).

La Corbeille de fleurs (Limoges, Barbou, 1853).

Drohojowska, Madame la comtesse, *Fleurs de l'histoire* (Lehuby, 1853).

Fleurs des champs, par un curé de campagne (Bayonne, Lamaignière, 1853).

Fleurs du désert, ou Hymnes à Marie (Grenoble, Prud'homme, 1853).

Fleurs et fruits, choix de poésies (Lille, Lefort, 1853).

Guérin, A., *Épis, bluets et coquelicots* (Beaulé, 1853).

Guillon des Tremblayes, L. E., *Des fleurs parmi les ronces* (Breteau, 1853).

Hautefeuille, E. de, *Fleurs de tristesse* (Caen, Hardel, 1853).

Lacou, J., *Fleurs des landes* (Bordeaux, Moulins, 1853).

Louis, G., *Épines et roses* (Dentu, 1853).

Mouret, N., *La Reine du Château-des-Fleurs* (Beaulé, 1853).

Perribère, V., *Fleurs d'automne* (Masgana, 1853).

Renaud, A., *Les Fleurs de l'éloquence — ou recueil en prose* (Tours, Mame, 1853).

Romigny, C., *Les Fleurs fanées* (Dondey-Dupré, 1853).

Saint-Gabriel, Mademoiselle J., *Fleurs du désert* (Clermont-Ferrand, Pérol, 1853).

Ségalas, Madame A., *Les Violettes et les abeilles* (Schiller aïné, 1853).

Tardif, A., *Fleurs d'automne* (Aix, Aubin, 1853).

Thiébaud, *Fleurs choisies dans les litanies de la sainte Vierge* (Besançon, Tubergue, 1853).

Abadie, R., *Roses et dahlias* (Toulouse, Sens, 1854).

Adelbert, *Violettes* (Lyon, Vingtrinier, 1854).

Auvert, J., *Les Primevères et les soucis, poésies* (Nolet, 1854).

Astouin, L., *Gerbes et épis, poésies* (Dentu, 1854).

C. B., *Les Fleurs de Marie* (Rouen, Mégard, 1854).

Célarier, A. *Fleurs de famille, ou Hélène et Julia* (Picard, 1854).

Chartier, A. J. B., *Gerbe poétique* (Châtellrault, Varigant, 1854).

Delanoue, A., *La Fleur des nouvelles* (Passard, 1854).

Essarts, A. des, *Fleurs du paradis* (Courcier, 1854).

Les Fleurs (Lille, Lefort, 1854) (7 editions by 1879).

H. P., Madame, *Fleurs d'outre-tombe* (Prenaud, 1854).

Lacroix, Madame, *Fleur de serre et fleur des champs* (Janet, 1854).

Lelion-Damiens, *Pervenches* (Desoye, 1854).

Levain, A., *Bluettes* (Montargis, Chrétien, 1854).

Mesnage, C., *Fleurs d'avril* (Laval, Godbert, 1854).

Poujol, A., *Fleurs et jeunes filles, ou Les Fleurs animées* (Raynal, 1854).

Quinsac, E., *Pensées et violettes* (Toulouse, Sens, 1854).

Raynal, L., *Feuilles et fleurs* (Lille, Danel, 1854).

Saffray, Madame M., *Les Marguerites*, poésies (Dentu, 1854).

Wiers, B. de, *Les Violettes du Nord* (Ledoyen, 1854).

Badoche, E., *La Fleur des champs* (Cellier Dufayel, 1854).

Une fleur de plus à la couronne de Marie (Amiens, Imp. Caron, 1854).

Corday, Madame A. de, *Les Fleurs neustriennes* (Mortagne, Loncin et Daupelay, 1855).

Les Fleurs de mai ou Chants en l'honneur de la Vierge immaculée (Auch, Foix, 1855).

Fleurs du désert ou Hymnes à Marie (Grenoble, Prud'homme, 1855).

Fleurs du mois du Sacré-Coeur de Jésus (Lyon, Pélagaud, 1855).

Grimaud, E., *Fleurs de Vendée, poésies* (Dentu, 1855).

Robion, l'abbé, *Les Fleurs de la poésie française* (Tours, Mame, 1855).

Roze, E., *Fleurs de printemps* (Nolet, 1855).

Saint-Victor, J. B. de, *Fleurs des saints* (Vermot, 1855).

Decroix, A., *Fleurs d'un jour, poésies* (Garnier, 1856).

Depéry, Mgr. J. I., *Les Fleurs du Laus* (Gap, Delaplace, 1856).

du Molin, J. B., *Flore poétique ancienne* (Baillière, 1856).

Fleurs de juin, ou le mois eucharistique (Lyon, Pélagaud, 1856).

H. C., Madame, *Les Fleurs du Carmel* (Montpellier, Seguin, 1856).

Limagne, É. de, *Fleurs religieuses* (Mandeville, 1856).

Pernelle, l'abbé, *Fleurs poétiques de mai* (Paulmier, 1856).

Fleurs et fruits, Choix de poésies (Lille, Lefort, 1856).

La Fleur de la famille (Les Librairies protestantes, 1857).

La Fleur des chansons populaires (Delarue, 1857).

Fleurs d'Armorique (Dinan, Huart, 1857).

Fleurs de l'Inde, comprenant La Mort de Yazadate (Duprat, 1857).

La Fleur des Gasconnades (Passard, 1858).

Fleurs des champs, fleurs du monde, vers et prose (Garnier, 1858).

C. D., *Fleurs de poésie anglaise* (Amyot, 1859).

La Fleur chansonnière, nouveau chansonnier universel (Le Bailly, 1859).

Fleurs des Saints Pères de l'Église latine (Toulouse, Privat, 1860).

Les Fleurs du chanoine Schmidt (Limoges, 1862).

Fleurs de la terre et fleurs du paradis (Josse, 1862).

Fleurs de Savoie (Lyon, Perrin, 1863).

Fleurs de la littérature française (Vermot, 1863).

Une fleur de patience ou Vie de sainte Lidwine (Avignon, Aubanel, 1863).

Une fleur moissonnée (Librairie française et étrangère, 1866).

Fleurs d'Ars (Lyon, Vingtrinier, 1867).

Fleurettes de monastère (Goupy, 1868).

Une fleur chaque matin dans le parterre de la perfection chrétienne (Tournai, Castermann, 1868).

Fleurs de la solitude ou chemin de la croix, (Poussielgue, 1869).

P., Mme Emilie, *Fleurs d'Avril* (Lyon, 1872).

Fleurs du Chablais (Poésies intimes, Annecy, Burdet, 1872).

Le langage des fleurs, offert à Marie, en mai 1873 (Montbard, Blesseau, 1873).

Fleur de Grenade, nouvelle par Madame A. J. (1873).

Flore mystique de Saint François de Sales ou la vie chrétienne sous l'emblème des plantes (1874).

Fleurs d'hiver, Dernières feuilles du journal d'un curé de campagne (Lyon, Storck, 1875).

Leroy, C., *Flore poétique du jeune âge, ou Nouveau choix de poésies* (E. Belin, 1878).

Les Fleurs de l'autel (Tours, Mame, 1879).

Fleurs indulgentes offertes à l'indulgente amitié (Larguier, 1879).

Fleurs poétiques du Séraphique Saint Bonaventure (Aubeuil, 1881).

Les Fleurs du rosaire (Roussel, 1882).

Les Fleurs félibresques, poésies provençales ou languedociennes modernes (Union générale de la librairie, 1883).

La Fleur de la littérature grecque (Garnier, 1884).

La Fleur de la littérature latine (Garnier, 1886).

Fleurs de charité (Librairie catholique, 1886).

INDEX